The Shell Book of the
Islands of Britain

The Shell Book of the
Islands of Britain

David Booth and David Perrott

Guideway/Windward

© Guideway Publishing Ltd 1981

Produced by Guideway Publishing Ltd
Willow House, 27-49 Willow Way, London SE26

Published in 1981 by Guideway Windward

Windward is an imprint owned by
W.H. Smith & Son Ltd
(registered No 237811 England)
trading as WHS Distributors
St John's House, East Street, Leicester LE1 6NE

Booth, David & Perrott, David
The Shell book of the islands of Britain.
1. Islands - Great Britain
2. Great Britain - Description and travel - 1981 -
Guide-books
914.1'04857   DA668

ISBN 0 7112 0087 4

Printed and bound in Great Britain by
William Clowes (Beccles) Limited,
Beccles and London

Original concept: David Perrott
Researchers: Clare Crawford, Graham Oakley,
Morag Perrott, John Pickwell
Line drawings: Pamela Dowson

The publishers would like to thank the following for
their help in producing this book: J.D. Allman; Ian
Archibald; Dr A. Bebbington; George Bramall;
Dennis Butcher; Bet Davies; Peter Duke; Howie
Firth; Jeanne Geddes; Mildred R. Holgate; Bedwyr
Lewis Jones; Elsie Karbacz; Jean Martindale; Mike
and Maureen McCormick; Robert McDonald;
Duncan McIntosh; National Library of Wales,
Aberystwyth; E.C.A. Sheppard; Lea Speake; A.L.W.
Stevens; Lisa Tyler; Tynwald Library, Isle of Man;
Major Peter Wood.

Front Cover: The Islands of Rum and Eigg from
Arisaig. *W.F. Davidson.*
Back Cover: Lindisfarne (Holy Island),
Northumberland. *R. Thomlinson.*

Photography: all photography by the authors except
the following: Aerofilms: 185 (top); Airviews Ltd:
178 (top); R. W. Arnold: 178 (bottom), 179 (top left);
British Tourist Authority: 31 (bottom), 94 (top), 116
(bottom), 175 (bottom), 177 (top), 183 (bottom), 184
(top); R. V. Collier: 62 (top), 65 (bottom), 67 (top),
85 (bottom); A. Gilpin/RSPB: 36 (bottom); C.
Graham: 154 (top); D. Hardley: 96 (bottom), 97 (top
& bottom), 98 (bottom), 99 (top); P. Harrison/RSPB:
51 (bottom); *Holiday Which?:* 87; Isle of Man Tourist
Board: 160 (top); Manx Press Pictures: 158 (top), 159
(top & bottom), 161 (top); National Trust for
Scotland: 64 (bottom), 65 (top), 68 (top); Philipson &
Son Ltd: 121 (top), 123 (top); Phoenix Photos,
Kirkwall: 27 (top), 29 (top), 30 (bottom), 32 (top), 35
(bottom); F. Pölking: 181 (top); Scottish Tourist
Board: 93 (top), 111 (bottom), 113 (top), 117 (top);
D. C. Thomson: 37 (bottom); B. Tulloch: 180
(bottom); R. Vallintine: 63 (top); West Air
Photography: 182 (top).

Contents

Introduction

When the first Christian missionaries came from Ireland to Britain in the fifth century, they chose to establish many of their monastic settlements on islands – Iona and Lindisfarne are two well-known examples. Why was it they did not go directly to the mainland, since it would seem more practical to live among those whom they were to convert?

An area of land, with a natural boundary easily recognised by all, would have provided both isolated sanctity and a measure of security, the sea acting as a defensive barrier. Other considerations may have included a ready supply of food from the surrounding water, and a climate moderated by the warming effect of the ocean. But their mission was to change men's minds and uplift their spirits. Where better to find inspiration than surrounded by huge vistas of sea and sky? And where better to retreat for quiet meditation and regeneration? In all respects an island answered their needs.

Now that the lives of most of us centre on the urban and industrial complexes, it is not surprising we feel drawn towards an island when we view it from the mainland. The desire to cross the natural boundary and step outside the usual hustle of life is still strong in us all. We still look for what the missionaries found fifteen centuries ago.

The islands around the shores of Britain are amazing in their diversity and all have something to offer. The great majority of them are part of Scotland and remain relatively unspoiled. Others have their share of industry, some are devoted to tourism, and one or two are indistinguishable from the mainland. In this book we have surveyed all those we consider to be of note. We have not tried to produce a catalogue of them all – such a listing would, in our opinion, be needlessly repetitive. It would also have presented us with the thorny problem of defining an island, something we have chosen to avoid.

An island is not simply 'a piece of land surrounded by water', as a dictionary would describe it. When is a rock, surrounded by water, *large* enough to qualify as an island? A survey conducted in 1861 approached the problem in an original way, stating that an island had to have a minimum area of grass sufficient to provide summer pasturage for one sheep. Unfortunately this takes no account of the fertility of the soil or the length of the growing season, vital factors which dictate the area of land required by livestock, and which varies a great deal according to latitude and exposure to the Gulf Stream. We have made *our* decisions on the basis that an island is easier to recognise than define, and have trusted our eyes.

As diverse as the islands are the people who inhabit them. Most remarkable are the small communities which thrive under conditions that would drive a city dweller, reliant on readily available goods and services, to despair.

The Outer Hebrides is Scotland's Gaelic stronghold, where the language and traditional values remain a part of everyday life. The Inner Hebrides generally show more mainland influence but life there is still well balanced and community based. Both suffer from depopulation and lack of self-determination. To the north are some of Britain's most remote inhabited islands, still retaining their strong Norse heritage and now adjusting to an influx of oilmen and the paraphernalia of exploration and exploitation – the nation's 'Klondike'. The quiet and holy north-eastern isles of England contrast with the industry of the north-west, and the holiday spirit which prevails in the south. Wales is blessed with Anglesey, a stronghold of Welsh language and culture, the saints' isle of Bardsey and the wildlife havens off Pembroke. Staunchly independent are the Isle of Man and the Channel Islands, proving that small island communities can run their own affairs successfully under the British umbrella.

All of these islands we must cherish. Every visit to one is special; to many it is an adventure. We hope this book will tempt you over the sea to share in this unique experience.

In the course of our two years work we have been fortunate enough to visit, or to peer at, the great majority of the islands covered by this book. Working side by side, we divided the load as follows: David Booth – Orkney, Shetland, England and the Channel Islands; David Perrott – western Scotland, Wales and the Isle of Man (we have not included the islands of Northern Ireland, feeling that these would be better served by a separate book). Clearly a book such as this can not be written solely from the knowledge of two people. We have consulted many books and have relied on the help given, knowingly or otherwise, by experts and by local people. If we are to extend *special* thanks, they must go to John Pickwell, our 'devil's advocate', to Nancy Duin for her inexhaustible patience, and to Eric Jones for his enthusiasm and support.

Opposite: *The mountains of Arran from the summit of Mullach Mòr, Holy Island.*

Note to the reader

The maps which accompany the text are intended to familiarise the reader with the 'lie of the land' and clarify the description. They have been drawn in a series of scales dependent upon each island's size, complexity or importance. Areas of dark shading indicate ground over 1000 feet high. Serious island exploration merits more detailed maps, and we recommend the Ordnance Survey 1:50,000 series as being particularly suitable.

Within the text and on the maps we have given heights and distances in imperial measure, realising many younger readers may not approve. It is our belief that more people in Britain relate to the 'old' system rather than metric; to have given both would be cumbersome. However, conversions may be effected by using the following factors: feet to metres, multiply by 0.3048; miles to kilometres, multiply by 1.609.

All place names are as they appear on Ordnance Survey maps (1:50,000 series) unless otherwise stated and except for those of the Channel Islands for which the map published by John Bartholomew & Son was used. All the names of wild flowers follow the spelling recommended by the Botanical Society of the British Isles.

The order of the book is geographical so that neighbouring islands appear together in the text. To locate a specific island the listing in the index should be used.

The Country Code

Guard against fire risks.
Leave gates as you find them.
Keep dogs under control.
Keep to paths across farm land.
Do not damage fences, hedges and walls.
Leave no litter.
Safeguard water supplies.
Protect wildlife, wild plants and trees.
Go carefully on country roads.
Respect the life of the countryside.

The Botanical Society of Great Britain
produce a leaflet detailing a Code of
Conduct for the conservation of wild
plants, which we heartily recommend.

'Take only pictures, leave only footprints.'

Scotland

This section, by far the longest, begins in the far north with Shetland, followed by Orkney and the myriad islands of the west, from Dunnet Head to the Solway Firth, as far into the Atlantic as Rockall, to finish in the east in the Firth of Forth.

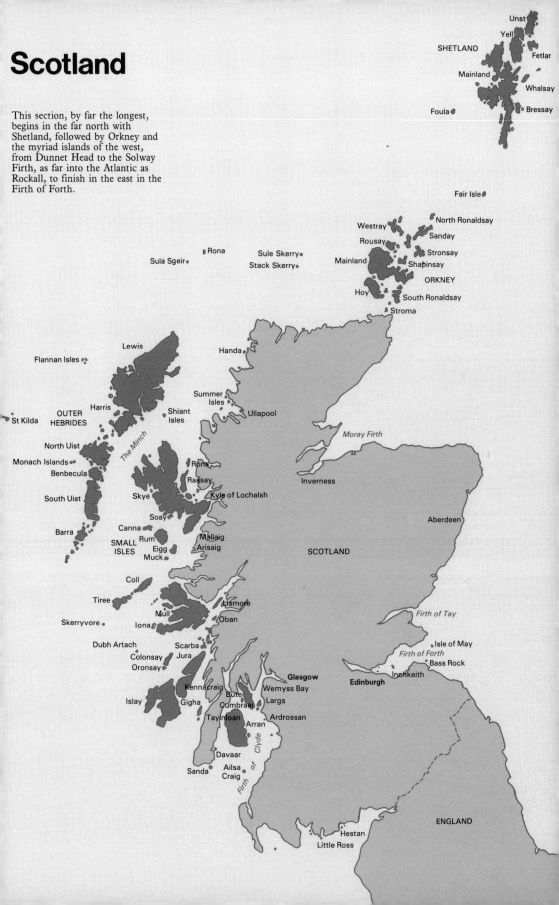

SHETLAND
Unst
Yell
Fetlar
Mainland
Whalsay
Foula
Bressay

Fair Isle

North Ronaldsay
Westray
Sanday
Rousay
Stronsay
Mainland
Shapinsay
ORKNEY
Hoy
South Ronaldsay
Stroma

Rona
Sule Skerry
Sula Sgeir
Stack Skerry

Handa

Lewis
Flannan Isles

Summer Isles
Ullapool

Harris
Shiant Isles

OUTER HEBRIDES
St Kilda

The Minch

North Uist
Rona
Monach Islands
Raasay
Benbecula
Skye
Kyle of Lochalsh

South Uist

Soay

Barra
Canna
Rum
Mallaig
SMALL ISLES
Eigg
Arisaig
Muck

Coll

Tiree
Lismore
Mull
Oban
Skerryvore
Iona

Dubh Artach
Scarba
Colonsay
Jura
Oronsay

Islay
Kennacraig
Wemyss Bay
Bute
Largs
Gigha
Cumbraes
Taynloan
Ardrossan
Arran

Davaar
Firth of Clyde
Sanda
Ailsa Craig
Little Ross
Hestan

Moray Firth
Inverness

Aberdeen

SCOTLAND

Firth of Tay
Isle of May
Firth of Forth
Bass Rock
Glasgow
Edinburgh
Inchkeith

ENGLAND

Shetland

The most northerly of all Britain's islands, the group numbers over 100 in total, ranging in size from hundreds of square miles to very tiny islets of just a few square yards, covering (in total) an area of 552 square miles. Only 14 of the islands are inhabited: Mainland, Unst, Yell, Fetlar, Whalsay, Out Skerries (Bruray and Housay), Trondra, East Burra and West Burra, Bressay, Fair Isle, Foula and Papa Stour. The total population is 20,794 of which 16,040 live on Mainland, the largest of the islands.

Shetland, according to geologists, is the mountainous area of the pre-Ice Age Scottish/Scandinavian continent. This vast area, over the course of millions of years, was gradually eroded by rivers and the sea, and the weight of the ice under which the land lay during various ice ages caused the land to sink until all that was left, of what once was part of the European continent, was Shetland.

The variety of different rocks and minerals is quite remarkable. The most common sedimentary rock is old red sandstone, found mainly on the eastern side of the islands. Limestone is also present in two parallel bands across the middle of Mainland between Scalloway and Girlsta. The main backbone of

Shetland is a ridge of hard metamorphic rocks stretching from the island of Unst in the north to the southern tip of Mainland, the two main types being schist and gneiss. Although Shetland has little in the way of commercially useful minerals, there are deposits of copper, iron, chromite, serpentine, talc and limestone, plus some small deposits of magnetite, platinum, iridium and nickel. However, because the rocks are of the non-porous type, this leads to drainage problems; as a result, the soils are of an extremely poor quality and peat covers a great majority of the area.

Because of the windy climate and the closeness of the sea there are, with the exception of one small experimental plantation, no trees on Shetland. However, the remains of tree stumps have been found in the peat bogs, indicating that there has been, long ago, a great climatic change with the weather becoming colder and wetter and the winds stronger. The present climate differs very little between the seasons. Average summer temperatures very rarely exceed 60°F, and there are mild winters, with average temperatures not dropping below 39°F, warm for such northern latitudes. The wind, however, is exceptionally strong, and several gales have been recorded in recent years with gusts in excess of 97 mph. The highest ever recorded in Britain – a gust of 177 mph – was measured at the top of Saxa Vord on Unst on 16 February 1962. The record is

The Shetland coast.

unofficial, since the wind carried off the measuring device and therefore the evidence!

The general weather conditions are also extremely changeable. One moment it's fine and sunny with no wind at all then, without warning, a wind of gale-force strength springs up and clouds form in what was a clear blue sky. These winds, in the summer, are very mild but can literally blow you off your feet. It's interesting to note that, in a land with such strong winds, anything tall is obviously at a great disadvantage; there are no native trees, the ponies are miniature and the old native cattle and pigs were also very small in stature.

Shetland's scenery is magnificent.

The west coast of Mainland.

If you're looking for that 'get-away' place, with unspoiled views and a panorama of cliffs, sea, caves, lochs and moorland, then Shetland should be near the top of your list. There are truly spectacular cliffs wherever you go and, surprisingly, extremely good beaches, most of them in sheltered bays or coves. But it is the sea that is the dominant factor, affecting all Shetland life as well as the landscape.

The earliest inhabitants of the islands came by sea, some time between 2000 BC and 1500 BC and, by comparing the remains and relics with those of other neolithic communities in Europe, their origins can be traced back to the Mediterranean. Over 60 neolithic dwelling places have been found in Shetland. Two important finds are

circular in plan with a thick hollow wall enclosing a central courtyard. The diameter of the tower becomes narrower towards the top, where it contains galleries, and the whole structure is not unlike present-day water-cooling towers but on a smaller scale. There are over 500 broch sites in the world, almost all of

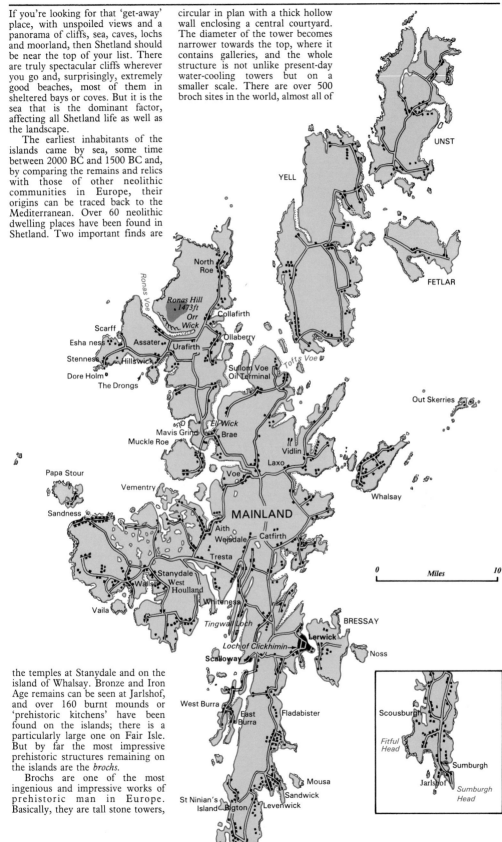

the temples at Stanydale and on the island of Whalsay. Bronze and Iron Age remains can be seen at Jarlshof, and over 160 burnt mounds or 'prehistoric kitchens' have been found on the islands; there is a particularly large one on Fair Isle. But by far the most impressive prehistoric structures remaining on the islands are the *brochs*.

Brochs are one of the most ingenious and impressive works of prehistoric man in Europe. Basically, they are tall stone towers, them concentrated in Shetland, Orkney and the north-east of Scotland. The most complete are situated on the island of Mousa and at Clickhimin on Mainland.

Since all the brochs are within signalling distance of each other, it has generally been accepted that they were used as an early-warning system against impending attacks, and that, in the event of an invasion, the towers would protect the local population and their livestock. But since the internal area of even the largest broch would not have been more than a few thousand square feet, including galleries and staircase, it would not have held many people and certainly not their livestock as well. Also there is the problem of why the brochs were so tall, averaging about 40 ft. Anyone who has visited the Northern Isles knows that great distances can be seen from ground level, and a height of 40 ft would add very little extra warning time to prepare for an invasion. Eric Linklater, Orkney's most distinguished writer, in his book, *Orkney and Shetland*, postulates an alternative theory. He states that, since prehistoric times, these islands have been subjected to wave after wave of seaborne invasions and the only way to prevent a superior military force from overrunning the inadequate defences was to prevent it from landing. That being the case, the brochs were ideal platforms for a primitive form of catapult which, given the height, would enable the defenders to fling rocks at the invading boats and sink them before the enemy could land.

Who exactly the broch builders were is not known but they are commonly believed to have been the Picts, a race of people of which little is known as they left no written records of their way of life. They probably arrived in Shetland about AD 100 and either fled from or were

Lerwick Harbour, Mainland.

finally subdued by the Vikings around 900. At the height of their power their control of Britain extended from Shetland to Northumbria with occasional raids as far south as London.

Although the Norsemen probably arrived in Shetland as early as AD 700, it was not until Harald Fairhair, King of Norway, landed on Unst in the 10th C that they took control of Shetland and Orkney. The islands were then handed over to Earl Rognvald of Möre who in turn gave them to his brother, Sigurd Eysteinsson, who became the first Jarl (Earl) of Orkney and Lord of Shetland. The rule of the jarls was to continue for the next 500 years. Our knowledge of those years is derived from Norse sagas, the Orkneyinga Saga being the main source.

In 1469, the islands, by now under the rule of Denmark, were pledged to James III of Scotland in lieu of a dowry for King Christian's daughter, Margaret, when she married King James, and they have been part of Scotland, and later of

Great Britain, ever since, despite several attempts by Denmark to redeem the pledge. In 1564, Mary, Queen of Scots, granted the islands to her half brother, Lord Robert Stewart, and for the next 50 years he and his son, Earl Patrick, abused their position to enrich themselves and oppress the local population. After Earl Patrick's death the islands were assimilated into the rest of the Scottish kingdom. However, the effect of 500 years of Norse rule far outweighs the effect of a similar period under Scottish rule, and there persist, even today, place names, native dialects and local events that have more in common with Scandinavia than Scotland.

Mainland

Mainland covers an area of 378 square miles and is about 55 miles long with a maximum width of 20 miles, but the coastline is so indented that no point is more than three miles from the sea. The isthmus connecting the districts of Northmaven and Delting at Mavis

Sullom Voe oil terminal, Mainland.

Grind is only 100 yards wide, with the Atlantic Ocean on one side and the North Sea on the other.

Just under half of the population live in Lerwick, the chief town. Mainland's other population centres are Scalloway, Stenness, Sandness, Walls and, with the development of the offshore oil industry in the North Sea, Sullom Voe. Before the advent of the oil boom, the principle industries were crofting and fishing and, to a lesser extent, knitting. Physical evidence of the oil development has been confined to Sullom Voe, a deepwater inlet, or fjord, which can easily accommodate the largest oil tankers. An oil storage terminal has been built on the eastern side of the voe, where crude oil, pumped through submarine pipes from the rigs, is taken ashore and transferred to tankers. Sullom Voe may soon become the largest oil terminal in Europe.

Mainland is composed of old red sandstone in the east and sandstone interfolded with volcanic rock in the west. The limestone strip in the centre is the most fertile part, although there are other fertile patches in the heather and peat moorland. In the north-western Northmaven district, there are some of the oldest rocks in the world - pre-Cambrian, at least 2000 million years old. The north-west coast also has the wildest and most spectacular scenery in Shetland. In contrast to the sea and landscape, the houses and buildings on Mainland are, in the main, drab and uninteresting and yet, considering its varied past, you tend to expect something a little different. It's almost as if it's 'sinful' to brighten up the island. Only on the smaller islands can you see the Shetland of old: stone-built crofts scattered across a bleak landscape, the church or chapel standing out, alone and isolated from the rest of the community.

It's impossible to see Shetland without some form of transport unless you have several weeks in which to do it. The public bus service, although perfectly adequate for the islanders, is not really developed for the tourist. Either bring your own car on the ferry or hire a car in Lerwick. Although public transport may not be ideally suited to the tourist with only a few days to spare, there are, during the summer months, regular coach tours from Lerwick to Jarlshof, to the oil terminal at Sullom Voe and trips to see the various local craftsmen at work.

Lerwick is the centre of the fishing industry, well-equipped with fish-processing plants and accommodating a large number of foreign vessels. Its prosperity is based on the situation of its harbour, sheltered by the neighbouring island of Bressay. First used by the Vikings, Lerwick's

advantages were later recognised by the great fishing fleets of the Dutch, who set up small huts on the beach so that the fish merchants could trade. These huts, or 'booths' as they were known, quickly developed into a small town, later developed as a naval garrison by Cromwell in the war against the Dutch. Fort Charlotte, begun in 1665, is Lerwick's oldest building. The barrack block was added in the 18th C and the view from the ramparts takes in the whole of Bressay Sound.

Lerwick is the ideal place to base oneself to see all of Shetland. From here you can reach ferries that can take you to the other islands, and Lerwick airport, only a few miles from the town, has an excellent air service to most of the inhabited islands. The local Tourist Information office is extremely helpful in planning any trip you wish to make.

First stop should be the museum and library on Hill Head. The museum has a unique collection of Stone Age implements, Celtic ornaments and a wealth of exhibits from Norse times. The library, situated in the same building, contains a special 'Shetland' collection of literature. A few hundred yards north of the museum, in St Sunniva Street, is the oddly named 'Up Helly Aa' exhibition containing a full-size replica of the Viking longship that is sent up in flames on the last Tuesday in January of each year. The festival, started in 1889, is a declaration of the islanders' Viking past, saluting the Norse spirit in a pagan fire festival.

Before leaving this part of the island, you should walk the half mile down to Sumburgh Head. Looking over the Sumburgh Roost, a fierce ocean current that is at most times a turbulent rage of white water, you can see Fair Isle and, on a clear day, the island of Foula far out to the

west. We will come back to these two islands later. Heading back up the same road, turn left at Skelberry and take the road to Bigton where, connected to Mainland by a sweeping stretch of white sand, lies **St Ninian's Isle**. Since excavations began on the island during the 1950s, a priceless collection of Celtic silver has been found, together with a pre-Norse church and a Bronze Age burial ground.

The west coast of Mainland is not as indented as the eastern side and from Bigton up to Scalloway it is fairly straight. It's well worth the 12-mile hike over the Clift Hills to Scalloway. All the way up you will have fabulous views of the islands of Havra, Burra and Trondra and the small islands beyond - Oxna, Papa and Hildasay.

Six miles from Lerwick, on the west coast, is the old capital of Shetland, Scalloway. From the top of Scord Hill the view is a panorama of Shetland - hills, voes, islands, fishing villages, crofts and that ever-present force, the sea. The 17th-C castle dominates Scalloway, just as its builder dominated its people. The Royal Bastard, Earl Patrick Stewart, used forced labour from this area to build his castle, and from here he instituted a rule of terror and oppression throughout Shetland. Scalloway today is a thriving little fishing town, the harbour often crowded with fishing boats from many countries. On the west shore is a large fish-processing plant which can be visited to see what happens to the fish between landing and reaching the shops.

Scalloway lies at the southern end of one of the few fertile areas on Mainland, the Tingwall valley. A few miles from the town is Tingwall Loch, and at the north end of this loch is a peninsula, once the small islet **Law Ting Holm**, where the Norse parliament met to dispense justice. Following the A971 north,

Scalloway from Scord Hill, Mainland.

Weisdale Voe, Mainland.

the road climbs steeply to the top of Wormadale Hill. On a clear day you can see just about all of Shetland, certainly the whole of south Mainland and possibly as many as 50 or 60 islands or islets, including Fair Isle over 40 miles away. Down in the valley to the north-west is the Weisdale Voe and a few miles from the head of the voe is the only tree plantation in Shetland, containing mainly larch and spruce. The distance from Weisdale to Sandness, on the west coast, is only a matter of 16 or 17 miles via Bridge of Walls, but between those two points, on the north side of the road, there are at least 40 lochs.

Half a mile from Bridge of Walls, south of the main road, are the remains of a neolithic temple – Stanydale, heel-shaped in plan with a 12-ft-thick outer wall enclosing an oval area about 40 ft by 20 ft. In the rear of the chamber there are six shallow recesses. Similar structures have been found on the island of Whalsay and at Mnaidra in Malta.

Walls (Old Norse for 'two voes') is a fine natural harbour sheltered by the island of Vaila. Once an important fishing port, the village now shows the familiar signs of depopulation and decline - old and roofless crofts, damaged and decaying boats. Recently, however, the knitwear industry has given Walls a new lease on life and perhaps the decline can be stopped.

In order to reach north Mainland, visible across St Magnus Bay, you will have to go back to Bixter. The road twists and turns through Aith over bleak moorland, inhabited only by sheep and a few birds, until the road joins the main road north at Voe. Once you are past Mavis Grind, the landscape changes into wild and rugged terrain. Over towards Hillswick and Eshaness, the cliffs and offshore rocks are truly spectacular, one of the most impressive features being **'The Drongs'**, a series of jagged rock pinnacles in St Magnus Bay.

Further west at Stenness, scattered around the little pebble beach, are the remains of an old *haaf* (deep-sea) fishing station, the little stone huts now deserted. In days

Dore Holm, near Stenness.

gone by this was a thriving community and fishermen lived in the cottages throughout the season, salting and drying the fish on the beach. A little further east, towards the headland at Fiorda Taing is a large blowhole, about 60 ft deep and 40 ft from the cliff edge. From this point you get a marvellous view of **Dore Holm**, a giant rock about half a mile offshore having a tunnel cut by the action of the waves and looking like a giant archway. Rabbits abound in this part of Mainland, with rabbit holes every two or three feet over acres and acres of cliff-top moorland.

Back on the main road again, heading east, you come upon a little track which takes you up to Ronas Voe. The road here runs along the south side of the voe and affords a good view of the highest point in Shetland, Ronas Hill (1486 ft), but the view from here does not compare with that which can be seen from the top. All of Shetland and more is visible from up there. It's a long hike from the road but worth the climb. Back down to Brae, a sharp left turn leads you alongside Sullom Voe all the way to the oil terminal. To complete the trip of north Mainland the run back to Lerwick is more interesting via Laxo and Nesting, an area with many brochs, burnt mounds, standing stones and cairns (ancient burial sites).

Although Shetland offers much to the archaeologist and the geologist, it is the naturalist who will benefit most from these islands. For the birdwatcher in particular, Shetland is unique in the British Isles; divers, dunlins and merlins are all breeding birds of Shetland. Snowy owls can be seen on Ronas Hill, king eider and surf scooter in the voe below. Kittiwakes from Dore Holm fly to and from the little loch behind Stenness. Arctic skuas nest in many places in the hills and Sullom Voe is a good place to see Slavonian grebes and velvet scooters. Red-throated divers are common, tufted ducks nest in a few places and the moorlands support the curlew, lapwing and wheatear. The trees in Weisdale attract jackdaws, wood-pigeons, fieldfares, redwings and lapwings. In Weisdale Voe red-breasted mergansers and herons can be seen in winter. In the south, peregrines and fulmars glide over Fitful Head and whooper swans winter in the valley below. Even in Lerwick, eider ducks, shags and black guillemots feed within sight of the harbour. Other breeding birds include mallard, shelduck, whimbrel and glaucous gull. Migrants and winter visitors include the barnacle goose, hen harrier, jack snipe and the little auk.

Shetland's mammals are not so numerous as the birds and most of them have been introduced by man. Hedgehogs were introduced about 1860 and are fairly well distributed throughout Mainland. Some time during the 12th C the rabbit arrived. Myxomatosis is prevalent in the islands but the population is still large, especially on sea cliffs in isolated areas. The blue hare may be found on Ronas Hill as well as on the island of Vaila. Shetland long-tailed field-mice (also called wood-mice) seem to be the only indigenous mammal in the islands and have developed certain characteristics in isolation which at one time led it to be classified as a separate species. The otter, or 'dratsie' as the is-landers call it, is widespread, usually living by the sea or inland around the lochs.

Marine mammals include the grey seal, the population estimated at 3000, found mainly in the north of Unst, on the east side of Fetlar and at Fitful Head in south Mainland. There are numerous sightings of dolphins, killer whales and porpoises, mainly out to sea but occasionally near the headlands.

With over 2500 freshwater lochs, it's not surprising that the islands are famed among anglers. The brown trout and sea trout are numerous in all but the smallest lochs. There are some sites for salmon, and rainbow trout have recently been introduced. There is no charge for fishing in most waters but a permit is required. The Tourist Information office has a list of the free lochs and can also issue

Shags drying out.

permits. The brown-trout season is from 15 March to 6 October, sea trout from 25 February to 31 October.

Sea angling is also extremely rewarding in these waters with current records for rod-caught fish standing at 450 lb for shark, 226 lb for common skate and 190 lb for halibut. Boats are available for hire, and tackle and bait is on sale in Lerwick. Clear water, a varied marine life and an abundance of old wrecks make the islands an ideal place for sub-aqua divers. The local sub-aqua club welcomes experienced divers and compressor facilities are available.

Sailing is unfortunately limited for the visitor. The waters around the islands are dangerous and unpre-dictable to all but the most experienced yachtsman. However, both Lerwick and Scalloway have boating clubs which offer club-house facilities to visitors. Other sports available are golf (Lerwick has an 18-hole golf course just a few miles out of town towards the airport), tennis and bowling; putting facilities are also available.

Although only 14 of the Shetland islands are inhabited and therefore easily accessible, there are a few more islands that deserve a visit. Getting to them is not too difficult and, if you ask in the harbour on any of the large islands, there should always be a local fisherman willing to take you across.

Bressay

Lying half a mile across the sound from Lerwick is Bressay, six miles long and two-and-a-half miles wide with a population of 307. The whole island is dominated by the Ward of Bressay, a conical hill, 743 ft high, which is situated in the south of the island. Further south, a sheer cliff – The Ord – drops 500 ft to the sea below. The island is different from most of the other smaller islands in that it has a 'suburban' look about it: there are farms, not crofts; terraced houses look out over the small harbour; and in the square near the jetty is a public toilet, the only one to be found outside Lerwick. Fishing is the main industry and a fishmeal and fish-processing factory accounts for much of the island's work-force.

This is an island for walkers. There are no forms of public transport, although most local car drivers will stop for you should you

Bressay Harbour with Ward of Bressay in background.

need to get back to the ferry quickly. The roads are good and there is plenty of open moorland. Bressay has been inhabited since ancient times and has its fair share of broch sites, burnt mounds and standing stones plus the remains of three medieval churches. Heading south from the ferry terminal at Maryfield, the road leads to the ruins of the church at St John at Kirkabister. From then on it's a steep climb up over the Ord cliffs and down to Bard Head at the southern point of the island. Below the headland is a large cavern called the Cave of the Bard but known locally as the Orkneyman's Cave. The climb back over the Ward of Bressay is long and arduous but there is a wonderful view, spoiled only by a television transmitter.

The northern part of Bressay looks flat and uninteresting but, since most of the antiquities are to be seen there, it's not an area to miss. Just past the golf course near the Lochs of Beosetter is a standing stone and further north at Gunnista are the ruins of the medieval church of St Olaf. Over on the east coast at Cullingsburgh is an early Celtic church, St Mary's, and it was in this area that the famous 'Bressay Stone' was discovered. The stone, inscribed with ogham writing which reads 'The Cross of Naddod's Daughter, Child of Maqqddrroann', is now in the National Museum of Antiquities of Scotland in Edinburgh, but a facsimile can be seen in the Lerwick museum.

From a hill south-east of St Mary's church on Bressay, you can look down on Noss Sound and over to the little **Isle of Noss.** It has towering sandstone cliffs along its eastern and southern shores, the narrow ledges of which are packed with thousands of birds during the nesting season. Noss (its name is from the Old Norse word meaning 'point of rock') is one mile long and about half a mile wide. It was inhabited from early times, and in 1881 had a population of 24, but has been deserted since 1931 with the exception of the wardening staff –the Isle of Noss is now a National Nature Reserve. Visitors to the island must contact the Tourist Information office to find out if a crossing to the island is possible. The currents running through Noss Sound are fierce and the only boat available to make the crossing is a small inflatable dinghy manned by the Reserve staff. However, to really see Noss and its birds from the most impressive viewpoint - the sea - regular boat trips around the island are organised by a local boatman departing from the little harbour south of the ferry terminal at Lerwick.

Whalsay

About ten miles north of Bressay, lying about one mile off the east Mainland coast, is the island of Whalsay. Five-and-a-half miles in length and two-and-a-half miles wide, it has a population of 1005, almost all of which are directly or indirectly concerned with the fishing industry, although there are a few farms. Whalsay has a prosperous appearance, and is basically low-lying with three hills, the highest being the Ward of Clett at 360 ft. Its four main villages are Sandwick, Isbister, Brough and Skaw, with Symbister as the main town and port.

Fishing has always been important to Whalsay and the links with the older fishing days are still to be seen. Near the pier at Symbister is an old trading booth, the only complete example of its kind in Shetland, evidence of the days when the fishing industry was in the hands of the Hanseatic merchants.

Archaeologically, the island claims the most ancient site in all Shetland, the Standing Stones of Yoxie, a temple dating from 2000 BC. The courtyard and main structure measure 61 ft by 36 ft, and the inside chamber, unlike that at Stanydale, has a small annex making the general plan a figure-of-eight. 100 yards west is the Benie Hoose, a neolithic dwelling place believed to be the home of the priests who officiated at the temple. Further south in the Loch of Huxter, about one-and-a-half miles east of Symbister, is an island on which is a good example of an Iron Age fort. The island is joined to the shore by a man-made causeway and the situation is comparable in its position to the Broch of Clickhimin on Mainland. There is a regular car ferry service from Laxo on Mainland to Symbister and there is an airstrip at Skaw.

Between Whalsay and Mainland is a small islet called **West Linga** and about a dozen small holms. On the eastern side of Whalsay about a mile off the coast, there are some 12 to 15 other holms and skerries (varieties of islets and rocks), some with delightful names such as **Trota Stack**, **Nista**, **Mooa** and **Grif Skerry**. Although all of these are uninhabited, most of them have sheep grazing on the small areas of grass. At the end of the summer the farmers round them all up to bring them back by boat to a more hospitable area on Mainland or one of the other larger islands for the winter.

Noss Sound.

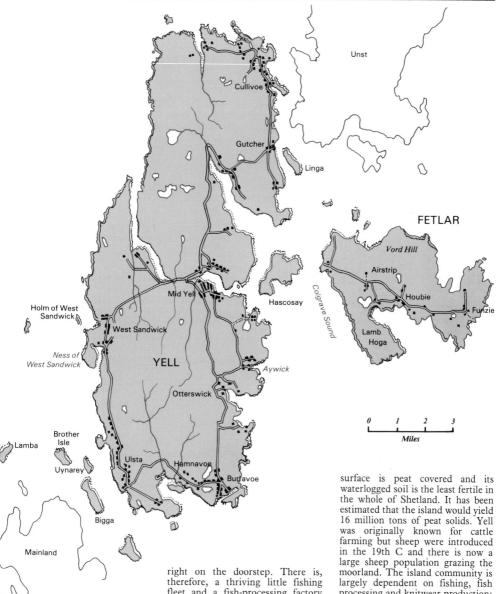

Out Skerries

About eight miles north-east of Whalsay lies the most easterly of all the Shetland islands - Out Skerries, a group of about 25 islets and rocks. Only two are inhabited, **Bruray** and **Housay**, locally known as the East Isle and the West Isle. These islands are joined to each other by a road bridge and, although the whole group covers an area of less than one square mile, the population is a staggering 91. The main reason for this is that the Skerries have a natural almost landlocked harbour and some of the best fishing grounds

right on the doorstep. There is, therefore, a thriving little fishing fleet and a fish-processing factory which, between them, employ nearly all the population. The north-isles ferry makes a weekly visit and Loganair have an airstrip on south Housay. Being so isolated, it seems that the whole community are pleased to see any visitor and they go out of their way to make you feel welcome - altogether a delightful place to visit.

Yell

North-west now to the island of Yell, the second largest in Shetland. 17 miles long from north to south and six miles wide, Yell covers an area of 83 square miles. The population numbers 1185, most of whom live in Cullivoe, Mid Yell, Burravoe and Ulsta. Two-thirds of the island's

surface is peat covered and its waterlogged soil is the least fertile in the whole of Shetland. It has been estimated that the island would yield 16 million tons of peat solids. Yell was originally known for cattle farming but sheep were introduced in the 19th C and there is now a large sheep population grazing the moorland. The island community is largely dependent on fishing, fish processing and knitwear production; there is some farming but mainly only on small crofts.

A car ferry operates from Toft on Mainland to Ulsta and from there the east road (B9081) runs through Hamnavoe to Burravoe at the south-eastern corner of Yell and then on up the east coast. Sightseers should be prepared to leave the road at several points on the way to Mid Yell, as there are many caves and natural arches, dozens of rock stacks and the remains of two brochs all within half a mile of the road. At Moss Houll, a brisk walk over the moorland to the cliff top will be rewarded by the sight of many impressive natural arches. It's better to stay on the coast road, through Aywick, Tow and finally up to Mid Yell; the landscape

The west coast of Yell.

on this route is really worth seeing. The motorist should then leave his car at Mid Yell and do some walking.

Mid Yell has a superb natural harbour, almost totally landlocked. At this point Mid Yell Voe to the east and Whale Firth to the west almost meet, with just a few hundred feet of land preventing Yell from being divided into two separate islands. The coastline from Ulsta north to Mid Yell, through Setter and West Sandwick, is not as interesting as the east side, nor are there as many crofts but, as on the east coast, there are two brochs, one at the Head of Brough just north of Everhoull, and the other at West Sandwick. This road hugs the coastline and affords splendid views across Yell Sound over numerous islets and skerries - **Brother Isle, Uynarey, Lamba, Little Roe** and **Muckle Holm**. At West Sandwick there is a beautiful white sand beach sheltered by the tiny islet of **Holm of West Sandwick**. From here to the northern tip of the island, the scenery is magnificent.

Yell is the ideal place for anyone who wants to do some hiking and birdwatching. There are miles of heather-covered moorland, with nothing in sight but the sheep and the birds. The breeding birds of Yell are the same as those of Mainland.

Fetlar

Lying east of Yell and south of Unst is Fetlar, 15 square miles in area with good fertile soil (it is known as the 'garden of Shetland') and a strong farming tradition. No evidence exists of early (neolithic) activity on the island and it seems that the first inhabitants were the

Picts. There has been a steady decline in population since the 1830s, a situation made worse by the Clearances. In 1872 the Truck Commission tried to stem the flow of emigrants from the isles as did the Crofters' Act of 1886 which gave them security of tenure. In many places the population stabilised, but not, it seems, in the case of Fetlar, where the trend to seek a new life free from the hardships of island life continued; in 1841 there were 761 inhabitants, in 1901 there were 347, and by 1978 the island population was down to 103.

Much of the northern part of the island is a nature reserve run by the Royal Society for the Protection of Birds (RSPB). Fetlar is well known for its snowy owls and anyone wishing to see them should contact the warden at Bealance; visits can only be arranged if conditions allow so as not to disturb these beautiful birds. Visitors should always realise, wherever they are, that to cause any bird to leave its nest, even for a few minutes, will invite egg robbing by gulls and skuas, or may even cause the bird to desert the nest completely. In addition, it is illegal to visit the nests of the red-throated diver, the whimbrel and the merlin without first getting written approval from the Nature Conservancy Council.

Apart from the birds, grey seals breed on several beaches between East Neap and the Kirn of Gula, and it is best to see these magnificent animals in late autumn when the pups are born. The otter is still to be found on Fetlar; large numbers have been located at Brough Lodge and also at Urie. Good fishing can be found on and off the island. Small

boats may be hired in Houbie and a day's fishing just off the coast will prove most enjoyable, the likely catch being saithe, mackerel and whiting. There are also several lochs on Fetlar, all well stocked with brown trout and eels.

Because the island is very fertile there is a fine and varied selection of wild flowers including the northern gentian, frog orchid, insectivorous sundew and monkeyflower. Fetlar has more caves than any other island in the group, numerous stacks and natural arches, beautiful bays and impressive cliffs. Getting to the island is no problem; it is connected to Yell by the ferry service and also has its own airstrip. Boats and cars can be hired, and there are several guest houses and a general store.

Before moving on to Unst, there are two small islands worthy of a mention in this area. **Hascosay**, lying between Yell and Fetlar, has an area of about 750 acres, and **Uyea** (598 acres) is just south of Unst. Both islands were inhabited until recently and Uyea contains the smallest and best-preserved pre-Reformation chapel in Shetland.

Unst

For many visitors the attraction of Unst lies in the fact that it is the most northerly place in Britain. Its population is 1050, scattered over an area 12 miles long by six miles wide. There are a considerable number of antiquities including heel-shaped and chambered cairns, several standing stones and 11 broch sites. A number of Viking sites have been excavated at Clibberswick and Sandwick, and a complete Viking longhouse at Underhoull.

But by far the most impressive

been completed at Baltasound to cater for the growing number of helicopters taking men and supplies out to the oil rigs in the North Sea, the Ninian Field being only 82 miles away.

Since public transport is virtually non-existent on Unst, it's wise, if you are not taking a car, to arrange for a taxi to pick you up at the airport or ferry terminal to take you to your base. Baltasound is ideal, right in the middle of the island with easy access to all parts. This island is perfect for the walker; you are never more than a couple of hours away from any starting point. Some suggested walks are: from Balta-sound over Vallafield to Westing; from Westing up the coast to the Dale of Woodwick; the Hermaness National Nature Reserve; from Haroldswick to the top of Saxa Vord and along the cliffs to Skaw. There are numerous skerries and holms on the west, and near Herma Ness in the north is a series of rocks, culminating in one called **Out Stack** – the most northerly point in the British Isles.

Wherever you go you can not fail to see the Shetland ponies; Unst exports more than any other island in Shetland. Each year in October at the pony sales at Baltasound over 200 of these delightful animals are sold, most of them to be exported to the British mainland and the Continent. Most species of Shetland birds are to be found on the island.

West Coast Islands
Leaving Unst and heading down the west coast of Mainland we come to St Magnus Bay which contains no fewer than five islands and several dozen small holms. **Muckle Roe** is the largest. Circular-shaped with a diameter of three-and-a-half miles, it is connected to west Mainland by a bridge, 360 ft long and 5 ft wide. Most of the population (about 90) live along Roe Sound and down the east coast. South Ward hill, situated right in the middle of the island,

monument on the island is the castle built by Laurence Bruce, half brother to Earl Robert. Muness Castle is situated on the south-east tip of Unst about two miles from the village of Uyeasound. It has three rooms on the first floor: one large central room with a large fireplace, and two smaller rooms, one on either side of the main hall. Down below on the ground floor are a series of passageways and several cellars and storerooms. The main door to the castle is always locked but visitors only have to ask at the small croft next door for the key and a torch for the cellars.

About 100 yards away is another croft and living there is one of the very few women who spin by hand and make the fine lace shawls for which Shetland is famous. It takes her about a year to complete one shawl and, because the young people of the island are leaving to make more money in 'civilisation', there will very soon come a time when the craft will disappear. Unst is a craft island, with baskets, sealskin products, knitwear and fine lace shawls all being produced here.

There are, however, many empty crofts and, with the recent wetter summers, many more crofters will have to leave this island unless help is given. There is a large RAF station at Saxa Vord, manned by 800 men, which also provides work for many islanders both directly and indirectly. A new airstrip has just

Muness Castle, Unst.

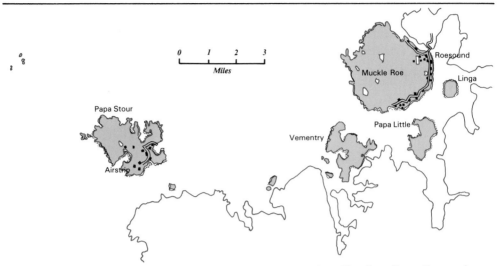

is 557 ft high, and there are at least 20 lochs. There are no brochs or cairns but the west-coast scenery, particularly between North and South Ham, is among the finest in Shetland.

Muckle Roe has two attendant holms: **Linga** ('heather isle'), a circular islet of about 170 acres, lying between Muckle Roe and Mainland, and **Crog Holm**, a tiny islet of no more than ten acres lying in Roe Sound. South of Muckle Roe are two smaller islands, **Papa Little** and **Vementry**. The former was inhabited until 1828. We can assume that, as with all other islands with 'papa' in their names, it would have been colonised by Celtic priests about 2000 years ago. It is quite fertile and rises to a height of 250 ft. Vementry is the largest of all the uninhabited islands, 959 acres. It has so many 'arms' and 'legs' (voes, lochs, headlands and attendant holms) that looking at this little island is almost like seeing the whole of Shetland in miniature. Cairns and mounds tell of ancient occupations and two six-inch guns from World

War I show that it had a certain military importance at that time. The two larger holms on the south side of Vementry are **Linga** (not to be confused with the holm near Muckle Roe) and **Gruna**, each about 40 acres in extent.

About eight miles west of Vementry lies **Papa Stour**, the 'big isle of the priests'. Three square miles in area, the island has a population of 42. Its volcanic rock formations contain one of the finest sets of sea caves in Britain and they are accessible at most times. Sandness is the nearest point on Mainland and boat trips can be arranged from there. Papa Stour has a lot to offer the geologist; there are several subterranean passages on the south and west coasts. The only inhabited part of the island is the settlement around Housa Voe on the east coast. The island was a leper colony during the 18th C; in addition, sufferers of a particularly bad type of scurvy were sent there. Papa Stour has several nearby holms: **Forewick Holm**, **Holm of Melby**, **Fogla Skerry**, and **Ve**

Skerries, five miles north-west, with its notoriously dangerous current.

Sheltering the entrance to Walls harbour on Mainland is the little isle of **Vaila**, 757 acres in size and inhabited until quite recently. The watch tower is the only prominent feature, although there are also caves, burnt mounds, natural arches and a cairn. The island has obviously seen more prosperous times and, in the days of haaf fishing, it must have fairly bustled with activity.

Off the west Mainland coast between Whiteness and Scalloway are about 35 skerries and holms, ranging in size from tiny rocks of only a few square yards to islands such as **Hildasay** and **Oxna** with over 100 acres. Some of the smaller ones - **Flotta**, **Hoy**, **North Havra**, **Papa**, **Sanda Stour** and **Langa** - are mentioned here only because they are very pretty; one does not need to visit them to appreciate the natural beauty of these little emeralds since all of them are only a few hundred yards off the west Mainland coast.

Down the west coast of Mainland, along the Clift Hills, are the islands of Trondra and East and West Burra. **Trondra** (population 65) is approached from Mainland by way of a bridge. The island is two miles long by about half-a-mile wide and is rather bleak and barren. It has no fishing industry and no harbour but, being connected to Mainland, its inhabitants can cross to Scalloway without difficulty for employment. Another bridge connects Trondra with **Burra**. This island looks like a giant capital H, with East and West Burra separated by a narrow channel over which a bridge has been built. West Burra is five miles long by about 600 yd wide and East Burra

Muckle Roe.

Opposite: *Pool of Virkie, Sumburgh, Mainland.*

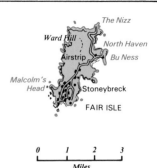

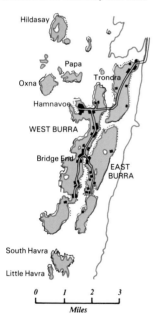

North Haven harbour, Fair Isle.

about three miles long by 1000 yd wide. The total area of both is less than five square miles and the population is 797. Its prosperity depends almost entirely on fishing, with some crofting, although the soil is not good. The main population centres are Hamnavoe in the north of West Burra, and Bridge End on the west side of the central bridge.

Hamnavoe has one of the most delightful sheltered harbours in Shetland and the sight of half-a-dozen fishing boats sheltering in the little voe on a stormy day is worth the visit for that alone. Both East and West Burra have lots to offer the hiker, with over 25 miles of rugged coastline, indented by many voes and bays, and lots of caves and natural arches. There is a standing stone and two cairns at Norbister on East Burra.

A little further south is a small (147 acres) islet called **South Havra** and its attendant holm, **Little Havra**. You can hire a boat to South Havra at Maywick on Mainland. This little island sums up most people's idea of a desert island and just to walk over it with nothing to see or find other than what nature has provided is well worth the boatman's fee. South of St Ninian's Isle, already mentioned, is an islet called **Colsay**, which must have been used as a burial place in ancient times since there are the remains of a cairn on the south-east side. 54 acres in size, Colsay shelters the Bay of Scousburgh.

Fair Isle

About 25 miles south of Sumburgh Head lies an island known to every ornithologist in the world – Fair Isle. Three miles long and one mile wide, the northern half of the island is barren moorland, the south is fertile and has many crofts. The population

of 79, after many years of decline, seems to be holding steady. The National Trust for Scotland purchased the island in 1954 and since then an extensive modernisation scheme has been carried out, many crofts have been improved and electricity provided. Most of the modernisation work has been carried out by young people from the International Voluntary Service.

The National Trust for Scotland have also created alternative work for the crofters by providing a weaving shed and by employing the islanders on construction work. Fair Isle knitwear is famous the world over and, although knitting is also a major industry on the other islands in the group, only Fair Isle still uses the traditional colours derived from native plants instead of the new chemical dyes used elsewhere.

The largest burnt mound in Shetland is situated on Fair Isle, 122 ft long, 88 ft wide and 10 ft high. There are over 200 of these grass-covered heaps of stones in Shetland, some broken and discoloured by heat, the accepted explanation being that they were a prehistoric type of kitchen.

In 1588, the flagship of the defeated Spanish Armada, *El Gran Grifon*, was wrecked at Sivars Geo. The crew of 600 were saved and spent six or seven weeks on Fair Isle, eating most of the islanders' food and nearly causing a famine before they could be transported to Mainland.

Most visitors to Fair Isle come to the bird observatory situated at North Haven. The hostel, where visitors are expected to help in the general upkeep and running, accommodates 24 people and is open between March and November, with May being the best time to see breeding birds. Because of its isolated geographical position on the migratory routes, more rare birds have been recorded here than in any other part of the British Isles. Since the observatory opened in 1948, over 119,500 birds of 227 different species have been caught, examined and ringed. At most times throughout the year the island is alive with birdwatchers from many countries and conversation at the hostel seems to consist of only what birds have been seen or not seen during the day; to the uninitiated it's almost like a foreign language.

The island has an airstrip and a weekly service is operated by Loganair. There is also a ferry service (*The Good Shepherd*) operating between North Haven and Grutness on Mainland. Anyone wishing to book at the observatory hostel should write directly to The Warden, Bird Observatory, Fair Isle, Shetland.

Foula

The most isolated island in Shetland is Foula. Three-and-a-half miles long by two-and-a-half miles wide, it is without doubt one of the loneliest inhabited islands in the British Isles. It has a population of 41 who maintain their own weekly boat service to Walls on Mainland. Foula has no harbour and is often cut off for weeks during the winter. The island rises to 1372 ft with cliffs around the entire coast reaching a maximum height of 1220 ft. The name means 'bird isle' in Old Norse and there is an immense wealth of bird life to be seen. Visitors should remember that a trip to Foula means one week on this lonely outpost and, unless you can persuade one of the islanders to offer accommodation, you must take a tent.

Shetland is a land controlled by the weather. Good weather means good crops, happy fishermen and dry peat. Most of the smaller islands and many people on Mainland rely on this fuel for heating and cooking; even on Mainland, peat cutting is a major activity. It is of great value, clean to handle, has a pleasant smell and will give heat two-thirds that of coal but without soot and dirtiness. From early May onwards people can be seen on the moors cutting peat. When a suitable 'bank' is found, the turf is cut off, and then, with a special tool known as a 'tushkar', the peat bricks are cut from the bank and laid out to drain. After a few weeks the bricks are built into small stacks to allow the air to circulate between them. When completely dry, they are transported back to the croft, ready for winter. Peat used to be transported by Shetland ponies but now it's usually done by car or hand cart. Wet summers can wipe out the winter fuel stocks, just as it can destroy winter feed for the cattle and sheep as happened during the latter part of the 1970s when many crofters had to sell their stock. If the islanders can't provide for themselves, then everything has to be imported at extremely high prices and, in the majority of cases, the prices are too high.

One of the main problems in Shetland is the attraction of working for the oil companies instead of on the croft or by fishing. High salaries offered to young people mean fewer people to work the land and man the boats. When the oil runs out (and run out it eventually will), who will want to return to the croft or to the fishing boats? As long as more can be made elsewhere the old way of life will deteriorate and depopulation will set in on a grand scale until eventually the islands die. For them to become empty would be a tragedy. Shetland has a uniqueness that should be kept forever and not just as a few uninhabited islands off the north coast of Britain.

Regular sea and air service to Shetland are operated by British Airways, Loganair and P & O Ferries. For full details on all transportation and accommodation, contact the Tourist Information office at Lerwick.

Orkney

Situated just six miles, at the nearest point, from the extreme north of Scotland, but separated by one of the most turbulent stretches of water in the British Isles – the Pentland Firth – Orkney consists of over 70 islands, of which only 18 are inhabited: Mainland, Graemsay, Hoy, Flotta, South Ronaldsay, Burray, Gairsay, North Ronaldsay, Shapinsay, Eday, Egilsay, Wyre, Stronsay, Rousay, Sanday, Westray, Papa Westray and Cava. The total population is 18,118 and the total sea area covered measures 53 miles from north to south and 30 miles from east to west, a total land area of about 240,000 acres. Orkney (never 'the Orkneys' or 'Orkney Islands', since the suffix 'ey' is Old Norse for 'islands') has a relatively simple rock structure, with mainly sedimentary rocks of the old red sandstone period. The upper beds consist of gritty sandstone which give rise to poor acid soils; the middle beds are flagstones and whinstones, some with a high proportion of lime, some with a sandy texture and some weathering to clay.

Orkney has, over long periods of prehistory, experienced many changes in sea level. Even as recently as the end of the last Ice Age the islands were joined to the Scottish mainland. Like Shetland, it is almost treeless but the evidence of forests in the peat mosses and submerged foreshores indicates substantial growths during the post-glacial boreal period, between 7500 and 5500 BC.

Neolithic man arrived shortly afterwards around 3500 BC. Bones have been found that show that he was short in height with a medium-to-long skull, of the Mediterranean or sub-tropical species. He was followed by Bronze Age man whose burial system was similar to that of the 'beaker folk' of Europe. Greek and Latin historians recorded that the islands were inhabited by two races – the Picts and the Papae, the latter being Celtic clergy. In AD 43 the Roman fleet of Claudius negotiated a non-aggression pact with the people of Orkney suggesting that the Picts had considerable power and influence at that time. St Columba visited the 'King of Orkney' about AD 500 to ask for safe conduct for his missionaries. That an effective passport was issued proves the existence of a strong and stable government.

The Norse invasion of Orkney began in about AD 700. According to the Orkneyinga Saga, written in 13th-C Iceland, the power of the

Peat stacks.

Norse 'jarls' (earls) reached its peak about 1100. Earl Thorfinn the Mighty ruled Orkney and Shetland, the Western Isles, much of northern Scotland and a large part of Ireland from a small tidal island off the west coast of Mainland (the largest island in both Orkney and Shetland is known by this name) called the Brough of Birsay. The remains of the cathedral and palace he built can still be seen.

Thorfinn's grandson, Magnus Erlendsson, became joint-earl with Haakon Paulson. Magnus had a reputation for kindness and understanding while his co-earl was a typical war-loving Viking. Haakon, dissatisfied with only half the power and wealth, tricked Magnus into a meeting on the island of Egilsay at Easter in 1117 and had him murdered. However, such was the

popularity of Magnus that stories quickly surfaced of miraculous healings at places with which he had been connected, particularly at the site of his death. In 1130 Magnus was canonised and a few years later his nephew, Earl Rognvald, founded St Magnus Cathedral in Kirkwall.

The body of Magnus, with an axe wound in the skull, has lain in the cathedral ever since.

In 1468 the Norse link was broken when King Christian of Denmark pledged Orkney and, in 1469, Shetland to King James III. Under Scottish rule many tyrants

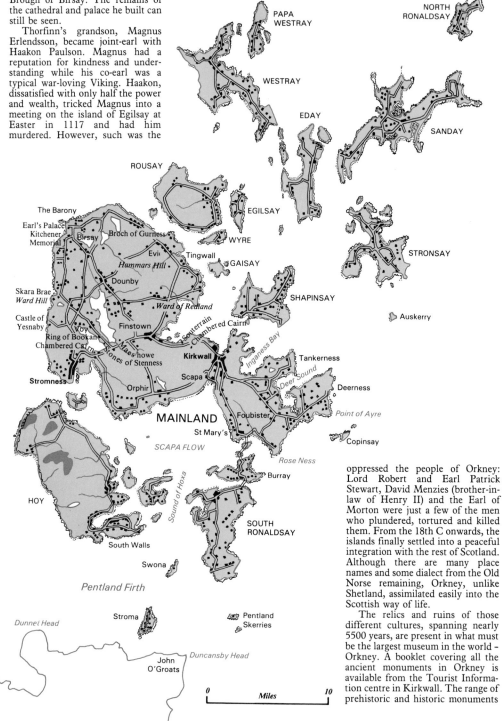

oppressed the people of Orkney: Lord Robert and Earl Patrick Stewart, David Menzies (brother-in-law of Henry II) and the Earl of Morton were just a few of the men who plundered, tortured and killed them. From the 18th C onwards, the islands finally settled into a peaceful integration with the rest of Scotland. Although there are many place names and some dialect from the Old Norse remaining, Orkney, unlike Shetland, assimilated easily into the Scottish way of life.

The relics and ruins of those different cultures, spanning nearly 5500 years, are present in what must be the largest museum in the world – Orkney. A booklet covering all the ancient monuments in Orkney is available from the Tourist Information centre in Kirkwall. The range of prehistoric and historic monuments

Kirkwall Harbour, Mainland.

and treasures is vast. The houses and tombs of neolithic man, the barrows of the Bronze Age, the brochs of the Picts, the churches of the Papae, the settlements of the Viking and the castles of the Stewarts are all there for the visitor to see, some of them in a well-preserved condition and others no more than a few battered and broken stones on the ground. The settlement sites, such as Skara Brae and Knap of Howar, have survived more by chance than by design. Medieval farmers needed either the land or the stones, or both, more than they needed a monument to a distant culture and many sites are now no more than indentations or mounds in a farmer's field.

There are over 100 brochs in Orkney. Their condition is not as good as those in Shetland, but two of them, at Gurness and Midhowe, have been reasonably well preserved. Apart from the brochs the most distinctive Pictish objects are the decorated symbol stones, but the most impressive and best-preserved monuments are the Stone Age tombs.

The general appearance of Orkney is, apart from the island of Hoy, flat and mainly agricultural, and the difference from Shetland is immediately apparent: well-laid-out fields, farms rather than crofts and a distinct 'green' look about it. The Orkadian has been well described as 'a crofter with a boat', whereas the Shetlander is 'a fisherman with a croft'. The weather, however, is generally the same as in Shetland, with winter and summer average daily mean temperatures differing only by about 17 degrees Fahrenheit, and with violent winds. The average annual rainfall is 37.1 inches, with few air frosts and much less snow than the Scottish mainland.

Mainland

Mainland, the largest island, has a population of 13,931 and covers 121,000 acres, measuring 23 miles east to west and 17 miles north to south. The capital and administrative centre is Kirkwall (Old Norse *kirkiu-vagr* meaning 'church bay'), situated on the north side of the narrow waist of Mainland by a small lagoon called the Peerie Sea. The little harbour, triangular in shape, provides a safe mooring for small boats. The visitor staying at one of the hotels in Harbour Street will be amazed at the amount of activity that goes on in this area. From dawn until dusk there is the constant sound of boats entering and leaving the harbour, loading or unloading, men coming from and going to a day's fishing, passengers for the ferry and, above all this, the cries of the gulls.

Opposite the main pier is the gaunt, towering, Kirkwall Hotel, dominating the harbour. Down the eastern side of the hotel is the entrance to Bridge Street, the start of a long winding road which changes into Albert Street, Broad Street, Victoria Street and Main Street before running out of town west

St Magnus Cathedral, Kirkwall, Mainland.

along Wellington Street. Known locally as 'The Street', this is the centre of Kirkwall, full of shops, offices, cafés and silversmiths. Narrow and stone-paved, it fairly bustles with people at most times of the day but it's very attractive and clean, with one large tree situated in the middle of Albert Street. On the east side of Broad Street, dominating the town, stands the Romanesque-style St Magnus Cathedral. Constructed of red and yellow sandstone it seems surprising that such a magnificent chuch should have been built here at all and that it should have remained in such a splendid condition since 1137.

The Earl's Palace, Kirkwall.

Across the road, in Watergate, are two other impressive structures - the Bishop's Palace and the Earl's Palace. The former, now a roofless shell, was built in the 12th C for Bishop William the Old (1102 -1168). It was here that the Norwegian King Haakon died in 1263, after his defeat at the Battle of Largs. Although only the outer walls and the tower still stand it's not difficult to imagine the sort of stately life-style the Bishop enjoyed. A few yards away stands the Earl's Palace, constructed for 'The Black Pate', Earl Patrick Stewart, in 1600. This imposing residence consists of three main apartments; a great hall and two smaller rooms at first-floor level; and some rather magnificent cellars and store rooms below. The most impressive parts of the building are the beautiful Renaissance doorway, the bow windows and the fireplace in the great hall, and there is an Elizabethan-style carved decoration throughout.

Back in Broad Street, opposite the cathedral, is Tankerness House and gardens. Built in the 16th C for the merchant family of Baikie, the house is a fine example of an Orkney mansion. Open to the public it contains beautiful furniture, paintings and household items depicting the life and times of an Orkney family. Behind is a fine, well-laid-out and secluded garden.

There are many little houses and gardens in Kirkwall worthy of a visitor's time, particularly at the northern end between Junction Road and Shore Street, and a peaceful walk around will allow the visitor to see much of the old world charm of Kirkwall so often bypassed during the hustle and bustle of a busy day. Two miles south of the town is one of the great malt whisky distilleries of Scotland - Highland Park - founded in 1798 by Grant of Speyside. It is possible to tour it if you first obtain permission.

From Kirkwall, taking the A965 west, one can begin to see the wide range of archaeological remains that make Orkney unique. About one mile from the town, near Hatston, is a particularly fine underground earth house. This 'souterrain' has the unusual feature of a flight of steps leading down to the passage and central chamber. Further west at Rennibister is another earth house which, when excavated, yielded the bones of 18 people. To the south of Rennibister on top of Wideford Hill is a chambered cairn, and an interesting example of a chambered tomb is at Cuween Hill, a mile south of Finstown. The masonry is of a high quality but the low passageway makes it difficult for visitors to appreciate.

Finstown derives its name from David Phin of Limerick, an Irish drummer who came to Orkney in 1811 with the 19th Royal Veteran Battalion and eventually built an inn, the Toddy Hole, in the area. North of Finstown on the A966, past the Ward of Redland and Hammars Hill, a little road leads off right to Evie. Half a mile from the pier, overlooking Eynhallow Sound, is the Broch of Gurness. Although not as well preserved as the brochs of Clickhimin and Mousa in Shetland it is nevertheless well worth visiting. Within sight of the Broch of Gurness, across the Eynhallow Sound on the island of Rousay, there are three other brochs, all of them guarding this narrow stretch of water.

The A966 now runs up the coast around the shores of the Loch of Swannay and into the parish of Birsay. At the end of the 16th C, Earl Robert built a palace in this delightful little village and, although now in a much dilapidated condition, the remains show that it was once a fine, noble building. Historical records reveal that the palace had barns and stables, peat stacks and cornfields, flower and herb gardens, a rabbit warren plus archery butts and a bowling green, all within its precincts. Along the shore to the north is Earl Thorfinn's island, the Brough of Birsay, of about 50 acres. A narrow causeway, covered at high tide, runs across to the isle. From the causeway the

island slopes steeply up to the cliffs of the western side. Near the cliffs are the ruins of an early 12th-C chapel dedicated to St Peter and the remains of a Viking settlement. Birsay gets its name from the Old Norse *byrgi* meaning fortress and *ey* meaning island. Today it's difficult to imagine why anyone would want to fortify this little rock.

A few miles down the coast, off the B9056, are the magnificent cliffs of Marwick Head which rise to nearly 300 ft. It was here that, on 5 June 1916, the cruiser *Hampshire* sank after hitting a mine. Nearly all were lost, among them Lord Kitchener, and on top of the headland a monument has been erected to their memory. Now travel down through the fertile Marwick Valley to the Bay of Skaill, one of the most attractive bays and certainly one of the best beaches in Orkney. Here there stands the most remarkable prehistoric settlement in Britain - Skara Brae. The houses, streets and alleyways of a small village, built around 3500 BC, are so well preserved that even the stone furniture inside the houses still survives. The inhabitants of this neolithic village were forced to abandon their homes when a great sandstorm covered the area. The unique degree of preservation of this site and the everyday items in use at the time is due entirely to this covering of sand.

Above Skara Brae stands the 17th-C house of Bishop Graham. This imposing mansion is one of the oldest houses on the island still in occupation. From Skaill down to Stromness, the coastline is rugged and rocky and contains many strange sea stacks. One such stack is called the Castle of Yesnaby so named because of its castle-like shape. The highest point along this coast is Black Craig which rises to 360 ft. Coming into Stromness one can immediately see that it is a very different town from Kirkwall, having only a single incredibly narrow street over one mile long. The houses on the seaward side have all been built with the gable ends protruding out toward the sea and many will have a sea door with a pier or jetty. There is an excellent museum which displays the historic life of the town in a well-planned and entertaining way. The Vikings called this place Hamnavoe, meaning Haven Bay, and to visitors arriving on the ferry from Scrabster on a summer's day, that's exactly what it looks like.

Three miles north of the town is one of the best fishing lochs in Orkney, the Loch of Stenness, separated by a narrow isthmus from the Loch of Harray. At one end of this strip of land stands the Ring of Brogar and at the other, the Standing Stones of Stenness. The

Stromness, Mainland, with Hoy in background.

Ring of Brogar is perhaps the most impressive of the two large monuments, being 340 ft in diameter and originally consisting of 60 stones. Only 27 stones of varying heights still stand, but, nevertheless, the circle, stones and mounds around the site leave one with the impression that the whole complex could have been, as has been suggested, a neolithic lunar observatory. The Standing Stones of Stenness on the other hand are not quite so grand, only four stones having survived out of a possible 12. It is, however, interesting to stand in the middle of both circles and ponder the problems of quarrying, transporting and erecting such giant monoliths around the year 3000 BC.

Maeshowe, Mainland.

Back on the Kirkwall road we come to the finest Stone Age tomb in the British Isles, Maeshowe. Encircled by a dry moat 45 ft wide and 6 ft deep stands a dome-shaped mound 24 ft high and 115 ft in diameter. The interior of the tomb is one of the great architectural achievements of prehistoric man. Whatever treasure these people buried with their dead we shall never know since the Vikings carried it off. They also recorded their presence in the tomb by a series of runic inscriptions. These inscriptions, or 'graffiti' as we call them today, have been deciphered as reading: 'The Pilgrims to Jerusalem broke into Orkahowe' (*Orkahowe* meaning 'the tomb on the island of Ork') and

'Haakon alone bore the treasure out of this tomb.' From other inscriptions it's clear that, like man throughout the ages, the 12th-C Viking too liked to write rude things on walls and they also show that Maeshowe was used for other things as well as burials. One reads: 'Thorny was bedded, Heigi says so.' Ironically, these runic characters, and also, incidently, some inscribed pictures, are now estimated by archaeologists to be far more valuable than the treasure carried off by the Vikings for their insight into the nature and habits of the Norsemen.

Before you head back to Kirkwall there is one other interesting place to visit in west Mainland - Orphir Church, just off the A964 on the shore of Scapa Flow, the only circular medieval church in Scotland. Built in the early 12th C and dedicated to St Nicholas, the church was built by Earl Haakon after his pilgrimage to the Holy Land and was modelled on the Church of the Holy Sepulchre in Jerusalem.

East Mainland is not as interesting nor as rich in remains as the west. Mainly flat agricultural land, the principle livestock is Black Aberdeen Angus cattle and any crops produced are used mainly for animal feed. Deerness has some spectacular cliffs and beautiful sandy beaches which, even at the height of the holiday season, remain uncrowded. In fact, it would be unusual to see more than two dozen people on any half-mile stretch of beach. At Skaill boat trips can be arranged to sail into The Gloup, an awe-inspiring natural cleft in the rock face. The skill of the boatman in negotiating the small entrance into this vast chasm is impressive, especially if there is a slight swell at the time. On a sunny day the light reflected inside the cave is very beautiful.

The South Isles

Although very definitely islands the eastern group of the South Isles are joined to Mainland by a giant concrete barrier known as the Churchill Causeway. In the early part of World War II, the eastern defences of Scapa Flow, an important British naval base, were protected by submarine nets laid betwen the islands of Lamb Holm, Glims Holm, Burray and South Ronaldsay. Many of the islands' sounds contain ships which were sunk to form a 'boom'. However, in October 1939, a German U-boat slipped through the defences and torpedoed the battleship *Royal Oak*, and over 800 men died when she sank. It was obvious that the defences of Scapa Flow were inadequate and Winston Churchill ordered the building of the concrete barrier between the islands to prevent any further penetration from the eastern approach. 2000 Italian prisoners-of-war were employed to construct thousands of five- and ten-ton concrete blocks, which were then dropped into the water until all the channels were closed. Later a road was built along the top of the barrier. In their spare time, these Italian prisoners built a small chapel on **Lamb Holm**. The chapel, converted from two Nissen huts, is so beautiful that each year it attracts thousands of visitors to this tiny islet.

The Churchill Barrier.

Burray with a population of 270 is about two miles from north to south and four miles from east to west. It has some fine cliffs and caves on the eastern side and golden sands on the west. Many old rusting boom-ships are visible on both sides of the causeway, especially at low water. Connected to Burray by a small stone causeway is the tiny islet of **Hunda**, a breeding site for a large number of birds including, storm petrels, ducks and gulls.

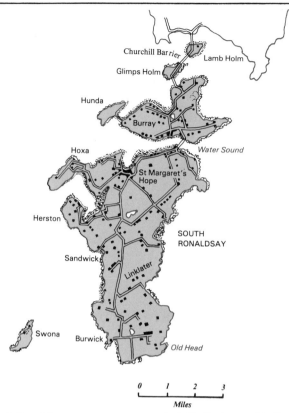

South Ronaldsay

0   1   2   3
Miles

South Ronaldsay

This island has a population of 824 and measures about seven miles by three-and-a-half miles, with cliffs on the east rising to about 200 ft. These cliffs are indented by small bays with white sandy beaches and thousands of sea birds nest on the ledges. The main population centre is the relatively unspoiled village of St Margaret's Hope. West of the village, out on Hoxa Head, are the ruins of a broch, reputed to be the burial place of the notorious Viking, Thorfinn the Skullsplitter. There are also medieval churches on the island but, apart from these, there is little else of antiquity to see. It is, however, ideal for a family outing, with good beaches, boating and safe swimming in many of the little bays.

Ramblers and birdwatchers will find lots to interest them since there are plenty of cliff walks and nesting birds in the area. There is also a rather charming festival which takes place in the little sandy bay on the Hoxa isthmus. The 'Boys' Ploughing Match and the Festival of the Horse' is held in mid-August when the boys and girls of the island, dressed in vividly colourful costumes, plough the sands with miniature replicas of ancient ploughs.

The island of **Swona** is situated two-and-a-half miles off the south-west coast of South Ronaldsay. One-and-a-half miles long and half a mile wide, the island is surrounded by treacherous currents. Boat trips can be arranged but there is little on the island that cannot be seen elsewhere.

Three miles south of South Ronaldsay, lonely and isolated in the North Sea, lie the **Pentland Skerries**. The main islet is **Muckle Skerry**, oval in shape and 103 acres in size, on which the only buildings are the lighthouse and the foghorn tower. Three smaller skerries in the group are situated about half a mile to the east. The largest of these, **Little Skerry**, is a breeding ground for the grey seal, and the whole group is a resting place for a variety of migrant birds.

The islands of the western group of the South Isles are not joined together like their eastern counterparts. But from Stromness regular ferry services operate to Graemsay, Hoy and Flotta, and boats can be hired to visit Cava, Fara and Switha. Loganair also operate an air service to Hoy and Flotta. **Graemsay** (population 40) is a green and pleasant little isle about two miles long and three-quarters of a mile wide, lying between Stromness and Hoy. Fishing and crofting are the only industries and there are no ancient monuments to attract the visitor.

Hoy

Across Burra Sound, which is littered with wrecks, is Hoy, the second largest island in Orkney, thirteen miles long and six miles wide with a population of 448. 'Hoy' is Old Norse for 'high island', and it is well named since it has the highest hill in Orkney, Ward Hill at 1565 ft. There are two parishes, Hoy and Walls; the latter forms the southern part of the island and is almost split into two by a long inlet called Longhope in the east and North Bay in the west. South Walls is connected to North Walls by a narrow isthmus just a few yards wide. The contrast between the island of Hoy and the other islands in the group is immediately visible. Hoy has cliffs over 1000 ft high and 80 per cent of the island is a vast moorland covered in heather and rough grass, unlike the neat, tame, agricultural look of most of the other islands.

From the ferry terminal and airstrip in South Walls, the island road runs along the south side of

Boys' Ploughing Match and Festival of the Horse, South Ronaldsay.

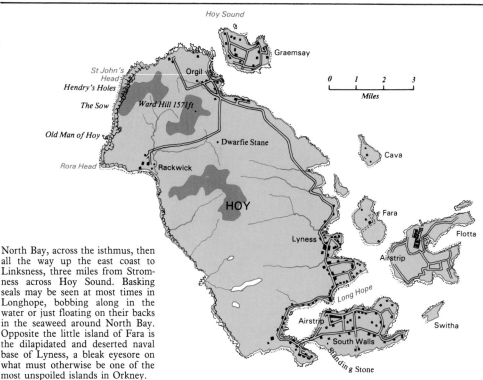

North Bay, across the isthmus, then all the way up the east coast to Linksness, three miles from Stromness across Hoy Sound. Basking seals may be seen at most times in Longhope, bobbing along in the water or just floating on their backs in the seaweed around North Bay. Opposite the little island of Fara is the dilapidated and deserted naval base of Lyness, a bleak eyesore on what must otherwise be one of the most unspoiled islands in Orkney.

Seven miles north of Lyness a small side road cuts across the island to Rackwick on the south-west coast. About one mile down this road, on the left-hand side, is the famous Dwarfie Stane, the only rock-cut tomb in Britain. Dating from about 1900 BC the tomb is 28 ft long by 18 ft wide and 6 ft high. Inside is a passage and two cells that have been cut out of solid rock. Legend has it that the stone was hewn by a giant, one cell for him and the other for his wife. Rackwick lies at the head of the sweeping bay of Rack Wick, nestling between Ward Hill, Mel Fea and Moor Fea. The village, once a prosperous fishing community, is now almost a ghost town, deserted except for the few people who still maintain their traditional way of life. However, most visitors to Hoy pass through Rackwick on their way to the famous **Old Man of Hoy**, a towering rock stack just north of Rora Head. This stack, 450 ft high, was first climbed in 1966, taking three days, and it became known to millions when, in 1967, television cameras filmed six mountaineers climbing it by three different routes.

Further north is one of the highest perpendicular cliffs in the British Isles, St John's Head, rising to over 1000 ft. From here round to Braebuster, on the northern point of Hoy, the scenery is truly breathtaking and the view one of the best anywhere in Britain. One can see all of Orkney and most of Shetland to the north and much of Caithness in

Scotland to the south. Because of the numerous sea birds that nest here and the immense variety of flowers (including some rare alpines), Hoy has been designated a Site of Special Scientific Interest. There is some accommodation available and a taxi service if required, but visitors should check with the Tourist Information office before commencing a trip to the island.

The island of **Flotta** (population 114) is just three quarters of a mile from Hoy but it's hard to imagine two such dramatically contrasting islands lying so close to each other. Flotta, as its name suggests, is flat and only about three-and-a-half miles long by two miles wide. Heavily defended and fortified during both world wars, much of the debris still litters the island. There is a large oil terminal on the northern shore and large tankers lie off the

The Old Man of Hoy.

southern end of Scapa Flow. The island has an airstrip and is also served by the Mainland ferry.

There are three other small isles in Scapa Flow - Cava, Fara and Switha - with not more than 340 acres between them. **Cava** (100 acres) was inhabited by a few families up to 1945 but now only two people live there. **Fara** (200 acres) is the largest and in 1891 had a population of 76; now the crofts are deserted except for the rabbits. **Switha** is about 40 acres of low-lying light soil. There is a standing stone on the islet but it's not worth hiring a boat to go there.

Copinsay, the largest of a small group near east Mainland, is about 70 acres in size. The islet is pleasant and green and dominated by the lighthouse. Sloping steeply to the 200-ft cliffs on the east the fertile area once supported a farm which used the four attendant holms for grazing sheep. Copinsay is now a bird sanctuary and is populated in summer by kittiwakes, guillemots, shags and razorbills. Boats can be hired from Skaill in Deerness for a trip to the island. About ten miles north-east of Copinsay is a small island called **Auskerry**. For many years the lighthouse keepers were the only people on the island but when the light was automated they were withdrawn. There are some standing stones and the ruins of a medieval chapel plus the birds to be seen if you can find a boatman to take you there.

The North Isles

Shapinsay

Across the bay of Kirkwall is a low fertile island of 6761 acres - Shapinsay. The island is highly cultivated with a population of 324 and, like Bressay in Shetland, very suburban with little in the way of spectacular scenery. Its attraction is Balfour Castle, set on the south-west corner of the island against a background of tall (for Orkney) trees. The castle was built by Colonel David Balfour in 1847 and contains family heirlooms and other treasures.

Between Shapinsay and the larger island of Rousay are four islets and their attendant holms. **Gairsay** (population 5) is approximately one mile wide by one-and-three-quarter miles long and is presently occupied by only one family, the owners of the island. The island rises to 334 ft in the centre with fertile land on the southern slopes. **Wyre** is situated between Gairsay and Rousay. Two miles long by three-quarters of a mile wide, the island has eight farms and a population of 20. Two attractions draw visitors to this island. One is the 12th-C church and

Balfour Castle, Shapinsay.

the other is the ruins of a castle, known locally as 'Cubbie Roos Castle' and thought to have been built by a notorious Norseman called Kolbein Hruga. The rest of the island offers little, except to the naturalist, with many acres of uncultivated heather moorland to wander over.

Eynhallow (from the Old Norse meaning 'Holy Isle') is a small islet lying between Rousay and north-

west Mainland. The only surviving building is a church which was rebuilt as a dwelling house in the 16th C. One thousand years ago the island supported a thriving monastery, the ruins of which can still be seen - just. Eynhallow is one of the few pretty islands in Orkney and, when viewed against the dark brown landscape of Rousay, it's not hard to think of leaving the city and its problems for a life on just such an island. One mile east of Rousay is a flat arrow-shaped island called **Egilsay** which has two small holms, **Kili Holm** and the **Holm of**

Scockness. Egilsay (population 20) is about three miles long and about one mile at its widest point. It was here that the most famous of all the Orkney earls, Magnus, was murdered, and the little church of St Magnus stands a few hundred yards from the spot where he died, now marked by an inscribed stone.

Eday

This island (population 137) occupies a central position in the North Isles. It is eight miles long by two-and-a-half miles wide, with six attendant holms: the **Calf of Eday** (the largest), **Faray, Holm of Faray, Muckle Green Holm, Rusk Holm** and **Little Green Holm**. 'Eday' means 'isle of the isthmus' and the island does in fact have a narrow waist with Fersness Bay on the west and the Bay of London on the east, separated by less than half a mile of land. The northern half of the island is scenically more attractive. Red Head in the extreme north rises to 200 ft and overlooks Calf Sound and the Calf of Eday. It was in this fast-moving sound that the pirate, John Gow, was captured, later hanged in 1725. (Sir Walter Scott immortalised Gow in his novel *The Pirate*.) The ferry passes through the Sound on its way to Westray, and sailing between Red Head and Grey Head on the Calf is an experience to be remembered. The cultivated area of Eday is small in comparison to the total area as most of the island is bleak, heather moorland with several high hills; Ward Hill at 334 ft is the highest. There are several burnt mounds in the south, at Backaland, Quarryhouse and Greentoft. Chambered cairns are to be seen in the north near Carrick House, named after John, Earl of Carrick, younger brother of Earl Patrick Stewart.

West of Eday lies **Faray**, less than two miles in length and half a mile wide. The island used to be prosperous, supporting a population of between 60 and 70 people. Today it's deserted with only the sheep and the ever-present birds left to enjoy the pleasures of this pretty little isle.

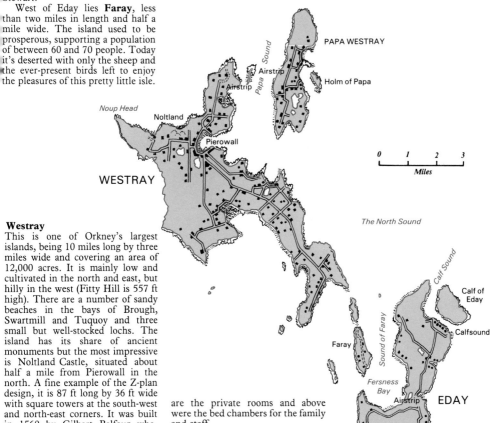

Westray
This is one of Orkney's largest islands, being 10 miles long by three miles wide and covering an area of 12,000 acres. It is mainly low and cultivated in the north and east, but hilly in the west (Fitty Hill is 557 ft high). There are a number of sandy beaches in the bays of Brough, Swartmill and Tuquoy and three small but well-stocked lochs. The island has its share of ancient monuments but the most impressive is Noltland Castle, situated about half a mile from Pierowall in the north. A fine example of the Z-plan design, it is 87 ft long by 36 ft wide with square towers at the south-west and north-east corners. It was built in 1560 by Gilbert Balfour who, with his brothers, was implicated in the murder of Lord Darnley, and was finally hanged for treason in 1576. The ground floor is entered through the south-west tower and contains the kitchens and store rooms. Ascending the tower to the first floor by way of a fine stairway, believed to be of a later period, we come into the great hall with its impressive fireplace. At the far end

are the private rooms and above were the bed chambers for the family and staff.

The island's population (717) is fairly well distributed over the lowland areas with the picturesque village of Pierowall as the main centre. Apart from the ferry service the island is also served by Loganair, the little airstrip being situated at Aikerness in the extreme north-east.

Papa Westray
Papa Westray (population 100) lies one mile east of Aikerness across

Noltland Castle, Westray.

Papa Sound. Four miles long by one mile wide, the island is fertile and extremely attractive. This 'isle of the Papae' and its neighbouring holm are rich in plant and animal life, especially on the rough moorland in the north. On the west shore is one of the earliest settlements in Orkney – the Knap of Howar – dating from 3500 BC. At Holland, in the middle of the island, stands the old mansion home of the Traills of Holland, an important Orkney family who at one time owned this island. Papa Westray has the doubtful honour of being where the last great auk in Britain was killed, shot here in 1813, now stuffed and on display in the British Museum. The island is served by both ferry boat and Loganair.

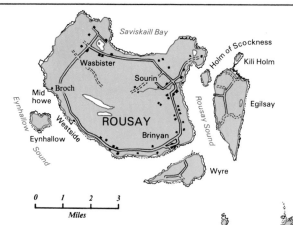

Rousay

With a population of 212, the largest of the inner North Isles is circular in shape and about six miles across. Much of the island is moorland and, apart from the south and south-west, it has very little arable soil. Rousay reaches a height of 821 ft, with cliffs on the west side rising to 200 ft. There are four small lochs and the general appearance is one of uncultivated, brown hilly moorland; however, that's not what brings the thousands of tourists here each year. Rousay is rich in archaeological remains - brochs, cairns, chambered tombs and a Stone Age village –many of the sites being in a good state of preservation.

Stronsay

With its attendant holms of **Papa Stronsay**, **Linga Holm** and **Holm of Huip**, Stronsay has a total acreage of 8736 of which nearly 93 per cent is cultivated. The highest point is Burgh Head, some 154 ft above sea level. The island has nothing of any great archaeological interest but it does have some rather nice secluded

beaches on both the east and west coasts. Two excavated broch sites, one at Lambs Head and the other at the Hillock of Baywest on the western arm, are not particularly noteworthy.

Sanday

Sanday (population 486) is half an hour from Stronsay by ferry. The island is 13 miles long (north-east to south-west), but with so many 'arms' and 'legs' it's difficult to give the breadth. As the name implies, it's an island of beaches with miles of golden sand, dunes and low headlands. There are not many beaches in Britain to rival Whitemill Bay, Sandquoy or Lopness on Sanday. Much of the island is cultivated, growing oats, turnips, barley and potatoes. Prehistoric sites are few since the demands of agriculture have reduced nearly all

the sites to a few broken stones. There is, however, one chambered tomb, dating from 2000 BC, at Quoyness. Being low, the island is difficult to see in hazy or foggy weather, especially from the deck of a ship, and the eastern shore has claimed more wrecks, with the exception of North Ronaldsay, than any other island in Orkney.

North Ronaldsay

The most northerly island in Orkney is North Ronaldsay (population 114), situated about two-and-a-half miles north of Tafts Ness on Sanday. Three-and-a-half miles long by one mile wide, the island is very fertile and low-lying with no place more than 50 ft above sea level. A wall has been built all round the island just above the high-water mark to a height of six feet, designed not to keep the sea out but to prevent sheep from grazing on cultivated land. This may seem a little cruel but, in fact, the rather small and goat-like sheep live on the rocky shore and eat seaweed. Their wool is extremely soft and fine and their meat has a delicious delicate flavour. They are probably the only true-bred descendants of the primitive sheep found by the Norsemen when they arrived in the 8th C. The people of

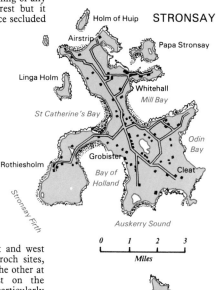

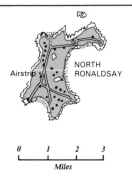

NORTH RONALDSAY

Airstrip

```
0    1    2    3
Miles
```

North Ronaldsay bear more resemblance to Shetlanders than to Orkadians, dialect and traditions having been maintained here. The island is almost totally cultivated and therefore there are not many prehistoric sites left standing.

The last island in the Orkney group is also the most isolated: **Sule Skerry**. Situated 37 miles west of Brough Head on Mainland, this remote island of 35 acres is one of the main breeding grounds for puffins and storm petrels in Orkney. Five miles to the south-west stands **Sule Stack**, a towering granite outcrop rising 130 ft above the sea. This rock has Orkney's only gannet colony.

Transport facilities to Orkney are similar to those of Shetland, but for detailed information contact the Tourist Information centre at Kirkwall.

Stroma

Caithness. Situated in the Pentland Firth about two miles north of Canisbay on the Caithness coast is Stroma, about four miles long by one mile wide, rising to a height of 167 ft at Cairn Hill. In 1920 Stroma had a population of 300 but since then there has been a steady decline, and in 1959 only 130 people were left. Several attempts were made to prevent depopulation, and a new harbour was constructed at Uppertown in 1960, but this did not stem the flow and within ten years the island was totally deserted. Today, it has an eerie atmosphere, with many empty houses (some habitable), rusting agricultural equipment lying in the fields and a general impression that some evil spirit had just recently driven the inhabitants away.

There is a chambered cairn near the lighthouse at the northern end of the island which once contained natural mummies. George Low on his tour of Orkney in 1774 visited the tomb but found only two skulls and a few leg bones. The islanders told him that many people had come to the island to see the mummies and that some, out of 'mere wantonness', had shattered the bodies and trampled them to pieces. Stroma is privately owned but boat trips can be arranged by Thomas & Bews from Huna, two miles west of John o' Groats.

Kettletoft Harbour, Sanday.

North-west Highland

Of the many islands off this coast, few were ever inhabited as the soil is poor and access difficult. Many of the larger islands were used for summer grazing.

Sheltering Skerray Bay is the grassy **Neave** or **Coomb Island**, rising to 230 ft and separated by the narrow channel of Caol Beag. At the entrance to Tongue Bay are the red sandstone group known as **Eilean nan Ron** ('seal island'), cliffbound with some fine natural arches, and two summits over 240 ft. In 1840 they were inhabited by a few tenants who dried fish in the salty wind, but were last occupied in 1938. To the west of Tongue Bay are the green humps of the tidal **Rabbit Islands**; **Sgeir an Oir**, the most northerly, has a natural arch. The coast between Tongue Bay and Loch Eriboll is inaccessible by car but beneath the steep cliffs are numerous islets and stacks, natural refuges for seabirds.

The low-lying, fertile **Eilean Choraidh** lies sheltered in the deep waters of Loch Eriboll, once a fleet anchorage; German U-boats assembled here after the surrender in 1945. The island was once used for burials, to avoid the unwelcome attention of wolves then prevalent on the mainland. **Eilean Hoan** lies to the west of the entrance to the loch, about a mile from the mainland, and it too was used for burials. It has an area of 100 acres, and rises to a height of 83 ft. In 1840 it supported four families – the remains of their dwellings can still be seen – but now it is used for grazing. In 1980 the island became an RSPB reserve, an undisturbed nesting place. Landing is difficult, and permission must first be obtained from the RSPB. Species present include eider ducks, oyster-catchers, ringed plovers, lapwings, arctic terns, lesser black-backed gulls, black guillemots, storm petrels and many other birds. In winter, as many as 400 barnacle geese have been counted and, in the spring, great northern divers, in their breeding plumage, mass before migrating to Iceland.

West to Cape Wrath and south to Handa Island, the coast is bare and exposed, with only a few islets. **An Garbh-eilean**, near the cape, is used as a bombing target by aircraft from Lossiemouth. The broken shoreline of Loch Laxford is made up of poor Lewisian gneiss, and the islands in the loch are typically low-lying.

Handa Island

Highland. This is a mainly cliffbound island of 766 acres, a Torridonian sandstone outcrop standing off a Lewisian gneiss foreland, less than a mile south-west of Tarbet. The sea cliffs on the north and west rise to 400 ft, and there is an impressive rock known as the Great Stack, resting on three pillars. The interior is mainly rough pasture, peat bog and heather. It was once inhabited by seven families who had a 'queen' and, as on St Kilda, the menfolk used to hold a daily 'parliament' to decide the work. The people emigrated to America during the potato famine of 1848. This island, too, was used as a burial place by mainlanders to save the corpses from scavenging wolves.

Although privately owned, Handa is run as a nature reserve by the RSPB who maintain a warden

The sheer cliffs of Handa.

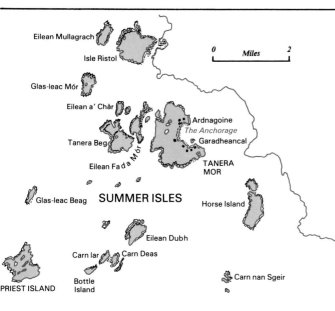

Eilean Mullagrach

Isle Ristol

0   Miles   2

Glas-leac Mór

Eilean a' Chàr

Ardnagoine
The Anchorage
Garadheancal

Tanera Beg

Tanera Mór

Eilean Fada

TANERA
MOR

Glas-leac Beag   SUMMER ISLES

Horse Island

Eilean Dubh

Carn Iar   Carn Deas

Carn nan Sgeir

PRIEST ISLAND

Bottle
Island

John Mackenzie of London, whose business thrived when the seas were full of herring; there were other stations on **Isle Ristol** and **Isle Martin**. Barrels of the salted fish were exported as far afield as the West Indies, and as many as 200 vessels were at one time to be seen anchored in the bay. During the 19th C the island was a centre for the illicit distilling of whisky. Tanera Mor rises to 405 ft at the summit of Meall Mor, affording fine views as far as the Outer Hebrides. Holiday accommodation can be booked through the Summer Isles Estate, and a regular ferry operates from Achiltibuie. There are facilities for boating, sailing and fishing among other things, amid excellent scenery and seclusion.

during the summer. 141 species of bird have been recorded, with 35 breeding regularly. Of most importance are the colonies of sea birds. The last white-tailed sea eagles nested here in 1864. Of great notoriety was an eccentric albino oystercatcher with a deformed bill, which died on 9 July 1967 and is now in the Royal Scottish Museum, Edinburgh. 216 species of plants have been recorded plus more than 100 species of mosses. Small plantations of lodgepole pine and alders have been established, and there are many rabbits.

A 'bothy' (a stone hut) provides shelter on the island, and boats may be hired from Tarbet, three miles north of Scourie.

Scourie to Loch Broom

Highland. The foreland of Eddrachillis Bay and the many islands, rocks and skerries in the bay are of Lewisian gneiss, the oldest rock in Europe and also one of the poorest. This area, once described as 'the roughest low ground in Britain', is inhabited only by sea birds. The area around **Oldany Island**, which is used for grazing, is fished for lobster. The **Old Man of Stoer**, a 200-ft-high sandstone stack, once declared unclimbable, stands just west of the Point of Stoer; it was climbed in 1966.

Summer Isles

Highland. These are a group of islands and skerries spread over 30 square miles, lying north-west of Loch Broom, consisting of Torridonian sandstone covered with peat.

The largest island in the group is **Tanera Mor**, with an area of 804

acres. In 1881 its population numbered 119 people, who lived in the settlements by The Anchorage, one of the best natural harbours in the north-west. The population declined until, in 1931, the last tenants left. Sir Frank Fraser Darling farmed the island between 1939 and 1944, and wrote about this period in his book *Island Farm*. Then once again it was deserted until the mid-1960s, when the Summer Isles Estate decided to restore many of the cottages and the schoolhouse as holiday accommodation. The permanent population now numbers nine, and 250 sheep are grazed. The Summer Isles Post Office, which issues its own stamps (recognised by the Post Office) for conveying mail to the mainland, and the Offshore Islands Philatelic Society are both run from Tanera Mor.

Between the settlements of Ardnagoine and Garadheancal are the remains of a fishing station at Tigh-on-Quay founded in 1783 by Roderick Morison of Stornoway and

ISLE MARTIN

Loch Broom

The island of **Tanera Beg**, to the west, has a beach of coral sand, rare in this area. **Horse Island**, once inhabited, now supports only a herd of wild goats, first recorded in 1937. To the south-south-west is **Carn nan Sgeir**, two islets joined by a shingle spit. Orange, grey and black lichens hide the cliffs, and the ledges are covered with thrift, sea campion, scurvygrass and lovage.

The most westerly of the group are **Priest Island** (300 acres), and the much smaller **Glas-leac Beag** (34 acres). There is no proper landing place on Priest Island and its exposed position makes access difficult – in spite of this, it was at one time occupied by crofters.

The Summer Isles from Priest Island.

All of these islands are now rich in bird life — heron, shelduck, fulmar, snipe, and eider are among the species commonly seen - and many are still grazed by sheep. Boats may be hired from Archiltibuie and Ullapool, but most of the islands are privately owned.

Isle Martin lies to the east of the Summer Isles and north of Loch Broom, is composed of Torridonian sandstone with an area of 400 acres and a maximum elevation of 393 ft. In the late 18th C, at the start of the herring boom, the British Fisheries Society erected a curing station close by Ardmair Bay, the foundations of which still exist. In 1901 the population of the island was 33, but by the start of World War II the last resident had left. There is a legend about a cooper of Isle Martin who was miraculously transported to South Rona to cut brooms and then equally miraculously brought back - all, of course, arranged by the fairies.

Ullapool is the terminus for the Caledonian MacBrayne vehicle ferry to Stornoway, Isle of Lewis.

The Outer Hebrides

Western Isles. With an area of 716,000 acres and a population of 30,000, these are often called, as a group, 'The Long Isle'. It is an archipelago 130 miles long, lying in a crescent about 40 miles off the north-west mainland of Scotland. The west coast is pounded by the unbroken force of the North Atlantic. The name 'Hebrides' is derived from the Norse *Havbredey*, the 'isles on the edge of the sea'. They consist mainly of Lewisian gneiss, 'the oldest known fragment of Europe', cut with transverse sounds. Of the 200-plus islands in the group, only 13 are now inhabited, with about 80 per cent of the population living on Lewis and Harris.

Of the many physical aspects setting the islands apart from the rest of Scotland perhaps the most memorable is the quality of the light. Reflected off the clear water of the surrounding sea it accentuates edges and heightens colours with its luminosity. Other times the dark storm clouds come in procession from the west, or the sea mist envelops everything. The climate is mild, with no extremes of temperature or rainfall but the wind blows strongly two days in three, especially in the north.

Most visitors to the Outer Hebrides approach from the east. The first impression is that of a barren, rock-strewn land, broken by flooded glaciated valleys, narrow and steep sided. A Tarbert man once asked American visitors arriving on the ferry, 'Why send a man to the moon? He could have been sent here!' But if the approach were from the west, the first sight would be of long white beaches, backed with fertile grassland grazed by cattle and dotted with cottages. Between these two contrasting coasts lies peat moor and a landscape which, although appearing devoid of trees, has most types present. Over 800 plant species have been recorded on the islands.

There are many prehistoric stone structures throughout the islands, the most famous being the stone circles at Callanish, built about 4000 years ago when the climate was drier and warmer, and the inhospitable peat bogs were less extensive. Then, as now, the main areas of settlement were on the west coast.

The patterns of human population are very different between the northern and southern islands. Harris and the Isle of Lewis (together with Barra) reached their zenith in 1911 (35,000 people) due to the quite exceptional circumstances surrounding the herring fisheries. The pattern of North and South Uist is more comparable with that of the rest of the islands of Scotland, reaching over 14,000 in 1841, then succumbing to the 'clearances'. Much land is still held by absentee landlords, being left fallow for 'sporting' activities.

At the turn of the century the Gaelic language stood equal with English throughout Scotland. Today the Outer Hebrides is its last major stronghold, due probably to the physical distance of the islands from the mainland. In the Outer Hebrides a life-style and culture have survived that elsewhere have virtually disappeared under pressure from a centralised government that prefers standardisation, finding communities living at the edge of its administrative area 'difficult'. It is only now becoming recognised that people who live on islands, away from the 'mainstream' of society, are not anachronisms - they simply wish to continue a pattern of life developed over the centuries, in tune with their more demanding environment. Society has to decide if it wishes to finance suitable industries and develop natural resources on these islands in order to stem the flow of emigration to the already overcrowded urban areas. In terms of the nation's finances the cost would be insignificant; in social terms its value would be enormous. Whether or not Government attitudes will change significantly remains to be seen - meanwhile many of the communities are organising self-help schemes, to secure their future and keep the young people on the islands. The Lewis Development Fund is a prime example. Money is raised locally and is administered locally. Its object is 'to assist every worthwhile development on Lewis ... stem depopulation, and preserve our cherished way of life'. The Gaelic culture, once subject to derision on the mainland, is now actively promoted in the Outer Hebrides.

Lewis, Harris and North Uist are Protestant, South Uist and Barra are Roman Catholic, and Benbecula is a mixture of the two. There is no friction between the two religious communities - in fact the geography of the Sound of Harris has caused North Uist to have more contact with its Roman Catholic neighbours than with Lewis and Harris.

The main body of Protestants belong to the Free Presbyterian Church, with its strict observance of the Sabbath; Stornoway on Lewis is a major stronghold of the Lord's Day Observance Society. On Sunday, on the Protestant islands, all the bars, restaurants and shops close (making it difficult for those in bed-and-breakfast accommodation), public transport ceases and people go out only to attend church services, during which no hymns are sung. Traditionally, ministers have taken little part in secular matters, except to speak out loudly against behaviour of which they did not approve. More recently they have turned their attention to social problems such as heavy drinking among a section of the male population. As in much of Scotland alcohol is consumed by part of the community with a fervour that can be of benefit only to the distillers, and those who like the 'cosy' atmosphere of an English pub will find little of interest here. Sundays on South Uist and Barra are an altogether more lively affair.

The traditional form of entertainment is still the *ceiliah*, originally meaning 'gossiping house' but more recently a gathering for music and storytelling.

The Outer Hebrides appeal to visitors as a perfect place to get away from it all. There is a Hebridean saying that reflects the atmosphere of these islands: 'When God made time, he made plenty of it.' The people are friendly and helpful towards tourists, but they have done little to provide organised facilities. There is no need. Nature endowed them with lochs full of salmon and trout and sea fishing of equal quality. It provided rugged scenery under wide open skies. The west coast has beaches the equal of any in Europe, deserted even on warm days. The seas are clear and clean (but, naturally, a little cold). Archaeologists will find some of the finest sites in the country, and ornithologists can seek out rare and unique species.

Opposite: *Achmore, Lewis.*

Isle of Lewis

The name derived from *leogach* (pronounced loo-ach) meaning 'marshy'. The largest and most populous island, with 22,000 inhabitants, in the Outer Hebrides, it borders Harris to the north of the Forest of Harris, a natural barrier of wild moorland and mountain. The island is made up almost wholly of gneiss, rising to 1885 ft at the summit of Mealisval in the south-west, and to 1874 ft at the summit of Beinn Mhór in the south. Much of the gneiss is overlaid with glacially deposited boulder clay. There are small areas of Torridonian sandstone near Stornoway and several hundred acres of granite in the parish of Barvas.

The dominant feature of Lewis is the dark, undulating central peat moor, scattered with hundreds of shallow lochs. Although its appearance is uniform, its sheer size is impressive. Centuries of peat cutting have enlivened the surface of the moor with circles, squares and snaking lines, each cut having a herring-bone pattern. The cutting takes place in the early summer, when the moor becomes alive with families engaged in this work. Later, when the cut peat has dried, it is carried away from the banks in sacks, barrows, car boots and modified tractors and trailers to be used as fuel. 'Going to the peats' is very much a social occasion.

The peat began to form about 7000 years ago. Under generally cold, wet and acidic conditions the growth of sedge, moss, grass and heather outstrips the rate at which the dead plants decompose and the layer of peat - fibrous plant remains - begins to thicken. Lewis peat is a mixture of sphagnum and deergrass

which, on some parts of the moor, is still 'making'. The peat in the deeper, blacker layers is a fine fuel, clean and easy to handle when dry, but its calorific value is only two-thirds that of coal. In its natural state the water content can be as high as 90 per cent. The reserves of peat on Lewis have been estimated at 85 million tons, and it is still cut in the traditional way. A good worker, with helpers, can cut 1000 peats a day, which then have to be drained, dried and transported. A crofting family would use around 15,000 each year. The neatly stacked peats - the *cruach* - by the crofts and houses represent a large investment of time and labour and the islanders are justly proud of them.

Where the peat has been removed, revealing the boulder clay, the resultant areas are known as 'skinned land', or *gearraidh*. Treated with shell sand and seaweed, it can be turned into fertile soil.

The main pillars of the Lewis economy are weaving, fishing and crofting (there are about 3500 small crofts, generally worked on a part-time basis). Another more recent addition has been construction work for the oil industry. This variety has brought a measure of stability lacking on other islands which have less diverse sources of income. If a cold wind blows in one sector of the Lewis economy, there are others to fall back on.

Known worldwide is Harris tweed and the centre of production is Lewis. Harris tweed can only be sold as such if it is made in the Outer Hebrides from virgin Scottish wool, woven on hand-looms in the weavers' own homes. It must also bear the 'orb' trade-mark. The hard-wearing, warm and water-resistant cloth is produced 28½ inches wide,

in rolls of 38 weaver's yards (each being 72 inches). The tweed was originally produced for the crofters' own use until its wider applications were promoted by the wives of the landowners, such as Lady Dunmore of Amhuinnsuidhe Castle, who recognised its exceptional quality and durability.

Recent attempts to 'rationalise' production by using larger power-looms were resisted by the weavers, 95 per cent of whom voted to retain traditional methods, not only to protect employment but also to preserve their quality of life and independence. Working at home allows them time to tend the croft, look after the sheep and cut peat. Working in a factory would be far too rigid. Of course some things have changed in the industry. The wool is no longer sheared, dyed with crotal (natural dyes made from lichen) over a peat fire, carded and spun at the croft - all this is now done in the factory at Stornoway using modern methods. The prepared wool is delivered to the weaver, and the finished cloth collected by van from the factory. The finished bundles of tweed can be seen lying at the roadside, in all sorts of weather, awaiting collection.

The hand-looms are usually housed in small sheds; a rhythmic 'clacking' reveals work in progress. The weaver sits at the loom, his legs providing the power and his hands changing the shuttles. It looks, and is, hard work. There are about 600 such weavers on Lewis and Harris, the skill traditionally being passed down the generations, although it can now be learned at the technical college in Stornoway.

The first owners of Lewis were clans of Norse origin. Later, the island became part of Scotland, with the MacLeods being replaced by the Mackenzies of Kintail in 1610, who then held the island until 1844 when Mrs Stewart Mackenzie sold it to Sir James Matheson for £190,000. He invested £500,000 (earned from the China trade) on improvements -draining land, building schools and financing industries.

Lord Leverhulme then bought the island (along with Harris) in 1918, intending to develop the fishing industry. After spending £875,000 he gave up in 1923. On leaving, he gifted the 64,000-acre parish of Stornoway to the people, to be administered by the elected Stornoway Trust, and distributed crofts as free gifts. The slump resulting from his withdrawal caused the emigration of over 1000 able-bodied men to North America, some of whom returned during the Depression of the 1930s.

In the heyday of the herring fishing industry over 1000 boats operated from Stornoway, but the loss of men during World War I and

Stornoway harbour and oil-rig construction area at Arnish Point, Lewis.

Norwegian competition brought about its eventual demise. The white-fish industry suffered from steam trawlers fishing illegally and destroying the local line-fishing gear. Now, with the aid of loans and grants, the industry is on its feet again with over 40 local boats landing white fish and prawns.

The only town of burgh status in the Hebrides, and the only town in the Outer Hebrides, is Stornoway. It is the administrative centre of the Western Isles Authority and has a population in excess of 5500, steadily rising as a result of migration from the surrounding countryside. On its outskirts there is much new housing to accommodate this influx.

The fine natural harbour provides shelter in all conditions, and the quays are host to local and visiting fishing boats and traders as well as the Caledonian MacBrayne ferry from Ullapool. The lifeboat based here is responsible for one of the largest areas in the British Isles. A colony of grey seals has also made

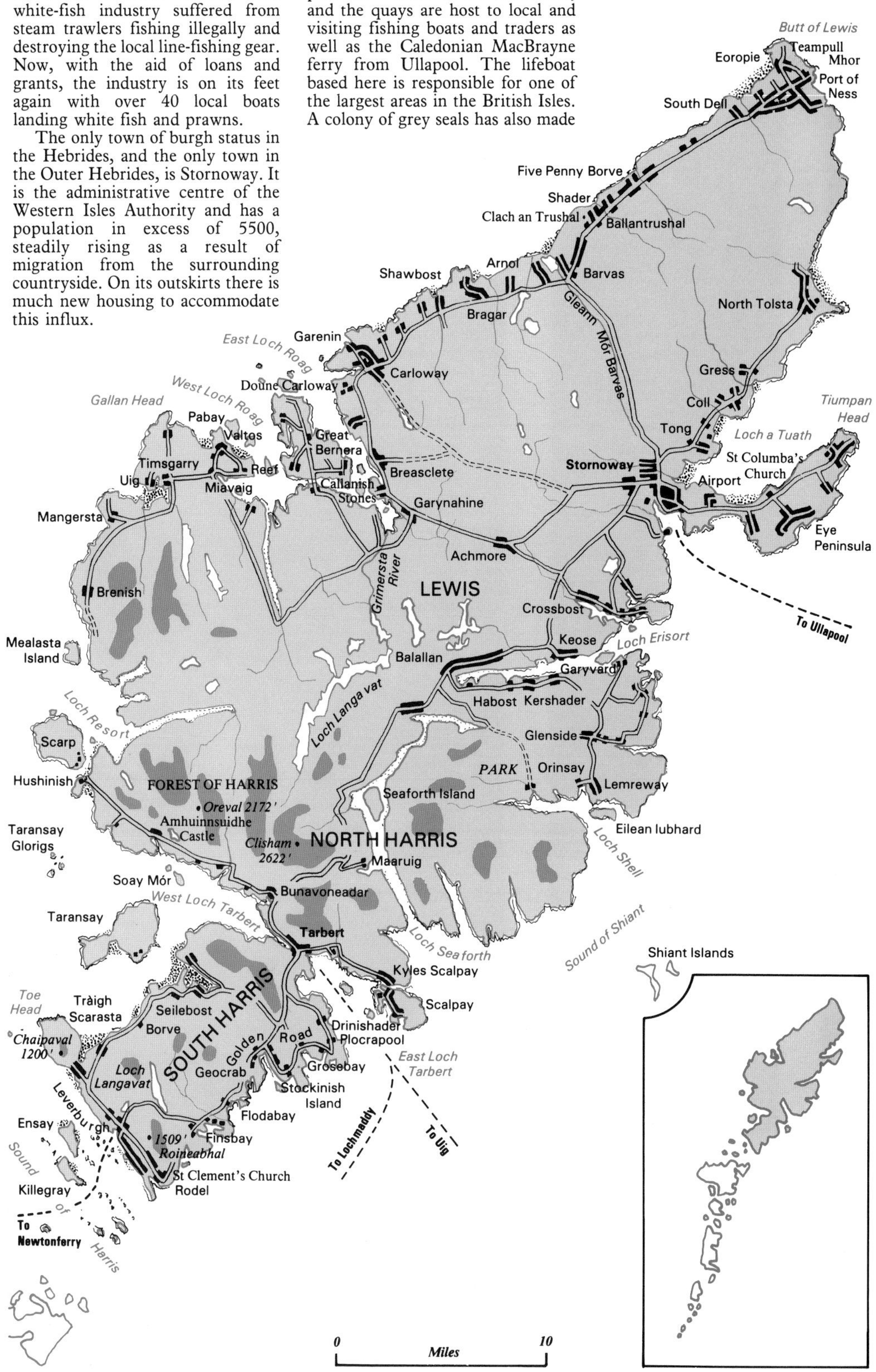

Butt of Lewis
Teampull Mhor
Eoropie
Port of Ness
South Dell

Five Penny Borve
Shader
Clach an Trushal
Ballantrushal
Shawbost
Arnol
Barvas
North Tolsta
Bragar
Gleann Mór Barvas
Garenin
East Loch Roag
Carloway
Gress
Coll
West Loch Roag
Doune Carloway
Tong
Tiumpan Head
Gallan Head
Pabay
Valtos
Great Bernera
Loch a Tuath
Timsgarry
Reef
Breasclete
Stornoway
St Columba's Church
Uig
Miavaig
Callanish Stones
Airport
Garynahine
Mangersta
Eye Peninsula
Achmore
Brenish
LEWIS
Grimersta River
Crossbost
To Ullapool
Mealasta Island
Keose
Loch Erisort
Balallan
Garyvard
Loch Langavat
Habost Kershader
Loch Resort
Glenside
Scarp
Orinsay
PARK
Hushinish
FOREST OF HARRIS
Seaforth Island
Lemreway
Oreval 2172'
Taransay Glorigs
Amhuinnsuidhe Castle
Eilean Iubhard
Clisham 2622'
NORTH HARRIS
Loch Shell
Soay Mór
Maaruig
Taransay
Bunavoneadar
West Loch Tarbert
Tarbert
Loch Seaforth
Sound of Shiant
Shiant Islands
Kyles Scalpay
Toe Head
Tràigh Scarasta
Seilebost
Scalpay
Chaipaval 1200'
Borve
Golden Road
Drinishader
Plocrapool
Loch Langavat
SOUTH HARRIS
Geocrab
Grosebay
East Loch Tarbert
Ensay
Leverburgh
Stockinish Island
Flodabay
To Lochmaddy
To Uig
Killegray
1509'
Finsbay
Roineabhal
St Clement's Church
Rodel
To Newtonferry
Sound of Harris

0   Miles   10

its home in the harbour. The new oil-industry construction yard, which has provided many new jobs and a boom in the bed-and-breakfast trade, is situated at Arnish Point. On **Eilean na Gobhail** ('goat island') opposite, there are ship-repair facilities and a slipway. To the north of the harbour entrance are 'The Beasts of Holm', rocks where 205 Lewis men returning from World War I were drowned on 1 January 1919, when the *Iolaire* was wrecked in sight of home.

The town has a fresh, cosmopolitan atmosphere, and offers a range of shops, hotels, bars, restaurants and services unique in the Western Isles. It even has a small Pakistani community – shopkeepers with a working knowledge of Gaelic. One of the most modern shops in the town is run as a charity for the old and infirm, a reflection of the caring nature of society in the islands. Vans leave Stornoway each day with supplies for the outlying communities. The tourist office is situated in South Beach Street.

The 18th-C net-loft on North Beach Quay is probably the oldest building still standing in the town. St Peter's Episcopal Church has the prayer book taken by David Livingstone on his travels. Martin's Memorial, the spired church in Francis Street, was built in the 19th C at the birthplace of Sir Alexander Mackenzie, the man who made the first overland crossing of Canada. The police headquarters, the Sheriff Court and two hospitals are also situated in the town, along with the Nicholson Institute, the only senior comprehensive school in the Outer Hebrides (founded in 1873 by a Lewisman subsequently killed in Shanghai). There is a sports centre and swimming pool, a golf course and a cinema. The sea fishing in this area is excellent and boat trips are arranged by the local sea-angling club.

Lews Castle

To the west of the town is the turreted Lews Castle, built by Sir James Matheson during the 1840s, and surrounded by a square mile of beautiful mixed woodland. These woods, unique in the Outer Hebrides, have been colonised by a

Clach an Trushal, Ballantrushal, Lewis.

wide variety of woodland birds and there is also a large rookery of about 150 nests. What were once private gardens are planted with berberis, azalea, fuchsia and rhododendron. The Stornoway Trust now uses the castle as a technical college, where navigation, weaving, building and engineering are taught.

To east of Stornoway is the comparatively densely populated Eye Peninsula, known as 'Point'. Stornoway airport, to the north of the road to Point, is both civil and military, being used as Nato base. There are plans to extend the main runway by 400 yd for military purposes, a proposal causing considerable alarm among local environmentalists, who predict problems from the sand spit (which could shift and continually bury the runway) and planes hitting birds.

At the very western end of Point by the north shore stand the walls of the now defunct 14th-C St Columba's Church and the graveyard of Ui, an important religious site said to have been built where St Catan had his cell in the 7th C. The graveyard is the burial ground of 19 MacLeod chiefs of Lewis. There is a fine effigy of Roderick MacLeod on the south side of the church and an impressive Celtic stone on the north. The last service was held here in 1828. The rest of the peninsula is of little interest, being undulating moorland shared by crofters and commuters. There are pleasant small beaches near Bayble and Garrabost, and a lighthouse at Tiumpan Head.

North-east of Stornoway the road passes the beaches at Coll and Gress, before ending near Tolsta by Tràigh Mhór, a fine sweep of dune-backed sands with caves and stacks nearby. Tolsta was built by Lord Leverhulme who intended the road to become part of a complete circuit of northern Lewis, connecting with Port of Ness. At present this section

of the coast remains inaccessible by car.

The road from Stornoway to Barvas crosses the central peat moor, following the north-west course of the River Barvas (a salmon river) until it meets the west coast road. This road, with its scattered crofting/weaving townships, follows a route about a mile inland, and little of interest can be seen without leaving it.

The first impression given by the townships is one of untidyness – old houses are left to crumble while new ones remain not quite finished. Cars stand abandoned right outside front doors. Little attention is paid to exterior colour schemes and all manner of materials serve as fences. Let it be said immediately that the interiors of the houses are given a great deal of attention and care. What we see has two explanations. The communities are virtually classless and non-competitive in the modern urban sense so there is no desire to 'impress' the neighbours with outside appearances. Secondly, while the people do wish to have new houses, cars, etc., they do not want to make a clear break with the past so old things that have served them well are left to just fade away.

It was from the townships of Barvas that the idea of re-seeding the barren moorland spread. Initially the surface of the moor is skimmed, after which lime-rich shell sand, nitrous phosphate and fertiliser are spread, seeds are sown, and worms and bacteria turn the whole lot into soil. Some 18,000 acres have been improved in this way under the Crofters Commission Land Improvement Scheme. It raises the grazing potential for sheep 30-fold and, where the reclaimed land adjoins the moorland, the contrast is quite dramatic. In March 1980 Barvas was the scene of a unique referendum to see whether the people wished to have licensed premises in the parish. The idea was defeated by two to one and drinking continues in *bothans*, illegal dens on common ground, tolerated by the police. Strangers are *not* welcome.

The tallest standing stone in the Hebrides, Clach an Trushal, stands overlooking the sea at Ballantrushal. To the east of Loch an Dùin at Shader is Steinacleit, a 50-ft diameter burial cairn encircled by stones, in a large oval enclosure. It stands on the skyline and can be reached via a rough track. From Dell to Port of Ness there are many crofts and the land is green and sandy. On the coast, between Dell and Eoropie, are several small sandy bays, from which the natural arch at Roinn a' Roidh can be seen. Just beyond the arch is **Luchruban**, the tidal 'pigmy's isle'. Its claim to occupation by small people is unfounded, as the bones found here were more likely the remains of food consumed by the occupant of an ancient stone cell, the remnants of which can still be seen. It is from the small harbour at Port of Ness that the men of the district leave every August to bring back guga (young gannet), considered quite a delicacy, from Sula Sgeir, 41 miles to the north.

The most northerly village in the Outer Hebrides is Eoropie. The key to the restored 12th-C Church of St Moluag (Teampull Mholuidh) in a field to the north can be obtained from the store.

The red-brick lighthouse and white fog-horn tower at the Butt of Lewis stand above the rocky northern tip of the island. 44 miles north-north-east is the tiny island of Rona (North Rona), and 200 miles north are the Faeroes. To the south-east of the Butt is the attractive tiny Port Sto.

Heading south-west from Barvas the road passes Loch Mór Barvas, a refuge for wildfowl, before reaching Arnol. At the far end of the township is the remarkable Black House museum. This *tigh dubh*, last occupied in 1964, has walls six-feet thick, with a roof of thatch over turf, weighted with ropes and stones. A peat fire burns in the centre of the floor, and there is no chimney. These structures were warm, dry and quiet when the wind outside howled. Visitors see authentic room settings, including straw-lined box beds. Arnol stands at the edge of the machair (*see* Harris), where the crofts are divided by stone dykes. The original settlement, along with others on this western seaboard of Lewis, was closer to the sea, on a site occupied since the 1st-C AD, but winter storms and the exhaustion of the peat beds resulted in re-siting during the 18th C. Nearby Loch na Muilne, a mill lock, powered several of the township's water-mills.

By the roadside at Bragar there is a whalebone arch some 20-ft high –

The Butt of Lewis lighthouse.

suspended from it is the harpoon that killed the whale. The children of Shawbost, the next village, made a splendid folk museum for the 1970 Highland Village Competition which is now housed in a converted church to the south of the road. These energetic young people have also restored a nearby Norse water-mill.

By the coast at Carloway is the village of Garenin. At the end of the road, above a sheltered shingle bay, is the last remaining 'street of black houses' in Lewis (in fact, some are 'white houses' – *tigh geal* – the dry stone walls having been cemented, and the roofs tarred). The last family left here in about 1973 and the

buildings are decaying, with old furniture and broken glass filling those most recently abandoned. There was a scheme proposed for restoring them to their original condition, but the expense would be considerable and perhaps the money better spent elsewhere on the island. However, the setting is unique and worthy of inspection; with the debris removed and the grass trimmed it would make a fine monument, attracting visitors who come to see Doune Carloway and Callanish nearby.

Doune Carloway is a well-preserved broch with the tallest part of the wall standing over 22 ft high and a diameter of 47 ft. The

The 12th-C Church of St Moluag at Eoropie, Lewis.

The whalebone arch at Bragar, Lewis.

Doune Carloway broch, Lewis.

galleries, staircase and entrance can be clearly seen, and the view from it is superb.

The main road now heads south along the side of East Loch Roag which is scattered with low-lying islands. Between Carloway and Breasclete the land becomes more hilly with many small lochs. Hidden by the shore is the pretty village of Tolsta Chaolais. The modern factory above the pier at Breasclete processes fish using a Norwegian method of drying to produce *stokfish* for export to Scandinavia, Eastern Europe and Africa. The factory forms part of a long-term scheme to tap the reserves of fish to the west of the Outer Hebrides, and the first landings were made here in May 1978. The work-force is local and the factory represents a major attempt to revitalise the Hebridean

fisheries, using fish caught by a new generation of automated 'long-line', boats. What was once the shore station for the Flannan Isles lighthouse stands in Breasclete.

At the head of East Loch Roag is Callanish, site of a stone circle probably erected 4000 years ago, equal in importance to Stonehenge. The monoliths make a rough Celtic cross 405 ft north to south, 140 ft east to west. 47 are now left, the tallest over 15 ft high, and within the central circle is a cairn where the remains of the cremation were found. It was not until 1857, when five feet of peat was dug away that the true height and extent of the stones was seen. Various theories exist regarding their true purpose – at present the astro-archaeological one seems the most credible. Professor Gerald Hawkins, an American astronomer, has used a computer to verify 12 significant astronomical alignments, one of the main ones being mid-summer moonset, south along the main avenue, over Clisham on Harris. Whereas Stonehenge seems to relate to the sun, Callanish seems to relate to the moon. There is still much more research to be done before firm conclusions can be drawn and such

studies will have to include the many other smaller stone circle in the area which also align with Callanish. A local legend claims that the stones are really giants, petrified by St Kieran for refusing to be christened. The views from the circle are very fine, especially towards the dark mountains of Harris to the south.

After Garynahine, the main road traverses the central moorland on its way to Stornoway, a minor road leaving it to head south-west to Great Bernera and Uig, and soon crossing the Abhainn Grimersta river, which is fed by the remote Loch Langavat and acknowledged as one of the best salmon rivers in Europe. To the north is the hilly and loch-strewn island of **Great Bernera** in Loch Roag. It is the largest of over 40 islands in the loch, the other notable ones, all uninhabited, being **Little Bernera, Vuia Mór, Vacsay** (population of nine in 1861), **Pabay Mór** (population of 17 in 1861) where there are the remains of a church, and **Drasay** which once had a population of two. This whole area surrounding Loch Roag is, without doubt, one of the most attractive parts of Lewis. The many freshwater lochs make good fishing for brown trout, and the mountains to the south-west are the haunt of golden eagles, peregrine falcons and buzzards. Great Bernera is a lobster-fishing centre and, in 1972, a fish-procesing plant was built at Kirkibost on the east side. The name most common on the island is MacDonald, said to be descendants of a watchman who was given the island as reward for his services to the MacAulays of Uig. The bridge was opened in 1953 after the islanders threatened to 'build' a causeway themselves by dynamiting the cliffs. There is a small sheltered beach, facing Little Bernera, beyond the deserted village of Bosta. To the north-west is the island of **Bearasay**, retreat of Neil MacLeod, who defeated the Fife Adventurers (merchants who tried to take over the island in the 16th C to exploit the herring fishing), but who later turned pirate and was eventually executed.

To reach Uig the road passes round Little Loch Roag through typical peat and rock scenery. At Carishader, on the west shore of Loch Roag, the scenery again becomes attractive. Behind Miavaig, where oysters are farmed, the road passes through the lovely steep-sided green and rocky Glen Valtos – an atypical sight on Lewis and a nice surprise. A minor road completes a circuit of Cliff, Valtos, Reef and Uigen. There are superb beaches here, especially the dune-backed shell sands of Tràigh na Berie, sheltered by Pabay Mór and Vacsay. To the north of Glen Valtos is the township of Aird Uig, and Gallan

The stones of Callanish, Isle of Lewis.

Tràigh na Berie, a superb beach in Lewis.

Harris

With a population of 2900, Harris is separated from Lewis by the deep incisions of Loch Seaforth and Loch Resort, and six miles of mountainous and treeless deer forest rising to a height of 2622 ft at the summit of Clisham, the highest point in the Western Isles. North Harris is separated from South Harris by the narrow neck of land at Tarbert, where two sea lochs almost cut the island in two.

Gneiss, the rock of the Outer Hebrides, is nowhere more apparent than on Harris, always visible even if covered here and there with peat or water or strewn with boulders. It is only on the west coast that a narrow border of machair brings some relief. Machair is the low-lying, sometimes undulating, land behind the dunes and the stabilising fringe of marram grass. It consists of as many as 50 types of flowering plants among grass, growing on wind-blown shell sand. Its fertility is enhanced by animal dung and the spreading of seaweed manure. It is easily damaged by overgrazing and the erosive effects of rabbits and of wheeled vehicles.

Untilled, the soil forms a layer about six inches thick, uniform and free from stones. With cultivation and the addition of seaweed it often reaches a depth of 12 inches. The wind is constantly spreading fresh shell sand over the machair - a natural dressing of lime. On these gneiss islands, the fertile machair is a vital land resource. In early summer, when in flower, it is brilliantly coloured and is so heady with perfume that it can flavour the milk of grazing dairy cattle. Against the blue sea and the white shell-sand beaches, it is magical.

The people of Harris, although said to have the same Norse ancestry as Lewis, have a different dialect, with fewer words of Norse derivation and spoken with a softer lilt. The island was held by the MacLeods of Harris from the time of the Norse surrender in the 13th C until 1779, when it was sold to Captain MacLeod of Berneray who invested in a fishing industry for the island. The Earl of Dunmore purchased Harris in 1834, later selling the north to Sir Edward Scott in 1868 and the south to Lord Leverhulme in 1919. After the latter's scheme to revitalise the island and its fishing industry failed, in 1923 much of the land was sold to absentee landlords, who sold off assets, built by Lord Leverhulme, with scant regard for the indigenous population. Eventually some of the land that was 'cleared' in the 19th C was purchased by the Government and returned to the crofters.

Before the Clearances (*see* Skye) the population had risen far beyond

Head. The Flannan Isles are 21 miles north-west into the Atlantic.

The Uig Sands are beautiful - wide, clean, flat and well sheltered - access is good, and the grassland at the back of the beach is flat enough for a football pitch. The whole is overlooked by the handsome cream-painted and slated Uig Lodge and the superbly sited school at Timsgarry. A hand-carved walrus-ivory chess set of Norse origin dating back to about 1150 was found in 1831 at Ardroil, by a herdsman whose beast uncovered it in the dunes. Parts of the set are now in the British and the Scottish National Museums.

The view inland from Uig, along the glen between Mealisval and Tahaval, is dramatic and a refreshing change from the peat moor of the north. The road ends at Brenish. Beyond here was Tigh nan Cailleachan Dubha ('house of the black old women'), a Benedictine convent possibly associated with Iona. To the south is **Mealasta Island**, lying about half a mile off the coast, where the mountains drop steeply to the sea.

To the south of Stornoway is the parish of Lochs, aptly named as, in parts, there seems to be more water than land. It is best seen early or late in the day when the water appears like mercury against the dark peat moor. The coast here is steep and rocky with no beaches, and narrow sea lochs cut deeply into the land -Loch Seaforth, for example, brings salt water some 12 miles inland.

The most rewarding areas of this parish of are well off the main road. To the north of Loch Erisort lies the smaller inlet of Loch Leurbost with the villages of Leurbost, Crossbost, Ranish and Grimshader all attractively sited to the north and

linked by a loop road. The seaward end of the lochs are littered with small islands.

Further south, a minor road connects with Keose and the alginate factory, where seaweed collected from around the island is processed. Alginate from here apparently went to the moon - fireproofing the astronauts' notepads. Beyond the crofting township of Balallan which straggles along the road for two-and-a-half miles, a splendid roadsign names no less than 11 villages to be found by following the route along the southern shore of Loch Erisort to Cromore, Marvig and Lemreway. The first habitations to be passed are Habost, Kershader and Garyvard, all refreshing places, with grass, conifers and rowan. The effects of re-seeding the moorland can be seen clearly along the course of the Caversta River, one side being the usual dark heather-clad moor, the other surprisingly lush and green.

At Cromore, **Eilean Chaluim Chille**, with its ruined church dedicated to St Columba and small burial ground, can be seen. The main road finishes at Lemreway, situated at the back of a bay sheltered by **Eilean Iubhard**.

To the south of Loch Erisort and to the east of Loch Seaforth, is the treeless Park Deer Forest, where herds of red deer roam freely. It was here, in 1887, that one of the last uprisings of the 'Crofters' War' (which began with the 'Battle of the Braes' on Skye) took place. The crofters, desperate for more land, killed 200 deer to draw attention to their plight - and entertained invited journalists to roast venison in order to obtain wide coverage by the press. The leaders of the 'Deer Raid' were later tried and found not guilty of 'mobbing and rioting'.

that which the land could reasonably support and living standards were intolerably low. Such were the pressures that the 'lazybeds', strips of fertile soil built by hand on top of the rock and used for growing potatoes and oats, were stretching 500 ft up the hillsides in places. In the 19th C depopulation was seen as the only possible way of raising living standards.

The main occupations today are crofting, weaving (Harris tweed originated here but the centre of production is now Lewis), knitting, fishing and little else. As a result, depopulation continues steadily, with many young people, already having had part of their education away from home, leaving to find employment elsewhere.

Tarbet is the largest village. There are a few shops, some selling knitwear and tweed, a post office, a hotel and an incongruous new 'motel' by the ferry terminal. A small tourist office is open in the summer.

North Harris
East Loch Tarbert is littered with many rocks and islands, the largest of which are **Scotasay** which had a population of 20 in 1911 but is now deserted, and the thriving Scalpay, reached via the small ferry from Kyles Scalpay. The road to the ferry winds along the north side of the loch, past crofts forged out of the barren ground. Many now have well-tended gardens – in one, two small palm trees grow! A path from Urgha leads north along the salmon-filled Laxadale Lochs to Maaruig on Loch Seaforth.

To the north of West Loch Tarbert are the high bare mountains of the Forest of Harris. On the shore, beneath Clisham, is Bunavoneadar where there are the remains of a whaling station built by Norwegians about 1912. It was utilised by Lord Leverhulme as part of his revitalisation scheme, but was finally abandoned in 1930.

The narrow road winds around the head of Loch Meavaig, where the view north along the glen, between the steep and craggy sides of Oreval (2172 ft) and Sròn Scourst (1611 ft), is quite dramatic. In a beautiful and isolated position above the township of Meavaig stands the corrugated-iron school, neat, tidy and painted cream. Here the children learn and play looking out towards **Soay Beag**, **Soay Mór** and **Taransay**, a fine prospect.

Beyond Cliasmol, with its maze of lazybeds, is the baronial-style Amhuinnsuidhe Castle (pronounced Amin-sewey), standing by the pretty inlet of Loch Leosavay. Built by the Earl of Dunmore in 1868, the castle is of attractive warm-grey stone imported into Harris. The road approaches the castle through white

Urgha, Harris: roofless black houses, lazybeds and crofts.

gates and passes the falls where the waters of Loch Leosaid tumble into the sea. Here, in June and July, salmon can be seen leaping. The west entrance to the grounds is through a fine archway, beyond which there is a sturdy terrace of stone houses and stables. The castle gardens are planted with shrubs and lilies, and pheasants wander among the trees. It was at Amhuinnsuidhe Castle that James Barrie, the Scottish author and dramatist, wrote *Mary Rose*, inspired, it is said, by one of the small islets in Loch Voshimid, four-and-a-half miles to the north-east.

Most of this part of Harris, including the castle, is owned by the proprietors of the North Harris Estate. The herds of red deer that roam the hills are carefully protected, the lochs are rich with salmon and trout, and golden eagles and ravens haunt the peaks.

A mile inland from Amhuinn-suidhe, Loch Chliostair feeds a new hydroelectric power station which supplies most of Harris. The 'arch dam' built here was the first of its type in the Outer Hebrides. The road continues north-west through an area of peat before reaching the small crofting community of

Amhuinnsuidhe Castle, Harris.

Hushinish. To the west of the superb beach, low cliffs of rose-coloured gneiss shelter guillemots, shags and fulmars. Cattle and sheep graze behind the dunes. When a strong southerly wind blows, the sands spread everywhere, sometimes burying the road. A short distance to the north a small pier serves the island of **Scarp**, first settled around 1810, but abandoned by its last remaining crofters in 1971. In the 1940s the population was still over 100, but the cottages are now used as holiday homes. This rocky island rises to a height of 1011 ft in the north; the 'village' is sheltered from the prevailing winds by a smaller hill in the east of the island. Several small islands lie offshore. Five miles to the south-west is the tiny low-lying islet of **Gasker**, which has a large seal colony. In 1934, well before the army brought its missiles to South Uist, an experiment was conducted here to see if mail could be sent to and from Scarp by rocket. On the first firing, celebrated with a special stamp issue, the projectile exploded on impact and most of the mail was damaged. The service ceased.

South Harris

The eastern coastline, known as 'Bays', is broken with narrow sea lochs and many small islands; inland the gneiss is spattered with hundreds of small lochs. The coast road (or 'Golden Road' so called because it was so expensive to build) winds through this dramatic heather-clad and rock-strewn landscape where boulders balance precariously on hill slopes and small dwellings nestle in dips and hollows.

Many crofters came here when the fertile land in the west was cleared for sheep, having to grow their food where none had grown before. They collected seaweed and mixed it with peat, arranging the whole in raised beds for drainage. The mixture weathered into compost and, on these 'lazybeds', oats and potatoes were grown. Gradually the beds were enlarged, running far up the hillsides in places, and the seaweed had to be carried further and further. A few sheep were grazed among the rocks. In the crofters' favour was the broken coastline which provided shelter for their boats and enabled them to catch herring and lobster, and the freshwater lochs which supplied trout.

But life was never easy, and neither was death. So intractable is the ground that the dead had to be taken to the west coast for burial. Here we are privileged to see a land where men and women have literally forged their existence on bare inhospitable rock and the sight is an inspiration. Now that life is a little easier, there is time to grow a few

East Loch Tarbert, Harris

flowers by the croft – an enjoyable sight among these bare hills.

At Drinishader, to the west of East Loch Tarbert, Mrs Alex MacDonald wove tweed that was presented to the Queen, Elizabeth II. Beyond Grosebay is Kyles Stockinish where the only youth hostel in the Outer Hebrides overlooks **Stockinish Island**. The small inlet on the island is used as a lobster pond.

From Loch Flodabay the Shiant Isles can be seen 18 miles to the north-east, their tall cliffs rising steeply from the sea. After Loch Finsbay the road rises around the foot of Roineabhal (1506 ft) from which the whole panorama of the coast and the lochs can be seen.

The Church of St Clement, Rodel.

The village of Rodel, one mile north of Renish Point, has a small harbour sheltered by the island of Vallay and overlooked by the famous St Clement's Church, the plan of which is cruciform, with a square central tower, making it unique in the outer isles. It was built in about 1500 by Alasdair Crotach, 8th MacLeod of Dunvegan in Skye, using mellow green sandstone, some imported from Mull. His effigy, sculpted in 1528, lies in a fine arched recess tomb, beautifully and simply

carved. The church has been twice restored, in 1787 and 1873. The key is available from the hotel nearby.

Two-and-a-half miles north-west of Rodel, through Gleann Shranndabhal where a few wind-blasted trees cling to life, is Leverburgh, formerly Obbe. The name was changed when Lord Leverhulme tried to revolutionise the fishing industry here. He chose Obbe, on the Sound of Harris, because it gave equal access to both the waters of the Atlantic and the Minch, so that his boats could always find sheltered water in which to fish. He planned to blast away many of the rocks and skerries that make the waters of the sound so treacherous, and he built factories and houses for his workers. The initial catches of herring exceeded expectation but the project never really worked well. He sold out in 1923, and within two years all activity had stopped. Leverburgh looks, sadly, like a failed dream, untidy and down at the heel. A small passenger ferry crosses the sound to Berneray and Newtonferry on North Uist.

At the eastern end of the Sound of Harris are the small green islands of **Gilsay**, **Lingay**, **Scaravay** and **Groay**. The two largest islands in the Sound were **Killegray** which once had a population of five, and **Ensay**, which once supported 15 people. Both have houses still standing, and attractive beaches. On Ensay there is a chapel by the house and Viking relics have been uncovered. In summer they are grazed by sheep, and visited, apparently, by the holidaying Royal Family.

After Leverburgh, the road passes through Glen Coishletter. As the summit is reached acres of glorious cream shell sand come into view, sheltered by the great bulk of Chaipaval to the west, rising to 1201 ft. It is an extremely pleasant walk through the crofting land and up to the top. The sight is splendid — on a clear day St Kilda can be seen some 45 miles to the west and the Skye

Seilebost, west Harris.

Cuillins 50 miles south-east. The small island of **Coppay,** which has a seal colony, can be seen one-and-a-half miles to the west.

The road along the west coast crosses the machair behind the beaches. The crofts look prosperous, with sheep and cattle grazing nearby. The beach at Borve is excellent; at its southern end there is a standing stone. Standing in a hollow sheltered by woods planted by the Earl of Dunmore, Borve Lodge was occupied by Lord Leverhulme during his time on the island. A mile offshore is the handsome island of **Taransay** – two large humps joined by a narrow neck of dunes – where cattle and sheep can be seen grazing by the shore. Taransay once had a population of 76.

There are more fine creamy shell sands at Tràigh Seilebost, backed by a spit of dunes, which in turn are backed by the estuarine sands of Tràigh Luskentyre. On the northern shore, behind the dunes, is the township of Luskentyre.

The road skirts the southern side of the estuary, passing saltings and then crossing a causeway before climbing between the South Harris Forest and the wild hills to the south. The view back towards Taransay is magnificent, especially in summer when the sea thrift is in bloom.

South Harris is an area of stark contrasts and is worthy of much exploration. There are fine rough walks along the harsh eastern seaboard and through the central hills and lochs. In summer, if the wind drops and the sun shines, the beaches on the west, backed by the machair in flower, are perfect for 'a day by the sea'. The whole is unspoiled, undeveloped and uncrowded.

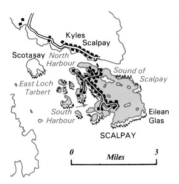

SCALPAY

0 _____ Miles _____ 3

Scalpay

Situated off Harris at the mouth of East Loch Tarbert, Scalpay has a population of about 450 and the main industry is fishing. All the habitations are on the western seaboard and the pressure of so many people on the land has resulted in extensive lazybed cultivation. A fine natural harbour is situated in the north-west with another on the west. On **Eilean Glas**, in the far south-east, there has been a lighthouse since 1788 – the first in the Western Isles.

The Scalpachs are a tight-knit and vigorous community with a strong attachment to their little island. Enlightened leadership and modest and timely investments in new equipment have allowed them to maintain their viability during periods of considerable change in the fishing industry. Bonnie Prince Charlie came here, on his way to Stornoway, after his defeat at Culloden in 1746. Donald Campbell, a farmer, gave him refuge and the use of his boat.

A small vehicle ferry, Caledonian MacBrayne's *Morven*, connects with Kyles Scalpay.

North Uist

With a population of 1850, and an area of 75,000 acres, this is a low-lying island, deeply incised in the east by sea lochs and so liberally endowed with freshwater lochs that half the area is covered by water, reflecting so much light that colours seem to glow and shimmer in the sun. Rising from this anglers' paradise are North and South Lee (860 ft and 922 ft respectively) and, further south, Eaval (1138 ft), the highest point on the island. In the north and west a few low hills give way to wide sandy bays with tidal islands, backed by tracts of machair, particularly attractive in the spring and early summer. With no high ground in the west, the prevailing winds blow unchecked.

After the period of Norse occupation, North Uist was ruled by the MacRuairidhs, followed by the MacDonalds of Sleat (Skye) whose official title was confirmed by James IV in 1495. They held the island until 1855, when it was sold to Sir John Powlett Ord who split the estate. It is now all owned by the enterprising Lord Granville, a cousin of the Queen.

In the early 19th C there were almost 5000 people living on the island, but a decline in population over the last 160 years has continued. Evictions were carried out around 1850 under the direction of Lord MacDonald of Sleat, whose conduct as a landowner did him little credit. Police constables were brought to the island, cottages were burned and a bloody fight took place between the police and the crofters near Malaclete. The church minister was conspicuous by his absence during this time.

In recent years the economy has been fairly well balanced, with a spread of activities including crofting, fishing, the production of alginates, weaving and knitting, and bulb-growing has also been tried. The crofts on North Uist are generally quite large, enabling them to be worked as a primary means of income, rather than on the part-time basis common elsewhere. There was once a large herring fishing fleet centred on Loch Maddy, but today the fishing industry is concerned mainly with lobsters and crabs, and is based on Grimsay. The alginate factory, opened in 1957, is at Sponish on Loch Maddy, where local collectors bring seaweed for processing. Knitwear and tweed are produced both on an individual and collective basis.

The islanders have been Protestant since the late 18th C, sharing their religion, strangely, with their more distant neighbours across the Sound of Harris rather than with the Catholics of South

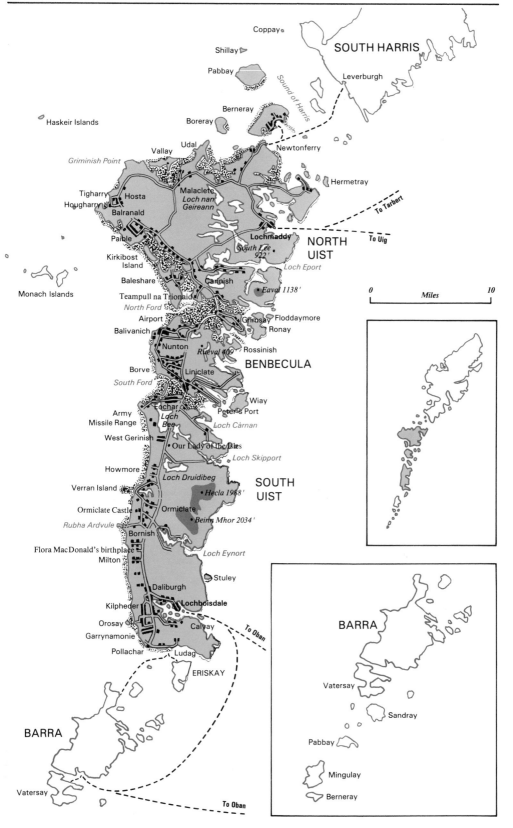

Coppay

Shillay

Pabbay

SOUTH HARRIS

Leverburgh

Sound of Harris

Berneray

Boreray

Haskeir Islands

Udal

Vallay

Newtonferry

Griminish Point

Hermetray

Tigharry

Hosta

Malaclete

Loch nan Geireann

Hougharry

Balranald

To Tarbert

Paible

Lochmaddy

NORTH UIST

To Uig

Kirkibost Island

South Lee 922'

Baleshare

Loch Eport

Teampull na Trionaid

Carinish

Eaval 1138'

Monach Islands

North Ford

Airport

Grimsay

Floddaymore

Balivanich

Ronay

Nunton

Rueval 409'

Rossinish

BENBECULA

Borve

Liniclate

South Ford

Wiay

Eochar

Peter's Port

Army Missile Range

Loch Bee

Loch Càrnan

West Gerinish

Our Lady of the Isles

Loch Skipport

Howmore

Loch Druidibeg

SOUTH UIST

Verran Island

Hecla 1988'

Ormiclate Castle

Ormiclate

Rubha Ardvule

Beinn Mhor 2034'

Bornish

Flora MacDonald's birthplace

Loch Eynort

Milton

Stuley

Daliburgh

Kilpheder

Lochboisdale

Orosay

Calvay

To Oban

Garrynamonie

Pollachar

Ludag

ERISKAY

BARRA

Vatersay

To Oban

0   *Miles*   10

BARRA

Vatersay

Sandray

Pabbay

Mingulay

Berneray

Vallay Strand, North Uist.

Uist and Barra. The different religious communities live in total harmony with each other.

The complex area of lochs in the east, salt and fresh, and the salmon, sea trout and brown trout they contain, are a major attraction to anglers. Fishing is controlled by the North Uist Estate and the Newton Estate. A good place to start enquiries is the hotel at Lochmaddy, the main village and terminal for the ferry from Uig, with a population of about 300. As well as the hotel, there are a couple of shops, a bank, post office, school and small hospital. The position of the village, at the back of Loch Maddy, is very attractive. There are two theories regarding the derivation of 'Maddy'. One claims it is from the two dog (maddy) shaped rocks at the entrance to the loch, the other that the loch is rich in a certain kind of shellfish called maddies. The village is the natural centre for touring the island and for fishing.

By the road, to the north-west, Blashaval rises to 358 ft. On its western slope are three standing stones called Na Fir Bhreige, 'the false men', said to mark the graves of three spies who were buried alive. The north side of Loch Maddy is reached across a narrow neck of land, and there are fine views over the many islands in the loch towards North and South Lee. The east coast of the promontory has a few small hills, and to the north, in the Sound

of Harris, are the islands of **Sursay, Tahay, Vaccasay** and **Hermetray**. It was on the last that Charles I planned to establish a fishing station, but the outbreak of the Civil War brought the scheme to a premature end.

In Clachan Sands, to the west of the Newtonferry road, are the remains of the pre-Reformation church of St Columba and a burial ground. Just behind Port nan Long is the broch, Dùn an Sticir, last occupied in 1602 by Hugh MacDonald of Sleat (*see* Duntulm, Skye). The causeway to it can still be seen, but the building is now little more than a pile of stones. The easy climb to the summit of Beinn Mhór (625 ft), is well worthwhile; looking to the south-west the contrast

between the loch-strewn east and the machair in the west can be clearly seen.

At the northern tip of North Uist is Newtonferry, where a small passenger ferry connects with Berneray and Leverburgh.

Of the three large islands visible from here – Berneray, Pabbay and Boreray – only the first is still inhabited. **Berneray** is three miles long, one-and-a-half miles wide and has a population of about 150 living in well-kept, white-painted houses on the eastern side. Although lying close to North Uist, it forms part of the Parish of Harris. The island is green (there is no peat) with superb beaches. Prior to the 16th C it was almost connected to Pabbay, but strong tides swept the sands away.

North and South Lee, North Uist.

Teampull na Trionaid, North Uist.

The people are crofters, lobster fishermen and knitters.

Pabbay, four-and-a-half miles off North Uist, once supported a population of over 300 who produced, among other things, whisky. The island was cleared for sheep and is now run as a single farm. It rises to a height of 643 ft on the northern side, and was once known as 'the granary of Harris'. On the southern shore is an old burial ground. A mile to the north are the small islands of **Shillay**, where grey seals breed.

Boreray, two-and-a-half miles north-west of Newtonferry, is one-and-a-half miles long by one mile wide, the highest point being 184 ft, and it has a large central loch. In 1841 it supported a population of 181, but it was evacuated by request in 1923, although one family changed its mind at the last minute, obtaining a holding of 87 acres. Until quite recently it was still being farmed by a resident family. Coins dating from the reign of James IV have been found in the sands.

The main road of North Uist skirts its north coast, passing between the white sands surrounding the tidal island of **Oronsay** and Loch nan Geireann. On one of the islands in the loch, **Eilean-an-Tighe**, the remains of a neolithic potter's workshop have been found. Acknowledged to be the earliest such example yet found in Western Europe, its size indicates it

must have served quite a wide area. North Uist is rich in ancient sites; standing stones, stone circles and chambered cairns are spread profusely over the island. To the north of Grenitote, on the narrow peninsula of sand and machair, a team of archaeologists have been excavating at Udal, a site occupied from the Bronze Age until the Clearances. In the sea cliffs at the northern tip, Aird a' Mhòrain, an incised cross and some cup marks (Bronze Age carvings of ritual significance) have been found. A freshwater spring here is known as the 'Well of the Cross'.

The tidal island of **Vallay** (which had a population of 59 in 1841) is reached across the white sands of Vallay Strand. The fine grey-stone house on the island was built by Erskine Beveridge and is now the property of the owner of the North Uist Estate.

At the north-west corner of North Uist is Griminish Point, where there is a natural rock arch 30 ft high. 41 miles west-north-west is St Kilda. Eight miles west-north-west are **Haskeir Island** and **Haskeir Eagach**, a small group with stacks and arches, frequented by grey seals and puffins. Lewis Spence based his book, *Island of Disaster*, around Haskeir Eagach, the most southerly of the group. In Loch Scalpaig a small castellated folly stands on a green islet. It was built by Alex MacLeod, chamberlain to the

MacDonald estates, who also erected the conspicuous Latin cross half a mile south-west at Kilphedder in 1830, after it was unearthed in a burial ground nearby. Beyond Loch Hosta (said to cover a drowned village) there is a vast area of dunes, and the small beach at Tràigh Stir, opposite the loch, is quite beautiful. In the cliffs at Tigharry is the 'Kettle Spout', a spouting cave.

The rare red-necked phalarope.

To the west of Balranald House, once the seat of the MacDonalds of Griminish, is the RSPB's Balranald Reserve. The varied habitat here includes the tiny island of **Causamul**, two miles offshore, a seal nursery and refuge for the winter duck population, and beaches, dunes, machair, marshes and freshwater lochs. A notable rarity often seen here is the red-necked phalarope. Access to the reserve is restricted; the summer warden resides at Hougharry.

Tigharry, Hougharry and Paible are the main west-coast

Benbecula, the 'mountain of the fords'.

communities, an area of well-kept crofts and grazing land. Many of the graves of North Uist's nobility are to be found in the churchyard at Hougharry. Inland, on the southern slope of South Clettraval (436 ft), is Cleatrbhal a' Deas, a wheelhouse and chambered cairn.

To the south of Paible there are wide expanses of white sand around the tidal dune islands of **Kirkibost Island** (across the sands from the solid, square Westford Inn) and the larger **Baleshare** reached by a causeway. Its name means 'East Township' - West Township was swept away by the same exceptional tide that widened the Sound of Pabbay, and also isolated the Monach Isles (eight miles west of Baleshare) once fordable at low tide. There are extensive beaches on Baleshare, and the remains of Christ's Temple. Hugh MacDonald of Baleshare is thought to have introduced the kelp industry (kelp, when burned, produces alkali) to the Hebrides in about 1735, which resulted in a period of prosperity until it collapsed in the first half of the 19th C.

The most important ecclesiastical remains on North Uist are at Carinish in the extreme south-west. Here stands the fine ruin of Teampull na Trionaid, a medieval monastery and college thought to have been founded by Beathag, daughter of Somerled, in the early 13th C, and later enlarged by the wife of John MacDonald of Islay, first Lord of the Isles, in 1350. It was rebuilt in the 16th C, destroyed after the Reformation, and rebuilt again in the 19th C. Many chiefs sent their

sons to be educated here. Alongside is Teampull Clan A'Phiocair, the chapel of the Macvicars, teachers at the college. Close by are the Slochdanan cup marks and Feithe na Fala, the 'Ditch of Blood', scene of a battle in 1601 between the MacLeods of Harris and the MacDonalds of Uist.

The main road south connects with Benbecula, but not before passing right through a stone circle on a slight rise, half a mile from Carinish. To the south of Loch Eport, the road through the small community of Locheport passes the five chambered cairns and stone circle of Croineubhal Craonaval, before finishing about one-and-a-half miles from the steep and rocky western side of Eaval which can only be climbed via its eastern slope (Loch Obisary cuts off any approach from the north and west). The view from its summit is more than adequate compensation for the steep climb.

The road to the north of Loch Eport passes Ben Langass (295 ft), the only hill between Clachan and Lochmaddy. Conspicuous on its slope is Langass Barp, a neolithic chambered cairn which, although partially collapsed, can, with care, be entered. Around the western side of the hill can be found Pobull Fhinn, 'Finn's People', a stone circle above Loch Langass.

The western tip of the low-lying island of **Grimsay** is linked to North Uist (and Benbecula) by the causeway opened in 1960. Prior to its opening, the sands of Oitir Mhór ('north ford') could be crossed at low tide, although not without risk as the

tide rises swiftly. Grimsay is a lobster-fishing centre, with a large storage facility built in 1968. Live lobsters can be taken to the airport four miles away to arrive fresh in the fish markets within a few hours. Tweed is also woven here at Balaglas.

To the east of Grimsay the largest of several islands is **Ronay**, rising to a height of 377 ft, and uninhabited since the 1920s, although it once supported 180 people before being cleared in 1831. Fishermen were buried by the Lowlander's (St Michael's) Chapel.

Benbecula

Benbecula's name derives from *Beinn a' bh-faodhla* ('mountain of the fords'), a reminder of days when the island was the stepping stone between the Uists. It is low-lying and windswept, with machair in the west and peat moorland in the east where the coast is deeply cut by sea lochs. The whole island is liberally endowed with freshwater lochs, making it, like its neighbours, a rewarding place for anglers and ornithologists.

There is a solitary hill, Rueval, a prominent landmark rising to 409 ft just north of the island's centre. On the south-east side of the hill is the cave where Bonnie Prince Charlie hid on 25 and 26 June 1746 while waiting for Flora MacDonald to organise his escape (*see* South Uist and Skye). The intrepid pair finally went 'over the sea to Skye' from Rossinish, east of here. The easy walk to the top of Reuval is an excellent way to see the island, laid out like a map.

The indigenous population, a harmonious mixture of Protestant and Catholic numbering 1300 (plus 500 military personnel), have recently enjoyed a measure of prosperity thanks to the presence of the army at Balivanich. Whether these benefits will be long-term, and anything other than material, remains to be seen. The army base was established in 1958; in 1971 the missile range on South Uist and attendant facilities were expanded at a cost of £22 million. Initially, and understandably, there was local resistance to the military presence, but now the base has become an accepted part of the island's life to a degree that would leave a considerable vacuum were the Ministry of Defence to decide it were no longer needed.

Balivanich is the 'capital' of Benbecula - a cluster of regimented houses around the NAAFI building, with shops, garages and other services, as well as a council office. To the north is the airfield, established by the RAF during World War II and now serving as an important link in the communications of these islands, with regular flights to Stornoway and Glasgow. It is manned by a small contingent of RAF technicians.

A main road crosses the island from north to south, but more interesting is the west-coast route which passes through the tidy crofts and farms. South of Balivanich is the Culla beach, beautiful cream sands backed by dunes, and behind these are the ruined walls of the 14th-C Nunton Chapel. It was from Lady Clanranald at Nunton House that Bonnie Prince Charlie obtained his 'Betty Burke' disguise before leaving with Flora MacDonald from Rossinish on 28 June 1746. The road continues by the shore to Borve, where the ruined walls of the 14th-C castle, once a Clan Ranald stronghold and occupied until 1625, stand in a field. To the south-west of the road are the barely visible remains of a chapel that once belonged to the castle. The MacDonalds of Clanranald held the island until 1839, when it was sold to Colonel Gordon of Cluny (*see* South Uist), whose family and trustees owned the island until 1942.

From Liniclate a minor road heads south-east to the pier at Peter's Port, with another road branching north to Loch Uiskevagh. The south-east coast here is in complete contrast to the west with many small coves and rocky islands, the largest being **Wiay**, a bird sanctuary, which in 1861 had a population of six, but has been uninhabited since 1901. The pier at Peter's Port was built in 1896; it was then found that there was no road to it, and access by sea was dangerous.

Later a causeway and a road were built, but the pier was hardly ever used - and remains a planner's folly. The main road passes through Creagorry, with its hotel and large food store, before crossing 'O'Regan's Bridge' (built in 1943 to serve the airfield) over the sands of South Ford to South Uist.

South Uist

The second largest island in the Outer Hebrides, having an area (including Benbecula and Eriskay) of 90,000 acres and a population of 2500, South Uist has a mountainous spine running almost the full length of its eastern side, rising to 2034 ft at the summit of Beinn Mhor and to 1988 ft at the summit of Hecla. Four sea lochs cut deep into the east coast: Loch Boisdale, Loch Eynort, Loch Skipport (joining with the non-tidal Loch Bee to make the north-east tip virtually an island) and Loch Sheilavaig. The west coast has 20 miles of virtually unbroken beach, white shell sand backed by dunes and the springy grass of the machair making for excellent coastal walking, usually with an invigorating salty breeze blowing off the clear, blue Atlantic. Between the mountains and the machair there is peaty moorland with many freshwater lochs, rich with salmon, sea trout and brown trout; however, fishing is strictly controlled. Here and there are deserted black houses 'growing' out of the ground, often looking more organic than man-made.

The main sources of income are crofting, fishing, alginates and the missile range. The island's major asset is the fertile strip of machair about a mile wide running the whole length of the west coast. Along with the usual crofting activities, many cattle are raised for export. Sheep are generally left to forage in the rough hill-grazing and moorland. Fishing activity centres on lobsters, with salmon and trout also being taken. Loch Càrnan is the hub of this

industry. Seaweed is processed at North Lochboisdale, the wrack or 'tangle' being collected from the east-coast bays, where great heaps are cast up after storms. Collection is done on a part-time basis, although the factory provides some full-time employment. The weed is also collected by crofters for their own use as fertiliser.

The Royal Artillery range is situated in the area west of West Gerinish and Loch Bee. It provides both direct employment, and work generated by the needs of the 500 or so military personnel. The islanders and soldiers are on good terms; compensation has been paid for land taken, and, when the range is not in use, the grazing is made available.

The Hebrideans of South Uist are mainly Roman Catholic - small roadside shrines are the visible evidence of this - and thus Sundays are a more lively affair than those on the Protestant islands further north. There is no secondary school in these islands, so the older children have to leave the island and live in hostels, providing an early trigger to emigration, the biggest problem in the Hebrides since the Clearances.

The only village on the east coast is Lochboisdale (population 300), where the Caledonian MacBrayne vehicle ferry from Oban and Barra calls. There are shops, a hotel, bank, school, police station and Tourist Information office (open in the summer). The village straggles westward to Daliburgh, with crofts seemingly everywhere and cottages built quite often on rocky outcrops with scant regard for shelter - where the land is poor, the dwelling had to be built on the least fertile part of the croft.

Colonel Gordon of Cluny, who bought the island together with Benbecula and Eriskay from the MacDonalds of Clanranald (descendants of Ranald, the son of John, first Lord of the Isles) in 1838, was a particularly

Loch Skipport, South Uist, where the steamers once called.

Hecla and Beinn Mhor, the 'spine' of South Uist.

insensitive man. He cleared the islands for sheep, evicting crofters and forcing emigration. A few were given land on Eriskay which was too poor for sheep. During this period over 1000 emigrants left Lochboisdale on *The Admiral*, only to arrive in America destitute. Some of those evicted took to the hills, pursued by police. Between 1841 and 1861 the population of South Uist fell from 7300 to 5300. Later militant action by the crofters won them their present holdings.

At the mouth of Loch Boisdale is the island of **Calvay**, with a ruined 13th-C castle where Bonnie Prince Charlie took refuge from the king's soldiers on 15 June 1746, and an automatic light replacing the light built in 1857. There is one main north-south road on South Uist which runs wide and straight beside the machair. It reveals little of the true character of the island, the most interesting parts of which are to be found by walking or driving down the narrow roads to the west and, occasionally, to the east.

South of Daliburgh, where there is a hospital, the main road finishes at Pollachar. There is an inn here, with fine views towards Barra. South-west of Daliburgh, near Kilpheder, are the remains of a wheelhouse dating from the 2nd C AD, excavated in 1952. It has a circular plan, the hearth being the hub and stone piers at the rim supporting the 'spokes' - wooden rafters. It was probably used as a

farm house. Where the track from Kilpheder breaks into three near the sea, take the middle track. Over the dunes is a beautiful white beach. Further south along the main road, on a slight rise, is the church of Our Lady of Sorrows, built by the Barra priest Calum McNeil in 1963. The Garrynamonie school nearby will be long remembered for Frederick Rea, the headmaster from 1890-1913, who refused to acknowledge Gaelic and taught only in English.

At Mingary, to the east of the road, a track leads to Barpa Mhingearraidh, a chambered cairn with a ring of pillar stones standing prominently on the slope of Reineval. Just north of Milton, a cairn inside low, ruined walls marks the birthplace of Flora MacDonald, the young woman who helped Bonnie Prince Charlie after his defeat at Culloden. The Prince left the mainland on 24 April 1746 with a price of £30,000 on his head. After many exploits in the Outer Hebrides, including being chased by a man o' war, and a three-day drunken 'Highland debauch', he met Flora MacDonald, who agreed to help him. The Prince, disguised as Flora's maid 'Betty Burke', left Benbecula in a small boat for Skye on 28 June 1746. The ruin is worth visiting only for its romantic associations - there is nothing of interest to see.

About two miles north of Milton, a minor road ends at Rubha Ardvule, the most westerly point on the

island. This promontory contains a small lochan, the haunt of many waterfowl. Beneath the shingle there is said to be an old Norse stone causeway, revealed once when exposed by a storm. By Loch Bornish there is a small Roman Catholic church with a simple and dignified interior, the only decoration being behind the altar. The minor road north through the crofts can be followed to Ormiclate Castle, a fine ruin standing in a farmyard. The unfortified building took seven years to build and burned down seven years later, on the eve of the Battle of Sherrifmuir in 1715, where the builder, Ailean MacDonald of Clanranald, was mortally wounded. Much still remains to be seen, including an armorial plaque in the north wall. Its site, overlooking the Atlantic, is superb.

The little church near the west coast at Howmore has an unusual central communion pew and a fine interior. Nearby are the remains of Caibeal Dhiarmaid church, (dedicated to St Columba), Caibeal nan Sagairt and Teampull Mor. On an islet in Loch an Eilein are the few remains of Caisteal Bheagram, a small 15th- or 16th-C tower.

The ridge between the peaks of Beinn Mhor and Hecla dominates the area; a walk along the top is a fine energetic day's work with, of course, excellent views, including Skye and the Cuillins to the east. On the southern slope of Beinn Mhor, beneath the lower summit of Spin

(1168 ft), is the wooden glen of Allt Volagir, full of birch and hazel, and brightened with violets and bluebells in the spring.

The Loch Druidibeg National Nature Reserve (total area 4145 acres) is just to the north of Drimsdale, stretching for four miles inland from the sandy shore, through the dunes and limy machair to the acid peat moorland around the loch. The shore of the loch is broken with many small peninsulas which, together with innumerable small islets, make an ideal habitat for many types of waterfowl. It is now the most important (and one of the last remaining) breeding grounds in the British Isles of the native grey lag goose. Also of interest is the differing flora of the two soil types; for instance the shallow calcareous lochs and marsh of the machair have a richer vegetation than their counterparts in the acid peat. A rarity, the American pondweed, has its only natural distribution in the British Isles in the Uists. A permit is required to visit the reserve; the Nature Conservancy Council hostel is at Grogarry Lodge.

The road east to Loch Skipport, along the northern edge of the reserve, is well worth exploring. The country is rugged heather, peat and boulders, with a small clump of conifers and rhododendrons hiding around a corner as a pleasant surprise. There are lapwings everywhere. The road finishes with a steep descent to the decayed pier (built 1879) in the sheltered waters of Loch Skipport, where the steamers once called. The lighthouse at Rudha Ushinish became operational in 1857.

Beyond the nature reserve, the army missile range begins to make its presence felt. A launching, if you happened to be there at the time

'Our Lady of the Isles', South Uist.

Eriskay.

(there are long periods of apparent inactivity), would be clearly visible from the perimeter. The missiles are tracked from St Kilda, over 40 miles to the north-west.

On the slope of Rueval, 'The Hill of Miracles', is the 30-ft granite statute of 'Our Lady of the Isles' by Hew Lorimer, erected in 1957 to commemorate Marian Year. The tall pillar-like Madonna and child look towards the missile range, and is itself overlooked by the range control installation (known as 'space city') at the summit.

The road crosses Loch Bee on a causeway. Mute swans can sometimes be seen on this large expanse of shallow water. It is noticeable that many of the small islets in the lochs throughout the Uists are covered with dense thickets of willow, hazel, rowan, and juniper growing among ferns, all thriving out of the reach of grazing sheep – an indication of what much of the island must have looked like before the hand of man fell so heavily upon it, clearing the trees and raising sheep.

Eriskay

Eriskay (from the Gaelic *Eirisgeigh*, 'Eric's isle') is a small island, two-and-a-half by one-and-a-half miles, with a population of 200. The island was made famous worldwide by 'The Eriskay Love Lilt' and other beautiful Gaelic melodies which originated here, and by the shipwreck of the SS *Politician*, which inspired Sir Compton Mackenzie's book, *Whisky Galore!* It also has its place in the romantic story of the ill-fated rising of 1745: the half-mile beach of Coilleag a' Phrionnsa on the west is where Bonnie Prince Charlie first set foot on Scottish soil, landing from *Du Teillay* en route from France to the Scottish mainland. The pink sea bindweed (*Calystegia soldanella*) which grows at the back of the beach, and on Vatersay, is said to have spread from seeds dropped by the Prince.

Eriskay belonged to the MacNeils of Barra until 1758, when it passed to the MacDonalds of Clanranald.

Eriskay, Barra, Benbecula and South Uist were sold to Colonel Gorden of Cluny in 1838, who cleared the island for sheep but allowed a few evicted crofters to settle on Eriskay as it was too poor for grazing. Like the crofters of Harris, they made lazybeds of seaweed and peat, raised for drainage, on which they grew oats, barley and potatoes.

The main area of settlement is on the north coast, with another small township by the fine natural harbour in the east. The people of this thriving community are Roman Catholic, take great pride in their well-maintained and brightly painted houses, and have a strong attachment to their native island. There is a shop, school, post office and church. The main occupations, supplemented with crofting, are fishing (a small fleet takes herring, lobster, prawn and white fish) and the production by the women of hand-knitted sweaters, with patterns peculiar to Eriskay.

The sea around the island is quite shallow and unsuited to large vessels. It was therefore surprising when the 12,000-ton SS *Politician*, bound for New York with 24,000 cases of whisky on board, foundered to the east of Calvay, between Eriskay and South Uist. The islanders felt it their duty to salvage such a valuable cargo, and soon nearly everyone on the island, and some say the livestock as well, was drunk. Such was the glut that the spirit was even found useful for lighting the peats! Compton Mackenzie based his book *Whisky Galore!*, set on the fictional island of 'Todday', on these events. The classic Ealing comedy film of the same name was made on Barra in 1948. The seaweed-covered hulk of the stern of the ship is still visible at low tide, and the occasional (and now undrinkable) bottle is still found.

The angelus at St Michael's Church, built in 1903 by Father Allen MacDonald, is rung on a bell recovered from the German battle-cruiser *Derfflinger*, scuttled at Scapa Flow, and the altar base is

Castlebay, Barra.

constructed from the bow of a lifeboat from the aircraft-carrier *Hermes*. Eriskay ponies, used on the island to carry peat and seaweed, are the nearest thing to a native Scottish breed still surviving. They stand 12 to 13 hands high, and have small ears.

The ruin of Weaver's Castle on **Eilean Leathan** in the **Stack Islands**, off the southern tip, was once the base of the pirate and plunderer of wrecks, MacNeil. A small passenger ferry connects Eriskay with Ludag on South Uist, and Barra.

Barra

Barra has a population of 2000, and an area of 22,000 acres (including Vatersay). It has been suggested that the name may derive from *Finbar*, (St Barr) a 6th-C saint. The island is a microcosm of the whole of the Outer Hebrides, with a rocky and broken east coast, fine sandy bays on the west backed with machair, and rising to a maximum height of 1260 ft at the tooth-like summit of Heaval. The whole is Archaean gneiss, heavily glaciated. Over 150 species of birds and 400 types of plants have been recorded here - figures comparable with the rest of the Outer Hebrides.

Following the Norse domination of the Hebrides, the MacNeils held Barra from 1427, receiving the charter from Alexander, Lord of the Isles. James IV confirmed this charter in 1495. During the 16th C they raided English shipping, and made forays into Ireland. Although taking no active part in the 1745 rising (*see* Skye), the chief of the Clan MacNeil was implicated in the revolt, imprisoned, but never

prosecuted; in 1747 the clan moved to Eoligarry. When in debt in 1838, Roderick MacNeil sold the island to Colonel Gordon of Cluny (who had also bought Benbecula, South Uist and Eriskay), who offered the island to the Government as a penal colony - a further demonstration of his total lack of sensitivity towards the islanders. Deciding he was receiving insufficient rent, in 1857 he undertook clearances with the help of imported policemen, confiscating the crofters' stocks and causing many emigrants to arrive destitute in the New World. Later land shortages led to discontent among the remaining crofters, with the result that the large farms were split.

The ancestral home of the MacNeils is the impressive medieval fortress of Kiessimul Castle, built on a rock outcrop in Castle Bay. A high wall encloses a keep, hall and chapel, providing shelter at the expense of any outward prospect. There has

been a fortification on this site since the 11th C - the present building dates from the 15th C. In 1937 Robert Lister MacNeil, 45th Chief of the Clan MacNeil, purchased his ancestral home together with 12,000 acres of Barra. An architect, he restored the castle, which has now become a focal point for MacNeils all over the world. He died in 1970 and is now at rest in the chapel. During the restoration, the old castle gate was found at Sponish on North Uist, being used as a base for a peat stack.

The basis of the island's economy is crofting, with both sheep and cattle being kept. There is a small fishing fleet catching white fish, prawns and lobster. With the building of a new hotel in 1974, it is hoped that tourism will begin to make a significant contribution - certainly the island's undoubted charm should make it a popular holiday place.

Deserted crofts, east Barra.

When James Methuen began using Castle Bay as a port in 1869, at the start of the herring boom, the associated curing and packing industries brought great prosperity. Within 20 years, as many as 450 boats, mainly from the east coast of mainland Scotland, were using the harbour, seeming to make a floating bridge to Vatersay. The resident fleet was ill-equipped to compete, but many Barra men were engaged as crew, and by 1911 the population of the island had risen to 2620. During the 1930s the industry declined, being halted finally by the outbreak of war.

The famous 'Sea League' was formed here by Compton Mackenzie, who was then living on Barra, and John Lorne Campbell of Canna, in 1933, to protect local

shell grit from Tràigh Mhór, for use as a building material and as chicken feed. This latter activity is at present the subject of some debate, as it is claimed that the continuing removal of shell is compromising the future use of the beach as the island's airstrip.

Most of the people are Catholic, and have been so since St Patrick founded the See of the Isles in the 5th C, which, until the 14th C, was united with the See of Sodor and Man (*see* Isle of Man). During the 17th C there was a degree of religious persecution, but the islanders clung steadfastly to their faith. Ministers of the Church of Scotland have been present since 1734, and have been, for the most part, servile to the landowners, Rev. Henry Beatson (1847-71) particularly so during Colonel Gordon's clearances. Gaelic is spoken, although all the inhabitants are bilingual. The people are hardworking and unashamed in their pursuit of pleasure in contrast to their counterparts on Lewis. It is a very cheerful place, seven days a week.

The 'capital' of the island and main ferry terminal is Castlebay,

fishermen from illegal trawling in the Minch by the English. It pressed the Government for protective legislation but came up against stiff opposition from the English fishing lobby. Many young Barra men still go to sea, but now in either the merchant or Royal Navy.

Other minor employment is found in the production of perfume, and knitwear, and the removal of

The Castlebay Hotel and Our Lady, Star of the Sea, Barra.

The daily flight, Tràigh Mhór, Barra.

with hotels, shops, post office, tourist office, schools, bank and a cottage hospital. A post bus connects with Eoligarry, via the east coast road. The bay faces south towards Vatersay. To the north is the mountain of Heaval, with a statue of the Virgin and Child, erected in 1954, on its south-east slope. It is not a difficult walk to the top, and the view of the islands to the south is very fine. The large church overlooking Kiessimul Castle, Our Lady, Star of the Sea, was built in 1889. Moored by the castle is the lifeboat, which serves some of the most difficult waters around the coast of Britain. During one emergency in the winter of 1979, both the Barra and Islay boats were overturned by mountainous seas when answering a call for help from a Danish coaster. Fortunately there were no serious injuries and both boats returned safely.

The other main areas of settlement are North Bay, Eoligarry, Borve and Earsary. Eoligarry, north of Tràigh Mhór (known also as the Cockle Strand), is joined to the main body of the island by a neck of dunes. A small passenger ferry operates from the pier here to Eriskay and Ludag on South Uist. Above the grassland is Cille-bharra, the MacNeil burial ground. There are two roofless chapels by the restored church of St Barr, all possibly 12th C; Sir Compton Mackenzie is buried here. The views over the Sound of Barra to the mountains of South Uist are quite beautiful.

To the north of the long white beach of Tràigh Eais, a few stones mark the site of Dun Scurrival, a prehistoric galleried fort. Off the northern-most tip is the low-lying island of **Fiaray**; to the east is the grassy island of **Fuday**, its name

possibly deriving from the Norse *utey* ('outside isle'). This latter had a population of seven in 1861, although it has been deserted since the turn of the century. It was used for Norse burials, and was the retreat of some of King Haakon's forces after their defeat at the Battle of Largs in 1263.

The coast around North Bay is rocky and deeply indented. On an islet not far from the road stands a statue of St Barr by Margaret Somerville, a local artist, erected in 1975. The largest offshore island, **Hellisay**, had a population of 108 in 1841, but it was last occupied in the 1880s. The name is Norse - 'caves isle'. Beyond Hellisay is **Gighay** ('Gydha's isle'), rising to a height of 305 ft; it also once had a small population. The road along the east coast winds around the many small bays, with lazybeds crammed in everywhere - very reminiscent of south-east Harris.

The west coast between Greian Head and Doirlinn Head is a series of white sand beaches, with Halaman Bay in the south being outstanding - a magical place at sunset. Behind the sands is the machair, rich with flowers and scent in the spring and early summer. At Allasdale, to the north, are the remains of Dùn Cuier. Between Halaman Bay and Castle Bay, a path leads down to Loch Tangusdale (also called Loch St Clair), stocked with trout; the stump of Castle Sinclair, a small square tower, stands on an islet in the loch.

Barra's increasing population has made it possible for all essential services to be maintained. Even though limited employment prospects for young people lead to a degree of emigration, many people are returning and the future should harbour no fears for this particularly bright jewel of the Hebrides.

Vatersay

This is almost two islands, joined by a narrow neck of dunes and machair, with fine beaches in the bays thus formed. With a total population of 116, the main settlement is in the south - a picturesque shambles of cottages, wooden council houses, abandoned vehicles and grazing cattle. There is a post office and a public call-box here. To the north is the junior school, community centre, chapel and a few scattered cottages all linked by narrow metalled roads. There is a grocer's van that also acts as the island's only off-licence.

The economy is based on cattle and sheep. Until quite recently the cattle were tethered to boats and swum across to Barra, to be taken by

Castlebay's 'main street', and Kiessimul Castle, Barra.

Opposite: *Crofts at Eoligarry, Barra.*

Vatersay Bay.

once known as the Bishop's Isles, are uninhabited, except for the lighthouse keepers at Barra Head, Berneray. The Western Isles Council run a sturdy passenger ferry from Castlebay pier to Vatersay. This stretch of water can, at times, be very rough.

Sandray

The name means 'sand isle'. It lies about one-half mile south of Vatersay, rising to a height of 678 ft at the summit of Cairn Galtar. A strip of dunes lies parallel to the east coast. In the early 18th C, the island was divided into nine farms; by 1881 the population had fallen to ten, but rose to 41 in 1911 due to resettlement. It had been deserted since 1934. There was once an ancient chapel, known as Cille Bhride, on the island. To the west, are the small islands of **Lingay**, **Greanamul** and **Flodday**, the last having a natural arch.

Pabbay

Two-and-a-half miles south-west of Sandray, this is one of the many 'Priest's Isles' in the Hebrides, with the summit rising to a height of 561 ft, and steep sea cliffs. In 1881 the population was 26 with the settlement being on the eastern side above a shell sand beach. It is now deserted. On the north-east corner are the remains of Dùnan Ruadh, 'the red fort', and above Bàgh Bàn there was once a chapel and burial ground – still remaining are three cross-marked stones and one with a cross, a crescent and a lily. All are possibly Pictish. Some small islands lie to the south-west.

Mingulay

Taking its name from the Norse for 'big isle', Mingulay lies two miles south-west of Pabbay, and is two-and-a-half miles by one-and-a-half miles. It was once owned by MacNeil of Barra, who took care of his tenants – finding new wives for widowers, new husbands for widows, and making good the loss of any milking cow. The settlement was on the east side, above the sandy Mingulay Bay; the population peaked at 150 in 1881 when the island had its own school, but fell rapidly in the 1900s when many of the inhabitants joined the 'Vatersay Raiders'. By 1934 the population numbered two, and it is now deserted. On the western side, the sea cliffs are magnificent, Biulacraig being a sheer 700 ft. Islanders once climbed these crags to harvest sea-birds' eggs. There are many sea birds, including a large puffin colony, nesting among the ledges, stacks and caves. Two islets off the west coast, **Arnamul** and **Lianamul**, were once grazed by

the Caledonian MacBrayne ferry to the market at Oban. They are now transported by barge, with the result that they arrive at the market in a better condition.

The population in 1861 was 32, but by 1911 it had risen to 288 due to an influx of immigrants from Barra and Mingulay. After falling to around 70 people and seeming to lose impetus in the early 1970s, the population is now rising healthily.

At the turn of the century Vatersay was run as a single farm by tenants of Lady Gordon Cathcart, who only visited the island once during her 54 years of ownership. This was at a time of severe land shortage on Barra and South Uist. After pressure from the crofters, the Lady grudgingly parted with a small area of land at Eoligarry on Barra. Continuing unrest forced the Congested Districts Board to try to buy land on Vatersay to rent to the crofters. Finally, in desperation, on the 19 August 1906, one crofter, within one day, erected a wooden dwelling on Vatersay Farm, thatched

it and lit a fire; under ancient law this gave him title to the land. Others followed suit. These 'Vatersay Raiders' were brought to trial, but were subsequently released after a public outcry. In 1909 the Board finally purchased the whole island and divided it into 58 holdings.

The island rises to 625 ft at the summit of Heishival Mór. Off the extreme eastern tip is the small tidal island of **Uinessan**, where once stood the church of Cille Bhrianain, known as Caibeal Moire nan Ceann, the 'chapel of Mary of the heads' – a short-tempered lady who decapitated those who upset her. Two miles to the east, the dark hump of **Muldoanich** rises from the sea. It once had a chapel and was known in Gaelic as Maol Domhnaich, 'the island of the tonsured one of the Lord'.

To the west of Vatersay, in 1853, 450 emigrants, many of them Hebrideans, lost their lives when the *Annie Jane* was wrecked. To the south of Vatersay all the islands,

Berneray and Mingulay.

sheep, the latter being reached by a rope bridge.

The highest point is Carnan, rising to 891 ft. Macphee's Hill (735 ft) is named after a rent collector who landed on the island and found all the inhabitants dead from the plague. His companions rowed away in fear, leaving the unfortunate man on his own for a year, but MacNeil of Barra gifted him some land when the island was resettled. A Bronze Age stone cist (burial chamber), Crois an t'Suidheachain, has been uncovered on the island.

Berneray

The southernmost island of the Outer Hebrides, Berneray's tall sea cliffs (over 600 ft at Skate Point) take the full brunt of the Atlantic waves, unbroken by shallow water. After severe gales, small fish are sometimes found on the grass at the top, and in 1836 a 42-ton rock was moved five feet by the force of a storm.

At the western end stands the Barra Head lighthouse, 680 ft above sea level, marking the end, or the beginning, of the Long Isle. Granite to build the tower was quarried on the island. Near the lighthouse are the remains of two promontory forts. In 1881 the population was 57; now there are only the lighthouse keepers. The name 'Berneray' is from the Norse, 'Bjorn's isle'.

The main Tourist Information office for the Outer Hebrides is at Stornoway, Lewis. Smaller, summer-only offices are at Tarbert, Lochmaddy, Lochboisdale and Castlebay. There are three vehicle ferry connections with the Outer Hebrides, all operated by Caledonian MacBrayne. They are: Oban to Castlebay (Barra) and Lochboisdale (South Uist); Uig (Skye) to Lochmaddy (North Uist) or Tarbert (Harris); and Ullapool to Stornoway (Lewis). Crossing times range from 2 hours (Uig to Tarbert or Lochmaddy) to 9 hours (Oban to Castlebay via Lochboisdale). The Ullapool to Stornoway service runs twice daily. There are no Sunday services on any route. Passenger-only ferries operate between Ludag (South Uist), Eriskay and Eoligarry (Barra), and Newtonferry (North Uist), Berneray and Leverburgh (Harris); and there are small ferries to Vatersay and to Scalpay.

Loganair operate an air service between Glasgow and Barra (landing on the beach of Tràigh Mhór, at low tide, is quite exciting), plus a Barra/Benbecula/Isle of Lewis (Stornoway) inter-island service. There are also services between Glasgow and Benbecula, and Stornoway and Inverness operated by British Airways. Again, there are no Sunday flights on any route.

The Hebridean Outliers

Rona

Often called 'North Rona' to distinguish it from the island of the same name ('South Rona') north of Raasay, *Ron-y*, the 'island of seals', is a National Nature Reserve of about 300 acres, 44 miles north-north-east of the Butt of Lewis. A natural haven for sea birds and a resting place for migrating birds, it has the largest colony (2000 pairs) of great black-backed gulls in Britain, as well as the largest grey-seal colony anywhere (estimated at one-tenth of the total world population).

It was probably first settled by Norsemen in the 8th C. In 1549 Donald Munro wrote that it was inhabited by a small number of 'simple people, scant of any religione' who caught 'grate fisches'. Their numbers gradually fell until by 1814 there was only Donald MacLeod, 'King of Rona', and his family left. In 1844 the island was finally abandoned.

The remains of the village, stone huts built low into the ground as shelter from the wind, can be found, overgrown, on the south side, near the ruin of the 8th-C Ronan's Cell, a dry-stone construction. The island was uninhabited for 15 years during the 17th C after a plague of rats, probably from a wrecked ship, starved the people out, and some unfriendly seamen stole their only bull.

After the final abandonment it was visited by naturalists, and the fishermen of Ness came to hunt seals. There is also the curious tale of two men exiled to Rona from Ness in 1884, after a religious dispute, who were both found dead a year later. Perhaps even stranger is the story of the German naval officer who died, sitting up in one of the houses, dressed in full uniform. He was found, and given a decent burial, by an RAF team sent to recover a crashed aircraft in 1940.

While the island was populated, the seals were not present in significant numbers as disturbance and hunting limited the population.

Barra Head, the southern extremity of the Outer Hebrides.

The gannetry on Sula Sgeir.

Flannan Isles

These are a group of cliff-bound islands also known as 'The Seven Hunters', rising steeply from the sea to 288 ft, 21 miles north-west of Gallan Head, Lewis. They are composed of hornblende gneiss, and have an area of a little under 100 acres.

On the largest island, **Eilean Mór** (38 acres), are the remains of the 8th-C Chapel of St Flannan, and a lighthouse built by 1899 by D. & C. Stevenson of Edinburgh – the scene of a mystery rivalling that of the *Marie Celeste*. On the night of 15 December 1900, a passing steamer, the *Archer*, reported to the Northern Lighthouse Board that the light was out. The *Hesperus* was sent to investigate. The landing party could find no trace of the three keepers: James Ducat, Thomas Marshall and Donald MacArthur. Ducat's logbook was complete up to 13 December, and a slate continued the record to 9.00 a.m. on the 15th. Ducat's and Marshall's oilskins were gone, a meal of cold meat, pickles and potatoes for three lay untouched, and one chair was knocked over.

The weather at the time of the disappearance was foul, to the extent that a crane was torn from its foundations 100 ft above sea level, and a concrete structure was demolished. The logbook told of damage to the west landing, an inlet finishing in a cave, called Skiopageo. The most common theory is that Ducat and Marshall went to inspect this landing. MacArthur, seeing a freak wave coming, ran to warn them. The wave burst into the inlet, exploded in the cave and swept all three away.

Other accounts tell of the meal half eaten, and all the oilskins still hanging up. It has been suggested that one of the keepers was an alcoholic who dragged his companions over the cliff during a suicide attempt. The story became well known in the early 1900s with the publication of Winifred Gibson's poem 'Flannan Isle': 'Three men alive on Flannan Isle/Who thought on three men dead.' The light is now automatic. An old rail track, used for transporting fuel, climbs steeply up the cliffs to the tower.

During the 16th C the MacLeods of Lewis used to visit the Flannans to hunt wild sheep and collect seabirds' eggs. A few sheep are grazed on the grassy tops by Lewis crofters.

They now breed on the peninsulas of Fianuis in the north and Sceapull in the south-west. The island's fertile grassland is grazed by sheep. Rona rises to a height of 355 ft at Toa Rona in the south-east and is composed mainly of hornblende gneiss veined with pegmatite, and covered with sandy soil. It is entirely cliff-bound with many sea caves, including the Tunnel Cave (which has a blowhole) in the middle of Fianuis. Permission to land must be obtained from Barvas Estates Ltd, Fochabers, and the Nature Conservancy Council Regional Officer must be informed.

Sula Sgeir

Deriving its name from *sula*, ('solan goose'), and *sgeir* ('rock'), this is a tiny island, half-a-mile long by little more than 200 yd at its widest point, lying 41 miles north of the Butt of Lewis. It is composed of hornblende gneiss, has little soil and rises to a height of 229 ft at the southern end. A sea cave runs right through it. At the centre of the island are the 'bothies' (huts) used by the men of Ness, who are legally authorised to

come each September to harvest up to 3000 gugas (young gannets) from the island's great gannetry. The gugas are taken under the Wild Birds (Gannets on Sula Sgeir) Order 1955, and the men of Ness co operate with the Nature Conservancy Council to ensure that stability of the gannet population. These trips are not without danger –landings can only be made in one place, Geodha Phuill Bhain, on the eastern side, and only in calm weather. In 1952 the men of Ness had to be rescued by the Stornoway lifeboat, when their own boat was lost. Traditionally sheep stealers were imprisoned on the island – presumably a fate as bad as death. Permission to land must be obtained from Barvas Estates Ltd, Fochabers, and the NCC Regional Officer informed.

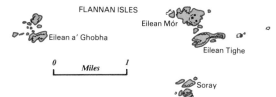

FLANNAN ISLES

Eilean a' Ghobha

Eilean Mór

Eilean Tighe

0   Miles   1

Soray

The Flannan light.

Sound of Shiant

Eilean Mhuire

Garbh Eilean   SHIANT ISLANDS

Eilean an Tighe

410

0   Miles   1

Shiant Isles

The name comes from *Na h-eileanan seunta* ('the enchanted isles'). This is a small group ten miles east-north-east of Scalpay, Harris. **Garbh Eilean** ('rough island') and **Eilean an Tighe** ('home island') are joined by a narrow neck of land; the third island is **Eilean Mhuire** ('Mary's island'). On the north and east sides there are spectacular sea cliffs of columnar basaltic formation rising to over 400 ft. Compared with the ancient gneiss of the Outer Hebrides, this is 'young' rock, a geological relative of the islands of Staffa and Mull.

They were last inhabited, by eight people, in 1901. In 1845 a whole family fell to their death while hunting sea birds on the cliffs of Garbh Eilean. The islands were owned at one time by Sir Compton MacKenzie, who renovated the

home on Eilean an Tighe and spent some time there writing. In 1937 they were sold to the author and publisher, Nigel Nicolson, for £1500.

The islands support large colonies of puffins (which burrow into the cliffs), guillemots and wintering barnacle geese. The scree at the foot of the cliffs harbours many brown rats, and the islands are grazed by sheep.

If a boat can be hired from Lochboisdale to visit the Shiants, beware

of the legendary 'Blue Men of the Minch', who live in the Sound of Shiant and are said to be not particularly friendly.

St Kilda

This is a spectacular group of islands and stacks, 41 miles west-north-west of Griminish Point, North Uist, and is owned by the National Trust for Scotland. The largest island, **St Kilda** - also called Hirta, possibly from the Norse *hirdo* ('herd island') - has an area of 1575 acres; **Soay** and **Dun** close by are 244 and 79 acres respectively. About four miles north-east are **Boreray** (189 acres), **Stac an Armin** (13 acres), and **Stac Lee** (6 acres). All the islands in the group are formed from volcanic rock - granite and gabbro - rising to a height of 1397 ft at the grassy summit of Conachair, St Kilda, 1225 ft at the summit of Soay and 1260 ft on Boreray. The isolated position of the group, exposed to the full force of the Atlantic, has resulted in the erosion of the rock to form sheer sea cliffs over 1000 ft high, the most magnificent in Britain. At the base of these walls of rock are many caves and stacks. In the Boreray group, Stac an Armin (622 ft) is the tallest monolith in the British Isles.

When you approach the anchorage at Village Bay (also called Loch Hirta) from the sea, the sheer scale of the scenery is awesome - the ground slopes steeply behind the village to the summits of Mullach Mór and Conachair, often enveloped in cloud, and Oiseval, 948 ft high to the north, with steep sea cliffs, looms over the boat. Dun, to the south, nearly a mile long and ragged topped, is dwarfed by the parent isle. In spite of the army encampment to the west of the bay, there is an air of mystery, and a strong sense of the past.

St Kilda was inhabited for possibly 2000 years by a hardy and, for the majority of that time, self-sufficient community, until the evacuation in 1930. It is known that the Vikings visited these islands. Their original settlement was at Glen Bay (known to the army as Seal Bay) on the north side, where there are 'shielings' (summer grazings with rudimentary shelters) to be seen. The latest population centre was at Village Bay, with some remains of a previous settlement behind. Arable land was enclosed by a dyke. Among the dwellings, and scattered up the mountain slopes, are the 'cleits' - small dry-stone and turf-roofed structures used for storing the dried sea birds which were the St Kildans' staple diet.

The earliest buildings at Village Bay were pulled down for the building of new 'black houses' in 1830. The present cottages along the main street, four of which having

St Kilda and the ever-present gannets.

been restored, are of the 'but-and-ben' type, built about 1860. To the west of the houses are the manse (occupied by the army), the school (built 1899) and the church (built in the 1830s), all lovingly restored by the working parties from the National Trust for Scotland that have been coming here for more than 20 summers. The remains of one rude hut are known as Lady Grange's House - an unfortunate woman exiled on the island for seven years from 1734 for threatening to reveal her husband's Jacobite sympathies prior to the '45 Rising. She died in 1745 and is buried at Trumpan, on Skye.

The population of St Kilda numbered 180 in 1697, but there was a steady decline from this peak, with several low points during cholera and smallpox outbreaks. From the 1750s to the early 1920s the community numbered over 70.

The islands were owned by the MacLeods of Harris and Dunvegan (in Skye) who were given them by a successor of Ranald, son of John, Lord of the Isles. Rent was paid by the St Kildans in the form of tweed, feathers, wool, dairy produce, stock, oil and grain. A steward was appointed by the MacLeods, and his deputy lived on the island, and once a year the steward himself visited to collect the rent.

The islanders held in common ownership everything that was vital to their existence, and all produce

was shared. Each day the 'St Kilda Parliament' would meet, latterly outside the post office, to discuss the day's tasks. With no one man having ascendency over the others, these discussions could go on all day, with nothing decided. There was no insobriety, but among the men there was a marked fondness for tobacco. Crime was unknown.

Along with the usual crofting activities such as peat cutting, tending the stock, fishing, harvesting, building, sewing, spinning and weaving, the St Kildan men collected thousands of sea birds and eggs. Working in teams, and using horse-hair ropes, they scaled the terrifying cliffs and stacks (including those of Boreray, a hazardous boat journey away) in their stockinged feet, with remarkably few accidents. Their ankles became thick and strong, and their toes prehensile. They took young gannets, puffins (for their feathers only) and, most importantly, fulmars, the bodies of which provided oil for their lamps, and for export - one-half pint of oil from each bird. Typical yearly harvests might be 5000 gannets,

The St Kilda 'Parliament', c.1926.

A recent picture of the Village, St Kilda.

20,000 puffins, 9000 fulmars. After plucking, the feathers were sorted, and the carcasses salted and packed for storage in the cleits. Nothing was wasted – even the entrails were used as manure.

There were two tests of climbing ability and agility used by the St Kildans. Young men had to scale Stac Biorach, 236 ft high, in Soay Sound, regarded as the stiffest climb in the group; and, before marriage, each suitor had to balance on one heel on the 'mistress stone' at the south-west of St Kilda, perched high above the sea, while grasping his other foot with his hands. This proved his prowess as a collector of food.

Apart from the ravages of contagious disease, the population was a healthy one, although it is not surprising that dyspepsia was common as their diet consisted largely of the oily flesh of sea birds. Perhaps the most tragic disease to afflict the island was 'eight-day sickness', *tetanus infantus*, which claimed eight out of every ten children born in the years before 1838. Various church ministers claimed it to be God's will, and the simple island people accepted this. Fortunately, Rev. Angus Fiddes did not. He took a course in midwifery and returned to St Kilda in the 1890s determined to eradicate the

disease. He found that St Kildans traditionally coated the severed umbilicus of an infant with a mixture of fulmar oil and dung, and were loathe to change their ways. After a protracted battle with the islands' 'knee woman' who performed this rite, he demonstrated that, by using sterile and antiseptic methods, this centuries-old blight could be eradicated.

The arrival of the first 'tourists'

aboard the steamship *Glen Albyn* in July 1834 marked the start of the St Kildan's increased dependence on the outside world, and their subsequent decline. They traded cloth, skins and birds' eggs and used the money thus earned to buy food, clothing and tobacco. This commerce, a new factor in their economy, depended on good communications with the mainland – communications that were difficult

Puffins.

Stac Lee and Boreray.

to maintain due to the weather conditions and their situation 'en route to nowhere'.

During the latter part of the 19th C, the St Kildans relied on the prevailing westerly winds to carry messages requesting help to the main Hebridean islands. They fashioned small wooden boats, with masts and sails, or used inflated sheeps' bladders, with the letters enclosed in bottles. Later, a loose arrangement was made with trawlermen to convey messages and mail. The post office on the island was opened in 1899, but there were never any scheduled deliveries or collections.

Other factors influencing the eventual evacuation were education, which began in earnest in 1884 and taught the young people that there might be a better life elsewhere, and a series of resident ministers who inspired such religious zeal that the islanders were in church every day of the week, at times when they should have been growing or collecting food.

After the community nearly starved in 1912, a wireless transmitter was installed the following year, although it soon broke down. It was repaired and used during World War I, resulting in a German submarine shelling the island on 18 May 1918, destroying the store and damaging the church, but harming no one. The submarine was later captured by an armed trawler. A cannon, which can be

seen to the west of the army camp, was later positioned to guard the bay. It was never fired.

Finally a decision was taken and the island was evacuated on 29 August 1930, when 36 St Kildans left on HMS *Harebell*, and those cattle and sheep that could be rounded up following on the *Dunara Castle*, a ship which had been bringing tourists out 'to the edge of the world' since 1875. Most of the St Kildan men, on leaving an island with no trees, were found work with the Forestry Commission.

The Nature Conservancy Council and the Army now manage

the islands, Britain's premier sea-bird breeding station, in partnership with the National Trust for Scotland. It has been estimated that 37 per cent of the total world gannet population is to be found there, particularly on Stac an Armin and Stac Lee. There were 59,000 breeding pairs counted during the period 1971-74, as well as 40,000 pairs of fulmars, the largest single British colony, and 150,000 pairs of puffins – about half the British total. Figures on the storm petrel are not clear, but the colony is thought to be one of the largest. Also to be found breeding are Manx shearwater,

St Kilda.

each's petrel, razorbill and great
skua, but there are only seven
species of land birds breeding on the
group, including the St Kilda wren,
a sub-species. There is also a species
of long-tailed field-mouse peculiar to
the group, although the St Kilda
house-mouse died out soon after the
evacuation. Between 600 to 2000
Soay sheep (the population is
cyclical) roam free on St Kilda; they
are a primitive species similar to
those kept by neolithic farmers.
Where the sheep cannot reach to
graze, the vegetation on Dun is
particularly lush. On Boreray the
sheep left by the St Kildans, blackface and cheviot crosses, have
reverted to a wild state. Over 130
flowering plants occur, including
some mountain types influenced by
the cool climate. Wind speeds of 130
mph at sea level have been recorded.

Since 1957, the army have
maintained a £1 million base of 40
men to run the missile-tracking radar
on top of Mullach Mór. Supplies
and mail are delivered by landing
craft, helicopter and air drop, and
the men are in constant radio contact
with the firing range on South Uist.
Even so, they are sometimes isolated
for weeks on end in bad weather.

St Kilda now has a new life. Each
summer, houses in the village are
lived in once again, and those who
have spent 24 hours or more on the
island can join the exclusive St Kilda
Club. But the St Kildans are no
more - a community that became an
administrative inconvenience and a
charge upon the mainstream of
society has been split up and lost for
want of many of the things that are
now provided for the army, at not
inconsiderable expense.

Those wishing to land on the
island, or join a working party, must
contact the National Trust for
Scotland. Caledonian MacBrayne
now make, in early May, an annual
St Kilda cruise from Oban,
circumnavigating the group but not
landing.

Isle of Rockall

The name derives from the Gaelic
sgeir rocail, the 'sea rock of roaring'.
An extremely isolated granite
outcrop rising 70 ft sheer from the
sea, its top measures just 100 ft by
70 ft. Being 184 miles west of St
Kilda, it is the most western point of
Great Britain. The first recorded
landing was made in 1810; on 18
September 1955 a party from HMS
Vidal landed by helicopter and
annexed it to the Crown. It officially
became the latest addition to the
territories of the United Kingdom
on 10 February 1972 with the
passing of the Isle of Rockall Act,
and an automatic navigation light
was installed. It comes under the
Western Isles administrative area,
and its position extends British

A Soay sheep, St Kilda.

fishing and mineral rights consider-
ably. The naturalists, F. Fraser
Darling and J. Morton Boyd, have
observed only six animal species: the rough periwinkle
(with a flatworm larva parasite), an
amphipod, two species of mite and
an unidentified orange rotifer. It is
thought that guillemot may breed on
a ledge near the summit.

Monach Islands

Also known as Heisker, these are a
group of four small islands about
eight miles west of Baleshare, South
Uist, with a total area of 836 acres.
The two main ones, **Ceann Iar** and
Ceann Ear (where there was once a
convent) are joined at low tide. On
Shillay, the most westerly, there is
a lighthouse, built in 1864 but now
disused; at one time a crude light
was maintained by monks who
inhabited the islands. In the 16th C,
sands that were passable at low tide
between the Monachs and North
Uist were swept away by the same
exceptional tide that formed the
Sound of Pabbay.

The islands have long been
populated. Before 1810 over 100
people lived there, but overgrazing
weakened the stabilising grass, and a
disastrous storm blew the top soil
away and the people left. By 1841,
19 people were re-established, and in
1891 over 100 people were again
living on the group with their own
post office and school. The numbers
then began to dwindle and the last
crofters left in 1942; the only cottage
still habitable is privately owned.
Occasionally the islands are visited
by lobster fishermen.

The Monachs are now a National
Nature Reserve, and permission to
land must be obtained from the
North Uist Estate, Lochmaddy, and
from the warden at Loch Druidibeg.
The habitat is a prime example of
shell sand, dune and uncultivated
machair over gneiss; the rock rises
only to a little over 60 ft. Barnacle
and white-fronted geese winter here,
and arctic, common and little terns,
fulmars and herons may also be seen.
The reef of **Stockay** is a grey-seal
nursery.

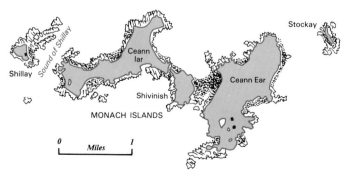

MONACH ISLANDS

Loch Broom to Maillaig

Gruinard Island

Highland. This island lies in the attractive Gruinard Bay, its name deriving from the Norse *grunna fjord* ('shallow ford'). During World War II this island was used as a test site for biological weapons. The last inhabitants had left long before these experiments were carried out. Soil samples are now taken regularly and tested by the Chemical Defence Establishment but, at the time of writing, landing is still prohibited. However, rabbits, sea birds and seals all appear unaffected, and each year a retired crofter visits Gruinard to repaint the warning signs, and he claims to have suffered no ill effects. But, until these notices are removed, DO NOT LAND.

A generally low-lying, sandstone island in Loch Ewe, half-a-mile from Aultbea, the **Isle of Ewe**, rises to 223 ft at its northern tip and 232 ft in the west. Its deep sheltered waters were used by the Royal Navy in both wars, and in World War II convoys bound for the Soviet Union assembled here before making their arduous and dangerous journeys. Royal Navy and Nato bases are still maintained.

In Loch Gairloch, **Eilean Horrisdale** shelters the jetties of Aird and Badochro, and to the north of the loch is the sandstone **Longa Island,** sheltering the beach of Big Sand. To the south are Lochs Torridon and Shieldaig, the latter containing tiny **Shieldaig Island** which was purchased by the National Trust for Scotland in 1970, and 'adopted' in 1974 by Mr and Mrs Armistead Peter III of Washington, D.C., who contributed a sum equivalent to the full purchase price. In the 19th C this island had been planted with Scots pine, which, with a few rowans and some holly, now make a welcome contrast to the surrounding barren hills. On the north-west corner there is a heronry.

The mainland coast to Applecross is bare and mountainous – splendid walking country. To the south of this village, **Eilean nan Naomh** shelters Camusterrach harbour. Little more than a rocky outcrop, this is the 'Holy Isle' where St Maolrubha is said to have landed in AD 671; he founded a monastery at Applecross, which was later destroyed by the Vikings. To the south there are a few islets and rocks. About a mile south-west of Loch Toscaig, the **Crowlin Islands** are reached, a volcanic outcrop with a north-south split giving a sheltered central channel 50-yd wide. The

Shieldaig Island is to the right.

largest of the three islands is **Eilean Mór,** rising to a summit of 374 ft, which has some ruined cottages in the north-east corner. A lighthouse stands on the smallest island, **Eilean Beag,** and its shoreline is rocky, with caves, and is inhabited by both common and Atlantic seals. Regular summer boat-trips are made from the Kyle of Lochalsh. The waters of the Inner Sound, to the north, are the deepest off the immediate coast of Britain; Royal Navy torpedo tests are made here.

The old fishing village of Plockton, on the southern shore of Loch Carron, is situated amid superb scenery and is surrounded by the property owned by the National Trust for Scotland (NTS), Balmacara. To the east, **Eilean na Creige Duibhe** is a Scottish Wildlife Trust conservation area where herons nest by fine Scots pines. Visits can be made by boat from Plockton. Beyond are the tiny **Strome Islands. Kishorn Island** and the forested **An Garbh-eilean**

lie at the entrance to Loch Kishorn, where oil rigs are assembled, a new industry in this quiet backwater.

Between Plockton and the Kyle of Lochalsh there are many small islands belonging to the NTS, the most interesting being **Eilean Bàn** (the 'white island'), with its light house and white-painted cottage built for the keepers and their families who once tended the, now automatic, light. The late Gavin Maxwell, author of *Ring of Bright Water*, bought the island in 1963 intending to turn it into a private zoo for Scottish wildlife. He converted the two cottages into one, and moved to the island in 1968 after his house at Sandaig on the mainland burned down, but ill-health prevented him realising this plan and, after living for a while at Kyle House, on Skye, he died in Broadford Hospital, Skye on 7 September 1969. His otter, Teko, the last survivor from the *Ring*, is buried beneath a boulder on Eilean Bàn.

Eilean Bàn, once the home of the late Gavin Maxwell.

The Cuillins from Elgol, Skye.

Island of Skye

Highland. The name 'Skye' derives from the Norse *skuy*, meaning 'cloud'; in Gaelic it is *Eilean à Cheo* ('isle of mist'). Easy access, breathtaking and varied scenery and romantic associations with Bonnie Prince Charlie have made Skye the most popular of the Western Isles from Victorian times, when the new railway to Stromeferry 'opened up' the island. The Victorians came to walk, watch birds, collect fossils and flowers and to paint, and it says much for the timeless quality of the island that visitors today do much the same.

The island (with a population of 7000) is 48 miles long, 24 miles wide (as far as its shape allows determination), and has an area of 430,000 acres with over 1000 miles of coast, due to the deeply indented sea lochs and mountainous peninsulas. Near the centre are the magnificent Cuillin Hills, the most dramatic manifestation of the volcanic activity that shaped the bulk of the island, formed from the now solidified reservoir from which the lavas flowed 50 million years ago. These gabbro mountains have narrow strips of brittle rock running through them, forming ridges like broken china above the dark grey slopes. This rock is extremely hard and was shaped not by weathering but by the abrasive effect of ice. The granite hills (the Red Cuillins), being less hard, have eroded into

more rounded shapes, with scree slopes of a warmer, pinker appearance. Gabbro and granite are essentially the same volcanic rock, but the former is harder due to slow cooling underground, whereas granite outpoured and cooled quickly.

The north of the island, including Duirinish, Waternish and half of Trotternish, was formed from a succession of lava flows, giving the land a stepped appearance, seen clearly on Macleod's Tables – Healabhal Bheag and Healabhal Mhor – where the softer outpourings have been eroded leaving the characteristic flat tops and tiered slopes. The oldest rock on Skye, gneiss, is found in Sleat (pronounced 'slate'), south of Isleornsay, with old red sandstone forming the rest of the peninsula.

In Trotternish, the Quiraing and the Old Man of Storr are the remains of volcanic rock which was left stranded on top of soft clays when the glaciers melted – the softer material giving way, leaving the blocks to slip down, creating cliffs, needle rocks and ravines.

Underlying sandstones, limestones and clays surface around the volcanic rock to give the best soils on the island, and this has generally determined human settlement. Northern Trotternish, Broadford and the west of Loch Slapin are typical of these areas, with many farms and crofts. Some places of lush green vegetation behind Broadford

mark the limestone outcrops. Where this limestone was baked by volcanic activity, marble has been produced, and it is still quarried near Torrin.

There are coral beaches at Claigan on Loch Dunvegan, formed by the seaweed *Lithothamnion*, and to the south of Duntulm Castle in Trotternish the sand has a green tint due to the sea eroding the mineral, olivine, from the cliffs. Gold has also been found on the island.

There are 20 peaks in the Cuillins, 15 over 3000-ft high (known as 'Munros') with the highest, Sgurr Alasdair, being 3257 ft. The first to be climbed, in 1836, was Sgurr nan Gillean (3167 ft), by a geologist named Forbes. Sgurr a' Ghreadaidh, at 3190 ft, is ascended from the Loch Coruisk side, one of the longest rock climbs in Britain.

Much of the island landscape is empty, with small crofting townships of scattered cottages only where the soil is workable. There are many ruined houses and empty glens, evidence of the Jacobites who were forced to leave after the unsuccessful rising of 1745, the bad harvests of 1881–85 and the Clearances.

A croft is a small farm usually of five to ten acres. The original crofters were self-sufficient, occupying arable land, divided into small areas, on a rotation basis, and sharing hill grazing. This was the 'run-rig' system (from *raoin-ruith*, 'running-share'), where all members of the community shared both the good and the bad land. Sheep were kept for wool, cattle for milk and meat; potatoes, oats and barley were grown and supplemented with fish, wild deer and rabbit. For fuel, then as now, they dug peat. Later the pattern changed, each crofter keeping his own area of arable land, but still sharing the grazing. They had no security of tenure and paid the laird (landowner) in rent and services.

This way of life ended for many with the introduction of profitable large-scale sheep farming and the 'clearance' of the crofters from the land. Whole townships were evicted and forced to emigrate to the New World, and between 1840 and 1888 over 30,000 people left. By 1882 over 365,000 acres of Skye were owned by absentee landlords, and in this year things came to a head when crofters at The Braes were denied grazing rights they considered theirs. A force of 50 Glasgow policemen was despatched to quell the riot that had developed and they fought a battle with the crofters. Later gunboats were sent and marines landed at Uig.

The result of this was a Royal Commission, set up by Gladstone, to investigate the crofters' grievances, and in 1886 the Crofters Act was passed, giving security of tenure at a fair rent. The present-day crofter usually has a full-time job or a pension, using his land to supplement his livelihood.

The sheep kept on the island are mainly Scottish blackface, an exceptionally hardy breed, and cheviots. Cattle are also kept, mainly for beef, and many of these are 'exported' each year. The Forestry Commission has over 8000 acres of trees, and much new ground is being prepared for planting; there is little natural woodland.

A small inshore fishing fleet operates around the island catching prawns for export to France and Italy and some white fish, which is sent to Aberdeen. Other shellfish, including scallops, are also taken. The once prolific herring catch has been ruined by overfishing, and 'foreign' trawlers still use techniques that waste immature fish and destroy the sea-bed.

It is tourism that has brought a measure of prosperity to the island, but even this has its drawbacks. The 'holiday-home' syndrome has pushed property prices beyond the reach of indigenous young married couples, and not enough jobs have been created to stem the flow of emigration. The high cost of living, due to transport costs, coupled with a lack of job opportunities, provides little incentive to stay.

In AD 585 St Columba visited Skye, and later Maolrubha became the patron saint of the central and southern areas - in the past, 25 August was celebrated in Broadford as his feast day. In the 8th C, Norsemen began raiding, and finally settled; their domination of Skye, under the Kingdom of Man and the Isles, lasted until three years after the Battle of Largs in 1263, when King Haakon of Norway was defeated (*see* Isle of Man). A legacy of Norse blood and place-names remains strong on the island.

John MacDonald of Islay (died 1386), a descendant of Somerled (who split the Kingdom of Man and the Isles in 1158), first adopted the title 'Lord of the Isles', with Skye as an administrative centre; the title lasted until 1748. The land was divided between the MacDonalds and the MacLeods, and the sites of their battles on the island are a reminder of their constant feuds. The inhabitants professed Catholicism until the Reformation in 1561; Evangelism spread from 1805, followed by the Free Church from 1843, with its dour teachings. In common with other Protestant western islands, Sunday is observed as the Lord's Day. Shops, pubs and restaurants close, and no work, unless absolutely essential, is done. There are those who will not listen to the radio, watch television, read a newspaper or even light a fire on a Sunday - but the influence of hundreds of thousands of visitors to the island has generally made for a slightly more relaxed approach here than on, say, Lewis in the Outer Hebrides. The Gaelic language is spoken, but most young people now use English.

Skye people once had a reputation for 'second sight': 'seeing' a person in a shroud prophesied death; 'seeing' a fire spark fall on someone's arm signified they would soon carry a dead child. The other 'people' on the island were the fairies, or *sithche* (pronounced 'sheeche') - from *sithchean* (the 'noiseless people') - who lived in any rounded grassy mound (a *sithein*, pronounced 'shi-en') and performed miraculous or mischievous deeds. If you wanted protection from these small people, you carried iron, steel or oatmeal.

The story of one of Scotland's popular and heroic partnerships unfolded on Skye. In 1745 Prince Charles Edward Stuart, Bonnie Prince Charlie, came to Scotland to attempt to depose George II and regain the crown of England for the Stuarts. After gathering together a small army, the Young Pretender enjoyed some initial success, but was finally routed at Culloden and his Jacobite army dispersed. Pursued by the King's forces, with a price of £30,000 on his head, he fled to the islands from whence he hoped to escape to Scandinavia or France. Disguised as 'Betty Burke', a maid,

To Lochmaddy

Waternish Point

Trumpan Church

Dunvegan Head   Isay

Loch Pooltiel   Borreraig

Neist Point

Ramasaig

Lorgill

Hallin

Glendale

Colbost

DUIRINISH

Macleod's Tables   •1538'   •1601'

Orbost

Macleod's Maidens

Idrigill Po

he was brought from Benbecula t Kilbride Bay in Trotternish by Flor MacDonald, a 24-year-old Edin burgh-educated Skye girl. Afte some close escapes, hiding in cave and cattle byres, he left Flora an went to Raasay the night after it ha been sacked by troops from th Royal Navy ship, *Furnace*, a retribution against the men of th island who had supported th Jacobites. After a short stay, waitin for a French ship that neve appeared, he went back to Skye, the on to Knoydart on the mainland Finally on 19 September 1746, French ship took him from Loc nam Uamh, and he died in Rome i 1778. Flora was arrested after hi escape and held prisoner in a privat house in London, but she was free after the passing of the Indemnity Act in 1747 and became the heroin of London society. Her grave an monument are in a simple buria ground in Kilmuir.

The bare rocks and peaks of th Cuillins and Trotternish and the se cliffs around Dunvegan Head an

The Storr and the Old Man of Storr, Skye.

Loch Harport are the habitat of the island's golden eagles. Sea birds and waterfowl inhabit the lochs, and many of these are fished for brown trout; the rivers run with sea trout and salmon, although these have declined due to overfishing at sea.

The richness of the island's flora was shown in a detailed study which revealed 589 species of flowering plants and ferns, 370 mosses, 181 liverworts and 154 lichens. Many alpines are to be found on the eastern side of the Trotternish ridge, including the tiny Iceland-purslane (*Koenigia islandica*), a relative of the sorrels, first discovered here in 1934. In the limestone crossing Strath Suardal behind Broadford, there is a birchwood where mountain avens, guelder-rose and helleborine grow. The rare red broomrape is found on grassy slopes above the sea, and rock whitebeam occurs on some of the low cliffs.

The largest wild mammal in Britain, the red deer, is found mostly around Loch Coruisk and in Sleat. Whales are sometimes seen off the coast, usually the herring whale (common rorqual), but killer whales have also been seen chasing seals.

Portree and Trotternish

The only town on Skye is its 'capital', Portree. The name is anglicised from *Port Righ*, 'Port of the King', so called in honour of a visit by James V in the 16th C. Prior to this it was called Kiltragleann, 'the church at the foot of the glen'. It is attractively sited with a fine sheltered anchorage, but apart from the usual services of a town – shops, hotels, library, schools, police station – there is little of architectural or historic interest, although the Royal Hotel does have associations with Bonnie Prince Charlie and Flora MacDonald (the room in which he bade her farewell is here). The tourist office is situated in the building that was once both courthouse and jail for the whole island; the present courthouse in Somerled Square was built in 1867. In the cliffs to the north of Loch Portree is Mac Coitir's Cave, said to run beneath the island to Bracadale.

Portree is the natural centre for touring the Trotternish, Waternish and Duirinish peninsulas and much of the centre of the island.

The coast road north of Portree to Trotternish is dominated by **The Storr** (2358 ft) and the **Old Man of Storr**, a rock needle 165-ft tall, precariously balanced among sheer cliffs and many smaller pinnacles, which was first climbed in 1955. The name 'Storr' is from *fiacaill storàch*, meaning 'buck tooth'. Here the ground is loose and treacherous and should be treated with caution. Below are Lochs Fada and Leathan, the reservoir for the 'hydro' which

Portree, Skye.

has supplied the island's electricity since 1952 (there is also an electric cable across the Kyle of Lochalsh). Before 1949 the only electricity was generated by a diesel engine belonging to the Portree Hotel.

In the cliffs east of Loch Fada is the cave where Bonnie Prince Charlie landed on his return from Raasay, and at Lealt there are spectacular waterfalls which can be seen by taking a not too difficult climb down the ravine. Three-quarters of a mile south, on the shore, is **Eaglais Bhreagach,** a church-shaped rock where the Clan MacQueen is said to have raised the devil, using an ancient ceremony called *Taghairm,* involving the roasting of live cats.

At Lonfearn the remains of 'bee-hive' dwellings (early Christian circular stone cells) were discovered – in Gaelic they are called *tighean nan druineach,* 'druids' houses'. To the west, on the Trotternish ridge, can be seen the summit of Beinn Edra (2003 ft); in the spring of 1945, a Flying Fortress bomber hit it in the midday mist – all on board were killed. Up the coast again there is a simple black-house museum at Elishader, and in the cliffs nearby can be seen the 'kilt rock', black basalt so called because of the folds and pattern of its strata.

A galleon of the Spanish Armada was reputed to have been wrecked near Staffin, some coins having been found, and there are people here said to be of Spanish descent. These crofting townships are overlooked by the fantastic Quiraing ('round fold') – awesome rock formations where whole herds of cattle could be hidden. The Table, the 120-ft-tall Needle and the Prison can all be explored by walking north from the Staffin-to-Uig road near its highest point.

In the bay below, a road signposted 'Staffin Slip' leads to some areas of dark sand among boulders, facing the low-lying **Staffin Island,** with its grazing sheep and bothy used by fishermen. **Eilean Flodigarry,** rising to a steep point at its eastern tip, once (according to legend) had its corn reaped in two nights by seven score and ten fairies. When they had finished, they asked for more work, so the owner set them to empty the sea! Behind the bay, the crofting land can be seen clearly divided into regular strips.

To the north of the Quiraing is the well-sited Flodigarry Hotel, a turreted building, once the home of Flora MacDonald after her escapades with the Prince. North of The Aird lies the grassy **Eilean Trodday,** the 'trolls isle', which once supported a herd of dairy cattle. This northern end of Trotternish was once known as the

The fantastic Quiraing, Skye.

'granary of Skye' due to its fertile basaltic soil.

As the road reaches the west coast the few craggy remains of Duntulm Castle can be seen at the top of a steep cliff, above the hotel. The main part of the castle is 15th C (it was occupied up to 1732), and a foot-path from the road leads to the ruin. In the bay lies **Tulm Island,** a narrow green hump, and about three miles north-west are the flat-topped **Lord Macdonald's Table, Gearran Island, Gaeilavore Island** and the largest of the group, **Fladda-chùain** with its ruined chapel dedicated to St Columba, the blue altar stone said to bring fair winds to becalmed fishermen. Sir Donald MacDonald of the Isles is supposed to have hidden title deeds here before taking part in the Rising of 1745.

The Skye Cottage Museum at Kilmuir consists of four restored black houses on an exposed site over-looking the sea, with typical room settings and a peat fire, Bonnie Prince Charlie and Flora Mac-

Donald relics and a particularly interesting collection of historical documents relating to life on the islands. Nearby in a small graveyard is the new memorial to Flora MacDonald; the original Mac-Donald mausoleum was gradually taken, piece by piece, by tourists. Close to this is a well-preserved crusader slab.

Between Balgown and the coast lies an area of marshy ground, once Loch Chaluim Chille which was drained in 1824, and on what were once islands are the remains of beehive dwellings. From the main road at Linicro a very rough track leads to the ruins of Sir Alexander MacDonald's once-fine house, Monkstadt. Flora and the Prince landed at Kilbride Bay and came to the house, only to find it occupied by the King's officers; the pair then fled through Kingsburgh to Portree.

The road descends steeply to the very pretty township of Uig ('bay' or 'nook'), sheltered by steep basaltic cliffs, its scattered crofts stretching back to the hills where there is,

Uig, Skye, looking along the glen.

along Glen Uig to Balnacnock, a Quiraing in miniature. The round tower opposite the Uig pier is a folly built by Captain Fraser, and there is also a youth hostel here.

At the head of Loch Snizort Beag, on the eastern side, stands Caisteal Uisdein ('Hugh's castle') built around 1580 by Hugh MacDonald of Sleat, who schemed against his chief and died entombed in Duntulm Castle with a piece of salt beef and an *empty* water jug. A farm track north of Hinnisdal Bridge leads towards the ruin.

The central region of the Trotternish peninsula is wild, inhospitable, heather-clad country with steep cliffs and peat bogs.

Loch Snizort Beag and Waternish

The road from Portree to the Waternish peninsula passes through a broad valley at the head of Loch Snizort Beag. On an islet in the River Snizort are the scant ruins of a chapel associated with St Columba, best seen from the old bridge by Skeabost post office (a path and stepping stones lead to the ruin), and the Skeabost Hotel, an imposing white castellated building. The village itself is notable as the birthplace of the poet, Mary MacPherson. On a hill above Clachamish stand the remains of Dùn Suladale, one of the best preserved of the 20 brochs on the island. (*See* Shetland for a further description of brochs.) Many are now reduced to barely recognisable heaps of stones.

The road then passes Edinbane, where there is a pottery, and on through peaty moorland to the Fairy Bridge with its legendary associations with the MacLeods of Dunvegan. As you head north along the Waternish peninsula, the well-sited village of Stein is reached, nestling on the east side of Loch Bay, backed by crofts and looking out towards the cliffs of Beinn Bhreac, and the low-lying islands of **Isay, Mingay** and **Clett,** once inhabited, but cleared in 1860. Isay was offered to Dr Johnson by the MacLeods, on condition that he built a house on it but, needless to say, such a comfort-lover did not accept the offer. More recently it was purchased by the folk singer, Donovan. Stein has a hotel, an attractive terrace, a fine stone house and a small jetty by a stony beach. In 1787 a fishing industry was started here, but the project was abandoned in 1837. The road passes through the 8600-acre Waternish estate, now Dutch-owned, where at present only sheep are being farmed. Above Hallin the remains of a broch can be seen, the walls standing about seven-feet high in places. To the east is Gillen, where there is a knitting workshop, and fine views of the uninhabited **Ascrib Islands,** where there is a colony of puffins burrowing into the basalt. Stone for Caisteal Uisdein is said to have been quarried there.

At the end of the road, above Ardmore Bay, stands the lonely and windswept ruin of Trumpan Church. It was here in 1578 that the MacDonalds of Uist barred the door on the congregation of MacLeods, and set fire to the church, to avenge the Eigg massacre (*see* Eigg). The only survivor in 1578, a girl, escaped by a window, severing one of her breasts as she squeezed through to raise the alarm. Other MacLeods arrived, carrying their legendary Fairy Flag, just in time to capture the MacDonald galleys, slaughtering all on board. The bodies were buried in a dyke; hence the battle is known as 'the spoiling of the dyke'.

In the churchyard are some ancient graves, including that of Lady Grange, who was exiled on St Kilda for eight years by her husband, and died three years after her return in 1742. A track near the church leads north towards Waternish Point.

Dunvegan and Duirinish

One mile north of the Fairy Bridge is Annait where there are remains of some early Christian cells. From the bridge the road continues south to Dunvegan, with its hotels, shops, boat trips to see the seals, and Dunvegan Castle, seat of the Clan MacLeod since 1200 - no other Scottish castle has been continuously occupied as long. The first building on the site is said to date from the 9th C, but the major part of the present one is 19th C, beautifully situated at the head of Loch Dunvegan and backed by mixed woodland planted since 1890. The castle contains many MacLeod relics including the 15th-C

Dunvegan Cup, Rory Mor's drinking horn and the legendary Fairy Flag (*Bratach shith MhicLèoid*), made of yellow silk from the Near East. Its miraculous saving powers can only be used three times, when the survival of the clan is threatened; there is now only one more opportunity left. Pregnant women should also take into consideration the myth that, upon seeing the flag, they may go into premature labour. The castle is closed from mid-October to March.

MacLeod's Tables from Bracadale, Skye.

Dunvegan Castle, Skye.

To the north is Claigan, where a sign-posted track leads down to the coral beaches – the first a small rocky bay, then on to a more dramatic sweep. Up a track behind Claigan Farm, the entrance to a souterrain (an Iron Age or earlier earth house or food store) can be found. There is another example near Loch Duagrich, to the east of Bracadale.

Duirinish is dominated by the twin flat peaks of Healabhal Bheag (1601 ft) and Healabhal Mhor (1538 ft) – MacLeod's Tables. It is an area of wild moorland, with the few roads keeping to the coast – the southern part is accessible only on foot. The main road rounds the head of Loch Dunvegan; a narrow track leads south to Orbost where a small art gallery has been established. From here, another track leads down to a small sheltered beach.

By heading north-west along the side of Loch Dunvegan, containing low-lying islands grazed by sheep, the tiny village of Colbost, with its Black House Museum (opened 1965) and Three Chimneys restaurant, is reached. Behind the museum, which depicts life around 100 years ago, is a replica of an illicit whisky still.

To the north, past Husabost, is Borreraig, where the legendary MacCrimmons, hereditary pipers to the MacLeod chiefs from 1500 to

1800, established their piping college. They were the first composers, players and teachers of *pibroch* (a tune with variations), and their history and folklore is recorded in the excellent museum, founded in 1975 in the unimposing cream house to the west of the road. On the promontory opposite, above the barely discernible remains of the original college, stands the beehive-shaped MacCrimmon Memorial Cairn, the focal point of an annual pilgrimage of MacCrimmons, and in the cliffs below is the Piper's Cave. The first piping school on Skye was established by the MacArthurs, who later went to Islay as hereditary pipers to the Lords of the Isles.

The main road from Colbost to Glendale passes the memorial to the Glendale Land Leaguers, 600 crofters who challenged Government forces and now own the Glendale Estate. The township of Glendale stretches back along the river valley behind Loch Pooltiel, where the hills to the west slope gently

Glendale Water Mill, Skye.

away and the scattered crofts are well tended and productive. Below the low cliffs at the water's edge is the Glendale Water Mill, a 200-year-old dry-stone grain mill with a thatched roof. It ceased operation in 1914, but was restored in 1971-72 to virtually its original working condition, the project being carried out on local initiative using local skills. Unfortunately the mill burned down in 1973, on the day the Skeabost mill stones were brought here: in legend, whenever these stones are moved, there is a disaster. The second restoration started immediately and the mill re-opened. Close by stands a dry-stone kiln, where peat was burned to dry the grain before milling, and there is a spectacular waterfall in the cliffs opposite.

The most westerly point in Skye is the sheer-sided and narrow Neist peninsula, where the well-made but steep path to the lighthouse makes a fine walk. There are some accessible small bays, towering cliffs with sea birds, and superb views of Waterstein Head, 967-ft high. On a clear day, North and South Uist and Benbecula can be seen, low on the horizon.

A narrow and bumpy road across rugged moorland and peat bogs leads to Ramasaig, an isolated settlement, from which a track goes to Lorgill, the 'glen of the deer's cry'. In 1830 all ten crofting families there were ordered to Loch Snizort to either board the *Midlothian* bound for Nova Scotia, or go to prison, and those over 70 years of age were to be sent to the county poorhouse. On 4 August that year, they all left. Idrigill Point can be reached on foot, but it is stiff walking.

Bracadale and Minginish

The south of Duirinish shelters Loch Bracadale, with its calm inlets and small islands, tiered cliffs and irregular hills. It is a magical part of the island, especially at sunset on a fine day, when the Cuillins are etched with deep shadows, and the sea glows between the headlands.

Above the township of Struan is Dùn Beag, the best-preserved broch on Skye – parts of the galleries may still be seen. Bracadale, established in 1772 by Thomas Pennant, stands at the head of Loch Beag, scattered crofts above a small beach. The view towards the lighthouse at Ardtreck Point and the crofts at Portnalong is splendid.

The main road to Sligachan passes through Glen Drynoch. At the head of Loch Harport a minor road crosses the River Drynoch and

The museum at Luib, Loch Ainort, Skye.

continues along the west side of the loch, passing the Talisker Malt Whisky Distillery at Carbost. Originally founded by Kenneth MacAskill of Talisker House at Snizort, it was first moved to Fiskavaig, then finally to Carbost in 1830. Talisker Whisky can be bought in some of the hotels on the island, but most of the product is blended and exported. There are conducted tours in the summer but, alas, no free samples. The road behind the distillery leads to Talisker Bay, reached through a steep-sided glen, where cattle and sheep graze, and crops grow on the fertile plain. In the cliffs to the north a fine waterfall spills to the sea, and a footpath leads to a secluded beach with views of the Outer Hebrides.

To the south, at the head of the loch, is Eynort, with its new wooden houses among conifer plantations, behind a sheltered beach. Further north along Loch Harport, the road finishes by the pier and sheltered small boat anchorage of Portnalong, a township of crofters from Lewis and Harris who came here in 1921, where salmon and trout are farmed in floating cages. To west is Fiskavaig, a crofting township above a stony bay, and to the north-west, across the mouth of Loch Bracadale, the three basaltic stacks of

MacLeod's Maidens can be seen, just off Idrigill Point, traditionally named after a MacLeod chief's wife and daughters who drowned near here. The views of the Cuillins from Loch Harport are dramatic, the stark black gabbro contrasting with the softer crofting land at the head of the loch.

From Carbost, a narrow road leads south between the Cuillins and the Glen Brittle Forest, ending by the sandy beach at Loch Brittle where, in summer, the campsite is full of brightly-coloured tents pitched by climbers tackling the sharp peaks, the surfaces of which appear barren and lunar – land stripped to the bone, beautiful and cruel. The rock is hard, making for some of the best climbing in the country. Those who do not climb can stare in wonder at the tiny figures traversing and ascending the steep slopes. Those who do are rewarded with a staggering panorama of the Hebrides, as distant as St Kilda. There *are* paths to the top (the summit with the best access for walkers is Sgurr Alasdair via Coire Làgan, also Bruach na Frithe via the north-west ridge from Sligachan), but it must be remembered that this is no place to get stranded in mist or a squall without proper equipment and

experience – the mountains do not forgive your mistakes. A Forestry Commission picnic site halfway along the glen overlooks Coire na Creiche, the scene of the last battle between the MacDonalds and the MacLeods.

Central Skye
South of Portree the road to Sligachan passes through Glen Varragill – unremarkable apart from good views of the Cuillins at the southern end. To the east lie The Braes, scene of a fight between crofters denied grazing rights and an expeditionary force of Glasgow policemen on 19 April 1882. This melée is sometimes romanticised as the 'last battle on British soil', and a small cairn by the roadside here commemorates the battle fought on behalf of 'the crofters of Gaeldom'. This road finished at Peinchorran: along its length are a few crofts where once there were many, and ruined black houses now stand beside the worst sort of modern chalet bungalows, yet the feeling is of peace, and the views of Raasay are good.

The hotel at Sligachan, beautifully situated at the head of the loch with a mountain backdrop, was once a climbing centre for the Cuillins. From the bridge, as you look south along Glen Sligachan, the difference between the gabbro to the west, spiky and angular, and the granite to the east, smoothed by erosion, can be clearly seen. A track through the glen leads to the isolated and dramatic glacial basin of Loch Coruisk (*coire uish*, the 'cauldron of water') at the head of Loch Scavaig. Loch Coruisk remains little changed since the thawing of the ice that scooped it out 100-ft deeper than the water of Loch Scavaig – a primeval, lonely place. At the seaward end of Loch Sligachan is Sconser, the ferry terminal for Raasay and site of the island's main nine-hole golf course. Of the two routes to Loch Ainort, the minor road by the coast is more pleasant.

Loch Bracadale, with the Outer Hebrides on the horizon.

Opposite: *The Cuillins of Skye from Portnalong.*

On the southern shore of the loch is Luib, with its folk museum, a regular coach-party stop that can become crowded quickly. It is a black house restored in 1978 by the energetic Peter MacAskill who has been responsible for saving other similar buildings on the island. There are room settings, showing interiors of about 50 years ago, a peat fire burning in the stove and some farm implements. During restoration two guns, dating from the 1745 rising, were found hidden under the roof. Outside roam a small flock of blackface tups, sheep noted for their longevity. There are other black houses in the immediate vicinity, one occupied.

Further south along the coast is Strollamus, where boats can be hired. Beyond the forestry plantations is Broadford, a formless village that serves as the main centre for the south of the island. There is little of interest, but all main services – shops, hotels, bed-and-breakfasts, bank, post office, garage, youth hostel and tourist information - are available. The beach is untidy stone and shingle, and at one time the steamer used to call here on the way to Portree. The village is dominated by Bienn na Callich (2403 ft), on the top of which is a large and conspicuous cairn with, reputedly, a Norwegian princess buried beneath. The walk to the summit is not difficult and the views of Skye and Wester Ross are just reward.

Across Broadford Bay can be seen the low-lying island of **Pabay** ('priest [or 'monk'] island') noted for limestone fossils, with its house, ruined chapel and burial ground. There used to be a flock of Shetland sheep kept here, and a holiday cottage was let, but the island has recently been sold and its future use is uncertain. Before 1969, when myxomatosis spread to the island, it was the home of 7000 rabbits.

Waterloo is the eastward continuation of Broadford; in 1815, over 1500 Skye men fought at the Battle of Waterloo and, on return, many veterans made their home here. Behind Broadford the road to Elgol

passes along Strath Suardal, a wide valley to the south of Bienn na Caillich. Below here, at Coire-chat-achan, are the ruins of the house where Mackinnon entertained Boswell and Johnson during their tour of the Hebrides in 1773. By the road on a small rise is the ancient graveyard and crumbling, over-grown walls of Cill Chriosd, where St Maolrubha founded a church in the 7th C – the last service was held in the mid-19th C.

As you approach Torrin, by Loch Slapin, there is a marble quarry, its spoil heaps gleaming white, and nearby a track leads to a small beach. To the south, a few ruined walls are all that remain of Suisnish, a once thriving crofting community that was cleared to Canada. Over the loch the bare rock, deep crevices and scree of Blà Bheinn (3044 ft) contrast dramatically with the gentle shore-line. Kilmarie, on the east of Strathiard, was once the home of the Mackinnon chiefs. From the main road, a well-signposted track leads west to the fine isolated beach at Camasunary and on over the new army bridge to Loch Coruisk, this walk made difficult by 'The Bad Step', a rock obstacle.

The main road ends at Elgol, passing a thriving area of crofts before descending steeply to the stone and shingle beach and jetty. Virtually on the beach, by a deserted cottage, is the school - a marvellous, if somewhat exposed, position, where the view across Loch Scavaig to the Cuillins is particularly good. At Suidhe Biorach, half a mile to the south, is the cave where Bonnie Prince Charlie was hidden before leaving Skye – childless women were supposed to become fertile after sitting on this promontory.

A narrow and winding road crosses the peninsula to Glasnakille, a village of crofts along a steep and mainly inaccessible shore; the Spar Cave, best explored at low tide with a torch, contains many stalactites. A new track leads down to a deep gash in the cliffs, and the path along the top affords fine views of Sleat.

Sleat

The road from Broadford to Sleat passes a low-lying area of moors, much of which is being planted with trees. A smaller road west of the main one leads to Drumfearn, a pretty crofting township, where a track leads down to the sheltered rocky head of Loch Eishort, with small fishing boats, and cattle and sheep grazing by the shore. The main road and the main centres of population are on the fertile eastern side of the peninsula, 'the garden of Skye', with woodland, forest plantations, crofts and farms, and a mainly rocky shore. At the southern end of Loch na Dal is Isleornsay, a very pretty village with a pier, rusting anchors and chains, and small moored boats. The small tidal island of **Ornsay,** to which you can cross at low tide, has a ruined chapel and an unmanned lighthouse, built in 1857. There is an attractive beach at Camascross to the south. The road rejoins the coast at Teangue, where the ivy-clad ruins of Knock Castle, built in the 14th C, stand at the edge of a small bay, many of its stones having been taken to build Knock House.

A Gaelic college has been established in the restored farm at Ostaig, part of a large estate owned by an Edinburgh merchant banker who aims to revitalise this part of the island. Gaelic language courses for up to 30 people are held in the summer, with piping courses in the spring and autumn, and there is a bookshop selling Gaelic books and souvenirs.

Armadale Castle, designed by Gillespie Graham and built 1815 - 19, stands above the road in fine grounds planted with North American hardwoods, conifers and Australasian and European trees. The castle is now the Clan Donald Centre, with a display of relics, crafts and books, and a restaurant. The pier to the south is the terminal for the Mallaig ferry, and provides shelter for the Skye Yacht Club moorings. South of Ardvasar the road narrows and becomes quite dramatic, with fine views of Knoydart, Morar and Moidart - all on the mainland - ending at the crofting township of Aird of Sleat where a track, impassable for cars, continues to the lighthouse at the Point of Sleat, the extreme southern tip of Skye, looking out towards Rum, Eigg and Ardnamurchan.

On the west of Sleat there are three settlements reached by a narrow scenic road through low irregular hills, in a loop from Knock to Ostaig. The most northerly of these habitations is Ord, where there is a hotel above a small bay of pebbles and a little sand. Further south is Tokavaig, with crofts, and the remains of Dunscaith Castle built into the rock and overlooking

Cill Chriosd, Skye.

The lighthouse island of Ornsay, Skye.

the bay, a stronghold of the Mac-Donalds during the 15th and 16th C, and in legend occupied by the Queen of Skye, who taught the art of war to Cuchulainn, an Irish hero. It is one of the oldest fortified headlands in the Hebrides and was last occupied around 1570; access to it is difficult. The largest of the three communities is Tarskavaig, with crofts to the north of a small beach with sand at low tide, and rocks and skerries out to sea. This isolated area of western Sleat is well worth visiting. It has great intrinsic beauty, and a superb view of the jagged peaks of the Cuillins, cloud-topped in a sweep above Coruisk.

Eastern Skye and the Kyles

Skye's most ancient ferry terminal is at Kylerhea, a small township over-looking Kyle Rhea. As recently as 1906, cattle were swum across the narrows to the mainland at slack water, tied nose to tail in strings of six or eight behind a boat – up to 8000 head a year were once taken off the island in this way. It is now the terminal for the Glenelg ferry, linked to the main Broadford to Kyleakin road by the steep and narrow pass through Glen Arroch, with its summit at 911 ft.

Kyleakin was once a fishing village, but it is now the main ferry terminal for Skye with a continuous seven-day-a-week service. The Sunday service was started in 1965 against a background of strong protest, led by Rev. Angus Smith, Free Church minister of Skeabost, who also instigated the narrowly

Caisteal Maol, Kyleakin, Skye.

defeated anti-alcohol poll two years later. The village overlooks the swift-flowing waters of Kyle Akin, where King Haakon moored in 1263 on his way to defeat at the Battle of Largs. The entrance to the harbour is guarded by the ruins of Caisteal Maol, used by the Mackinnons from the 12th to the 15th C. Apparently a Norwegian princess, resident in an earlier building on this site, stretched a chain across the Kyle to extract tolls from passing ships – an imaginative legend and an equally imaginative piece of engineering! The village has shops, hotels, restaurants and other services, and there are boat trips from here in the summer.

Four miles to the west of Kyleakin is the Skye airstrip, used by Loganair, and Bristow Heli-copters who have a new geodesic

hangar. Near here, where a stream crosses the shore, is the spot where St Maolrubha preached – keeping his scriptures in the rocks and hanging a bell from the branches of a tree. A graveyard at the end of the runway overlooks many small islands and skerries where cattle are sometimes stranded by the tide. A neat row of graves stands as a reminder of the sinking of the cruiser, HMS *Curaçao*, cut in two by the liner, *Queen Mary*, while acting as her escort on 2 October 1942. The scattered crofts of Upper and Lower Breakish (the name said to derive from *a'bhreac*, 'smallpox', that swept through the island in the 17th and 18th C) are of little interest, but the old schoolhouse on the main road is the office of the *West Highland Free Press*, a controversial campaigning newspaper started in 1972, and distributed throughout the isles.

Although much of Skye remains remote and unspoiled, it still has many facilities to offer visitors. There is good game fishing in both lochs and rivers (permits are issued by many of the hotels and the Portree Angling Club), and sea angling is arranged from several places. There are golf courses, pony trekking centres, sub-aqua facilities and skilled guides for walkers and climbers, as well as coach and boat trips, many craft workshops, and camping and caravan sites. Each year there is a Gaelic Mod – a gathering for music and poetry – and an agricultural show, Highland

Games and piping competitions. Up-to-date information and addresses are best obtained from the main tourist office in Portree or the small one, serving the south of the island, at Broadford.

Skye's close proximity to the mainland makes for easy and inexpensive access. The main Caledonian MacBrayne vehicle ferry operates virtually non-stop, from morning to night, seven days a week, from the railhead at Kyle of Lochalsh to Kyleakin: a five-minute passage. A Monday to Saturday ferry service is operated in the summer between Glenelg and Kylerhea by M. A. Mackenzie, carrying vehicles up to four tons: also a five-minute passage. Another Monday to Saturday, summer-only vehicle ferry is operated by Caledonian MacBrayne between Mallaig (a railhead) and Armadale: a 30-minute passage. In winter it carries passengers only.

Ferries operate from Sconser to Raasay, and from Uig to the Outer Hebrides, both carrying vehicles.

Loganair fly a daily service (not Sundays) during the summer from Glasgow to Broadford. Flight time: 55 minutes.

Raasay

Highland. With a population of 150, Raasay is 13 miles long by 3 miles wide, rising to a height of 1456 ft at the distinctive flat-topped summit of Dùn Caan upon which the ebullient Dr Johnson danced a reel.

The north of the island is composed of Archaean gneiss, the south being Torridonian sandstone with two large areas of granite. Some of the Torridonian shales contain the oldest plant remains yet discovered. A feature almost unique in the Highlands is the strong loam present between 600 and 900 ft at The Glam. The presence of this soil suggests that Raasay probably escaped glaciation leaving much ancient and rare flora on the east coast. The disused mineworkings in the south are evidence of ironstone deposits, no longer of economic use.

The present ferry service between Sconser and Suisnish, started by Caledonian MacBrayne in July 1976 after a long campaign by the islanders, has helped to stem the island's declining fortunes. Although there is full employment many of the people are elderly, and the boarding out in Portree of children over 11 during the school term does little to encourage them to stay in later years, splitting as it does families at a crucial time.

Raasay was once the centre of a breakaway section of the Free Church, formed in 1893 by a Mr MacFarlane, with an even more uncompromising doctrine than the original. All pleasure was suspect: music, dancing and poetry, once

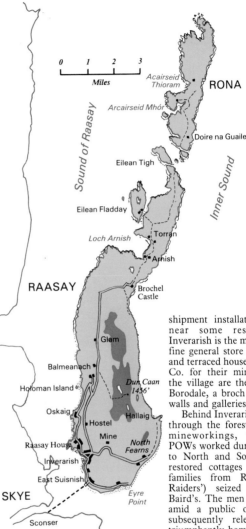

strong on the island, were banned. Today the original Free Church on the island has a few supporters, but most people belong to the church of the breakaway group, and this plays an important part in the island's life. The Sabbath is therefore strictly observed - no work, no play, and people going out only to church. The community is a caring one, sharing fortune and misfortune alike, and the people are happy to receive visitors - as long as their ways are respected. The main occupation is crofting, the language Gaelic. Accommodation is limited to the youth hostel, beautifully situated in an old hunting lodge above the western shore, and the Churchton Guesthouse near the War Memorial at Suisnish.

The ferry terminal at East Suisnish is an untidy place, with the remains of the iron-ore trans-

shipment installations conspicuous near some restored cottages. Inverarish is the main village, with a fine general store and a post office, and terraced houses built by Baird & Co. for their mineworkers. Above the village are the remains of Dùn Borodale, a broch with parts of the walls and galleries remaining.

Behind Inverarish the road passes through the forest and the disused mineworkings, where German POWs worked during World War I, to North and South Fearns, four restored cottages where, in 1919, families from Rona (the 'Rona Raiders') seized the land from Baird's. The men were put on trial amid a public outcry, but were subsequently released and piped triumphantly home. The view from here towards the Kyle is of immense beauty - layer upon layer of mountains in receding colours, often set against vast cloud formations swept in from the Atlantic. A path leads north from the Fearns to the waterfall by the shore at Hallaig.

On the north side of Churchton Bay stands Raasay House, a fine building backed by mixed woodland, but now dilapidated and boarded up. It stands on the site of a tower built in 1549, which was replaced with a house subsequently burned down (along with all the cottages on the island) during the reprisals after the 'Rising'. Raasay and Rona supported the Prince, and both paid dearly for it. This ancestral home of the MacLeods was again rebuilt, and was visited by Johnson and Boswell in 1773 during their tour of the Hebrides. They were suitably entertained with food and music: 'I know not how we shall get away,' said Johnson, in his contentment.

Raasay House.

James MacLeod improved the estate during the early 1800s and added the Regency frontage to the house.

The population on the island grew rapidly, poverty became widespread, and emigration began. In 1843, due to heavy debt, John MacLeod was forced to sell the island. The purchaser was George Rainy of Edinburgh, who paid 35,000 guineas (£36,750). Taking possession in 1846 after the last of the MacLeods had emigrated to Australia, Rainy genuinely tried to improve conditions on Raasay, but without success – so he turned to sheep farming and evicted over 100 families. On his death in 1863, ownership passed to his son, who before his premature death in 1872, aged 27, used the island as a holiday retreat.

Raasay then had several owners, each with little sympathy for the crofters, until Baird's bought it in 1912 to extract the iron-ore; the mine was worked from 1913 to 1919. The present owners of the island, the Scottish Department of Agriculture and Fisheries, bought it for £37,000 in 1922, following the exploits of the 'Rona Raiders'.

Raasay House was run as a hotel from 1937 to 1960, after which a doctor from Sussex bought it, together with the Home Farm and various other buildings. He allowed the house, its contents, and the garden to fall into decay and also refused to sell the more suitable pier at Clachan for use as a terminal for the badly-needed ferry. All this echoed the attitudes of the absentee landlords of the last century. After years of uncertainty, Raasay House has been sold and a trust set up, and there are now plans to turn it into an adventure school. Borodale House nearby is being converted into a hotel.

The narrow road north passes by the stables, now containing dumped cars, and beneath the clocktower where 36 men of Raasay assembled in 1914 to go to war. The clock stopped as they left and, despite many attempts at repair, has never been restarted: it was an ill omen –only 14 men returned and they found the island in a very poor state. Until recently the story has been one of continuous decline and decay. Behind the house stand the ruins of the 13th-C chapel dedicated to St Molnag on an ancient burial ground with two other buildings, the smaller of which possibly dating from the 11th C. One of the gravestones records the drowning off Rona in 1880 of Murdoch and Roderich MacLeod, brothers aged 26 and 24.

Beyond here, at the start of the sign-posted Temptation Hill, by a fuchsia hedge, stands an incised Pictish symbol stone, perhaps dating from the 7th C; another similar design is carved into a rock near the Battery, a small defensive structure built in 1807 in front of Raasay House, armed with cannon and two less-than-beautiful mermaids. These incised stones may have been part of a series marking an area of sanctuary.

The road winds around Balmeanach, with its crofts and a loch nestling in a sheltered valley. A path south-east to the summit of Dùn Caan leaves the road near here; the view from the flat top is magnificent.To the south of the mountains is Loch na Mna, the 'woman's loch', so named because a water-horse haunting it abducted a woman; the local smithy killed the monster, finding it to be made of 'jelly'. To the west is Loch Storab, taking its name from the nearby grave of a Norwegian prince.

The tarmac road ends at Brochel Castle, probably built by the MacLeods of Lewis in the 15th C, from which they raided ships in the Inner Sound, attracting many lawless men into the Clan. Iain Garbh was the last MacLeod chief to live here, dying in 1671. There are scant remains of the building, but the setting is romantic. One-and-a-half miles south, on the coast, are the remains of the township of South Screapadal, nestling in a steep valley. It is a good two-and-a-half hour walk from here through broken, rocky, heather-clad ground to Caol Rona. The first two miles of road were built single-handed with pick, shovel and wheelbarrow by Calum MacLeod, one of the island's most northerly inhabitants, to his home at Arnish. Through Torran, where the post office and school closed in 1960, **Eilean Fladday** is reached, where there were once four families with their own school, but now all the cottages are holiday homes. The island can be reached on foot at low tide. Off the north tip of Raasay is **Eilean Tigh;** at low tide, a rock ledge, joining it to Raasay and wide enough to walk across, is uncovered. The rough, rocky country here is the haunt of golden eagle.

The plant life on the island is particularly rich, with many ancient and rare plants making the island a venue for botanists. You can expect to find many alpines, saxifrages, ferns and mosses; also orchids, sea aster and bog asphodel. Mammals include red deer, otter, alpine hare, water shrew and a species of bank-vole, with a skull slightly larger than normal, unique to Raasay.

The only means of transport to the island is the Caledonian MacBrayne vehicle ferry from Sconser on Skye. There are up to five daily return journeys, Monday to Saturday: 15-minute crossing. There is no petrol for sale on the island.

The Fearns, Raasay.

Towards Eilean Fladday from Raasay.

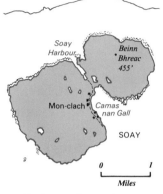

Island of Rona

Highland. Often known as South Rona, this is the northerly continuation of Raasay, separated from it by the half-mile channel of Caol Rona. Five miles long by about one-and-a-half miles wide, rising to 404 ft at the centre, Rona is composed of much glaciated Archaean gneiss. Its only inhabitants, apart from the seals and birds, are the lighthouse keepers who man the lighthouse, and the Royal Navy personnel who man the Nato signal station, both installations being at the far northern tip.

At one time there were three settlements, two schools and a church. During the 16th C, the island, then thickly wooded, was the retreat of robbers and pirates who raided shipping from the fine natural harbour of Acairseid Mhór - known at the time as *Port nan Robaireann,* the 'Port of Robbers'.

The island belonged to the MacLeods of Raasay until the time of the Clearances, when crofters evicted from Raasay settled at Doire na Guaile, Acairseid Mhór ('big harbour') and Acairseid Thioram ('dry harbour'), breaking the barren ground with picks and fertilising it with seaweed. In the mid-19th C there were 150 head of cattle kept on Rona in spite of the poor soil; now only sheep graze, tended from Skye.

By the end of World War I, Rona, like Raasay, was in a poor economic state and no Government help was made available to the crofters. In 1919 a group of seven families seized fertile land at Eyre and North and South Fearns on Raasay, rowing across Caol Rona with their sheep and 20 cattle; soon there was only one family on Rona who also subsequently left. The overgrown remains of the three settlements can still be seen.

Those who land on the island should visit the Church Cave on the east coast. A vast cavern with seats and altar of natural rock, the last service was held here in the 19th C.

Scalpay

Highland. Just off the east coast of Skye, below Raasay, Scalpay is about four miles wide and four miles long. To the east is **Longay,** rising to 221 ft at the southern end of a reef running parallel to Scalpay; to the south is the small low-lying **Guillamon Island.** Much of Scalpay is rough heather-clad hillside, rising to the 1298 ft summit of Mullach na Càrn, although the area around Scalpay House, in the south-east corner behind a small tidal harbour, is cultivated. There are several lochs and many streams, and large areas of conifers are being planted. 4000 acres on the north-west side have been fenced for intensive deer farming; carcasses will be exported to the Continent, where the demand for venison is high - a venture supported by the Highlands and Islands Development Board.

The island was developed in the 19th C by Sir Donald Currie who made roads and planted trees; it is now owned by a merchant banker and worked by his sons.

To the west of Scalpay House are the remains of a chapel, built on the site of a Celtic cell. Opposite Ard Dorch on the east coast of Skye, a cottage is let for holidays. At low tide the island seems almost to join Skye at Caolas Scalpay.

Soay

Highland. Three miles due west of Elgol, rising to 455 ft at the summit of Beinn Bhreac, Soay (pronounced 'soy') is pinched into a central isthmus by the narrow cut of the harbour on the north-west coast, and by the bay of Camas nan Gall on the south-east, where the islanders live. The island is composed of Torridonian sandstone, has many sea cliffs and is not very fertile.

Before 1823 only one family lived here, tending stock, but, as a result of the Clearances, crofters evicted from Skye settled on Soay and by 1861 the population had risen to 129.

In 1946 the author Gavin Maxwell bought the island and started a basking shark fishery, building a slip and a small factory. Lack of demand for shark oil brought it to an end three years later; the project was revived briefly by Maxwell's harpooner, Tex Geddes, in 1950 although the fishing was no longer based on Soay. By 19 June 1953, all except Geddes and his family had left the island, the final evacuation being made, in a blaze of publicity, aboard the SS *Hebrides,* the crofters re-settling on Mull. A succession of people seeking the 'quiet life' then came and went until the situation stabilised, with a total population of 16 in two large crofts. A boat from Arisaig on the mainland calls monthly. Happily, against all odds, this small island is now thriving.

Eilean Donnan

This is a tidal islet at the entrance to Loch Duich, upon which stands a beautifully reconstructed medieval fortress, among splendid and dramatic scenery. The original fortress was built in 1230 on the site of earlier defensive structures, but this was destroyed in 1719 after 45 Spanish allies of the Old Pretender surrendered to a squadron of British frigates commanded by Captain Boyle. After centuries of neglect, restoration - faithful to the original plans which had been kept in Edinburgh - began in 1912 and was completed in 1932 at a cost of £250,000. Access is gained by a stone bridge and the castle is open to visitors. To the west, in Loch Alsh, are the low-lying **Eilean Tioram** and **Glas Eilean.**

The many small islands in and around Loch Hourn are dwarfed by

The reconstructed medieval fortress of Eilean Donnan.

the grandeur of the surrounding mountains. The **Sandaig Islands,** to the north of the Loch, shelter the bay called 'Camusfearna' by Gavin Maxwell, who wrote *Ring of Bright Water* here in 1960. The cottage he occupied was destroyed by fire, and the ruin has been cleared. Boat trips run to here from the Kyle of Lochalsh.

There are a few islets before reaching Mallaig, ferry terminal for the Small Isles Parish and Armadale, Skye.

The Small Isles Parish

Canna, Rum, Eigg and Muck lie as a group to the south-west of Skye and to the west of Mallaig, and they are all inhabited. Their history is that of the surrounding isles – early conversion to Christianity, Viking raids then settlement under the suzerainty of Norway, finally becoming part of the Kingdom of Scotland in 1266. Then followed the rule of the Lords of the Isles until the end of the 15th C, then feuding by the clans vying for power, the '45 rebellion, the famines and the Clearances. Today Canna, Eigg and Muck are 'working' islands, with small communities proving that island life is viable and valuable. Rum, owned by the Nature Conservancy Council and, in spite of its size never really habitable, is a unique open-air laboratory.

Canna

Canna's population is now 24. Its name comes from the Gaelic, either *Canna* ('porpoise') or *Kanin* ('isle of rabbits'). It extends about five miles by one mile along an east-west axis, three miles north-west of Rum and halfway between Mallaig and Lochboisdale, South Uist. A steep-sided island, it is made up of terraced Tertiary basalt which breaks down into extremely fertile soil, on which some of the earliest crops in the West Highlands are grown. Rainfall is about 60 inches each year. At the eastern end is the harbour, with the only deep-water pier in the Small Isles Parish, sheltered by the tidal island of **Sanday** which is linked to Canna by a footbridge.

At the eastern tip of Canna is Compass Hill (458 ft), so called due to the high metal content of the rock and the effect this has on a ship's compass. A mile to the west is Carn a Ghaill, the island's summit, 690-ft high, and three miles south-west is the isolated basalt rock of **Humla.**

The island of Sanday is crofted; and Canna itself is run as a single farm by the proprietor John Lorne Campbell, who bought the island in 1938 from the widow of Robert Thorn, a Glasgow ship owner. Thorn had purchased the island from Donald MacNeil in 1881, after 60 years of drastic clearances during which the population fell to 48. Thorn was a benevolent and responsible man and Canna remained in good hands when John Lorne Campbell became the new owner. He is well known for his

work, with Compton Mackenzie, in founding the Sea League (*see* Barra), and, together with his American wife, he has done much to preserve and further Gaelic literature and culture. The people are Catholic, and Gaelic speaking; the island is viable and happy. There is a valuable stock of Highland cattle and Cheviot sheep, and early potatoes are grown on the farm.

Evidence of Viking occupation can be seen at Rubha Langanes on the north coast, where one of the finest examples of a ship burial was uncovered. The original township before the Clearances was A'Chill, to the north of the harbour, near the site of the 7th-C St Columba's Chapel. Only a Celtic cross, a column and the faint patterns of lazybeds remain. To the east of the harbour is An Coroghan, a ruined tower on top of an isolated stack, where a Clanranald chief imprisoned his wife to frustrate the attentions of her lover, a MacLeod from Skye. On the south coast is a ruined convent at Rubha Sgorr nam Bán-naomha – 'the headland of holy women'.

There is no holiday accommodation, but those who wish to camp may do so, with permission.

Rum

Rum's population is about 40 (fewer in winter) – all, apart from the schoolmistress, employed by the Nature Conservancy Council. The name is pronounced 'Room', possibly from the Norse *Röm oe* – 'wide island'. Commonly, and incorrectly, written as 'Rhum', this spelling was introduced by the

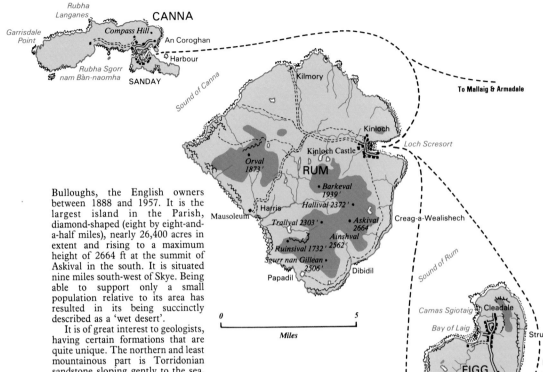

Bulloughs, the English owners between 1888 and 1957. It is the largest island in the Parish, diamond-shaped (eight by eight-and-a-half miles), nearly 26,400 acres in extent and rising to a maximum height of 2664 ft at the summit of Askival in the south. It is situated nine miles south-west of Skye. Being able to support only a small population relative to its area has resulted in its being succinctly described as a 'wet desert'.

It is of great interest to geologists, having certain formations that are quite unique. The northern and least mountainous part is Torridonian sandstone sloping gently to the sea, with a beautiful beach at Kilmory. The central high ground is a boss of gabbro, related closely to the Cuillins of Skye, with here and there a patch of Archaean gneiss. The western point is composed of steep-sided granite, with dramatic sheer cliffs where huge blocks have tumbled pell-mell to the shore. A half a mile to the north-east of Harris is the spot which has the strongest gravitational pull in the British Isles.

The only arable land consists of a few acres at Harris in the west, Kilmory in the north and Kinloch in the east, thus little of the island can be crofted. The climate is less mild than on surrounding islands and the average yearly rainfall is 93 inches, although this varies, being as low as 56 inches at Harris and as high as 122 inches in the mountains. The topography of Rum results in prolonged periods of cloud cover (when surrounding areas may be clear), and gusty winds.

In 1346 Rum was owned by John of Islay, passing to McKenabrey of Coll in 1549, then to the MacLeans of Coll in 1695. By the early 19th C it was vastly overcrowded, and the islanders were poor and unable to pay their rent. A clearance was arranged, and over 300 souls left bound for Canada and America to face a hard winter. With about 50 people remaining, MacLean rented the land for grazing and 8000 sheep were brought in. Crofters came to the island from Skye and, by 1831, the population had risen to 134. The

sheep proved unprofitable, and the island was sold in 1845 to the Marquis of Salisbury who stocked the streams with trout and the hills with deer. After being sold and resold, and with another attempt at sheep farming proving unsuccessful, Rum was finally bought in 1888 by the remarkable John Bullough of Oswaldtwistle, who had made his fortune designing milling machinery. It became his holiday retreat and self-contained sporting estate, with deer partly replacing the sheep.

John Bullough's son, Sir George, became the owner in 1891, and spared no expense in building Kinloch Castle, an extravagant monument to the Edwardian opulence which ended with the outbreak of war. Turtles and alligators were kept in heated tanks, a pure white Arab stallion was imported to 'improve' the stock of the native Rum ponies (said to

descend from Spanish ponies which swam ashore from a wrecked Armada galleon, but it is more likely they came from Eriskay), and two exotic Albion cars were used to transport guests. Muscatel grapes, figs, peaches and nectarines were grown under glass, and dances were held to the music of an electric organ in the sumptuous ballroom.

The island population stabilised at about 90 people until the outbreak of the war, and all regarded the Bullough family as kindly and courteous people, although the press labelled Rum 'The Forbidden Island' – a strange response to an estate kept no more private than those on the mainland. In 1957 the island was purchased from Sir George's widow, Monica Lady Bullough, by the Nature Conservancy Council to be used as a natural outdoor laboratory. Kinloch Castle has been preserved, and part is now run as a hotel.

Kinloch Castle, Rum.

Red deer, wild goats, domestic Highland cattle and ponies are maintained and studied. Sheltered glens are being replanted with native trees and shrubs, and open heathland is managed in order to preserve natural flora and fauna. Geology, ecology and conservation can all be studied in a unique environment, with little disturbance.

The main area of occupation is at Kinloch, where there is a shop and post office. There is no pier, and all cargo and passengers have to be trans-shipped to the jetty. Tarmac roads are also non-existent but a good track leads due west to the centre of the island, where it forks – north to Kilmory with its fine beach (and cemetery with a gravestone bearing the names of six children of the Matheson family, five of whom died in the space of a week), and south to Harris and the Bullough mausoleum, built in the style of a Greek temple and not a little incongruous. A rugged track leads south from Kinloch to the east of Hallival and Askival to Dibidil and

Papadil, passing near Creag-a-Wealishech – the 'Welshman's cliff', in memory of a gang of Welsh slate quarriers who widened a precipitous path.

The sea cliffs attract kittiwake, puffin, guillemot and razorbill and the mountain tops. Manx shearwater (over 130,000 pairs). In all, over 150 species of birds have been recorded, and the sea eagle has been re-introduced.

Plant life is prolific and varied, little disturbed on the cliffs and mountain summits since the last ice age. There are many alpines, including the rare arctic sandwort and penny-cress; roseroot, thrift, sea campion and Scots lovage on the cliffs; bog asphodel, heath spotted-orchid, sundew, butterwort and black bog-rush on the moors.

Day visitors are welcome. Those who wish to stay longer must make *prior* arrangements with the NCC Warden at White House, Kinloch. NCC accommodation is limited and priority is given to those engaged in research work. Climbers require a

permit and must be in organised parties. There is also accommodation at the hotel.

About nine miles west of Rum lie **Oigh-sgeir** and **Garbh Sgeir** (the 'maiden rock'), hexagonal basalt columns with an area of about 10 acres, rising 33 ft above sea level. The channel between the two outcrops has often provided welcome shelter for small boats caught by storms, the spray passing overhead as the craft lie in calm water. During the 19th C, Canna cattle were grazed on the islets' lush grass; now the three lighthouse keepers grow vegetables and flowers in what must be the country's most remote walled gardens.

Eigg

Pronounced 'egg', the name is probably derived from the Gaelic *eige* ('a hollow') and it once known as *Eilean Nimban-More* ('island of the big women'). It has an area of over 5000 acres and is dominated by An Squrr at the southern end, the largest mass of columnar pitchstone lava in Britain, rising a sheer 290 ft above the 1000-ft contour, best seen from the south, with a view from the top that is superb. A large colony of Manx shearwater has established itself on An Squrr, burrowing into the soil.

The northern plateau and southern moor are basalt and have weathered into excellent soil. Cliffs around the northern point are sandstone, eroded into fantastic shapes at Camas Sgiotaig, where the beach is composed of grains of quartz, white with black flecks, which creak underfoot – 'singing sands'! To the north of the pretty Bay of Laig there are limestone blocks and nodules, some trapped in rock cages and rattled by the waves. The packed crofting township of Cleadale lies behind the bay.

Eigg's main village is Galmisdale, on the south-east corner, its small pier partially sheltered by the columnar basalt **Eilean Chathastail** ('castle island') with its lighthouse. The harbour is not deep but can be used by launches.

Half a mile south-west of the pier is MacDonalds Cave or Uamh Fhraing ('St Francis Cave'), where, in the winter of 1577 (after an exchange of minor atrocities) the MacLeods of Skye suffocated 395 MacDonalds by burning brushwood at the narrow entrance. The MacDonalds were undiscovered until one of their scouts was spotted by the MacLeods who then traced his footprints in the snow leading to the cave. The feuding continued at Trumpan in Skye. A little further to the west is Cathedral Cave, used by Roman Catholics during the time of their persecution; a stone wall in the cave may have served as an altar. In the 7th C, a monastery was founded

Red deer stags feeding on seaweed at Kilmory, Rum.

by St Donnan, who, with his brothers, was killed by the islanders. The building was later destroyed by Norsemen, and the ruins of the 14th-C Kildonnan Church stand on the site of this earlier building.

MacDonald of Clanranald was given the island by Robert the Bruce in 1309. The Clan supported the Prince during the unsuccessful '45 rebellion. Captain John Ferguson of the King's ship, *Furnace*, later visited Eigg to arrest John MacDonald, who surrendered to avoid bloodshed. Ferguson gave an undertaking that, if the MacDonalds gave up their weapons, there would be no reprisals. After agreeing to this, those who were suspected of supporting the rebellion were taken, the island was sacked and the young men transported.

The MacDonalds sold Eigg in 1827 for £15,000 to Dr Hugh MacPherson, and several clearances took place. Upon his death the island passed to his children and became relatively prosperous during the 1870s, the population at this time being over 300. In the 1890s it was bought by Robert Thomson, and again the island prospered, but he died a sick and lonely man. He was buried beneath a marble slab at the summit of Eilean Cathastail on Christmas Day, 1913.

In the 1920s the island was purchased by the Runciman family, who developed the land, ploughed back profits, and made a self-sufficient and mechanised 2000-acre farm. In 1966 it was sold to Robert Evans, a Welsh Border farmer, who in turn sold it in 1971 to a 'Christian charity', which succeeded in alienating and demoralising the whole population with grandiose schemes that took no account of the island's needs.

In 1975 it was purchased for £250,000 by the present owner Keith Schellenberg, director of Udny and Dudwick Estates, a British Olympic bobsleigh team member, and a colourful and energetic man, determined to see the island prosper. With a population of about 80, Eigg is now actively promoted as a holiday island. There is guest-house, caravan and cottage accommodation available, but demand usually exceeds supply.

Muck

The name comes from the Gaelic, *eilean a muic* ('isle of the sow'), and was referred to by Buchanan in 1582 as *insula porcorum* ('pigs' island'). With an area of 1586 acres, rising to a maximum height of 451 ft at the summit of Beinn Airein, it lies about two-and-a-half miles south-west of Eigg and eight miles north of Ardnamurchan. A fertile island of Tertiary basalt, which receives beneficial dressings of wind-blown shell sand, it is a pretty and peaceful place with pleasant beaches, even if somewhat exposed to the weather. At the south-east corner is Port Mor, a small harbour with a difficult rocky entrance. Off the north-west tip, **Eilean nan Each** ('horse island'), where ponies were once kept, and **Eilean Aird nan Uan** ('the lambs' lofty isle') can both be reached at low tide.

Muck is run as a single unit by Lawrence MacEwan, a caring and tenacious laird who keeps cattle, sheep and a few ponies, and grows potatoes, oats and root crops – quite an achievement on what is truly an 'oceanic' island. The laird's house is at Gallanach.

In 1828, 150 kelp collectors were cleared and in 1854 Captain Thomas Swinburne, RN, the new owner, began a fishing industry, renting the land out for sheep. By 1861 the population was 58; today it is 24.

There are a few acres of woodland, and in spring and early summer the fields are coloured by cornflower, harebell, marigold and iris. Above Port Mor there is a ruined chapel by the graveyard, and at the entrance to the harbour are the few remains of a defensive structure, the 'Castle of the White Fort'. There is a limited amount of holiday accommodation.

The Small Isles Parish is served by a Caledonian MacBrayne ferry from Mallaig via Armadale on Skye, which does a round trip three times each week. There are also boats from Mallaig and Arisaig during the summer serving Eigg and Rum and a ferry from Glenuig and Lochailort to Eigg, also during the summer only.

Maillaig to Loch Linnhe

At the entrance to Loch nan Ceall ('loch of the hermit's cell'), there are many islands and rocks, the largest being the tidal **Eilean Ighe** and **Luinga Mhór**. At the head of the loch is Arisaig, beautifully situated and an embarkation point for boat trips to Rum, Eigg and Muck.

On **Eilean a' Ghaill**, to the south-east of Rubh' Arisaig, are the remains of a fort; there are others on Rubh' Aird Ghamhsgail, on the northern shore of Loch nan Uamh, and on **Eilean nan Gobhar** ('goat island') at the entrance to Loch Ailort. Loch nan Uamh ('loch of the caves') was the scene of the end of the '45 Rising, where Prince Charlie, after his adventures in the Outer Hebrides and on Skye with Flora MacDonald, finally left Scotland for the last time aboard the *Heureux*. A cairn has been erected to mark this historic event. On the southern shore of the Sound of Arisaig is the tidal **Samalaman Island** with a fine sandy beach and picnic area.

Eilean Shona ('island of the ford') splits the entrance to Loch Moidart, and is extensively forested on the eastern side; composed mainly of rugged igneous rock, it rises to a height of 870 ft. The *New Statistical Account of Scotland* of 1845 says that it was 'the only island worth noticing' in Ardnamurchan and that 'the dwelling house and surrounding scenery of the residence of a respectable family are very beautiful.' It is still inhabited by several families, is still very beautiful and is a private estate. Shona Beag is joined to Eilean Shona by a narrow neck of land.

To the south is the wooded **Riska Island**, and Castle Tioram (or *Tirrin*, the 'dry castle') standing on a rocky tidal islet off Cùl Doirlinn in the beautiful Loch Moidart. Built in the 13th C, it was the seat of the MacDonalds of Clanranald, and around 1600, some domestic buildings were added to the original massive curtain walls. This area was the centre of both Jacobite risings in 1715 and 1745. The castle was partly destroyed, at the orders of Clanranald, after the failure of the '45, although parts remained habitable. The unfortunate Lady Grange spent some time here *en route* to her exile on St Kilda.

There are a few isolated rocks and skerries off the shore of Ardnamurchan. In Loch Sunart are the islands of **Risga**, **Carna** and **Oronsay**; their position in the entrance to the loch causes the tide to flow swiftly around them. Oronsay, low-lying, barren and rocky, deeply indented with sea lochs, was once inhabited, as was Carna, recorded in 1845 as being a more fertile island, rising quite steeply to a height of 554 ft. Seals breed around **Eilean nan Eildean** to the west, and can also be seen in Glenmore Bay, sheltered by the tidal **Eilean Mór**.

The island of Risga has cup-marked rocks which may have been part of some kind of moon and sun calendar. It is the breeding ground of oystercatcher, merganser, eider duck and tern.

Mull

Strathclyde. The name 'Mull' means 'mass of hill', an apt description for this volcanic island, third largest in the Hebrides. With an area of nearly 225,000 acres, it lies to the west of Oban, its east coast roughly parallel to the Morven shore. In the south, the Ross of Mull extends as a long peninsula, with the

Opposite: *An Sgurr on Eigg.*

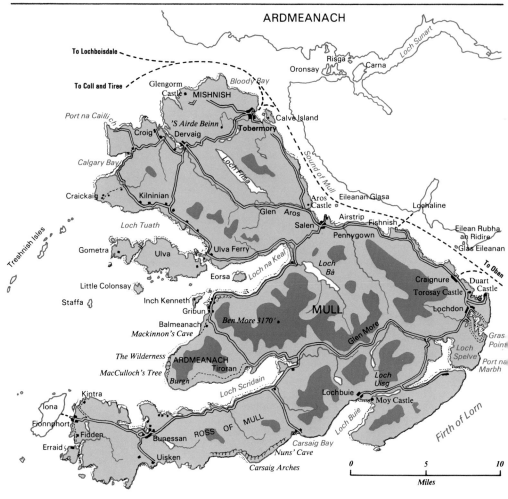

Torran Rocks

revered island of Iona off the tip, and the west is deeply indented with sea lochs leaving only a narrow neck of land between Loch na Keal and Salen.

The highest point, at the summit of Ben More, is 3170 ft, and there are several other peaks well over 2000 ft. Most characteristic of the landscape are the terraced hills known as 'trap' – Tertiary basalt plateau lavas, the volcanic outpourings of 40–50 million years ago, now much eroded. These stepped hillsides are best seen around Loch Scridain. The mountain of Ben More is the highest Tertiary basalt in Britain – the trap layers beneath the summit end in dramatic sea cliffs at Ardmeanach. Later eruptions, centred on Beinn Chàsgidle and Loch Bà, formed circular granitic dykes some five miles in diameter and 300-ft thick – the collapsed cores

of the vents. Dykes and sills from these two volcanoes can be traced as far south as Yorkshire.

Northern Mull is plateau basalt, flat wet moorland rising to the 'trap' layers, never higher than 1500 ft. 'S Airde Beinn is a volcanic plug. On the headland south of Treshnish Point there is a pre-glacial raised beach, 125-ft high and fertile, and in the south-east, Loch Spelve and Loch Buie are the end of the Great Glen fault. Glen More has many glacial features, including a terminal moraine above Graig Cottage.

Westward along the Ross of Mull the trap country gives way first to crystalline gneiss and then to a boss of pink granite, four miles square. Beneath the basalt lavas is a thin layer of chalk, exposed at Carsaig where lime-laden water washes over lias on a south-facing coast, giving extremely favourable growing conditions. Here, as in the chalk streams of southern England, watercress grows.

Columnar balsalt, which perhaps reaches its apogee on Staffa, is also

to be found on Ulva and Gometra, near Tavool on Ardmeanach and near Bunessan and at Carsaig. The east coast, sheltered from the erosive forces of the prevailing weather, consists of raised beaches above shallow bays.

Mull's climate is mild Atlantic, with very high rainfall in the mountains, making the growing season long. Wind is funnelled to the island's centre by the sea lochs.

The largest landowner and main source of employment is the Forestry Commission who have vast plantations of Sitka spruce and larch in the north-east, at Ardmeanach and on the Ross of Mull. There are a few large farms, a little crofting centred on the Ross and large areas of deer forest. Since the introduction of large-scale sheep farming in the 19th C and the consequent despoilation of cultivated land, Mull's considerable agricultural potential has never been fully realised - a fact reflected by the tiny population of 1600. The lobster fishing industry thrives (in the 1920s a 12-pounder was taken in Calgary

Ben More towering over Loch Scridain, Mull.

Bay) and there are, of course, tourists coming in ever-increasing numbers.

The first inhabitants of Mull left stones, circles and cairns scattered over the island. 'Crannogs' (lake dwellings) were built on stilts in Lochs Bà, Assapol, Frisa, Sguabain, Poit na h-I and na Keal. The Irish Celts came in the 2nd C, a turbulent period when many forts and duns were built; there are fine examples at Dùn Aisgain to the north of Loch Tuath; Dùn Urgadul (vitrified), one mile north of Tobermory; Dùn nan Gall ('fort of the stranger') on Loch Tuath; and An Sean Dùn (the 'bewitched fort'), south-west of Glengorm, the last two being brochs.

Christianity came to Iona with the arrival of St Columba in AD 563. The Norsemen raided then settled, and Mull came under Norwegian suzerainty until 1266 when, along with the other islands, it was controlled by Scotland under the Lord of the Isles. Following this period, the MacLeans became the dominant clan on Mull until the clan system was forcibly broken after the '45 rebellion.

During the 18th C the population increased rapidly, peaking at 10,600 in 1821. There was enormous pressure on the land, although the kelp industry alone sustained many people until it collapsed in 1852. Emigration began even before the lairds and newcomers began clearing the land for sheep, and many

evictions were made by owners with little regard for the hardships caused. An exception was the Duke of Argyll, who tried to find employment for his tenants. However, by 1881 the population had been halved, and the Crofters' Act of 1886 did little to help matters, many of the remaining crofts being amalgamated into larger farming units. When the grazings were ruined, the Victorians turned to the sporting potential of the island, stocking it with red deer, which are now to be seen around Torosay, Laggan and Ben More.

The main ferry terminal on Mull is at Craignure, where the new pier was built in 1964 to take the large vehicle ferry from Oban. To the north, beyond Scalastle Bay, is the terminal for the much smaller Lochaline – Fishnish vehicle ferry. The airstrip at Glenforsa was built in 54 days in 1966 by the 38th Engineer Regiment as an exercise.

At Pennygown only the walls remain of a medieval chapel; inside is the shaft of a Celtic cross, probably brought from Iona, showing the Virgin and Child. It is said that there were once benevolent fairies here who would complete any task that was left on their mound –spinning, weaving or the like – until someone left a short piece of wood, asking them to make a ship's mast. After that, no more favours were done.

Salen village sits in a wide bay at the mid-point of the Sound of Mull,

and is a convenient touring centre for the island. There is a hotel, and there are skin-diving facilities on the pier. At the north of the bay are the ruins of Aros Castle, built in the 14th C by the Lord of the Isles, and last occupied in 1608, beneath which treasure from the Tobermory galleon is said to lie buried.

There are several small islands in the Sound of Mull. At the southern entrance close to the mainland, beyond the lighthouse on **Glas Eileanan**, is **Eilean Rubha an Ridire**. In 1973 divers discovered the wreck of the 17th-C Royal Navy frigate *Dartmouth* off the north-west shore: she was torn from her moorings in the Sound during a storm and was wrecked on 19 October 1690. Off Salen is **Eileanan Glasa** where, on 25 January 1935, the cargo ship *Rondo* was wrecked, totally demolishing the original lighthouse.

At the northern end of the Sound is the beautiful harbour of Tobermory (*Tobar Mhoire*, 'Mary's well'), full of visiting yachts in the summer and sheltered by **Calve Island** (used as a summer residence) and the steep hills behind. This colourful town is one of the smallest to have had burgh status (from 1875 to 1975), with a population of about 700. The port was developed by the British Fisheries Society in 1788, who built the fine stone houses in the main street, now brightly painted, giving the town a Continental atmosphere. The

The fine harbour of Tobermory, Mull.

courthouse, built in 1862, serves as the police station and council offices. There are hotels, a museum, boarding houses, a tourist information office, a youth hostel, shops, bank, library, petrol stations, good junior and senior schools, and a fine public park - the Aros House Policies - given to the town by the Forestry Commission in 1969. There is also a nine-hole golf course.

Buried in the clay at the bottom of the bay lies the wreck of the *Almirante de Florencia*, a Spanish galleon from the routed Armada fleet, which anchored here to provision in 1588. When it became clear that the Spaniards were going to leave without paying for the stores, Donald MacLean went aboard to claim the islanders' due, and was imprisoned by the seamen. He escaped, reached the ship's magazine and blew it up; the Spanish officers who survived the explosion were held at Duart Castle. The wreck is said to contain 30 million ducats, still attracting treasure hunters, none of whom has retrieved anything of great value, and it has been suggested that Sacheverell, Governor of the Isle of Man, may have salvaged everything of value in 1688. To the north is Bloody Bay, scene of a sea battle between John, last Lord of the Isles, and his son Angus.

A minor road west from Tobermory passes Dùn Urgadul, a vitrified fort, before ending at the private Glengorm Castle (built 1860), well situated near the windswept Mishnish headland. Glengorm means 'blue glen', a name suggested to the unwitting owner which referred to the blue smoke of the burning crofts when the area was cleared. The main road to Dervaig passes the three Mishnish lochs, set in wild open moorland and well stocked with trout.

The pretty village of Dervaig (the 'little grove'), sitting at the head of Loch a' Chumhainn, was built by the MacLeans of Coll in 1799. By the road is the Kilmore Parish Church which has a 'pencil' steeple, more commonly seen in Ireland, and an attractive interior. The famous 'Mull Little Theatre' was founded in the village, and to the south is 'The Old Byre', with its unusual tableaux of crofting life. The road south-east to Aros passes Loch Frisa (a trout fishery) and, just before its summit, Druimtigh-macgillechattan, Mull's longest place-name and site of an ancient market which was held at 'the ridge of the house of the Cattenach fellow'.

At the mouth of Loch a' Chumhainn is Croig, a little rocky inlet where cattle from the outer isles were once landed *en route* to the mainland. At Calgary there is a fine sweep of pale sand backed by machair and, on the northern side, by the old pier, is a prominent basalt dyke which may have given the bay its name - *Calagharaidh*, the 'haven by the wall'. The city of Calgary in Canada was *not* so named by emigrants from Mull, contrary to popular belief.

The road south passes the gaunt ruin of Reudle schoolhouse, standing alone on the moor. About a mile south-west along the valley are the substantial remains of Crackaig and Clac Gugairidh, 'the hollow of the dark grazings', overlooking the Treshnish Isles; 200 people lived in these two villages until the end of the last century. The ash tree where a villager hanged himself still grows in the walled garden by the burn, and below, in the cliffs, is the 'Still Cave', where illicit whisky was made.

At Kilninian there is a small area of fine natural woodland, and beyond this, near Ulva Ferry, a waterfall. The view across Loch Tuath to the trap hills of **Ulva** and **Gometra** is excellent. These islands, with **Little Colonsay**, were the scene of an almost total clearance of 600 inhabitants by F. W. Clark between 1846 and 1851. Ulva ('wolf island') was held by the MacQuarries for 800 years until the 18th C; there was once a piping college founded by a MacArthur, a pupil of the famed McCrimmons of Skye, and Ulva House stands in fine woodland on the site of an earlier house once visited by Sir Walter Scott. Ulva and Gometra are joined by a bridge. The latter was once the home of Himalayan explorer Hugh Ruttledge. The islands now support sheep and some cattle, and are being steadily improved after the depredations which followed the

The 'trap' country of Mull.

Clearances. They are private, and permission to visit is at the discretion of the owner.

The island of **Eorsa**, in Loch na Keal (the 'loch of the cliffs'), once belonged to the Priory of Iona, and now is grazed by a few sheep, having a ruined bothy at the eastern end. The southern shore of the loch is dramatic, the slopes of Ben More (which is most easily climbed from Dhiseig) falling steeply to the water. At Gribun there are huge boulders which have fallen from the cliffs –one of these, now lying by a stone wall, flattened a small cottage in which two newlyweds lay sleeping.

Off the Gribun shore is **Inch Kenneth** - flat, fertile and farmed, once the 'granary of Iona'. There is a ruined chapel but no remains of the accompanying monastery. Sir Alan MacLean's grave in the burial ground is covered by an intricately carved slab showing the Chief in armour with his dog at his feet. The island is private.

One mile south of Balmeanach is Mackinnon's Cave, about 100-ft high and 600-ft deep, with stalactites in the deepest part. It can only be entered at low tide, and a torch is helpful. At Rubha na h-Uamha, which is the most westerly point of the boulder-strewn cliffs of the wild Ardmeanach peninsula, is Mac-Culloch's Tree, a fossil 40-ft high, engulfed by lava 50 million years ago. It was first described by Dr MacCulloch in 1819, and can be reached either from Balmeanach or Tiroran on Loch Scridain, where there is a National Trust for Scotland office. The walk along the shore is difficult but fascinating; try to arrive at half tide on the ebb.

The south-west end of Ardmeanach, known as the Burgh, was given to the National Trust for Scotland in 1932 by A. Campbell Blair of Dolgellau. It is a natural reserve for red deer, wild goat, otter, golden eagle, hen harrier, peregrine, sparrow-hawk, buzzard and numerous smaller birds.

To the east of Tiroran the road skirts Loch Scridain to join the main Craigmore–Fionnphort road. To the south of Craigmore is Torosay Castle, designed in the Scottish baronial style by David Bryce and built in 1856. The beautiful gardens, designed by Sir Robert Lorimer and sloping down to the shore, are open to the public.

Duart Castle stands on a dark headland, the imposing ancestral home of the MacLeans since about 1250. Overrun and put to fire by the Duke of Argyll in 1691, it was only returned to MacLean hands in 1912, and is now the residence of the 27th Chief and his wife, having been lovingly restored from ruins. It is open to the public who can explore the keep, battlements, and cells, examine MacLean relics, and see a scouting exhibition. On the coast to the south, at the entrance to Loch Don, is Grass Point, terminal for the old Oban - Kerrera - Mull ferry, and start of the pilgrim's path to Iona. Further south, at the entrance to Loch Spelve, is Port nam Marbh ('the port of the dead') where corpses

The deserted village of Crackaig, Mull.

Duart Castle, now beautifully restored.

were landed from the mainland for burial on Iona. A minor road west passes along the northern shores of Lochs Spelve and Uisg, through attractive scenery and mixed woodlands with masses of rhododendrons, to Lochbuie. Moy Castle, built in the 15th C by the MacLeans of Lochbuie, is a sturdy tower with a spring in the natural rock floor. Unfortunately, there is no public access.

The main road passes through the bare, glaciated Glen More, above the Lussa River. The Glen once separated the kingdoms of the Picts and the Scots (Dalriada). A cairn at Pedlars Pool marks the spot where a pedlar, who took care of two households with smallpox, died of the disease himself, and another cairn at Pennyghael commemorates the Beatons, hereditary doctors to the Lords of the Isles. A minor road south across the moor finishes at the fertile valley and farm at Carsaig. Along the shore to the west is the Nun's Cave, which contains early Christian carvings. Sandstone was quarried nearby until 1873, and was used in Iona Cathedral. Two miles beyond the cave at Malcolm's Point, beneath 700-ft cliffs, are the dark red basaltic Carsaig Arches.

The coast of the Ross is broken with many small bays and some fine beaches, such as that at Uisken; Bunessan is the touring centre for

this area. Inland is windswept, undulating moorland. The road finishes at Fionnphort, where the ferry leaves for Iona. Half a mile to the north granite was quarried until the late 19th C; stone from here was used to build Holborn Viaduct, Blackfriars Bridge and the Albert Memorial in London, and the Skerryvore and Dubh Artach lighthouses. Further north is the pretty harbour of Kintra. To the south, beyond the fine beach at Fidden, is the tidal island of **Erraid**, featured in Robert Louis Stevenson's book *Kidnapped*, which he is said to have written in one of the houses behind the row of granite cottages used as the shore station for the Dubh Artach and Skerryvore lighthouses (*see* Tiree) until 1967. In the book, David Balfour thought himself stranded on Erraid after the brig *Covenant* was wrecked on the seaward side – not realising that he could cross the sand at low tide. At the summit of Crioc Mor is the iron 'observatory' once used to signal to the lighthouses. The island is now occupied by members of the Findhorn Community.

The Dubh Artach lighthouse marks the end of a reef running south from Mull, which manifests itself as the **Torran Rocks** (*torunn* means 'a loud murmuring noise'). The lighthouse, which became operational in 1872, was designed

The tidal island of Erraid.

by Thomas and David Stevenson, R.L.S.'s father and uncle respectively. From base of the tower to the base of the lantern measures 106 ft, and it is built on a rock 35 ft above mean high water.

Although Mull's proximity to the mainland is making it increasingly popular with tourists, it is still easy, even in the summer, to find vast open spaces with no one else around.

Caledonian MacBrayne run a large vehicle ferry from Oban to Craignure, the voyage taking 45 minutes, and they also operate a smaller vehicle ferry between Lochaline and Fishnish taking 15 minutes. Their ferry from Oban to Coll and Tiree calls at Tobermory, for passengers only. Loganair fly to Glenforsa from Glasgow. Excursions are run from Oban to Mull and Iona. There is a bus service on Mull. The Tourist Information office is at Tobermory.

Treshnish Isles

These are a string of volcanic islands lying on a south-west/north-east axis, about three-and-a-half miles west of Gometra, off Mull. At the southern end, and separated from the rest of the group, is **Bac Mór**, the 'Dutchman's Cap', its old lava cone encircled by a lava rim – a distinctive landmark. The central and largest island is **Lunga**, rising to 338 ft at the summit of Cruachan, below which are the remains of some long-vacated black houses. On the west coast are the sea-bird cliffs and pinnacle of Dùn Cruit.

To the north-east of Lunga, across a profusion of rocks and skerries, is **Fladda**, once occupied each summer by a lobster fisherman. On the island of **Cairn na Burgh More** are the remains of a fort believed to have belonged to the Chief of Clan MacDougall, Lord of Lorn, on the site of an older Norse building. It once marked the division between the Nordreys ('northern isles') and the Sudreys ('southern isles') (*see* Isle of Man), and was given up to the Lord of the Isles in 1354. Religious books and records from Iona were said to have been hidden here at the time of the

Staffa: Fingal's Cave is on the far right.

Reformation; when Cromwell took the fort in 1650, the books were lost. In 1715 it was held by the MacLeans of Duart. There are the remains of a small chapel, and the freshwater 'Well of the Half Gallon'.

On **Cairn na Burgh Beg** are the ruins of a smaller fort occupied during the 1715 Jacobite rising.

Cruises around the Treshnish Isles are arranged from Ulva Ferry on Mull. The islands look quite spectacular when viewed from the ruined village of Crackaig on Mull. Permission to land must be obtained from the owner at Treshnish House on Mull.

Staffa

This is a tiny island that is known worldwide. It covers 71 acres, rising to a maximum height of 135 ft, and the name derives from the Norse *stafr-ey* ('pillar' [or 'post'] island'), after the wooden posts the Norse-men set vertically to build their houses. Staffa resulted from the same volcanic activity which formed the Giant's Causeway in Ireland and the Ardmeanach promontory on Mull, six miles to the south-east, and consists of grey-black fine-grained Tertiary basalt surmounted by amorphous lava, the basalt lavas having cooled slowly, resulting in patterns of three breaks radiating from single points equidistant over the surface, relieving the tension evenly. The results are the spect-acular hexagonal columns which gave Staffa its name.

Perhaps more famous than the island itself is Fingal's Cave, a cavern among the pillars at the southern tip, 65-ft high, 50-ft wide and 23-ft deep. Although flooded by the sea, it is possible to walk inside along natural causeways. It may be named after Fionn MacCaul, a legendary Celtic giant who is supposed to have built the Giant's Causeway, and in Gaelic it is known as *An Uamh Binn*, 'the melodious cave' – the sea makes strange noises among the pillars. A musical tribute was made to the cavern by Felix Mendelssohn in his *Hebrides Over-*

ture after he visited Staffa in 1829. From inside the cave, the view south is of Iona, and to the west of the cave is the Great Face or Colonnade, an expanse of columns about 55-ft tall, below which is Boat Cave. The cliff near Fingal's Cave was marked by a mine which exploded in May 1945.

On the west side of Staffa is Port an Fhasgaidh ('shelter bay'), a strange name considering its exposure to the prevailing weather. To the south is MacKinnon's Cave, nearly as grand as Fingal's and connected to Cormorant's Cave by a narrow tunnel. It is traditionally thought to be named after Abbot MacKinnon (died *c.* 1500), Abbot of Iona.

Off the south-east shore is **Am Buachaille** ('the herdsman'), a columnar rock separated from Staffa by 15 ft of water. Opposite the southern end is a peculiar formation known as the 'Wishing Chair'. A little to the north is the usual landing place, Clamshell Cave – its strikingly curved columns give it its name. Little of all this can be seen from the island's grassy summit; a boat affords the best view.

Staffa was, of course, known to the local people, and to the Norse-men, long before it was 'discovered' by the President of the Royal Society, Sir Joseph Banks, on 13 August 1772, while on his way to Iceland. After him followed a stream of visitors, and soon paddle-steamers were bringing hundreds of tourists. Among those who made the trip

Inside Fingal's Cave.

were: Sir Walter Scott in 1810, John Keats in 1818, Mendelssohn in 1829, J. M. W. Turner in 1830, William Wordsworth, Queen Victoria and Prince Albert in 1833, Jules Verne in 1859 (he featured Staffa in his book *The Green Ray* in 1885), Dr David Livingstone in 1864 and Robert Louis Stevenson in 1870. In August 1884 two tourists were drowned in Fingal's Cave. When Banks first came, the island had only one inhabitant, a herdsman living in a rough hut; by 1784 there were 16 people and livestock and in 1788 it was recorded that barley, oats, flax and potatoes were grown near the island's centre. Permanent habitation ceased at the end of the 18th C, although a herdsman continued to come for the summer grazing. In 1800 there were three red deer.

On the shore of Lake Zurich in Switzerland is the town of Stäfa, founded by one of Iona's monks who took memories of this extraordinary little island with him on his journey. Boat trips are run from Ulva Ferry and Croag, on Mull.

Iona

Strathclyde. An island of great Christian importance, Iona is three-and-a-half miles by one-and-a-half miles, lying three-quarters of a mile off the Ross of Mull. It consists of low-lying Torridonian sandstone, with Archaean gneiss on the western side – it is not related geologically to Mull. The highest point is Dùn-I (pronounced 'doon-ee') in the north, rising to 332 ft; there is another small hill in the south, and the valley between these two points is farmed, more so to the east. In the west, Camas Cuil an t-Saimh (the 'bay at the back of the ocean') is backed by

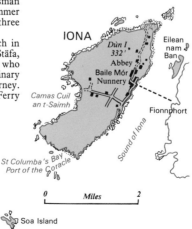

machair, and Iona marble was quarried near Cùl Bhuirg. The southern coast comprises cliffs and bays; the north has sandy beaches and machair. The main area of settlement and ferry terminal is Baile Mór facing Fionnphort, where there are hotels, shops, restaurants and a post office.

The island was used by Druids before the birth of Christ, and was known in Gaelic as *Innis nan Druinich* ('isle of the Druidic hermits'). It was also called *Ioua* and, later, *I-Chaluim-cille* ('island of St Columba'); during the 1500s it was once again known as Ioua, finally to become Iona. St Columba landed here from Ireland in AD 563 to found a monastery, a centre from which the mainland Picts could be converted. St Columba lived on the island for 34 years until his death in AD 597. Under his influence, Iona became the Christian centre of Europe (the *Book of Kells*, now in Dublin, was begun here), but was later destroyed by the Norsemen who raided in the years 795, 801, 806 (killing 68 monks at Martyrs Bay near the jetty), 825 and 986 (when the abbot and 15 monks were massacred at the White Strand).

In 1074 the monastery was rebuilt by St Margaret, Queen of Scotland, for the Roman Catholic order of St Augustine, and it was again rebuilt in 1203 by Reginald of Islay, King of the Isles and Somerled's son, for the Benedictine order. He also built the convent; much of this fine pink granite building remains, covered with grass and wild flowers. In 1430 the Bishopric of the Isles was created, with a seat in Iona, and in 1500 Iona achieved cathedral status. During the Reformation, all the ecclesiastical buildings were dismantled and nearly all the island's 350 crosses were destroyed. Taken by MacLean of Duart in 1574, the island was re-taken by Argyll in 1688. The ruins of the abbey church were gifted to the Church of Scotland in 1899, and were restored by 1910.

The monastic buildings were restored by the Iona Community between 1938 and 1965, and there is currently an appeal to raise £500,000 to preserve the fabric of the buildings. Recently the island, excluding the cathedral area, was bought on behalf of the Scottish nation from the Duke of Argyll by the Fraser Foundation, and now is administered by the National Trust for Scotland.

The Cathedral Church of St Mary is a simple cruciform building with a short tower, built in scale with its surroundings. The 10th-C crosses of St Martin and St John (a replica), both standing near the west door, are beautiful, but no equal to the Kildalton High Cross on Islay;

Baile Mór, Iona.

behind them is the tiny St Columba's shrine. The infirmary museum houses a collection of carved slabs, and along the marble causeway known as the 'Street of the Dead' is St Oran's Chapel. It was recorded in 1549 that 60 kings - 48 Scottish, 4 Irish and 8 Norwegian -were buried in the graveyard, Reilig Odhrain, including Duncan who was murdered by Macbeth. The tombs have long since vanished.

The Iona Community was founded in the 1930s by George MacLeod (now the Very Rev. Lord MacLeod of Fuinary), and was known as the 'Rome Express' by the Scottish Presbyterians. Their work in rebuilding Iona was to make possible 'an experiment in full Christian living'. Today the Community numbers 150, with 600 associate members worldwide. It is especially concerned with what it calls 'industrial evangelism', its members working in industry, depressed city areas and new towns. A summer youth centre is run on the island, accommodating 1000 young people during the course of the year. For the Community, Iona is a place of retreat, regeneration and inspiration.

Each year, 500,000 visitors, mainly day-trippers, come to the island. Most stray no further than the village and the cathedral and, with such an influx to cope with, it is inevitable that this area has a 'touristy' feel. But wander further, and peace and natural beauty can be found.

On the south coast are St Columba's Bay and the Port of the Coracle, where St Columba landed. Along here are beautifully coloured pebbles of green serpentine, and one-and-a-half miles offshore is the low-lying **Soa Island.** South of the village are two fine white shell-sand bays, backed by heather and wild flowers. From the modest summit of Dùn-I may be seen a panorama of the Inner Hebrides and, to the south of this hill below a hillock called Tor Abb in the 'Secluded Hollow', are the foundations of a hermit's cell, traditionally considered to be a spot frequented by St Columba. **Eilean nam Ban**, in the Sound of Iona, is said to be where St Columba sent all the women from Iona during his lifetime.

The island's main income is derived from visitors, but the main source of employment is crofting. On the fine west-coast farmlands, with sandy beaches backed by machair and secluded bays with semi-precious stones, Iona's other, more typically Hebridean, life goes on untouched by the thousands of visitors. The permanent population (excluding the Community) now numbers 100.

Compared objectively with other Hebridean islands, Iona is pleasant but not outstanding. Surrounded by trippers, a spiritual feeling may be elusive, but its importance to Christians can never be diminished.

Iona is reached by Caledonian MacBrayne passenger ferry from Fionnphort, Mull, and there are trips from Oban in the summer.

The Cathedral Church of St Mary, Iona.

Tiree

Strathclyde. The north-east corner of Tiree is 15 miles from Treshnish Point, Mull, and is separated from its island partner, Coll, to the north-east, by the two-mile wide Gunna Sound. It lies as far west as Harris in the Outer Hebrides, and measures a little over ten miles long by about six miles at the widest point, with an

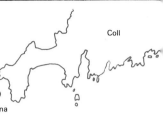

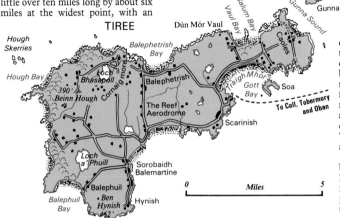

TIREE

area of 19,000 acres. It was called *Tir-lodh* (the 'land of corn'), and was once known as 'the granary of the isles' for, although the bedrock is Archaean gneiss, a poor infertile rock, over two-thirds of it has been deeply covered with wind-blown shell sand, which has blessed the island with fertile, well-drained machair, deep enough for the plough.

The landscape of Tiree is unique among the larger Hebridean islands, being one of houses, not hills. It is flat, for the most part a hairline on the horizon, with only two high points: Ben Hynish in the south rising to 462 ft, and Ben Hough in the north-west rising to 390 ft. Average rainfall is low, about 45–50 inches, and there are more hours of sun in the spring than anywhere else in Scotland, with an average of 223 hours in May. But Tiree's fertile soil was brought by the wind, and there

is no shelter from it – in February 1961 it gusted at 116 mph, a record at the time – and living on Tiree has been likened to 'living on the deck of an aircraft carrier'.

The population peaked at 4450 in 1831; 50 years later it was 2700, following the potato famines and forced evictions. In 1885 there was a revolt against the landowners, when landless families took over a vacated farm and demanded it be turned into crofts. The government sent two ships, the *Ajax* and the *Assistance*, and marines to deal with this disturbance; five men were arrested and imprisoned for a short while, but there was no fighting, and the marines became great friends with the islanders. With the passing of the Crofters' Act in 1886 (*see* Skye) the farms were split into the present 270 or so small crofts, maintaining a higher population (now 870) on the island than if amalgamated and rationalised. Cattle and sheep are grazed on the fertile machair, and crops provide winter fodder. There is a lobster-fishing industry, which has benefited from the building of a pier at Caoles. Trawling ceased due to over-exploitation.

Evidence of occupation on Tiree dates back to 800 BC – pottery and tools uncovered at Dùn Mór Vaul date from this period. A broch was built on the site of this earlier settlement. In AD 565 Batheine, a follower of St Columba, founded a monastery at Sorobaidh. St Columba also visited Tiree; in legend he cursed a rock in Gott Bay to remain 'weedless', after his boat struck it and nearly sank.

The Vikings raided Tiree – they burnt Sorobaidh in AD 672 – then later settled; Norse burials have been found at Cornaigbeg. Control then passed to the Kingdom of Man and the Isles (*see* Isle of Man) and, in 1123, Reginald, son of King Godfrey, ruled the area which included Tiree.

In 1164 upon the death of Somerled, his son Dougall inherited the island (along with Coll and Mull) which he in turn passed on to his son Duncan. After the defeat of the Norwegian force under King Haakon at the Battle of Largs in 1263, control of the isles passed to Alexander III of Scotland who confirmed ownership upon the MacDougalls. The Scottish Wars of Independence brought changes in ownership, with the MacDonalds acquiring Tiree (and Coll), only to return it to the MacDougalls in 1354. Their influence was negligible and, by 1390, Lachlan MacLean was Baillie of Tiree and Coll, his descendants disputing ownership until the 16th C. In 1562 and again in 1578, Tiree was invaded by the MacDonalds of Islay; in the latter part of the 17th C the present owners, the Argylls, took control.

The traditional homes on Tiree were of the 'black house' type (*tigh dubh*), with dry-stone walls up to nine-feet thick, rounded corners and a thatched roof resting on inner walls – all designed so that the gales sweep over them. These have now been converted into 'white houses' (*tigh geal*) with cemented stones, tar and felt roofs and a fireplace at one end, and the outside painted white.

The main pier and ferry terminal, sheltered in most conditions, is in Gott Bay, to the west of the Tràigh Mhór which is a fine beach, the longest in Tiree. Scarinish, the main village behind the old harbour, has a post office, shops and hotel.

At Tiree's flat centre is The Reef an airfield built by the RAF in 194

Balephuil Bay, Tiree.

Towards Balemartine from Hynish, Tiree.

on the site of a grass landing-strip, from where Hudsons, Wellingtons and Liberators flew. With the airfield came good roads and electricity, and it is now used for civil aviation, with a regular daily service from Glasgow operated by Loganair. The weather station here, which reports regularly for the BBC shipping forecasts, is a legacy of the early work done by D. O. MacLean, Head of Cornaigmore School, who started keeping records in 1926.

To the south of Sorobaidh Bay is Balemartine, the largest village, with many 'white houses'. At the end of the road to the south is Hynish, with granite houses built for the workers on the Skerryvore lighthouse, standing ten miles south-west of here, 138 ft from the base to the lantern, on a rock only ten feet above mean high water. It was built in 1838–43 by Alan Stevenson, another uncle of Robert Louis Stevenson, and the 4308 tons of granite used in its construction were quarried on the Ross of Mull. First lit in 1844, it was extensively damaged by fire in 1954, following which new diesel generators were installed. The sea area between the rocks and reefs of the Skerryvore and Tiree can be extremely rough during north-westerly gales. Above the Hynish is a granite tower, once used to signal to the lighthouse.

The pretty white houses of Balephuil stand to the east of a mile of beach backed by flat machair, in the midst of which Loch a' Phuill glistens. Above the village is Ben Hynish, from the summit of which there is a fine view of Skerryvore. On the west coast there are extensive areas of dunes grazed by cattle and sheep, and behind these grow crops of barley and corn.

Off the north-west corner of Tiree there are numerous rocks and skerries. Behind the shell-sand bay of Cornaigmore is Loch Bhasapoll, surrounded by machair, and known for its duck population. On its north side it is said that there was once a township called Baile nan Craganach ('the town of the clumsy ones'); five men each with 12 fingers lived there. The next bay east, Balephetrish Bay, takes its name from *Baile Pheadairich*.

Clacha Choire, the 'ringing stone'.

('the township of the storm petrel'), and is where Tiree marble, pink flecked with green, was quarried between 1791 and 1794 and again briefly in 1910. On the coast is the Clacha Choire, the 'ringing stone', a glacial erratic which originated on Rum, said to contain a crock of gold – but if it is ever split, Tiree will disappear beneath the waves. Such legends were collected by John Gregorson Campbell, minister of Tiree from 1861 to 1891, and published in his *Superstitions of the Scottish Highlands* in 1900.

On the rocky coast to the west of Vaul Bay is Dùn Mór Vaul ('fort of the big wall'), built in the 1st C. On the east of the island, at Caoles, there are attractive outcrops of pink orthogneiss. Across Gunna Sound lies the island of **Gunna**, once inhabited, now grazed by cattle.

Tiree can fairly lay claim to being the 'sunshine island', and in the spring and early summer the extensive machair lands are thick with blossom and heady with perfume. The island's large and robust population imparts a feeling of activity rare in the Western Isles. Good communications and an amenable climate should attract increasing numbers of visitors.

A Caledonian MacBrayne vehicle ferry runs from Oban to Gott Bay – a four-and-a-half hour journey via Coll. It is the only ferry between these two islands. Loganair operate a daily flight (not Sundays) from Glasgow to The Reef airfield and on to Barra. There is a post-bus service.

Coll

Strathclyde. With an area 18,300 acres, Coll measures thirteen-and-a-half by four miles, lying two miles north-east of Tiree and seven-and-a-half miles to the west of Caliach Point, Mull.

The northern two-thirds of the island are Lewisian gneiss, showing itself everywhere, its low hummocks infilled with peat bogs and lochans. The remaining third of Coll, apart from the extreme south-west tip which is also gneiss, consists of very ancient metamorphosised sandstones containing quartz and marble, particularly beautiful by the shore at Gorton. The west coast has a covering of wind-blown shell sand, forming dunes over 100-ft high and machair suitable for grazing. The summit of Ben Hogh (341 ft) is the highest point; on its northern side are two glacial erratics, boulders of gabbro, probably from Mull. There are raised beaches at Arinagour and Arnabost.

The climate, like that of Tiree, is favourable, with many hours of sunshine early in the summer, mild winters and rainfall that is less than 50 inches each year. It is, of course, windy.

The early history of Coll is

closely linked to that of Tiree – Norse settlement followed by the rule of Somerled and then Clan Donald. By 1841, the population had risen to 1440 and the laird, MacLean, given the island by Clan Donald, was unable to support such numbers and, during the next 15 or so years, half the population was cleared to Australia and Canada. In 1856 MacLean sold the island to the Stewarts, and now two-thirds are owned by a Dutch millionaire.

The shock waves of such a drastic solution as clearance continued for many years with further clearances and continued depopulation. The emphasis of agriculture turned to dairy cattle and the production of the famous Coll cheese, with farmers from Kintyre being brought to the island. With this came the virtual demise of Gaelic culture and language on Coll. At the turn of the

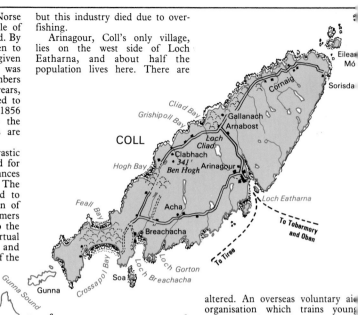

century the market for dairy produce collapsed, and a gradual shift to stock-raising began. Today there are about 1000 beef cattle, a few dairy cattle, and 7000 sheep, and the current population is about 140 people. There is a lobster-fishing industry, the numerous rocks and skerries off the north-east tip providing the breeding grounds. At one time ling were caught and salted,

but this industry died due to over-fishing.

Arinagour, Coll's only village, lies on the west side of Loch Eatharna, and about half the population lives here. There are shops, a church, post office, hotel, school and bicycles for hire. The pier, built in 1967, is a stopping point for the Oban and Tiree ferry. The coast to the north-east, and the land behind, is empty.

The road to Breachacha lies a little less than a mile inland from the south-east coast, which is deeply bayed and attractive. The ancient Breachacha Castle, standing by the shore of the loch, was thought to have been the 14th-C home of the MacLeans, part of the defences of the Lords of the Isles, but recent excavations now suggest 15th-C constructon. It is a good example of such a medieval fortress, little altered. An overseas voluntary aid organisation which trains young people has its headquarters in the fortress, which has been carefully restored.

The newer castle close by was built in 1750 by Hector MacLean and visited by Boswell and Johnson on their tour of the Hebrides in October 1773, being entertained there by Coll's last hereditary piper. Confined to the building by a series of gales, they condemned it as 'a mere tradesman's box'.

After a battle in 1593 between the MacLeans of Coll and the invading Duarts, the burn that flows into Loch Breachacha was choked with Duart heads, and ducks swam in the blood – it is now called *Struthan nan Ceann*, 'the stream of the heads'.

To the west a neck of marram dunes separates Crossapol Bay from the very beautiful Feall Bay to the north. Two miles away, beyond Gunna, lies Tiree – close, but unreachable from here. The west coast is broken into sandy dune-backed bays by low rocky headlands, the valleys between these headlands sheltering the farms. The golden sands of Hogh Bay are fringed with rose- and ochre-coloured gneiss glistening with mica. The tiny Clabhach Bay has white sand, Grishipoll Bay is rocky, Cliad Bay has shell sand. At Arnabost the school, now in ruins, was built over an earth house where the islanders hid during Viking raids; the entrance was beneath the school porch

The coast north of Gallanach Farm, Coll's largest, is one of pretty and secluded coves, the haunt of many seabirds. Cornaig Bay was once the centre of the ling fisheries; it is now an area of prosperous farms intersected with trout streams, and off the north-east tip are rocks and skerries which are fished for

Arinagour, Coll.

Breachacha Castle, Coll.

19th-C farmhouses. An influx of younger people into the farming community has begun to revitalise the island, which has probably never reached its full potential as a rearing ground for cattle and sheep.

Until half a century ago limestone was quarried at An Sailean and shipped to the surrounding islands and mainland, and two quarrymen's cottages and some lime kilns can still be seen on the tiny **Eilean nan Caorach** off the northern tip. Many lime-carrying boats operated from Port Ramsay close by, where there is a sheltered anchorage and attractive rows of neat cottages, now, regrettably, mainly holiday homes. The view from here along Loch Linnhe towards Ben Nevis is superb.

Lismore was the seat of the diocese of Argyll from the 13th C until 1507, the bishops receiving the title *Episcopi Lismorenses*. Incorporated into the tiny parish church are parts of the choir of the original medieval cathedral, and on the west coast, facing **Bernera Island**, are the ruins of the Bishop's Castle, Achadun.

In the 6th C a legendary race for possession of Lismore took place between St Moluag and St Mulhac:

lobster. To the east a lonely dwelling is all that remains of the community of Sorisdale, and between here and Arinagour there is little but wet and rocky moorland, lochs and streams.

Coll is reached by the Caledonian MacBrayne ferry from Oban, which also provides the link with its green and populous neighbour, Tiree.

Lismore

Strathclyde. Covering 10,000 acres, Lismore measures nine-and-a-half miles by one-and-three-quarter miles, and lies in Loch Linnhe to the north of Oban. Its Gaelic name is *Ieis Mor* (the 'great garden'). It is composed of Dalradian limestone, with shallow longitudinal valleys that provide shelter for livestock, and good farming conditions on extremely fertile soil. The highest

point is Barr Mór (416 ft). There is now little natural woodland although, in 1596, the island was reported to have been thickly forested with oak; however, some splendid trees have now been planted around the well cared for

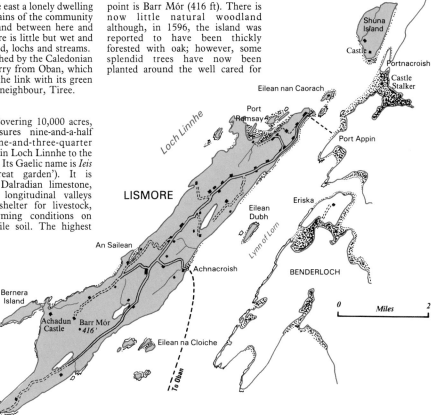

Lismore.

whoever made the first landfall would take possession. It is said that St Moluag, on seeing that his boat would not be first, cut off his finger and threw it ashore, thus securing the title. St Moluag did, however, found a monastery on Lismore between AD 561 and 564. Some 30 years ago the *buchull mor* (pastoral staff) of St Moluag was brought back to the island.

There is one main road running almost the length of the island, and most of the dwellings are sited by it, with the majority in the north; near the centre there is a post office, general store, and a junior school. Much of Lismore is owned by the Duke of Argyll, and is farmed by tenants, the present population numbering 160. There is no mains water, the houses being supplied by springs which are vulnerable should there be a long dry spell. Much of the shoreline is low sea cliffs, with some pleasant shingle beaches, and on the east side, and off the northern tip, there are some small islands, rocks and skerries.

The island of Lismore, as a platform from which to view the surrounding sea and landscape, is unequalled. On the mainland to the north are the mountains of Kingairloch, to the north-east Ben

Nevis, to the east Port Appin, Loch Creran and Benderloch, and to the south and west the islands of the Firth of Lorn, and Mull – surely one of the most stunning settings in the west Highlands.

A Caledonian MacBrayne vehicle ferry operates from Oban to Achnacroish, taking about one hour. A passenger ferry makes a much shorter crossing to the northern tip from Port Appin, where the ferryman lives.

Shuna Island, one-and-a-half miles north-east of Lismore, is owned by a Glasgow industrialist and run as a farm; to the south the substantial ruin of Castle Shuna. To the north-east of Shuna is the small **Eilean Balnagowan**. At the entrance of Loch Creran is the island of **Eriska**, reached via a narrow bridge. The fine turreted Eriska House is now a luxurious 'Highland' hotel.

In Loch Laich, on the tidal 'isle of the falconer', stands the beautiful rectangular **Castle Stalker,** ancient seat of the Stewarts of Appin, built in the 15th C and used by James IV as a hunting lodge. It later fell into ruins, but has recently been restored. It is private.

The lighthouse island of Eilean Musdile, Lismore.

Oban to Kintyre

Kerrera

Strathclyde. Four-and-a-half miles long by two miles wide, Kerrera lies to the west of Oban – a natural breakwater for one of the best harbours on the west coast of Scotland. The island is green and hilly, composed of a mixture of Secondary basalt, graphitic schists and old red sandstone.

The island has belonged to the MacDougalls since the founding of the Clan by Somerled in the 12th C. In 1249 King Alexander II of Scotland, with his fleet, anchored in The Horse Shoe bay, determined to wrest the Hebrides from King Haakon of Norway, but Alexander died quite suddenly, his army dispersed and his body was taken to Melrose. His visit is commemorated in the name of the land behind the bay - *Dalrigh*, 'the field of the King' Later, in 1263, King Haakon rallied his fleet in the bay, *en route* to the Battle of Largs where he was defeated, and the remains of his force once again anchored off Kerrera before travelling home to Norway. King Haakon never completed the journey, being taken ill and dying in Orkney.

Gylen Castle, the ruins of which now stand at the southern end of Kerrera, was built on the site of an earlier fortification in 1587 by Duncan MacDougall of Dunollie the 16th Chief. The building, a handsomely detailed tower standing above the cliffs, was besieged in 1647 by General Leslie during the Covenanting Wars and subsequently burned. It has never been restored.

Kerrera was used for many years as a stepping stone between Mull and the mainland. Cattle were once swum to the mainland from Ardantrive Bay at the north-east tip of Kerrera, where there are a jetty and moorings. The prominent memorial at the north end above the bay commemorates David Hutcheson, one of the founders of what is now Caledonian MacBrayne By 1861 the population of the island was 105, in 1879 a post office was established, and the present schoolhouse and church, over looking the Sound of Kerrera, were built in 1872. The population is now about 50.

In 1910 a lobster-trading business, which became one the largest on the west coast of Scotland was founded in the old slate quarriers' cottages behind The Little Horseshoe, where the lobsters, taken from the storage pond at Cullipool on Luing, are held in floating tanks then packed and despatched from here.

This compact and attractive island is ideal for gentle walks in attractive scenery, having fine views of Mull and Lismore to the west and north. It is easily reached by the small passenger ferry which operates from Gallanachbeg, to the south of Oban.

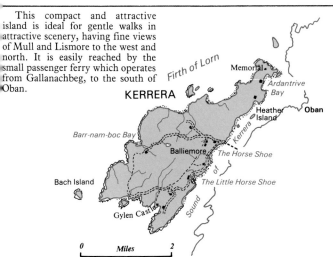

grave before I died'. At the island's centre is a school, a new church, and a ruined water mill, and the population now stands at 200. The view from the west side of the island's modest summit (285 ft), towards the Isles of the Sea and the Ross of Mull, is ample reward for the easy climb. To the east of Toberonochy lies **Shuna**, wooded and grazed by sheep, on which is the castellated Shuna House at the north-west corner, used as a youth adventure centre. To the east of Cuan Sound is the green island of **Torsa**, reached from Luing at low tide, with a farmhouse in the south and a ruined fortress in the north.

Luing is served by both passenger and vehicle ferries which operate from the south of Seil across the swift-flowing waters of Cuan Sound.

Seil

Strathclyde. A 'slate island', Seil has been joined to the mainland since 1792 by Thomas Telford's Clachan Bridge, upon which grows the fairy foxglove, *Erinus alpinus*. The ancient inn by the bridge was used by the Highlanders after the '45 rebellion to change from trousers into the forbidden kilt which could be legally worn only 'overseas'. The remains of disused slate workings can be seen at Balvicar which closed down in 1965, and at Ellanbeich where the sea once flooded one quarry with the loss of 240 lives. The island is farmed, lobsters are fished, and there is now a population of 500.

The island of **Easdale**, reached by a small passenger ferry from Ellanbeich, has workers' cottages around a harbour which can only be entered at very high tides. Most of these dwellings are now holiday homes, and the island, owned by an Englishman, is reminiscent of North Wales. To the south-west is the tiny island of **Belnahua**, itself once a slate quarry, and to the west is the cliff-bound and grassy **Insh Island**, with caves at the northern end. In 1873 a herd of 192 pilot whales were left stranded by the tide in Clachan Sound which separates Seil from the mainland.

Luing

Strathclyde. Pronounced 'ling', this is, like Seil, a 'slate island'. The main village is Cullipool on the west coast, where the quarries which closed down in 1965 once employed 150 men and produced 700,000 slates each year. Slates from here were used to re-roof Iona Cathedral. It is now a lobster-fishing centre, with the lobster pond at Fraoch Eilean being one of Scotland's largest. Luing is also well known for the prize beef cattle bred by the island's owner.

David Hutcheson memorial, Kerrera.

A road runs from the ferry at Cuan Sound to Toberonochy on the east coast. Above the village is the ruined chapel of Kilchattan, surrounded by some magnificent slate gravestones, including that of Alex Campbell, who 'digged my

The Isles of the Sea

Strathclyde. These islands are commonly known as the Garvellachs, deriving from *Garbh Eileach* ('rough isles'). Lying about three miles west of Luing, their

The flooded quarries and old slate workings at Easdale, Seil.

remoteness is made greater by the rocks and reefs of the surrounding seas. The north coasts comprise steep cliffs with sea caves, sloping to the more sheltered south sides, where landings can, with caution, be made.

Eileach an Naoimh (pronounced 'ellan nave') is the most southerly. It has some substantial remains of beehive cells from the original monastery founded by St Brendan in AD 542, 21 years before Iona. Landings are made at Port Columcille, where there is a small shingle beach and a freshwater spring. Nearby are a ruined chapel and burial ground – a stone slab is supposed to mark the grave of Eithne, St Columba's mother, although this is unlikely. This island is thought to have been St Columba's secret retreat, as close to his heart as Iona; it was referred to as Hinba from the Gaelic *Na In Ba* ('isle of the sea').

The small island of **A' Chùli** is reputed to have been St Brendan's resting place. Landings can also be made at Rubha Mór on **Garbh Eileach**, where there is a small burial ground. The northern-most island is **Dùn Chonnuill,** where the ruined 13th-C castle is said to stand on the site of an earlier fortress built in the 1st C by Conal Cearnach, an Irish king.

Lunga

Strathclyde. Lunga is situated to the north of Scarba, separated by the Grey Dog tide-race. The grassy top of the island rises to a height of 321 ft and is grazed by sheep, and the northern extremity breaks into several smaller tidal islands. The graves of some of its past inhabitants can be found in the burial ground of Kilchattan on Luing.

To the west are the low-lying islands of **Eilean Dubh Beag** and **Eilean Dubh Mór**, beyond which rise the mysterious Isles of the Sea. To the north are the tiny lighthouse island of **Fladda**, and **Belnahua,** one of the 'slate islands', with its

deserted quarries and cottages, all grey and windswept. To the east is Luing, across the swift-flowing waters of the sound.

Scarba

Strathclyde. The name derives from the Norse *Skarpoe* ('rough isle') Three miles long by two-and-a-half miles wide it lies to the north of Jura across the Corryvreckan tide-race separated from Lunga, to the north by another tide-race, the Grey Dog Although it is grazed by cattle and

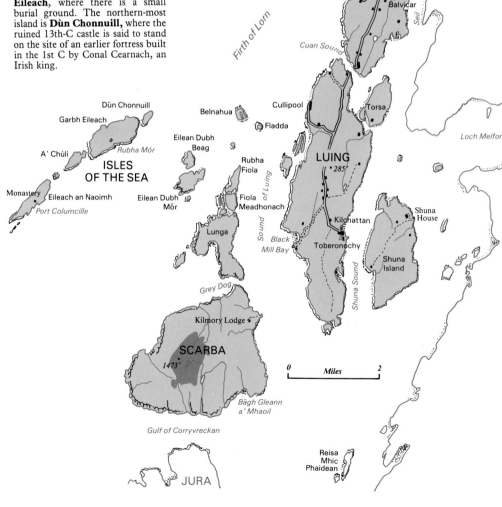

The Isles of the Sea and Belnahua, to the west of Luing.

sheep, the island is basically rough and craggy - graphite schist in the east, and quartzite in the west where it rises to a height of 1473 ft - and the coast is rocky, with many caves.

On the east side, above woodland, is the recently refurbished Kilmory Lodge. Bàgh Cleanh a' Mhaoil in the south has a good beach, but further round to the west are the whirlpools of the Gulf of Corryvreckan.

Jura

Strathclyde. Jura's name comes from the Norse *Dyr Öe* ('deer island'). It has an area 93,700 acres (including Scarba), and is 28 miles long by eight miles wide, lying just half a mile from Islay. As well as a narrow strip of schist along the east coast, Jura has the largest area of metamorphic quartzite - a poor, infertile rock - in the Highlands.

Loch Tarbert almost bisects the island. In the southern half are the Paps of Jura, prominent landmarks for miles around: Beinn a'Chaolais ('mountain of the Sound [of Islay']) rises to 2408 ft, Beinn an Oir ('mountain of the boundary', often called the 'mountain of gold') to 2572 ft, and Beinn Shiantaidh ('holy mountain') to 2477 ft. The slopes are barren and scree-covered, but the views from the top are splendid - on a clear day Ireland and the Isle of Man are visible. To the north-west of Beinn an Oir is a large rock scar called Sgriob na Caillich, the 'witches' scrape'. The majority of the island is trackless blanket bog, with about 5000 red deer, some wild goats and, of course, birds. It is extremely difficult country to cross, and is totally uninhabited.

Along the west coast are raised beaches, long stretches of white stones among the grass and heather, formed when the sea level was higher. Notable are those at Bàgh Gleann Righ Mór, Rubh' an t-Sàilen and Shian. There are many caves, used for shelter by both the deer and their hunters, as sheep folds and, in the past, by the islanders transporting their dead to Iona and Oronsay. Rudimentary altars were built in some.

A large cave about 180-ft deep, at the northern end of Jura in Bàgh Gleann nam Muc, overlooking the Gulf of Corryvreckan, is said to be the burial place of a Norwegian prince named Breacan, whose galley was consumed by the treacherous waters between here and Scarba. This tide-race runs west on the flood and east on the ebb at speeds of up to 10 knots (11.5 mph). A pinnacle of rock rising from the sea bed causes violent overfalls and breakers, with whirlpools on the Scarba side. Spring tides, and a westerly blowing against the flood, results in the maelstrom that can be heard many miles away. There is only a short period of slack water, when craft will sometimes pass through, travelling from west to east and hugging the Jura shore. The gulf is presided over by the legendary 'Caillich', an old woman who decides which ships shall sink and which shall survive, and indeed there have been terrible disasters and some remarkable escapes. St Columba is said to have navigated it in full flood, calming the waters 'with words alone'.

The island of Jura was owned by the Clan Donald before being sold to the Campbells of Argyll in 1607, who later sold it in 1938. During the 18th C and early 19th C it was a centre for breeding Highland cattle, and the population rose to over 1300 in the 1840s. The glens were, at this time, green with grass. There then followed the widespread introduction of sheep, the despoliation of good land and mass emigration. Farming and crofting are now the main means of employment, with beef cattle and sheep being kept, but the major part of the island is used for sporting activities and is owned by five landlords.

All Jura's 250 inhabitants live on the east coast, and the main centre of population is at Craighouse, in the south of Small Isles Bay. There is a post office, shop, hotel, school, doctor and distillery - a new building, replacing the original built in the mid-19th C by the Campbells, which opened in 1963, with the product, a malt whisky, first being bottled in 1974. One of the two piers was built in 1814 by Thomas Telford, and in Craighouse churchyard a stone commemorates Gillouir MacCrain, who saw '180 Christmasses' before dying in 1645. To the north of Craighouse, Loch na Mile has a fine beach, and two-and-a-half miles offshore is the Skervuile Lighthouse. At the southern end of the island, Jura House stands among woods and rhododendrons. On the small island of **Am Fraoch Eilean** ('heather isle'), lying to the south-west, are the ruins of Caisteal Claidh ('castle of the trench') built on the square Norman plan about 1154 by Somerled to defend the Sound of Islay.

Jura's only road finishes at Inverlussa, passing through areas of moorland and patches of attractive woodland above the mainly rocky shoreline, although at Tarbert there

The Paps of Jura, surrounded by barren peat moor.

is a fine sheltered beach. In the graveyard at Inverlussa lies Mary MacCrain, another member of a family noted for its longevity; she died in 1856, aged 126. A track continues towards the north of the island, passing close to Barnhill, the white farmhouse where George Orwell wrote *Animal Farm*.

Jura stands in complete contrast to the fertile land of its well-endowed neighbour, Islay, but it is blessed with a sheltered position and a mild climate - palm trees and fuschias grow in the open. It is unlikely that it will ever be much more than trackless moor and mountain, but its rugged beauty will continue to tempt visitors on to the small vehicle ferry which plies between Port Askaig and Feolin Ferry.

Islay

Strathclyde. Islay (pronounced 'i-la'), the 'green isle', measures 25 miles north to south and 20 miles east to west, and has an area of 150,500 acres. It lies 14 miles west of Kintyre, and a mile south-west of its close neighbour, Jura.

The geology of Islay is quite complex and, as a consequence, the landscape is varied. The southern end of the Rinns of Islay peninsula is Archaean gneiss with patches of hornblende, typically rough treeless grassland with rock outcrops. The northern part of the Rinns, around the head of Loch Indaal to Bowmore, is calcareous Torridonian sandstone with deposits of good loam; this is the agricultural heart of the island. The northern tip is Cambrian quartzite with belts of Dalradian limestone running through it, and from Port Askaig to the Mull of Oa (pronounced 'o') there is a strip of mica schist intersected with limestone. To the south-east of this is the mountainous belt of Dalradian quartzite - a continuation of the rocks of Jura also containing similarly barren sporting estates. On the extreme south-east coast, between Port Ellen and Ardtalla, there is a fringe of mica schist and hornblende, giving a beautifully broken coastline of bays and islands, backed by areas of woodland and scrub.

Coasts exposed to the west have benefited from deposits of wind-blown shell and the machair grassland this promotes. There are also extensive deposits of peat, used both as domestic fuel and for preparing malt in the island's eight whisky distilleries. It is also worth noting that Islay has some mineral potential; indeed, lead and silver were mined in the 19th C to the west of Port Askaig, and copper and manganese are both known to be present.

The tidal range on the east coasts of Islay and Jura is less than anywhere else in the British Isles. The spring range rarely exceeds five feet and may be as little as two. At neap tides the sea level seems to remain constant for days. The climate of Islay is typically oceanic. There is little shelter from the weather, and Loch Indaal tends to funnel the prevailing winds right to the centre.

There are prehistoric remains scattered all over the island, and written records are available for Islay from an earlier time than any other Hebridean island. The Irish came in the 3rd C, and St Columba is said to have founded a chapel at Kilchiaran on the west of the Rinns.

On two islets in Loch Finlaggan to the south-west of Port Askaig there once stood castles from which the Lord of the Isles ruled the

Port Ellen, Islay.

Hebrides, but there is now little left to be seen, and the land is private. John, first Lord of the Isles, erected the beautiful 14th-C Celtic cross in the churchyard at Kilchoman (the 'cell of Comman', long since vanished) in the west in memory of his second wife, Margaret. It is eight-feet high, slim and elegant. At the base is a wishing stone, to be turned by expectant mothers who wish to have a son; the hollow in which it rests has been worn deep. To the north-west the foundations of the summer palace of the Lord of the Isles have been discovered, and it is said that the famous Skye piping family, the McCrimmons, derived their art from the magic black chanter (part of a bagpipe) obtained on Islay.

The main industries are farming, distilling, tourism and fishing.

about 180 years ago, with many distilleries being built on the sites of old stills. For a period there was no duty payable on whisky produced and consumed on Islay, and drunkenness was rife, the standard of husbandry went into a decline and the ministers complained. There are now eight distilleries left, each employing about 20 people and making spirits with strong and distinctive flavours. A total of four

There are about 500 farms, and nearly all the farmers are the tenants of large estates. Sheep and beef and dairy cattle are kept – a mellow cheese is produced from surplus milk at the Port Charlotte Creamery, established in 1939. Barley was once grown for the distillers, but this raw material is now imported. The island's modest fishing fleet takes mostly shellfish, processed on the island.

On Islay, and throughout the Highlands, whisky was once distilled illicitly. Legitimate distilling began

million proof gallons are produced each year, of which 75 per cent is exported. The remaining 25 per cent, consumed in the British home market, results in the Exchequer receiving almost £7000 duty each year for every man, woman and child on the island. The distilleries are: Ardbeg, established on a site used by smugglers in 1815, producing a malt mostly used in blends; Bowmore, established in 1779 and the oldest legal distillery on Islay, producing malt; Bruichladdich, established 1881, producing malt; Bunnahab-

hainn, established in 1881, used in blends; Caol Ila, established in 1846, mostly blended; Lagavulin, built in the early 19th C on the site of an illegal still, producing malt; Laphroaig, established in 1820, producing a strong peaty malt, also used to blend Islay Mist, a milder flavour; Port Ellen, established in 1825, closed 1930 and re-opened in 1965 – it also provides malt for some of the island's other distilleries.

The Laphroaig distillery, Islay.

Bowmore, Islay, dominated by the church of Kilarrow.

The 'capital' of Islay is Bowmore, near the head of Loch Indaal, with a population of about 900. It is dominated by the unusual round church of Kilarrow, built that way in 1769 by the Campbells of Shawfield so that there would be no corners in which the devil could hide. A pleasant wide street of shops and bars leads downhill to the small harbour. Islay's administrative centre, Bowmore has a school for over 500 children, a police station, hospital, hotels and tourist office.

To the north, at the head of the loch, is Bridgend, where a private road to Islay House crosses the main road. There are woods, and the area is covered with flowers in the spring and summer – daffodil, bluebell, celandine, primrose and wild hyacinth. On a hill nearby stands a memorial to John F. Campbell, collector of Islay folklore.

The main road passes some pleasant beaches, a distillery and a small lighthouse before reaching Port Charlotte, a pretty village of neat pastel-painted houses, known as the 'Queen of the Rinns', where there is also a museum and a small pier.

At the exposed western tip of the Rinns of Islay are Port Wemyss and Portnahaven, separated by a burn and sheltered by two islands, the larger of which, **Orsay**, has a ruined chapel and a lighthouse. The west coast of the Rinns is rocky with some fine sandy bays, namely Lossit, Machir and Saligo. To the north of Saligo there are dramatic steep cliffs, and behind the bay is Loch Gorm, with the stump of a ruined castle on an islet, the largest expanse of water on Islay, where every winter there are enormous numbers of geese – barnacle (as many as 8000), greylag and Greenland white-fronted.

To the west of Loch Gruinart the land undulates towards the sand and machair of Ardnave Point, with low-lying **Nave Island** off the tip. Many fine stone farmhouses around here have been allowed to fall into ruin. At the head of the long sandy Loch Gruinart, a bloody battle was fought on 5 August 1598 between Sir Lochlan Mor MacLean of Duart and Sir James MacDonald of Islay, owing to a dispute over the ownership of land. It is said that the MacDonalds of Islay won with the magical help of *Du-sith*, the 'black elf'. The remains of Kilnave Chapel with its 8th-C cross, lying on the shore of the loch about two miles south of Ardnave Point, is where, after the battle, the MacDonalds burned to death 30 of the MacLeans of Duart, mistakenly believing they had killed their leader, Sir James. To the south of Loch Gruinart are extensive deposits of peat.

The area to the north of Ballygrant (on the road to Port Askaig), where limestone is quarried, is a hilly wilderness, the haunt of sportsmen: there are herds of deer, many pheasants, and lochs well stocked with trout. On either side of Rubha a'Mhail, the northern-most tip of Islay, there are raised beaches.

Port Askaig is one of the terminals used by the Caledonian MacBrayne ferry from Kennacraig. A small 'landing craft'-type ferry plies across the swift-flowing Sound of Islay to Jura. There are a few houses, a store, an attractive hotel (dating from the 16th C) and a lifeboat station, all overlooked by Dunlossit House. To the north are two distilleries, to the south the coast is rocky with small bays, a haven for sea birds and seals. There is no road until Ardtalla. The lighthouse at McArthur's Head marks the southern entrance to the Sound of Islay.

To the west of the trackless mountains of Islay is the six-mile shell-sand beach of Laggan, backed by dunes and machair, with a golf course at the southern end. To the south-east is Port Ellen, a simple workman-like village and Islay's other ferry terminal, the largest centre of population, built 100 years ago, with shops, a bank and hotels. To the west of Port Ellen, Kilnaughton Bay has a fine beach. The point of Carraig Fhada is guarded by a curious white light tower built in 1832 and dedicated to Lady Eleanor Campbell. The Oa peninsula, the most southerly part of Islay, has a rock and cliff coastline with many caves, once the scene of illicit distilling and smuggling. At the Mull of Oa, above sheer cliffs with views of Antrim and Rathlin Island, stands the American Memorial, built by the American Red Cross to commemorate U.S. servicemen lost when the *Tuscania* was torpedoed in February 1918 and the *Otranto* was wrecked in a gale in October 1918. Many bodies were washed ashore here.

To the east of Port Ellen the road heads north-east to Ardtalla, through one of the most attractive and interesting parts of the island, with white-painted and tidily kept distilleries of Laphroaig, Lagavulin and Ardbeg standing by the shore. To the south of Laphroaig is the small island of **Texa**, a rocky hump with a ruined chapel, a ruined cottage and two wells. Somerled anchored his fleet in Lagavulin Bay in the 12th C. To the east stands the fine ruin of Dunyveg Castle, built into the rock in the 13th C by Donald I and at one time a stronghold of the Lord of the Isles. The magical Loch a' Chnuic is overlooked by Kildalton Castle, standing in woodland, once owned by John Ramsay MP, who carried out forced evictions in the 19th C, and for his trouble received a curse

The Mull of Oa, Islay.

from an old woman bound for America. Whether or not as a result of this, he and his wife both died prematurely, and his estate attracted bad fortune.

Kildalton High Cross, Islay.

Two miles further north, by a ruined chapel, stands Kildalton High Cross, possibly the finest in the Hebrides. It dates from about AD 800 and was carved in local blue stone by a sculptor from Iona. On one side is the Virgin and Child, and David and the Lion; on the other are carved animals and bosses.

Between Aros Bay and the superb sand and shingle Claggain Bay is Trudernish Point, upon which stands a vitrified *dùn* ('fort'). Inland, and to the north-west of Ardtalla, a scrubby woodland gives way to barren private sporting estates, where herds of deer roam and where there are many pheasants and lochs full of trout. With such a variety of habitat, and so much land left wild, it is not surprising that Islay has the richest bird life in the Hebrides, with over 180 different species having been recorded – an ornithologist's paradise.

Islay's population peaked at nearly 15,000 in 1831; it is now 4000. There are few job opportunities and many young men go to sea – Islay has been called 'a nursery of sea captains'. Many of the farms have been taken over by Lowlanders and Gaelic culture has declined; although Gaelic is taught in the schools and spoken by the older folk, English still predominates. Islay has great agricultural potential, never fully realised, but Islaymen still believe that their island is the 'Queen of the Hebrides'.

The island is served by the large Caledonian MacBrayne vehicle ferry which operates from Kennacraig to Port Askaig and Port Ellen. Western

Ferries run a small vehicle ferry from Kennacraig to Port Askaig. Loganair fly to Islay from Glasgow. There is a bus service on the island.

Colonsay and Oronsay

Strathclyde. With a joint population of 130, these two islands, joined by sand passable at low tide, cover 11,075 acres, and are 10½ miles long by 3¾ miles wide, lying a little over eight miles to the west of Jura. They have been inhabited for 7000 years: neolithic flint tools and the bones of domesticated animals were found in Uamh Uir (the 'cave of the grave') on the south side of Kiloran Bay. In the dunes a Viking ship burial was uncovered, the warrior having been buried along with his weapons, horse and coins dated AD 831-854.

The name Colonsay probably derives from *Chaileiney* ('Colin's island'). The land is lower mudstone strata of Torridonian sandstone containing lime, and breaks down into

good soil. There are some basalt dykes, and much of the higher ground is broken moorland and scrub inhabited by shaggy wild goats. There are raised beaches on the west coast (fine examples are seen to the north of Kiloran Bay behind Port Sgibinis), evidence of a time when the sea level was higher, and Colonsay was in fact four islands. There are also beaches backed by machair on the west – the Tràigh Bàn, Kiloran, and Plaide Mhór are particularly notable. The valley by Rubh' a' Geodha in the north is dune-filled – a rabbit warren culminating in a beautiful beach facing east.

To the west of Kiloran village, the coast around Pig's Paradise (where pigs were once kept) is all craggy high cliffs cut by deep ravines – a superb place from which to view Mull, Iona, the Torran Rocks and Dubh Artach lighthouse. The highest point is Carnan Eoin (the

Crofts at Kilchattan, Colonsay.

Oronsay priory and farm: in the distance is Eilean nan Ron.

'hill of the birds'), rising to 470 ft to the north-east of Kiloran Bay. The Piper's Cave, on the coast beneath Beinn Bhreac, is the cavern where, in legend, a piper went in search of hell. He was never seen again, but his dog appeared from another cave four miles south, with all his hair singed off.

The first known owners of Colonsay were the MacPhees, followed by the Campbells of Argyll, and in 1701 it was purchased by Malcolm McNeil of Knapdale. In legend the McNeils of Colonsay are descended from a family that, with their cattle, came across from Barra in an open boat. McNeil's wife gave birth on the trip, one of the beasts being slaughtered and the mother and child placed inside the carcass for warmth and shelter. Malcolm McNeil built Colonsay House in 1722, using stones taken from Kiloran Abbey.

In the 19th C the McNeils planted many trees in Kiloran Valley, which provided shelter for the fine gardens developed by Lord Strathcona, who bought the islands in 1904, planting rhododendrons, azalea, eucalyptus, acacia, maple and magnolia. The woods have elm, ash, beech, sycamore, spruce, larch, silver fir and pine. Palm trees and bamboo grow in the open, sheltered by the gentle valley which creates a mild micro-climate. Lord Strathcona took a great interest in the island and its people, stemming depopulation and giving stable management that ensured long-term prosperity. Colonsay House is now converted, for the most part, into holiday flats, and the gardens are a pale shadow of their former glory – the woodlands are unkempt and the azaleas are gone, killed by disease; the kitchen garden is overgrown and the greenhouse is collapsing. The present Lord Strathcona is apparently less concerned than his predecessor, and rarely visits.

The economy of Colonsay is based on crofting and farming with a little fishing, supplemented by a limited amount of tourism. Milk and butter are produced for home consumption. There is a hotel, some summer cottages and bed-and-breakfast accommodation. For the peak holiday period, it all is usually fully booked.

The ferry terminal is at Scalasaig, the main village, where the pier was built in 1965. There is a post office/store, petrol pump and resident doctor here as well as the hotel. The other areas of population are Kilchattan in the west, and Kiloran. Electricity is diesel-generated on the island, and sold at a very high price; some crofters find it less expensive to run their own generators. The island has its own junior school, and there is a minister, but no police. Gaelic is the predominant language.

To the east of the bays of Tobar Fuar ('cold well') and Port Lobh (apparently 'Port Stink', from the rotting seaweed, but definitely not always so), there is a simple 18-hole golf course. The large central Loch Fada and many coastal locations provide excellent birdwatching, and there is much fine walking. Off the west coast of the grassy Ardskenish peninsula, there is a small colony of seals among the skerries.

The island of Oronsay is reached across The Strand, a wide expanse of dull shell sand which is dried out about three hours either side of low water – it is advisable, however, to seek local advice before making the crossing. Halfway, in the sand, can be found the 'sanctuary cross' – a fugitive fleeing from Colonsay was rendered immune from punishment when he reached the cross, provided he remained on Oronsay for a year and a day.

The name 'Oronsay' derives from that of St Oran, a disciple of St Columba, who came here from Ireland in AD 563. It is said that, when St Columba found he could still see his homeland from here, he moved on to Iona; as Ireland can also be seen from Iona, we must presume he did not bother to look again. He did, however, found a monastery on Oronsay, and the present ruined Augustinian priory is thought to have been built on the same site in 1380. The buildings are very fine, rivalling those on Iona, although on Oronsay farm buildings are uncomfortably close. In the chapel there is a high altar, in which are kept human remains which have surfaced in the graveyard nearby. Outside stands a Celtic cross, 12-ft high and of considerable beauty, and in a roofed building alongside the chapel are slab-shaped tombstones, carved with knights and various other figures.

Celtic cross, Oronsay.

Oronsay Farm was built by the McNeils using stones taken from the priory. The island, run as one farm, was sold by Lord Strathcona (who kept Colonsay) to Andrew McNeil, who has in turn sold it to a businessman.

The highest point is Beinn Oronsay (305 ft), from which there are excellent views, including, of course, Ireland. There are two good beaches on the west coast, and rocks and skerries to the south. On **Eilean nan Ron** ('seal island') there was once a kelp-gatherer's cottage, and there is still a colony of grey seals.

The Oronsay community is well balanced, and the island appears well tended. Those who wish to find peace in beautiful and unspoiled surroundings should seriously consider a visit.

A vehicle ferry, operated by Caledonian MacBrayne, runs from Oban. The tourist office for these islands is at The Pier, Campbeltown, Argyllshire, and you can ask at the hotel on Oronsay for information about golf, boat trips and the island's antiquities. There is a post bus.

There are about 20 small islands and skerries in and around Loch Craignish, some covered in scrub forest and grassland and used for grazing. The largest, **Eilean Righ**, has a small jetty, and the remains of three forts, and one of the smallest, **Eilean na Nighinn**, also has a fort, strategically placed to defend the anchorage. **Eilean Mhic Chrion** provides shelter for the yachting centre at Ardfern. On the west of Craignish Point is the old Jura ferry pier, beyond Craignish Castle, and to the south is Loch Crinan and the entrance to the Crinan Canal, a good spot for watching boats.

In Loch Sween, and to the west of Kilmory there are many small low-lying islands. The most remote of these is **Eilean Mór**, the retreat of St Abban mac ui Charmaig (died AD 640) who founded a monastery at Keills on the mainland. On the island is a medieval chapel, once used as an ale house, built around an older building; it was visited by John Paul Jones during the American War of Independence. There is a standing cross close by, and a replica of another to the south on higher ground, and there is also a small sanctuary cave.

It may be possible to hire a boat to the island from Keills, Castle Sween, Crinan, Ardfern or Ormsary.

Gigha Island

Strathclyde. 'Gigha' is pronounced 'gee-ah' with a hard 'g'. Although it has been suggested the name may derive from the Norse *Gjedöe* ('goat island'), a more apt and descriptive alternative is *Gud-ey* – 'good island' or 'God's island' – for what appears barren and rocky at a distance is a fertile and productive island with much good grazing (900 acres of arable land out of a total of 3600 acres) and a mild climate.

A ridge of epidiorite runs the length of Gigha, and the surrounding land is lime-free sandy loam, which is best on the east. The highest point is 331 ft, at the summit of Creag Bhan, and there are some fine sandy beaches.

The island is divided into about a dozen farms and half a dozen crofts. A large stock of Ayrshires produce over 250,000 gallons of milk a year, and Gigha cheese is made at the Achamore creamery. There are also some beef cattle and sheep, but there is no longer a commercial fishing industry.

The island was purchased in 1944 by the late Sir James Horlick (maker of the well-known beverage), who modernised the farms and converted 50 acres of woodland into the supremely beautiful and well-tended Achamore Gardens, transplanting many specimens from his garden near Ascot. Rare plants from Achamore are now being propagated and planted at Brodick, Arran.

There are, among varied deciduous woodland, laburnum, *Primula candelabra*, azalea, hybrid rhododendron and various sub-tropical plants including palms and palm lilies (*Cordyline australis*). The gardens were gifted to the National Trust for Scotland in 1962 and are open during the summer.

The main area of population (which totals 190), the only village and the ferry terminal is Ardminish. Here there is a shop, post office (where bicycles can be hired and Gigha cheese bought) and an attractive hotel. The church has a stained-glass window dedicated to Kenneth MacLeod (born on Eigg in 1872), translator and composer of songs, including 'The Road to the Isles'. South of the village is the ancient chapel of Kilchattan, with an ogham stone nearby.

Over 70 species of birds have been recorded on Gigha; **Eun Eilean**, off the west coast, is noted for its sea birds and there is gullery on Eilean Garbh, to the north. None of the usual mammals exists on Gigha – deer, stoat, weasel, mole, fox and hare have never established themselves, and the rabbits were almost completely killed off by myxomatosis. Grey seals play off the rocky shores and around the numerous outlying reefs and skerries, and wild flowers bloom everywhere. The Gaelic-speaking community is well balanced with a high proportion of young people –testimony to the far-sightedness of Sir James Horlick. Gigha is a rare mixture of stability, viability and beauty. It should not be missed.

Passenger and vehicle ferries to the island run from Tayinloan, Kintyre.

To the south of Gigha is barren **Cara Island** (from the Norse *Karoe*, 'coffin island'), uninhabited for over 30 years. On it are an empty house and a ruined 15th-C chapel; it is grazed by sheep and goats, and there are also otters.

Sanda Island

Two miles off the south-east tip of Kintyre, this is a group of islands and skerries, including the small Sheep Island. Sanda consists of old red sandstone rising to a height of 405 ft, and was farmed until 1946. On it are the remains of the 'Bloody Castle' and a chapel dedicated to St Ninian. It was much visited by the Vikings; in the burial ground is an old Norse grave. On the most southerly point is a lighthouse.

Achamore House, Gigha.

Sheep Island and the tiny **Glunimore Island** are the most important breeding stations in the Clyde area for the puffin.

In 1946 the lifeboatmen of Campbeltown made a remarkable rescue off Sanda, using the reserve boat *The Duke of Connaught*. Over a period of 18 hours, in terrible conditions, 54 passengers and crew and a dog were rescued from the 7000-ton *Byron Darnton*. The ship broke in two just as the lifeboat pulled clear and, despite engine trouble, returned safely.

Island Davaar

Sheltering Campbeltown Loch, this tidal island is linked to the mainland by a shingle causeway, treacherous when covered by the tide. On the northern tip of the island is a lighthouse, and on the southern side, in the fifth of the seven caves, is a wall painting of Christ crucified, executed in secret in 1887 by local artist Alexander Mac-Kinnon, which caused a sensation when first 'discovered'. MacKinnon was 33 when he painted the picture – he returned in 1934, aged 80, to retouch it. It is now a tourist attraction.

The Clyde Islands

Island of Arran

Strathclyde. The Island of Arran covers 105,600 acres, and is 20 miles long by 11 miles wide, lying three miles east of Kintyre in the Firth of Clyde. The name means 'high island'.

Arran was described by Sir Archibald Geike, the eminent geologist, as 'a complete synopsis of Scottish geology'. James Hutton, the 18th-C geologist, confirmed his theories of igneous geology on the island, and today Arran is visited regularly by scores of students who come to study the various rock formations. The island's most striking feature is the high spiky peaks and corries of Goat Fell (2867 ft), an igneous intrusion into the surrounding Devonian sandstones and schists. This has resulted in a ring of upturned strata around the granite.

The south of Arran is new red sandstone, and in the north-east there is an area of carboniferous limestone. Throughout there are basaltic dykes, which form ridges where the surrounding rock is softer (in the south), and fissures where the surrounding rock is harder (in the granite). Ice Age glaciers deposited many erratics, and spread boulders of northern granite all over the south. A raised beach at the 25-ft

level is easily recognised, virtually encircling the island.

Climate is mild Atlantic, with the low hills of Kintyre providing little shelter. Average rainfall varies from 50 inches in the west to 100 inches in the mountains, with the east receiving 70 inches. Snow generally lies only on the mountains, and frosts are rarely severe, and palm lilies, a sub-tropical native of New Zealand, grow in the open in the south and west.

Beef and dairy cattle and blackface and Cheviot sheep are kept, and potatoes are grown, but Arran's main industry is tourism. There is plenty of accommodation, and much to see and do in a relatively small area.

The history of Arran has much in common with the Hebrides. There are cairns, standing stones are to be found all around the coast and in the glens, and Bronze Age cists (burial chambers) have been found inside a stone circle on Machrie Moor. By 200 BC the Celtic people had arrived. Kilpatrick is thought by some to be one of the earliest Celtic Christian sites in Scotland, visited in AD 545 by St Brendan; it was probably sacked by the Vikings in 797. St Mo Las (born AD 566) came to nearby Holy Island during the 7th C; it was later called Eilean Molaise after him, then becoming Lamlash, its name until 1830 and now the name of the village on Arran facing Holy Island.

Viking raids were followed by settlement. The Norsemen separated the island from the kingdom of Dalriada and held it until Somerled took it in 1156. After the Battle of Largs in 1263 the islands became part of the Kingdom of Scotland, under the Lord of the Isles.

In 1503 the island was awarded to the Hamiltons by Royal Charter. The Jacobite rebellion of 1745 hardly touched Arran at all, but the Highland clearances which followed caused massive emigration and the desertion of villages and crofts. The introduction of large-scale sheep farming which brought quick profits to the landlords eventually laid waste to large areas. As land was enclosed for sheep, the people moved to small coastal holdings; when these were exhausted, they left for the industrial centres or the New World. Gaelic life and culture on Arran suffered a blow from which it was never to recover. Between 1821 and 1881 the population fell from 6600 to 4750; it currently stands at 3450. Arran is now owned by the family of the Duchess of Montrose, jointly with the National Trust for Scotland, and the Forestry Commission who hold between them 22,500 acres.

There are at present about 2000 red deer roaming wild, but at the end of the 18th C the herds had been hunted almost to extinction. Wild goats, once common, are now found only on Holy Island. There are no foxes, grey squirrels, stoats, weasels or moles, badgers are rare and adders are no longer as common as they

Brodick Castle, Arran.

were. All characteristic moorland birds are represented, and golden eagles are seen in the high peaks.

Most types of deciduous trees are present, and there are two protected species unique to the island, rare whitebeams – *Sorbus arranensis* and *Sorbus pseudo-fennica*. Among the expected species of plants to be seen are some less common varieties – alpine lady's mantle grows in Glen Sannox, and alpine enchanter's-nightshade is sometimes found in areas of deep shade.

The great majority of Arran's thousands of visitors arrive at Brodick, the 'capital' to the south of the bay, which has all main services and a new Tourist Information office near the pier. The village is unremarkable but its central position makes it an ideal touring centre. To the north of the bay is Brodick Castle and grounds, with Goat Fell behind, the summit of which can be reached after a pleasurable stiff walk. The castle and the mountain are both owned by the National Trust for Scotland. Although part of the castle, the Round Tower, dates from

the early 15th C, the vast majority owes its existence to the Hamiltons, who began building on to the earlier structure in 1558. In 1652 Cromwell's forces (later massacred by the islanders at Corrie) built the Battery and an additional wing. The final additions, including the Great West Tower, were started in 1844 by the architect Gillespie Graham, who was commissioned by William, son of the tenth Duke and his new wife, Princess Mary of Baden, a great-niece of the Empress Josephine. When the direct line of the Hamiltons finished in 1895 Brodick passed to the Duchess of Montrose.

The castle has an elegant simplicity, a fine example of the indigenous Scottish baronial style which belies the richness of its interiors. The drawing room is furnished with Italian marquetry and French gilt and ormolu pieces, and has a rich plaster ceiling. Other rooms contain Hamilton treasures, paintings by Watteau and Turner, and the Hamilton collection of sporting pictures, including works

by Rowlandson, Pollard and Reinagle. The Victorian kitchen has been recently restored. The informal woodland garden of 60 acres, rich with rhododendrons, was started in 1923; the walled garden dates from 1710, now containing an area devoted to specimens from the late Sir James Horlick's garden at Achamore, Gigha. Brodick Castle and gardens are open from Easter until late September, and over 30,000 visitors come during that period.

To the north of Brodick is Corrie, a village of gaily painted cottages around two tiny harbours. Stone used in the construction of the Crinan Canal was quarried in the hills behind. The road follows the coast to Sannox Bay, then turns north-west through North Glen Sannox and Glen Chalmadale to Lochranza. At the mouth of Glen Sannox are the remains of the old barytes mines, last worked in 1938, and there is a fine walk up the Glen beneath Cir Mhór on up to the high peaks.

At the northern end of Arran is an area of wild moorland, the haunt of red deer, and a dramatic stretch of coastline, with great rockfalls dating from the mesozoic and palaeozoic periods. The large sandstone outcrop at the northern-most point is the Cock of Arran.

Lochranza is Arran's other ferry terminal, connecting with Claonaig, Kintyre. The village and youth hostel sit comfortably to the south of the loch, dominated by the ruined tower of Lochranza Castle, standing on a shingle spit. The existing building dates from the 16th C, with fragments of an earlier fortification, first recorded by Fordun in the late 14th C. In the early 15th C it was held by John de Mentieth; by 1450 it had been granted to Alexander Lord Montgomery by James II of Scotland. A key is available for those who wish to enter. The village was once a herring port, the anchorage well sheltered by the enveloping hills.

The west coast offers fine views of Kintyre across Kilbrannan Sound, and the shoreline is also extremely attractive – bright pebbles with the occasional sandy beach. At Catacol (from the Norse for 'ravine of the wild cat') are the 'Twelve Apostles', a pretty terrace of identical cottages overlooking the bay at the mouth of a steep-sided glen. At the summit of Glen Catacol, beneath the wild hills around Beinn Bhreac (2332 ft), is Loch Tanna, the largest loch on the island. On the coast to the west of the mountains is Pirnmill, where pirns (bobbins) were once made; there is a fine beach here. Past the palms of Whitefarland and Imachar, Iorsa Water empties into the sea by Dougarie Lodge, built by the Hamiltons and where Arran's first telephone was installed

The Drawing Room, Brodick Castle, Arran.

in 1891. The terraces of glacial material below the lodge are of great geological interest. Iorsa and Machrie Waters both contain salmon and trout, the island's most expensive fishing.

At Machrie Moor the hills retreat and evidence of the distant past is profuse. A stone circle above the road at Auchagallon, standing stones and circles on the moor, and remains of burial chambers, all can be clearly seen. A large cairn at Blackwaterfoot, spoiled during the 19th C, contained relics, including a dagger, which suggest a connection with the culture of southern England that conceived Stonehenge. From Tormore there is a fine walk above the stony shore to the King's Caves, eroded into the sandstone on the level of the 25-ft raised beach, on the walls of which early Christian or Viking carvings can be discerned. Traditionally the caves are associated with Robert Bruce, who came to Arran to try to oust the English, but it is unlikely that Bruce ever stayed in any of them. In the 18th C the Kirk Session met there, and in the 19th C they were used as a school. In legend they were occupied by 'Fingal', Fionn MacCaul.

The village of Shiskine, on the south of Machrie Moor, is said to be the burial place of St Mo Las. The String, the road across the island to Brodick, was built by Thomas Telford in 1817, passing through bare moorland and rough grazing.

The village of Blackwaterfoot stands in the centre of Drumadoon Bay, around a minuscule harbour. Towards the south the scenery becomes gentler and more pastoral, and a minor road follows Sliddery Water through the green glen to Lamlash. At Lagg, a supposedly haunted inn stands among trees by Kilmory Water, and at Torrylin the creamery produces Arran cheese. The rocky coast, once the haunt of smugglers from Ireland, lies a short walk to the south.

Three miles north-east of Lagg, in the valley of Allt an t-Sluice, a tributary of Kilmory Water, is Carn

Whitefarland, Arran, where palm lilies grow in the open.

Ban, 950 ft above sea level. This chambered cairn, 100-ft long by 60-ft wide, dates from the neolithic period and has been little disturbed.

Kildonan overlooks the low-lying lighthouse island of **Pladda**, beyond which the triangular lump of Ailsa Craig looks deceptively close; to the south-west the Mull of Kintyre and Sanda can be seen. There are some good areas of sand below the remains of Kildonan Castle, a mysterious 14th-C ruin.

At Dippin Head the road rises high above the basaltic rocks of the shoreline, then descends to Whiting Bay, a sprawling village of cafés and craft shops, with a mainly stony beach. A mile up Glenashdale Burn, which enters the sea by the youth hostel, there are dramatic waterfalls, tumbling 100 ft down a lava sill, and to the north-east are the remains of a fort. A track leads from the village of Kingscross to Kingscross Point, where there are the substantial remains of a Viking fort and burial mound.

Lamlash is a sea-angling and sailing centre, spread along the north-east shore of Lamlash Bay facing towards Holy Island. The line of houses, hotels and shops are backed by trees and high moor, and by the beach there is a green. It is a delightful, relaxing place, where the hospital, council offices and high school are intermingled with craft shops and cafés. The large mooring

buoys in the bay remain from the time when this was a fleet anchorage. In 1263 King Haakon moored here, *en route* to the Battle of Largs.

In summer there are boat trips across the bay to **Holy Island**, a brooding hump rising to 1030 ft at the summit of Mullach Mòr. Above this island's small pier is the farmhouse, now used as a field research station. There is a story that a farmer murdered his wife here, driven to it by her bearing him 15 daughters; she is supposedly buried under the kitchen floor. The two rusty hulks below the house were once used as island ferries, just after World War II. On the west side is the cave used by St Mo Las in the 7th C, with early Christian and Viking carvings on the walls. Below, near the shore, is the Judgement Stone, a flat sandstone table, and St Mo Las Well is nearby. Beyond the cave, at the south-west tip, is the larger of the island's two lighthouses. There are traces of a 12th-C fortress built by Somerled, and in the early 14th C a monastery was established; the remaining small chapel was used for burials on Holy Island until 1790. The seaward side falls steeply to the sea, and a small lighthouse marks the south-east coast. The rocky cliffs are inhabited by wild goats, and peregrines breed. The island is occupied in the summer by the warden and visiting students, naturalists and even skin divers, and all year round by the lighthouse keepers.

Arran claims to be 'Scotland's holiday isle', and indeed there is plenty for the visitor to do: golfing, fishing, pony trekking, walking, climbing, skin diving, bowling, following nature trails, watching Highland games – these are just a few examples.

The major Caledonian vehicle ferry runs from Ardrossan to Brodick, taking one hour to cross. The smaller 'landing-craft'-type ferry between Lochranza and Claonaig takes half an hour, operating only in the summer. Buses run on Arran, and cars and bicycles can be easily hired. The tourist office is at Brodick.

The 'haunted' Lagg Inn, Arran.

The last paddle steamer on the Clyde, the Waverley.

Bute

Strathclyde. Bute measures 16 miles by 4 miles, with an area of 31,000 acres. Its northern half is enclosed by the Cowal peninsula which seems, in places, only a stone's throw away across the Kyles of Bute. The Highland Boundary Fault splits the island along the line of Loch Fad – to the north is Dalradian schistose grit, to the south more recent old red sandstone with some basaltic lavas. To the north of Ettrick Bay the island is quite hilly, rising to 911 ft at the summit of Windy Hill.

Apart from the southern tip, the rest of the land undulates gently, and much is green and fertile. There are some areas of mixed woodland; Torr Wood, north of Kingarth, is particularly pleasant. As Bute is highly cultivated, the bird life is not outstanding. The long-tailed field-mouse on the island is a sub-species of the mainland race, with a shorter tail and smaller ears.

Prior to the local council re-organisation, Rothesay was capital of the County of Bute, which included Arran and the Cumbraes. Rothesay attained the status of a Royal Burgh in 1403, and the charter was extended by James VI of Scotland in 1584. The Bute family have for a long time taken an active interest in

the affairs of the Burgh, often occupying the position of Provost. The history of the island is centred on the massive circular, moated Rothesay Castle, first recorded in 1230 when it was besieged by Norsemen, a portion of the eastern wall still showing signs of the breach made when they eventually captured the fortress, and in 1263 it fell to King Haakon of Norway. The wars of independence touched the castle little, although it was taken from the English by Sir Colin Campbell in about 1334. During the 15th C it was attacked by the Lord of the Isles.

During the reigns of James IV and James V it became an important base during their campaigns to subdue the Hebrides, a lawless part of the realm, and improvements were made to the fabric of the building, including the construction of the great tower, completed in 1541. In 1498 the Bute family were appointed hereditary keepers of the castle (an office still held by the present Marquess, although the Department of the Environment now maintains the building). The castle was successfully defended in 1527 against the rebel Master of Ruthven; however, the surrounding burgh was destroyed, a common occurrence each time the castle was attacked, and a hindrance to the continuing development of the town. In 1544 the Earl of Lennox took it for the English. When Cromwell withdrew his garrison in 1659 much of the building was dismantled; what was left was

burned during the Duke of Monmouth's rebellion in 1685. The second Marquess of Bute began restoration in 1816, and further work was done by the third Marquess in 1872 and 1900.

Inside the massive sandstone curtain walls stands the chapel of St Michael; to the north-east of this is a well. The great hall, renovated in 1970 by the sixth Marquess, has a fine fireplace along one side, and a tapestry of the 'Prayer for Victory at Prestonpans' on the wall. The castle is open to the public daily, and is well worth visiting, as is the museum to the south. At the top of the High Street is the ancient chapel of St Mary's, once part of the Bishopric of Man.

Rothesay's population accounts for three-quarters of the island's total of 8100. It is a pleasant holiday place with a fine winter garden and all the facilities a million visitors each year would expect, including visits from the *Waverley*, the last sea-going paddle steamer on the Clyde.

In 1882 the Rothesay Tramways Company began a horse-drawn tram service between Guildford Square in Rothesay and Port Bannatyne and, after considerable success, the line was electrified in 1902 and extended to Ettrick Bay in 1905. The Company's eventual demise began with competition from motor coaches in the 1920s, and it eventually became a summer-only service in 1931 before the last tram ran on 30 September 1936. It was unique in being the only such service on a Scottish island, comparable with that which still exists on the Isle of Man.

Rothesay harbour, an important ferry terminal, was built during the 17th C for the fishing fleet, and subsequently rebuilt and enlarged during the heyday of the Clyde steamers. From 1940 to 1957 the bay was a naval anchorage.

Prior to the advent of tourism as the main industry, Bute was a major supplier of agricultural produce to the surrounding mainland, and it is still very productive, concentrated on dairy farming. The first cotton mill was built in Rothesay in 1779

Rothesay Castle, Bute.

and this industry flourished in the early 19th C. Along with the rest of the west coast of Scotland, there was a great deal of prosperity during the herring-fishing boom. Present industries, as well as tourism and agriculture, include weaving and shellfish processing.

Kerrycroy, Bute.

To the south of the capital is Kerrycroy Bay, with very pretty houses among tall trees at the back of a green, a sand and pebble beach and a small stone jetty. Mountstuart, to the south, has been the home of successive earls and marquesses of Bute for over 250 years. At Kilchattan, red sandstone houses match the sand and stones of the beach, and a track from the end of the road leads to the lighthouse at Rubha'n Eun, with fine views of the Cumbraes.

St Blane's Chapel, Bute.

The southern tip of Bute is marked by the steep St Blane's Hill, rising to 403 ft above a rocky shoreline. A path from the road's end leads to St Blane's Chapel, among the ruins of a 6th-C Celtic monastery in a beautiful and secluded wooded glade. Established by St Catan, the monastery took the name of his nephew, St Blane. Remains of the cells are still visible, and the chapel shows fine 12th-C craftsmanship. Dunagoil, a vitrified Iron Age fort, stands on a promontory nearby.

The west-coast bays of Scalpsie, St Ninian's and Ettrick all have sand, if only at low tide. The low-lying island of **Inchmarnock** (675 acres) lies three-quarters of a mile west of St Ninian's Point and chapel.

Bute's gentle west coast, towards Garroch Head.

It is divided into two farms, worked by residents, surprisingly isolated considering their proximity to Glasgow. Remains of the monastery founded by St Marnoc in the 7th C can be seen, and cross fragments have been uncovered around the ancient chapel. A Bronze Age cairn containing three burial cists has been excavated; in one was the skeleton of a young woman and a fine lignite collar. Except for a short period during World War II when it was used for commando training, the island has remained a haven of peace, with prolific bird life including the largest herring-gull colony on the Clyde.

The main road skirts the low land behind Ettrick Bay. At St Colmac, near the chapel, is the Cross of Kilmachalmaig, possibly an old preaching cross. To the north-west of the bay, the road ends at Clate Point; inland, the hills are empty and unpopulated. At the north-west corner are the remains of Kilmichael Chapel, destroyed by the Norsemen, and higher up the hillside is the burial cairn of Glenroidean.

Port Bannatyne is a northerly extension of Rothesay. Kames Bay has a little sand, but beyond this the shore is stony. The road ends at Rhubodach, where a vehicle ferry across the Kyles to Colintraive was established in 1950. The **Burnt Islands** to the north are a natural haven for birds.

Bute is easily reached by Caledonian MacBrayne vehicle ferries sailing between Wemyss Bay and Rothesay (one-hour crossing) and by a small ferry between Colintraive and Rhubodach (five-minute crossing). There is a bus service on the island, and a Tourist Information office in Rothesay.

The Rothesay ferry.

Millport, Great Cumbrae.

The Cumbraes

Strathclyde. The total population of the islands is 1200, and the total area 5120 acres. Great Cumbrae, part of the Bute Estate, lies one mile west of Largs and just over two miles east of Bute. Little Cumbrae is half a mile to the south across The Tan; between Rubha'n Eun on Bute and Little Cumbrae passes all the Clyde shipping.

Great Cumbrae Island measures just four miles by two miles, and attains a maximum height of 416 ft, the summit of the ridge of hills being marked by the Glaid Stone. The coast is rocky and broken, with low cliffs. Central and northern areas are old red sandstone, with carboniferous limestone around Millport, and there are many igneous dykes, the outcrop known as The Lion on the south-east coast being particularly notable.

Millport wraps itself around the back of the bay, facing south towards Ailsa Craig and giving a spectacular view of Arran to the south-west. It offers all you would expect of a small resort, including golf, bowling, riding, boating, sea fishing, a cinema and an attractive new museum of local history, and has sandy beaches and attractive gardens. A popular way of seeing the island is to cycle its 12-mile circumference, and bicycles can be hired in the town.

During the late 19th C and early 20th C, the harbour was a regular port of call for the many Clyde

steamers. In 1906 the steamer companies who objected to 'excessive' pier dues, refused to call during the holiday season, and Great Cumbrae became a deserted island until Lloyd George arranged a compromise, just before the annual Glasgow holidays. The Episcopal

church was consecrated as the Cathedral of Argyll and the Isles in 1876, and is the smallest cathedral in Britain. It was in Millport Bay in 1812 that Dr MacDougal first identified the roseate tern *(Sterna dougallii)* as a separate species.

The University Marine Biological Station is situated to the east of the town by Keppel Pier. The rich marine life around the islands has been studied since the 1840s, when David Robertson, the 'Cumbrae Naturalist', made frequent visits, eventually establishing a floating laboratory in Kames Bay. The present buildings date from 1896, and were the headquarters of the Scottish Marine Biological Association until 1970 when it was transferred to Dunstaffnage, near Oban. The station is now controlled by the Universities of London and Glasgow. There are two research vessels and diving facilities, including a decompression chamber. Undergraduate and post-graduate courses are run, and independent research projects can be accommodated. For visitors there are an interesting aquarium and the Robertson Museum to be seen.

Close to the ferry terminal on the east side is the Scottish Sports Council's National Water Sports Training Centre, where sailing, sub-aqua and canoeing are taught. At the north-east tip – Tormont End – there are thought to be graves of Norsemen killed at the Battle of Largs in 1263. The rocky west coast is punctuated by the pleasant sand and shingle crescent of Fintray Bay.

Kirkton, in the south-west, was the first village on Great Cumbrae. There has been a chapel there since at least the 13th C – the present church dates from 1802. The 'inner road' traverses the island's backbone, and the views of Bute, Arran and the mainland are superb.

Little Cumbrae Island is privately owned, topped, at the western tip, by a disused lighthouse (the first light signal was built here in 1750). The house and farm buildings on the east, used as a holiday retreat, look over the remains of a tower on **Castle Island**. The Hunters of Hunterston were the castle's hereditary keepers until 1515, and in 1653 it was sacked by Cromwell. In the 14th C, Robert II and Robert III maintained the island as a deer forest. In 1845 Little Cumbrae supported four families, and over 5000 rabbits were taken each year.

In 1880 John Blain, a local historian, wrote: 'The islands of Larger and Lesser Cumbray intervene between Bute and the Continent.' The local minister also considered the islands of not a little importance, praying for 'the inhabitants of Cumbrae and the adjacent islands of Great Britain and Ireland'. Their closeness to the mainland, and indeed to major population centres, seems, by contrast, to enhance the 'island' qualities of the Cumbraes, and they remain remarkably unspoiled.

Caledonian MacBrayne operate a vehicle ferry service to Great Cumbrae from Largs, where there is a Tourist Information office.

Ardrossan to the Solway Firth

Ardrossan is the ferry terminal for Arran. The tiny low-lying **Horse Isle** just outside the harbour is a refuge for five species of gull. **Lady Isle**, three miles south-west of Troon, is a natural haven for sea birds, with colonies of common, arctic and sandwich terns nesting. Roseate terns have also been seen, their numbers fluctuating from year to year.

Ailsa Craig

Strathclyde. This is a volcanic hump in the Firth of Clyde, ten miles west of Girvan and inhabited only by lighthouse keepers. It is two miles in circumference, and rises to a height of 1114 ft. In Gaelic its name means 'fairy rock' and it is affectionately known as 'Paddy's Milestone'. It has been mentioned in poems by both Keats and Wordsworth. It is composed of microgranite, acid igneous rock with fine-grained crystals of quartz, felspar and mica, and was quarried until quite recently. The quarrymen's cottages and the old trans-shipment pier, to the north, remain. The granite is famous for its use in the manufacture of curling stones.

Landings are made around high tide at the jetty by the lighthouse at Foreland Point in the north-east, and a narrow gauge tramway runs from here to the quarry. Other man-made relics include a forge, disused foghorns and the castle, a square tower about 300 ft up the slope

behind the lighthouse. The building has little history, but it is said to have been used by the monks of Crossraguel Abbey near Maybole in Strathclyde, and was once held by Catholics on behalf of Philip II of Spain. Halfway up the eastern side of the hill there is a lochan, and from the top the view takes in the hills from Renfrewshire to Galloway, and Kintyre, Jura, Arran, Cowal, the Isle of Man and Ireland.

In the south-west corner is the Water Cave, approachable at low tide when it is also possible to walk right round the base of the island. There has been a colony of gannets on Ailsa Craig since at least 1526; between 1971 and 1974 their numbers were estimated at 9500 breeding pairs (about five per cent of the world gannet population), seen mainly on the southern side.

Boat trips are run from Girvan, weather permitting.

The **Isle of Whithorn**, on the south-west side of Wigtown Bay, is now joined to the mainland by a causeway which encloses a small harbour, its little grey stone fishing village being quite attractive. St Ninian built a church in Whithorn in AD 397, making it one of the earliest footholds of Christianity in Britain, and the 12th-C St Ninian's Chapel stands to the south of the harbour.

The **Scares**, rocks in the centre of Luce Bay, support a small gannetry on the largest of the stacks: 482 pairs were recorded between 1971 and 1974. On the east side of Wigtown Bay, to the south of Fleet Bay, are the tidal **Islands of Fleet – Murray's Isles**, **Ardwall** and **Barlocco Isle** - grassy-topped and once used for grazing.

At the entrance to Kirkcudbright Bay is **Little Ross** island. The lighthouse here was built in 1843 and is 175 ft from the high-water mark to the light. In 1960 it came into the news when the keeper, Robert Dickson, killed his 64-year-old workmate, Hugh Clarke, in what the press labelled 'a perfect murder'. Dickson was sentenced to be hanged, but this was commuted to life imprisonment; he later committed suicide. In 1961, the light was made automatic.

Hestan Island is reached at low tide by a shingle causeway from Almorness Point, to the east of Auchencairn Bay. The island has a lighthouse, and a 19th-C farmhouse once occupied by an organ builder who liked the acoustics.

To the north-east, in Rough Firth, is **Rough Island**, a bird sanctuary owned by the National Trust for Scotland. It is a tidal island, and has an area of 20 acres. Wader, scaup, shelduck, merganser and tern are to be seen there.

Ailsa Craig.

Islands of the Firth of Forth

North Ness

ISLE OF MAY

Altarstones

Lighthouse

The Pillow

Priory

Maiden Hair

South Ness

0   Miles   ½

Bass Rock.

Isle of May

The largest of the Firth of Forth islands is situated five miles south-east of Anstruther Easter on the Fife coast. One mile long and half a mile wide, 'The May' (Celtic *magh* meaning a 'plain') consists of greenstone or basalt of a dark grey colour tinged with green. The shores are steep and rocky all round except at the northern end. On the west the cliffs rise to a height of 160 ft and the interior surface of the island is flat. The soil is fertile and provides good grazing for sheep. Earliest recorded history tells of an Irish or Hungarian (it is not known which) missionary named Adrian who settled here with his followers about AD 860; ten years later the Danes raided the island and massacred all the inhabitants. King David I of Scotland (1124-1153) founded a chapel on the Isle of May, dedicated it to St Adrian, and gave the island to his sister, Queen Maude of England, for the Benedictine monastery of Reading, Berkshire, who in turn established a priory here. The island was sold 120 years later, in 1269, to William Wishart, Archbishop of St Andrews.

Scotland's first lighthouse was erected on The May in 1635; 21 years later, a larger beacon (40 ft high) was built. The light consumed one ton of coal each night but on stormy nights with gale-force winds three tons were used to keep the light burning. In 1815, the island was acquired by the Northern Lighthouse Commissioners for the sum of £60,000, and a new light-house was built by Robert Louis Stevenson's grandfather which still stands today. During the 18th C, some 15 fishermen and their families lived on the island. There used to be a custom of celebrating the end of the herring season and fishermen from Crail and Pittenweem on the mainland came to the island to join in the merrymaking. However, in 1837, one of their boats capsized and

13 lives were lost, mainly women, and the festivities were never held again.

Because of The May's strategic position in the Forth, there have been many naval battles there, the Scottish navy of the day fighting off invasions from the Picts, the Norsemen, the Danes, pirates and their long-time enemy, the English. Wreckage from warfare and other tragedies is strewn all along the east-coast shallows, including two steam-driven submarines, and the whole area provides a good day's diving for the many sub-aqua clubs that come here from all over the country.

Today, the island (uninhabited apart from the lighthouse keepers) is a sea-bird colony with a bird observatory fitted out with furnish-ings from the many shipwrecks. Apart from the lighthouse and the priory ruins, there is not much else to visit. Little vegetation grows there and the landscape is bleak, rugged and wind-swept. It was created a National Nature Reserve in 1956.

Bass Rock

Lying about two miles off the Lothian side of the Forth is one of the most famous rocks in Britain - Bass Rock. One mile in circum-ference and 350 ft high, the south side slopes down to the sea in a series of three terraces. It is composed of an igneous rock called phonolite and is part of an ancient volcano, the island being the 'plug' left after the ashes had eroded away.

The island was a retreat for early Christian hermits; St Baldred, a disciple of St Mungo, is supposed to have lived on the island in AD 600. The earliest recorded owners appear to have been the Lauder family who originally came to Scotland with Malcolm Canmore in 1056. The Lauders of the Bass were loyal to the house of Stuart throughout their history. The Laird of Bass accompanied Mary Queen of Scots to Carberry Hill and to the Ridge of Causland on her surrender in 1567. Charles Maitland held Bass Rock for James II after Parliament declared

his abdication, but surrendered the fort and the island in August 1689. In 1701, the fortress was destroyed on orders from the government, probably fearful of another Scottish uprising. In 1901, the lighthouse was built on the site of the old fortress which was situated on the lower terrace. The middle terrace contains the ruins of the chapel and the upper terrace was used as a vegetable garden for the garrison.

Since ancient times, gannets, or solan geese, have been a plentiful source of food, and without doubt it is the gannet that has made Bass Rock so famous. Today, seven per cent of the world's gannets are hatched on this little rock. In about 1650, they were sold for 1s-8d each (skinned and gutted) and large quantities were taken each year from here - 1118 birds in 1674 to nearly 2000 in 1850, after which the industry declined.

For its size the island has many interesting species of plant life. The soil is relatively fertile and supports a wide variety of flowers. One of the most interesting, occurring mainly in the shelter of the fortress ruins, is the Bass mallow (*Lavatera arborea*), or tree-mallow, which is found, apart from Bass Rock, only on Ailsa Craig, Steep Holm and some parts of south-west England. Other than the lighthouse keepers, there are no other people on the island. Permission to visit is required but regular boat trips around Bass Rock to see the birds are available from North Berwick during the summer months. For further details see the information at the end of this section.

Two-and-a-half miles west of Bass Rock is a round islet called **Craigleith**, which rises to a height of 168 ft and has very steep sides. History tells us absolutely nothing about this little island, and it has little to recommend it. Further along the coast are two more small islets, each no bigger than a football pitch, Lamb and Fidra. **Lamb** rises to about 80 ft above sea level and has

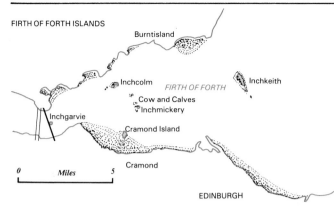

FIRTH OF FORTH ISLANDS

Burntisland

Inchcolm   *FIRTH OF FORTH*   Inchkeith

Cow and Calves
Inchmickery

Inchgarvie

Cramond Island

0   Miles   5

Cramond

EDINBURGH

many treacherous rocks on the southern side; boatmen usually give it a wide berth. **Fidra** is even smaller and reaches a height of 100 ft. A reef connects Fidra to the mainland on which the remains of a hermitage can be seen. The building was used by the nuns of the Cistercian convent at North Berwick as a retreat for meditation. A lighthouse is situated at the northern end of the island. The RSPB run both Craigleith and Lamb as bird sanctuaries and permission to visit either must be obtained from the society in advance.

Midway between Edinburgh and Kinghorn, at a point where the Firth of Forth narrows to about five miles, lies **Inchkeith**. Slightly triangular in shape, the island is 1000 yd long by 500 yd at the widest point. The general terrain is rocky and irregular and rises to 180 ft at the northern end, but there is a little wild and scraggy grass in certain areas. Geologically, the island consists of great sheets of igneous rock, chiefly of the stair-like trap type of formation. Between these sheets are thinner bands of shale, coal and limestone.

The island first emerges from the mists of history when the Venerable Bede wrote of 'Urbs Guida', standing in the middle of the eastern Firth. The name comes from Guidid Gaethbrechach, one of the Pictish kings who ruled Caledonia prior to the union of the Picts and Scots in AD 843. 'Inchkeith', the prefix 'Inch' signifying 'island', comes from one Robert de Keith, chief of the clan Catti, a warlike tribe from Germany who settled in Caithness (Keithness). In recognition of de Keith's gallant service to the Crown of Scotland during the Danish invasion of 1010, Malcolm II created him the hereditary Grand Marischal of Scotland and conferred upon him large estates including 'Urbs Guida', which then became the Island of Keith. The male line of the House of Keith lasted for seven centuries; the last of the line was Field Marshal James Keith, friend of Frederick the

Great of Prussia, who died at the battle of Hochkirchen in 1758.

The island was used several times as a refuge for the plague-stricken and an asylum for infected patients was built in 1497. In 1580, the ship *William of Leith* from Danzig was refused permission to land her plague-ridden crew anywhere except Inchkeith. Russian seamen who had wintered in the Firth of Forth during 1799 contracted an infectious disease and many of them died. All were buried on the island. The present lighthouse is situated on the site of the Castle of Inchkeith, built on the orders of Mary Queen of Scots in 1564. Nothing now remains of the castle which, in the words of Dr Samuel Johnson who visited the island in 1773, 'had bravely withstood the battle and breeze for upwards of two centuries'. Triple fortifications and batteries were built in 1881, each battery able to bring its guns to bear on any ship in the Firth of Forth.

By 1817, the population of this little island consisted of only 30 people: the lighthouse keeper and his assistant, their families and servants plus the men who manned the batteries. Inchkeith has three attendant rocks - **Seal Carr**, **Iron Craig** and **Long Craig**. The island is now a bird sanctuary run by the RSPB.

Seven miles west of Inchkeith and about two miles south of Aberdour on the Fife coast lies **Inchcolm**. Irregular in shape it measures about 800 yd long by 150 yd wide with both the rocky east and west sides elevated to a height of 90 ft. Composed of mainly greenstone with bands of steatite, pinchbeck brown mica and sandstone, the island also has areas of extremely fertile soil. The name comes from St Colme or Columba, who resided here during the 6th C. Alexander I of Scotland founded the abbey dedicated to St Columba, in 1123, the ruins of which can still be seen in the centre of the island.

Shakespeare immortalised the island in his tragedy, *Macbeth*. In

Act I, Scene 2, The Thane of Ross comes to Duncan's camp with news of the great victory Macbeth has had over the invading Norsemen: 'Sweno, the Norways' King, craves composition; nor would we deign him burial of his men, till he disbursed at Saint Colme's inch ten thousand dollars to our general use.' The historian Bellenden mentions many stones marked with the arms of the Norsemen on the west side of the abbey. All but one of these monuments have now disappeared.

Cramond Island lies opposite Inchcolm on the Lothian side of the Firth of Forth, at the mouth of the river Almond and is joined to the mainland by a causeway which is only covered at high tide. It was an important Roman station, housing the second and tenth legions under Lollius Urbicus. The name is derived from Caer Almond, the 'castle on the Almond'. Although 19 acres in size it's easy to miss.

Even smaller than Cramond is **Inchmickery**, lying midway between Cramond and Inchcolm. About three acres in size, the isle rises to about 50 ft. Little is recorded about this island and its attendant rocks, **Cow and Calves**, but it is possible that Inchmickery (Gaelic for 'isle of the vicar') was connected with the monastery of Inchcolm and was probably a dwelling place for one of the priests. Further west, where the Firth of Forth narrows to little more than one mile, over which spans the Forth Bridge, lies a small rocky islet called **Inchgarvie**; the name means, literally, 'rocky isle'. Inchgarvie stands about 40 ft above high water. Prior to the building of the Forth Bridge, the island guarded the entrance to the River Forth. The only historical feature was a castle, founded in 1491 by John Dundas. Cromwell captured the island in 1651, the castle was dismantled and the remains soon fell into a ruinous state. The stones were used to make concrete ballast for the caissons of the Forth Bridge, two of which are sunk into the rock of Inchgarvie. The island is now totally dwarfed by the bridge and many travellers pass over the Firth without even noticing it.

The islands and rocks of the Firth of Forth fall under different areas of control: Bass Rock, Craigleith, Lamb, Fidra, Cramond Island, Inchmickery and Cow and Calves are within the East Lothian District Council's domain; Inchcolm, Inchkeith, Inchgarvie and the Isle of May are situated in the district of Fife; and permission to visit any of these islands must be obtained from the relevant district council. However, for those islands designated as bird sanctuaries (Fidra, Inchmickery, Lamb and Craigleith), permission is only required from the RSPB.

England

A varied assortment of islands
scattered fairly evenly around the
coast, beginning with Lindisfarne
in the north-east and progressing
clockwise to the Isle of Walney in
the north-west.

SCOTLAND

Lindisfarne
Farne Islands
Coquet Island
St Mary's
Island

North Sea

Isle of Man

Walney Island

Irish Sea

Hilbre Islands

Scolt Head

WALES

ENGLAND

Havergate
Island
Hamford
Water Islands
Mersea Island
Foulness Island
Canvey Island
Isle of Sheppey

Bristol Channel

Steep Holm

Lundy

Straight of Dover

Brownsea
Island
Portsea Island
Hayling Island

Isle of Wight

Looe Island
Drake's Island
Great Mew Stone
Burgh Island

English Channel

Godrevy Island

St Michael's
Mount

Isles of Scilly

North-east Coast

Lindisfarne

Northumberland. There are several islands called 'Holy Island' in the British Isles, but the most famous is Lindisfarne. Located about a mile off the coast near Beal and about eight miles south of Berwick-upon-Tweed, the island covers an area of approximately 1150 acres. A causeway joins it to the mainland, but twice a day this road is covered by the tide. Lindisfarne is part of a dolerite dyke, formed by volcanic molten rock cooling in vertical towers, which gradually became exposed as the elements eroded the softer rocks around them. Apart from dolerite, the island also contains shale, limestone, sandstone and some coal.

The Northumbrian coast was the site of one of the earliest Anglo-Saxon settlements in Britain. Bamburgh was the capital and castle of the kings of Bernicia from AD 547 to 995, and the island was probably used as a military camp and safe harbour by the Saxons in their efforts to subdue Celtic resistance. Bishop Aidan came to Northumberland in AD 634, chose Lindisfarne as his seat and established a monastery; the island became a centre for Christiantiy for the next 200 years. In 664, Cuthbert was made Prior of Lindisfarne and, after many years of teaching and pastoral work, he gradually withdrew from the general activities of the monastery, first to live on Hobthrush Island (St Cuthbert's Isle) and later, in 676, on Farne Island (*see* Farne Islands). For the next nine years he remained alone on Farne, but was forced to give up his hermit's existence when he became Bishop of Lindisfarne, dying two years later on 20 March 687. The next ten years saw Cuthbert's canonisation and this, in turn, brought thousands of pilgrims to Lindisfarne.

During the early part of the 8th C, the finest book of the early Anglo-Saxon period was produced on the island - the *Lindisfarne Gospels* - one of the most important and beautifully hand-written books in the world. There are 258 pages of vellum with magnificent colour illustrations and over 22,000 lines of script being the four Gospels (St Jerome's version) together with the Eusebian Canons and two epistles. The original is now in the British Museum but a facsimile is kept in the parish church.

The first recorded Viking attack in England was at Lindisfarne in AD 793, during which the monastery was destroyed and many monks

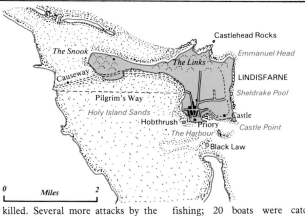

killed. Several more attacks by the Danes left the island in complete desolation and, in 875, the remaining monks took their treasures and fled. Nothing more is documented about the island until, in 1081, the Normans established a priory there. It was during this period that it became known as 'The Holy Island'.

In medieval times the island was the centre of activity in the north-east, with a thriving market and merchant ships calling regularly. Farming was done on a large scale and small industries grew up: iron smelting, coal mining, quarrying and fishing. The castle, essential for the island's safety, was built in 1549. Over the years the population has fluctuated a great deal: only 33 householders were recorded in 1560; the population then increased to 364 by 1790; and in 1861 the figure reached 614. However, over the next hundred years it fell to 190, and today it is still less than 200.

During the early 19th C, mining and quarrying proved extremely beneficial to the island. The large lime kilns, seen near the castle, were erected in 1860, and at that time over 20 per cent of the adult male population was engaged in lime working, but by 1920 all commercial mining had stopped. In 1850, half the population was occupied with

fishing; 20 boats were catching herring and three or four others concentrated on shellfish. By 1930, this had dwindled to just eight boats, and today, with only five working boats and ten or twelve people engaged in farming, the great majority of islanders now rely on tourism for a living.

The variety of wildlife and vegetation on such a small island is quite remarkable, with, for example, over 250 different species of birds having been recorded. A recent count records 44 resident breeding species, including the eider duck, arctic tern, fulmar, shag, guillemot, kittiwake and puffin. Of the visiting birds, mainly wintering on the island from the arctic regions, one can see widgeon, brent and greylag geese, dunlin wader and the bar-tailed godwit. From November through to February thousands of these arctic birds cover the bays and mud flats around the island, while in May and June, the resident birds are nesting in considerable numbers. The most common terrestrial vertebrate on Lindisfarne is the rabbit, although frogs, lizards, foxes and weasels all breed here.

Plant life varies according to location. The sand dunes are dominated by marram grass; other plants are sparse but include viper's-bugloss, hound's-tongue and

Lindisfarne Priory.

a rather unusual plant from Australia - the pirri-pirri-bur. On other parts of the island there are gentian, campion and common centuary. Coastal species include the sea aster and sea thrift.

The priory, right in the centre of the village, is an excellent place to start a tour of the island. It is extremely well maintained with splendid archways and the remains of the church, monks' dormitory and monastery bakehouse. To the west of the priory stands the parish church, dedicated to St Mary the Virgin. The facsimile of the *Lindisfarne Gospels* is kept here and it is well worth a visit just to see the beautiful illuminated manuscript. From the church Jenny Bell's Well Lane takes you down to the beach below The Heugh (hill) and from that point you can walk out to **Hobthrush Island** at low tide. A stone cross marks the ruins of St Cuthbert's Chapel and the walls of his cell, and traces of a second building, possibly a hospital, can be clearly seen.

Walking east over The Heugh and down to the harbour brings you in sight of the castle, towering above everything else on the island. Restored by Edward Lutyens in 1902 and given to the National Trust in 1944, the castle is open each afternoon except Tuesdays from April to September. From the castle, ramblers and birdwatchers can take the Old Waggon Way north past Sheldrake Pool up to Emmanuel Head and then west along the north coast of the island to Gull Bank. Along the way there are often plenty of grey seals to be seen, particularly at Emmanuel Head, as well as razorbill, sandpiper and cormorant. From Gull Bank the landscape changes to sand dunes which extend right out to The Snook.

Back in the village, visitors are able to sample and buy Lindisfarne mead, originally made by the monks and now produced by the islanders. Along with the castle and the priory, the Lindisfarne Liqueur Company is one of the most popular places on the island. Anyone wishing to spend a few days on the island should write to the Tourist Information centre at Berwick-upon-Tweed for a full list of hotels, inns and private guest houses. There are no caravan sites or provisions for camping but there are sites on the mainland between Beal and Berwick.

Berwick-upon-Tweed is the nearest railway station and buses operate from there to the island. The service is twice daily during July and August, and on Wednesdays and Saturdays only for the rest of the year. Times vary according to the tides so check the time tables at the bus station. For motorists, tide tables are posted at the Plough Inn at Beal and also at the beginning of the causeway. In case of trouble, engine stalling, etc., do not stay in the car if the tide is rising. A refuge box is situated on the bridge over The Low. For hikers and ramblers, there is a direct route of about three miles across the sands - Pilgrim's Way, marked by a series of wooden posts - from the coastline at Beal to Chare Ends on the island. Whichever method you choose, it is essential to consult the tide tables before crossing.

The Farne Islands, with Inner Farne in the foreground.

The Farne Islands

Northumberland. This is a group of 28 uninhabited islets and rocks located a few miles off the coast near Bamburgh and Seahouses. They are the eastern end of the outcrop of the Great Whin Sill, a volcanic rock (dolerite) that stretches across the north of England. Only 15 islands are visible at high tide, the largest of which is **Farne Island** (16½ acres at low water), also called Inner Farne. The other major islets and rocks are: **Staple Island**, **Brownsman**, **Longstone**, **Megstone**, **Big Harcar**, **Knivestone** and **Crumstone**.

On approaching the islands one is struck by the magnificent cliffs and sea stacks, rising to 70 or 80 ft in places, a characteristic feature of the volcanic rock of the Whin which produces steep cliffs on the south and west and sloping beaches on the north and east. The sea and wind have weathered the hard rock into an impressive seascape.

Historically, the islands have been used mainly as a religious retreat. St Cuthbert, in AD 676, chose Inner Farne as his sanctuary, and he spent more than eight years in comparative isolation on this small island. His fame spread all over Britain and, although Inner Farne was, by 7th-C standards, extremely remote, hundreds of pilgrims visited the island every year to see him. Bishop Aidan often visited the islands, from his priory on Lindisfarne, when he wished to be undisturbed, and Bartholomew was a notable hermit on Inner Farne around 1150. From time to time monks have farmed the island, growing barley and wheat. The Vikings obviously thought the islands worth a visit since records show several attacks by them in the 8th C.

There is, surprisingly, quite a lot to see even today. On Inner Farne there is a 'peel' (from the medieval word for 'palisade') tower, built by Prior Castell of Durham, reputed to be the site of St Cuthbert's cell. Castell also constructed a priory, a guest house and two chapels, one of which still stands - St Cuthbert's, rebuilt in 1370 and fully restored by Archdeacon Thorp in 1848. The ruins of the guest house - called 'Frisby House' - lie nearby. The stone font in the courtyard of the chapel did not originate on the island; it initially came from Gateshead parish church. The stone

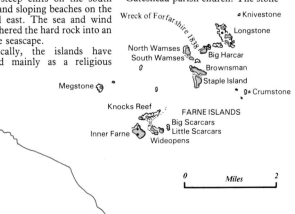

The Pinnacles, off Staple Island.

coffin is reputed to be that of Thomas Sparowe, master of the House of Farne from 1423 to 1430. The building behind the coffin occupies the site of the second chapel, St Mary's, and incorporates a little of its original stonework. It was used for many years as a store by the Trinity House lighthouse service, but today acts as an information centre. The round unmanned lighthouse at the southern corner of the island, near **The Stack**, was erected in 1800 and is still working today.

As far as the other islands are concerned, very little of antiquity remains. Part of a light tower, used as a beacon lighthouse in the 18th C and partially destroyed by a storm in 1890, can be seen on Staple Island. A small hut, possibly a seaweed cutter's home, stands on **West Wideopens**. On Longstone, one of the most famous lighthouses in England is still in operation. It was from here that the keeper, William Darling, and his daughter, Grace, saw the SS *Forfarshire*, a large luxury steamer, strike the rocks of Big Harcar on the 7 September 1838. Their subsequent heroic actions saved the lives of nine people and made father and daughter national celebrities. There is a memorial to her in St Cuthbert's Chapel on Inner Farne.

In 1927, the National Trust took over the islands and created a nature reserve. One of the world's rarest seals - the grey seal - breeds on Staple Island, Brownsman, Megstone and Crumstone. Throughout the year, and especially during the calving season in November and December, thousands of seals can be seen on the Farne Islands.

The islands are also a notable breeding area for sea birds. The eider duck has been called 'St Cuthbert's chicken', because of a special protection given by the saint to these birds; some 800-1000

usually nest on Inner Farne between late April and the end of June. The kittiwake is best seen nesting on The Stack along with the razorbill and the guillemot; kittiwakes and shags also nest on The Pinnacles, rock stacks to the south-east of Staple Island. On both **North and South Wamses** there are usually cormorant colonies. Herring gulls, puffins, four kinds of tern - arctic, common, roseate and sandwich - plus large numbers of lesser black-backed gulls, fulmars, ringed plovers and oystercatchers all nest here.

Vegetation on the Farnes is somewhat sparse. There are no trees at all and some of the smaller islands have no plant life whatsoever, but on Inner Farne and Staple Island many varieties of wild flowers can be found. In May both islands are covered with white-flowered scurvygrass and this is quickly replaced with pink thrift in June. Sea campion covers large areas and you can also find silverweed, hemlock, sorrel, red goosefoot and sea-milkwort, all flowering at different times. One of the most interesting plants to be found is *Amsinckia intermedia*, a native of lower California thought to have been accidentally introduced, possibly in a consignment of grain, by early lighthouse keepers. It can be found near the tower enclosure on Inner Farne and can be recognised by its tiny orange-yellow flowers.

Apart from the magnificent cliffs and sea stacks, one sight not to miss is the 'blowhole' at the western end of Inner Farne. When there is a storm from the north the sea rushes into The Churn and projects a column of water into the air, sometimes as high as 90 ft. The **Pinnacles**, off the south-east corner of Staple Island, are truly magnificent - three great rock stacks rising to between 45 and 55 ft above the sea; in June and July these are covered with about 1000 pairs of

nesting guillemots. It is difficult to see just how they all manage to stay on the rocks.

Two of the Farne Islands, Inner Farne and Staple Island, are open to the public - from April to September, between 10.00 a.m. and 6.00 p.m. However, during the breeding season, 15 May-15 June, Staple Island is open only for three hours in the morning, while Inner Farne opens only in the afternoon. Visitors should also make a note of the bye-laws governing the islands: always keep to the marked paths, do not take dogs on to the islands and do not collect any eggs or disturb a nesting bird. If you violate these last two points you could be fined a minimum of £20. In certain weather conditions, the islands are liable to be closed, so check at the National Trust Information Centre, Seahouses.

Coquet Island

Northumberland. Coquet Island is situated 19 miles south of Berwick-upon-Tweed, and about one mile off the Northumberland coast near Amble at the mouth of the River Coquet. A flat, uninhabited island about 500-yd long, it covers an area of 20 acres at high water.

The history of Coquet Island dates back to the Romans; several pieces of Roman jewellery and coins have been found on the island. During the 7th C, Benedictine monks lived in a small chapel which was the scene of an interview between Elfreda, the Abbess of Whitby, and St Cuthbert. The King of Northumbria, Egfrith, had offered St Cuthbert the bishopric of Lindisfarne and it was on Coquet that Elfreda persuaded him to accept. During the Civil War, Charles I stationed a small garrison here but the island was captured by the Scots in 1645.

Now owned by the Duke of Northumberland, the island is leased to the RSPB as a wildlife sanctuary. The sea-bird colony includes 2000 pairs of common terns, 500 pairs of arctic terns, 150 pairs of roseate terns and 600 pairs of sandwich terns. There are also 300 pairs of eider duck - the most southerly colony on the east coast of Britain. Access to the island is strictly prohibited due to its small size and to the threat of disturbance to the birds.

St Mary's Island

Northumberland. St Mary's Island lies just off the coast of the northern end of Whitley Bay, about five miles north of Tynemouth. Composed of sandstone, it is connected to the mainland by a natural rock causeway and is cut off only at high tide. Sometimes called 'Bait Island' or 'Bate's Island', it was a place of meditation; monks would retire to the island to seek solitude. MacKenzie, a local historian, says that, in the past, there was a small hermitage on the isle, and there seems to be little doubt that a chapel, dedicated to either St Mary or St Helen, was founded there but no trace of this exists today. According to tradition a lamp was kept burning in the chapel for the benefit of all those at sea.

Until the early part of the 19th C the island was quite bare of buildings and only visited by fishermen and wildfowlers but, after a house had been built there by a man named Ewen, the island became popular with nature lovers and painters. Later, an inn was built, attracting even more visitors, having a thatched and tiled roof, often a subject for local painters. The light-house and keeper's cottages were built in 1898 at a cost of £8000. St Mary's Island is an extremely pleasant and picturesque place to visit for anyone wishing to spend a few hours in tranquillity. There is a caravan site directly opposite the island, between Whitley Sands and Seaton Sluice.

St Mary's Island.

East Anglian and Essex Coasts

Scolt Head

Norfolk. Between Hunstanton and Cromer on the north Norfolk coast lie some of the most unspoiled sand dunes and marshlands in Britain, designated as an 'area of outstanding beauty', and over 17,000 acres have been made into National Nature Reserves or are Sites of Special Scientific Interest. There are ten reserves along the coast and, although the following will only deal with Scolt Head, the information relates to the whole coastline and visitors to the island should also try to visit the rest of the area to get a complete picture of this unique part of Britain.

Scolt Head was purchased from Lord Leicester in 1923 by the Na-

tional Trust, except for the extreme eastern end, which was sold to the Norfolk Naturalists' Trust in 1945. In 1953, the Nature Conservancy Council leased the whole island for a period of 99 years.

It is approximately four miles long and half a mile wide, running parallel to the coast about three miles from Burnham Market and 30 miles north-west of Norwich. Marshlands, some of them covered at high water, separate the island from the mainland.

Scolt Head was formed by wave action which built up sand and shingle ridges. Plant growth played an important part in the formation of these ridges, particularly a common dune grass called marram. As the grass gets a footing on the first layers of shingle, the sand, blown up from the low-water levels, becomes trapped in the grass, and dunes begin to form on top of the shingle. The marshes are composed of fine salt and mud brought in by each tide and deposited on the sand flats.

Shingle, sand and mud seem extremely inhospitable habitats for any living thing, especially when swept by salt water and gale-force winds, but Scolt Head and the surrounding marshes are alive with a multitude of wild flowers, shrubs, insects, sea and land animals and sea birds. One of the most interesting characteristics of this landscape, to

the natural history student, is the ever-changing aspect of the dunes and the marshlands. The visitor will notice, should he return to the island after a period of time, that the shapes of the ridges, dunes and even the coastline have altered since his last visit. Most of these alterations are produced by natural elements – the sea and the wind – but some are a direct result of the careless and unthinking who do not stay on the marked pathways, who collect wild flowers or dig in the sand. All these things will affect the ecology of the area and result in the sand being blown away. Considering that it has taken over 300 years for Scolt Head to form, it would be a shame to lose it because of a few unthinking people.

Scolt Head has an excellent nature trail, marked out so that visitors can view all that there is to see without disturbing the natural life of the area. The path runs through the ternery, where three types of terns breed, and past the nests of ringed plover, oystercatcher and black-headed gull. At low water the salt marsh bays are ideal for observing wading birds, some of which are resident breeders, others just migratory visitors. During the breeding season (May and June) access is not permitted to the western part of the island since even controlled visiting would create havoc among the nesting birds and lead to many abandoned nests.

The north shore provides an interesting area for beachcombers; much material is washed ashore after a storm and, apart from the bottles, cans and plastic bits and pieces, there are many interesting and unusual shells and stones to be found on the shingle. The sharp-eyed collector may find a variety of semi-precious stones including cornelian, onyx, amber and jet. There are many other marsh islands along this coast, but most are small and liable to change from being an

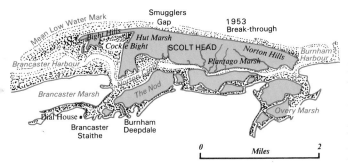

Mean Low Water Mark
Smugglers Gap
1953 Break-through
Bight Hills
Hut Marsh
Cockle Bight
SCOLT HEAD
Norton Hills
Burnham Harbour
Brancaster Harbour
Plantago Marsh
Norton
The Nod
Brancaster Marsh
Overy Marsh
Dial House
Brancaster Staithe
Burnham Deepdale

0   Miles   2

Scolt Head viewed from Brancaster.

island to becoming part of the mainland and back to being an island again. These include **Overy Marsh, Trowland Creek, Warham, Wells** and **Lodge Marsh**. Access is not easy and, without local knowledge of the tides and currents, it is not recommended for visitors to go wandering about in these areas.

For people wishing to spend a few days in the region, there are facilities on the mainland for camping and caravanning, and hotel or guest-house accommodation is available at Wells-next-the-Sea, Hunstanton and Blakeney. Norwich is only 30 miles away and there are coach tours to the coast during the summer months.

Havergate Island

Suffolk. About 18 miles east of Ipswich, on the coast near Orford, are a series of salt marshes: Lantern and Kings Marshes, Orford Beach and Havergate Island. There is no public access to any of these marshes with the exception of the last.

Situated in the middle of the River Ore, Havergate Island is two miles long and about 800 yd across at its widest point. It is open to the public only on certain days during the summer months, as it is a bird sanctuary run by the RSPB who organise full- and half-day trips to the island between April and August. Permits to join one of the

escorted tours must be purchased in advance by writing to the RSPB; the fee is very reasonable and includes boat transportation. A picnic lunch should be taken for a full-day trip since there are no shops or restaurants on the island. If you are interested in birds, particularly waders, it is well worth a visit.

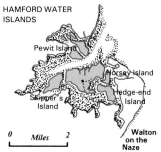

HAMFORD WATER
ISLANDS

Pewit Island

Horsey Island

Skipper's Island

Hedge-end Island

0   Miles   2

Walton
on the
Naze

Hamford Water Islands

Essex. Two miles north of Walton on the Naze are a series of low-lying marshy islands, situated in an area known as Hamford Water. The four main ones are **Skipper's, Horsey, Pewit** and **Hedge-end Islands,** and they cover a total area of about 700 acres. All are privately owned and therefore access is restricted. Skipper's Island is the most interesting to the naturalist; it is owned by the Essex Naturalists' Trust and managed as a nature

reserve. The island is about 160 acres in extent and mainly composed of London clay; about 50 acres is rough pasture with extensive thorn thickets and hedges. Breeding birds include the oystercatcher, shelduck and kestrel; winter migrants are numerous. The access route to the island lies over private land and prior permission, in writing, is required for anyone wishing to visit the reserve.

The Essex Naturalists' Trust owns, leases or manages 40 nature reserves in all and access to most of them is by permit only, although these are issued automatically to members. It is worth noting that, for anyone interested in natural history, membership of the various British conservation societies will greatly increase the number of areas you are allowed to visit. A list of the main societies has been included at the end of this book.

Mersea Island

Essex. Mersea, the 'isle in the Mere', nestles amid the salt marshes between the estuaries of the Blackwater and the Colne about nine miles south of Colchester. It is about five miles long by two miles wide and sea walls enclose virtually all but the southern side, which faces out to the North Sea. A causeway over the Strood Channel connects Mersea with the mainland.

The island is largely composed of London clay, well over 100-ft deep in places, which rests on a bed of sand and gravel; there are outcrops of this at the eastern and western ends of the island. The northern section, the marshy area, is composed of alluvial mud. There are a few chalk boulders on the beach, a result of glacial action.

During Celtic times the island had a fairly steady population, living mainly by farming and fishing. You can still see several of the famous 'red hills', heaps of burned soil, some covering a wide area, which are the remains of Celtic salt workings. The Romans established a *colonia* (a settlement) for retired veterans on land near to present-day Colchester, and for a long time this was their

The Barrow, Mersea Island.

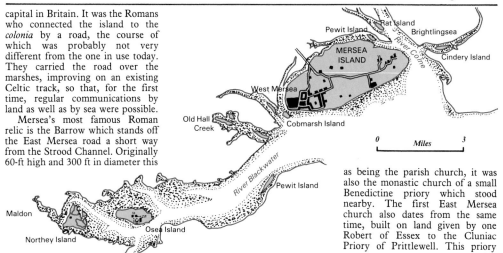

capital in Britain. It was the Romans who connected the island to the *colonia* by a road, the course of which was probably not very different from the one in use today. They carried the road over the marshes, improving on an existing Celtic track, so that, for the first time, regular communications by land as well as by sea were possible.

Mersea's most famous Roman relic is the Barrow which stands off the East Mersea road a short way from the Strood Channel. Originally 60-ft high and 300 ft in diameter this

mound enclosed a burial chamber which, when excavated in 1912, was found to contain a vault of red brick, enclosing a lead casket. The casket contained a fine glass urn in which the cremated bones of an adult were found. These relics are now in the Colchester Museum. The superior quality of the urn and the extent of the Barrow indicate that the person buried there must have been of considerable wealth and standing, most likely a Romanised Celt as the building of barrows was a Celtic custom and cremation a Roman one.

Although the Romans called the island *Maris Insula*, the island is known by its Saxon name, *Meres-ig* (the Saxons often used the first part of a Roman name but added a Saxon ending). The *colonia* became Colchester. The Norman Conquest made little difference to the inhabitants of Mersea, most of the land already being under the rule of the Norman house of St Ouen. The entry for West Mersea and the land owned by the Abbey of St Ouen in the *Domesday Book (c.* 1086) shows them consisting of 20 hides (about 2400 acres) and their possessions as: 22 ploughs, 36 villeins and 62

as being the parish church, it was also the monastic church of a small Benedictine priory which stood nearby. The first East Mersea church also dates from the same time, built on land given by one Robert of Essex to the Cluniac Priory of Prittlewell. This priory

The southern coast of Mersea Island.

bordars (both being categories of peasants tied to the land by various laws but higher in the social scale than serfs), and three serfs. The livestock of the manor is given as 300 sheep and a cash value of the church as £6.13s.4d.

The West Mersea church of St Peter and St Paul was built in 1046 (the lower part of the existing tower dates from this period) and, as well

was a cell of Lewes Priory in Sussex, which in turn was a daughter house of the famous Priory of Cluny in France.

The earliest specimens of domestic architecture are a group of cottages in Mersea Lane and the lower part of the Coast Road, some of which are 16th C. Originally fishermen's cottages, they are now much restored and modernised but retain their picturesque appearance and their beautiful old beams. There are many Georgian houses, ranging from small cottages such as Cherrytree Cottage and Myrtle Cottage in East Road, to fine large houses such as West Mersea Hall near the church and Yew Tree House in the Coast Road.

Generally speaking, the Mersea landscape is a mixture of old and new. The unchanging aspect of the marshes and creeks, the Celtic and Roman relics and every modern amenity all combine to make the island very popular with visitors. West Mersea is a busy seaside town, with a population of 6600. The centre of the town is around the church, where the High Street meets

Fishermen's cottages on Mersea Island.

the Coast Road. The older and more attractive part of Mersea is the southern coast. It is on this part of the island that one can really enjoy the Mersea of old.

Apart from the fishermen's cottages, the little boat yards and the sail-makers, there are many fishing boats to be seen setting out for sprat, cod, herring, shrimp and, of course, the famous Mersea oysters. Each year the Mayor of Colchester sails into Mersea waters to officially open the oyster season, and the oyster trade seems to be flourishing, Mersea oysters being exported all over the world. The fishermen grow the oysters in 'layings' in the various fleets and channels around the island and, when mature, the oysters are brought into pits, most of which are off the Coast Road, and kept there until they are sold. The Hard, off the Coast Road, is the harbour with the boat-builders' yards nearby. A great deal of produce used to be landed here and this trade continued up to World War I, but now it is used by only the fishermen and the many pleasure boats. A modern slipway has been built for launching,tying up dinghies, etc. Further to the east is King's Hard, the old landing place, now eroded and unused.

Off this south coast is **Cobmarsh Island**, used by the oystermen but inhabited only by gulls and cormorants. Other birds you are likely to see include heron, mute swan, mallard, grebe and pewit and, in winter, greylag geese, black-backed gulls and widgeon. Inland Mersea has much the same flora and fauna as any other part of south-east England.

East Mersea is almost entirely agricultural; wheat, barley and oats are grown, and pigs, sheep and poultry raised. The village, with only 300 inhabitants, is quiet and so small that, unless you keep your eyes open and drive slowly, it is difficult to know whether you have passed through it or not. The church, dedicated to St Edmund, stands near the sea away from the village. There are two other islands, apart from Cobmarsh, lying between Mersea and the mainland. **Pewit Island** in the Pyefleet Channel and **The Ray**, between Thorn Fleet and Strood Channel. The latter is run as a nature reserve by the Essex Naturalists' Trust and permission has to be obtained to visit the reserve.

The Mersea Regatta is an attraction not to miss, especially if you like sailing and boating. It is held in August, the actual dates depending on the tides, and covers a whole week of aquatic events. There are races for all classes of boats, water sports, a fair, a grand firework display, all culminating in the presentation of prizes and general

celebrations at the Yacht Club on the Saturday evening.

Tourist facilities on the island are much the same as any other seaside resort. There are plenty of hotels, guest houses, pubs and inns, several restaurants and cafés in West Mersea and caravan sites in both East and West Mersea.

Northey Island

Essex. Near the head of the River Blackwater about two miles east of Maldon lies Northey Island, covering an area of 330 acres and connected to the mainland by a causeway. Flint scrapers have been discovered here pointing to the probability that Stone Age man once inhabited the area. The mainland end of the causeway was the site of a great battle between the Vikings and the Saxons in AD 991 – the Battle of Maldon. During the 11th C the island was inhabited by at least seven people and 60 sheep. In the 18th C a sea wall existed, enclosing over 200 acres of land, but high tides in 1874 and again in 1897 severely damaged this and, although it was repaired, later storm tides finally put paid to any intensive agriculture. Today almost 60 per cent of Northey is covered at high tide.

The island is owned by the National Trust and managed by the Essex Naturalists' Trust and designated a Site of Special Scientific Interest. Visitors are allowed on the island only with a permit.

Osea Island

Essex. Osea Island is two miles east of Northey Island, midway between the north and south banks of the River Blackwater. Mainly agricultural land (330 acres) Osea has been inhabited since Roman times, and before the Norman Conquest was known as *Uvesia*. William the Conqueror gave the island to his nephew, Hamo Dapifer, who held it as a 'Manor and four Hides of Land'. The *Domesday Book* lists the island as belonging to the Bouchier family, later to become the Earls of Essex. During and after the

Middle Ages the island had a succession of owners: the Earl of Gloucester (1315), Sir Hugh Stafford (1420) and a Mr Charles Coe (1760).

In 1903 the island was purchased by Mr F. N. Charrington, of the brewery family, who opened a home for 'gentlemen inebriates'. Osea Island then became a retreat for alcoholics and it is said that the local boatmen made more money ferrying illicit supplies of whisky and gin to the residents than they did from fishing. Ownership has subsequently passed to Caius College, Cambridge, and public access is not permitted.

Foulness Island

Essex. A few miles north-east of Southend-on-Sea, and separated from the mainland by the River Crouch in the north and the River Roach, Paglesham Pool and Potton Creek in the west, lie six marshy islands. Foulness Island, the largest of the group, is about six miles long by three miles wide and covers an area of 5800 acres, the greater part of its land mass having been 'inned', reclaimed from the sea, during the past few hundred years. Evidence of several Romano-British settlements have been found on the islands: barrows, burial urns and pottery, plus several 'red hills'. The latter occur in several parts of coastal Essex and were most likely to have been part of Iron Age and Roman salt works.

The name Foulness derives from the Old English *Fugla* ('wild birds') and *Naess* ('promontory'), the latter offering support to the theory that Foulness was once part of the mainland. The first mention of Foulness Island is made in 1235 when the 'Manor of Fulness' was described as covering an area of 1500 acres of marshland held by Hubert de Burgh, Earl of Kent, the income from the land being worth about £19 a year. Sir Thomas Boleyn, father of Anne Boleyn, obtained the estate in 1527, but in 1549 the manor was sold to Sir Richard Rich, Lord Chancellor of England (1548-1551).

William Camden visited the

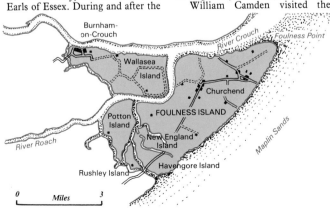

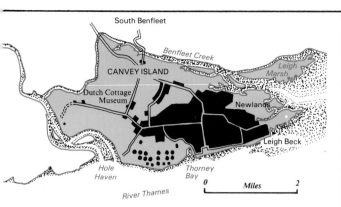

South Benfleet
Benfleet Creek
CANVEY ISLAND
Leigh Marsh
Dutch Cottage Museum
Newlands
Leigh Beck
Hole Haven
Thorney Bay
0   Miles   2
River Thames

marshlands in 1607 and said they were 'plentifull in grasse and rich in cattaile, but sheepe especially where all their doing is in making of cheese ...' In 1688, there were five farms on Foulness with rents totalling £1351 a year, and by the mid-18th C the island had more arable land than pasture. Arthur Young, writing in 1814, stated that it had the richest soil in the county.

In 1855, the War Department established an artillery range on Shoebury Sands on the mainland and in 1915 purchased the title to Foulness - the 'Lordship of the Island'. The population reached its peak in 1871 with 754 people living in 129 houses. Figures are not available more recent than those of the 1961 census which record a total population of 316, but an estimated 200 civilians still live on the island. However, access for the general public is prohibited by the Ministry of Defence. Foulness hit the headlines a few years ago when it was announced that an area comprising the island and the adjoining Maplin Sands was one of the proposed sites for the third London airport.

The five other islands in the group are **Wallasea, Potton, Havengore, Rushley** and **New England**. Havengore and New England are no longer true islands since the sea channels separating them from Foulness have been closed by the sea walls. Potton and Rushley are, like Foulness, controlled by the Ministry of Defence, which leaves Wallasea, joined to the mainland by a causeway, the only openly accessible island in the group. Originally called Wallfliet, it is four miles long by one-and-a-half miles wide and is completely enclosed by sea walls.

The whole area is rich in wildlife, particularly wildfowl; one-third of the world's population of brent geese winters in Essex, mainly around Foulness Point. Maplin Sands are teeming with seashore life; over 60 per cent of all cockles sold in Britain come from this area. One hundred years ago an unnamed naturalist wrote of the area: 'an idyllic paradise

of wild life, with swans reflected in the still blue waters of the fleets; as the sea lavender bursts into flower, a purple glow would steal over the marshes, and creek and pool were royally fringed with sea aster.'

Canvey Island

Essex. Canvey Island lies on the north side of the Thames Estuary, 26 miles from central London and five miles west of Southend-on-sea. Four miles long by two miles wide with a circumference of 13 miles, Canvey has 4351 acres of low-lying flat marshland, the entire island enclosed by a high sea wall and separated from the mainland by Benfleet Creek on the north-east, running into East Haven Creek on the north-west. The latter can be forded at low tide.

Composed of London clay and lying below the level of the spring tides the island was, for centuries, wholly or partly submerged by the sea. At the time of the Roman occupation of Britain, Canvey was about 20-ft higher than it is today and may have been part of the mainland. Essex was then inhabited by the Celtic tribe of Trinobantes who probably had settlements on Canvey for producing salt by evaporating sea water. At about the end of the 2nd C, there seems to have been a sudden fall in the land level by about 15-20 ft, resulting in the submergence of

the island and much of the surrounding mainland. After that there was a gradual elevation of the land which reached its peak about AD 1100.

The Norman Conquest did little to disturb the residents of Canvey Island who continued to graze sheep, which were not only kept for wool and meat but also for milk which was used for making cheese. Little of historical interest happened on Canvey Island until, in 1667, the Dutch attacked. One squadron of ships under Van Gent anchored at Hole Haven and fired several buildings and stole some sheep. Later on the same day Van Gent joined de Ruyter's main force and attacked Sheppey, capturing Sheerness and Queenborough.

About 30 years prior to the Dutch attack, work had begun on enclosing the island. A young Dutch engineer, Cornelius Vermuyden, suggested that he and a group of Dutch workers should build a wall around the saltings of Canvey Island and, in return, would receive one-third of all the land reclaimed from the sea. Considerable numbers of Dutch workers were employed by Vermuyden and, when the wall was complete, they settled on the island and became farmers, working the very land they had reclaimed. In 1648, over two hundred 'Low Country Strangers' lived on Canvey and one of their little octagonal houses can still be seen today, the Dutch Cottage Museum, standing just off the main island road near the industrial estate.

Canvey Island's development as a seaside resort and residential area began at the start of this century. Prior to World War I, the population was about 600; by 1947 this had risen to 10,030. In 1953, with the population numbering over 12,000, a disaster of immense proportions struck. On the night of 31 January, the island, along with the whole of the east coast of Britain, was flooded. Huge tides, whipped into a frenzy by strong winds, breached the sea walls and crashed

The Dutch Cottage Museum, Canvey Island.

Smallgains Creek, Canvey Island.

down on to a sleeping Canvey. Homes and shops were flooded, industry devastated and stock ruined. Most people had no warning; they were awakened by the sudden roar of the sea as it rushed through the breaches in the wall and swept over the island in minutes. Within one hour, the island was many feet under water, and the current was so strong that objects such as garden sheds were carried along 'travelling as fast as a bus'.

The heroism and courage of the people of Canvey can never be adequately recorded, but one story, told in Hilda Grieve's book, *The Great Tide*, sums up the horror of that fateful night. A young woman, living with her husband and three children in a house near the Central Wall, was awakened by the sound of rushing water and the baby crying and, jumping out of bed, she found the baby's cot floating in several feet of water. Since her husband could not swim, the woman climbed out of the window to attempt to reach the road and to fetch help. The water was so cold and the current so strong that about halfway across she realised that she would never make it and turned back. At no time could she touch the bottom. Reaching the house she climbed the outside staircase to the attic, found some blankets and bedding, proceeded to tear them into strips and made a rope. Then, leaning out of the attic window, she let down the rope to her husband who tied it round each of

the three children and the wife hauled them up one at a time.

This family was lucky; many were not. 58 people died on Canvey Island in one night of terror. Although the sea walls have been rebuilt to a greater height than before, many experts believe that, under certain meteorological conditions, surge tides, which are getting higher each year, could breach the sea defences once again.

Canvey Island today, with a population of 33,500, is more of a residential area than seaside resort and, although the sea front between Thorney Bay and Leigh Beck contains a holiday camp, hotels, guest houses and amusement parks, the area is not a Southend or Clacton-on-sea. The island has 530 acres of parks and open spaces, 3900 acres of nature reserves, a golf course, sports centre, swimming pool and over 215 small-boat moorings. There is a good open-air market which operates five days a week (including Sundays) in the summer. The industrial area is confined to the south and south-east parts of the island and, other than when visiting the Lobster Smack Inn at Hole Haven which happens to be situated right alongside an 85-acre methane-gas terminal, the gas and oil storage tanks do not appear that intrusive or noticeable.

The most pleasant part of the island is the area of mud flats and marshland on the eastern edge, from Canvey Point around Smallgains Creek and Tewkes Creek up through

Sixty Acres and Lakeside right up to the bridge at South Benfleet. The whole area is very pretty and is the western boundary of the Nature Conservancy Council's wildlife reserve. The northern limit of the reserve is **Two Tree Island**, just a few hundred yards from Canvey across Hadleigh Ray. This island consists of about 170 acres with its adjacent saltings and about 500 acres of intertidal mudflats. The western part of the island is used partly as a yachting centre and partly as a council rubbish tip.

The Kent Coast

Isle of Sheppey

Kent. The Isle of Sheppey is first mentioned in *Geographike Huphegesis*, written by the Greek historian, Ptolemy, in AD 161, when it was regarded as a stategic point of defence, situated as it is at the mouths of the Rivers Thames and Medway. The island is about nine miles long and four miles wide and contains some 22,400 acres, consisting of London clay and marshland, formed millions of years ago by ancient rivers when rich alluvial soil was washed down into the delta. In this London clay have been found deposits of fossilised tropical vegetation 10 to 20 million years old.

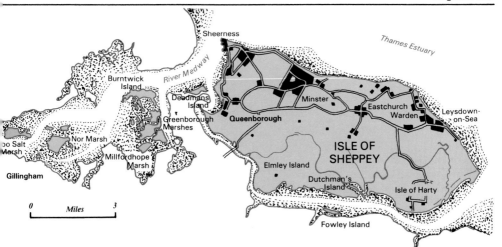

The remains have been found of 220 kinds of fish, birds and insects, the greater number of which are now extinct.

The presence of early man here has been proved by the discovery, at Harty, of a complete Bronze Age foundry (now in the Ashmolean Museum, Oxford), a tumulus near Borstall Hall and three earthworks at Queenborough. Although Sheppey was known to the Romans, who called it *Insula Ovinium* ('isle of sheep'), there is not much remaining evidence of Roman occupation. It is probable that they had a 'specular' (look-out post) at Minster, and a quantity of Roman tiles can be seen in the Sexburga Chapel in Minster Abbey Church; a kiln was discovered near Shell Ness point. The Saxons settled in Sheppey, changing the name to *Scaepige*, and built fortifications and an abbey at Minster. In AD 675, Sexburga, Queen of Kent, became its first abbess. She was canonised in 709 and the abbey became a place of pilgrimage.

For over 100 years the monastery prospered, then came the marauding Danes, first in 798, and later in 852 when the abbey was totally destroyed and the nuns put to the sword. By 893 the Danes had come to stay; a Danish prince, Hoestan, built a fort at Shurland and another at Queenborough, and planned to use the island as a base from which to conquer England. Prince Hoestan was finally defeated by King Alfred at Farnham and he retreated back to Sheppey. After several more abortive ventures he accepted defeat, embraced Christianity and settled on the island for good. In 1004, King Sweyn of Denmark invaded and was more successful than Hoestan, being crowned King of England. His son Cnut (Canute) succeeded him and lived for part of his reign at Shurland and, once more, civilised conditions prevailed. The abbey was restored and a few years of tranquility ensued.

After the Norman Conquest, Sheppey was divided up among several Norman barons - de Northwoode, de Shurland, de Cheyne and de Fiennes. They and their descendants became principle actors in the history of the island. Robert de Shurland accompanied Prince Edward on a Crusade in 1271, and when he became king, Edward I made de Shurland a Knight Banneret for his gallantry at the battle of Caelaverock in 1300.

It was around this Robert de Shurland that the legend of 'Grey Dolphin' is woven. Lord Robert was a man with a violent temper, and it is said that one day, when returning to Shurland Hall, he came upon a group of mourners who were arguing with a priest. Upon dismounting, he enquired into the cause of this unseemly conduct and was told that the priest had refused to bury the corpse unless he was paid first. Lord Robert was so angered that he drew his sword and slew the priest on the spot. When he reached Shurland Hall, he had grave misgivings; he knew that, when the news reached the monarch he would be severely punished, so he resolved to see him at once. He saddled his powerful horse, Grey Dolphin, and rode to where the King's ship lay at anchor, riding the horse far out from the shore to reach the ship. The King was impressed by this remarkable feat, and having a great liking for Lord Robert, he granted him a pardon. Upon reaching the shore once again, Lord Robert was accosted by an old woman, known as the Witch of Scrapsgate, who cursed him and said, 'This horse, which this day has saved your life, will one day cause your death.' Upon hearing these words Lord Robert once again flew into a rage and, drawing his sword, he killed the faithful Grey Dolphin. Some time later he was walking along the beach with some companions and, seeing the skull of the old horse lying there, proceeded to tell them the tale, contemptuously kicking the skull as he spoke. A bone pierced his foot and soon after he died of blood poisoning. Thus was the old witch's prophecy fulfilled. He died in 1310 and his tomb is in Minster Abbey Church; the head of Grey Dolphin, carved in stone, rests by his side.

In 1509, the newly crowned Henry VIII appointed Sir Thomas Cheyne to the Privy Chamber, and by 1539 Cheyne was Treasurer of the Royal Household, Warden of the Cinque Ports, Constable of Queenborough Castle and Lord Lieutenant of Kent. He lived to serve four monarchs, changing his religion to suit, and held high office and his possessions to the end.

On 11 June 1667 the Dutch fleet invaded and Sheerness was captured. The Mayor of Queenborough, in order to prevent further bloodshed, ordered the town to surrender and the Dutch flag was hoisted above the courthouse.

The gatehouse, Minster Abbey, Isle of Sheppey.

Queenborough, Isle of Sheppey.

During the mid-17th C, smuggling was rife in Sheppey and the headquarters of the gang was at the Old Royal Oak at Minster. Sir John Sawbridge, who lived at Warden Manor is reputed to have been the leader of the gang and it is said that his ghost can still be seen galloping through the woods on his way to supervise the unloading of an illicit cargo.

In 1901, Mr. J. T. Moore-Brabazon (later to become Lord Brabazon of Tara) formed a ballooning club at Muswell Manor, Leysdown-on-Sea, which, five years later, the Short brothers joined and soon began experimenting with designs for aeroplanes. They built six Wright biplanes, under licence, at a factory nearby and, in 1910, the factory was moved to Eastchurch. All the great names of aviation flew from here and from this modest beginning grew the Royal Flying Corps, which eventually became the RAF.

In 1960 a dramatic and depressive event took place on Sheppey: the dockyards of the Royal Navy officially closed. The financial loss to shops, services and to the people of Sheppey was devastating. However, since then, the people of Sheppey have slowly begun to rebuild the island's financial base; a new ferry bridge has been built and tourists are encouraged, new

industries have been started and Sheppey is once again a thriving, prosperous island.

For the visitor to the Isle of Sheppey, now with a total population of 32,000, the first stop must be Sheerness, the largest town on the island, which has strong associations as a naval base. The origins of Sheerness centre largely on its dockyards which were first laid out in 1665, Samuel Pepys noting in his diary: 'to Sheerness, where we walked up and down, laying out the ground to be taken for a yard, to lay provision for cleaning and repairing ships and most proper place it is for the purpose.' Before the coming of the docks, little existed at Sheerness, the port of Queenborough being the most important place on Sheppey. Today, the naval base has gone, in its place a trading estate and commercial docks, and almost all of the ancient historical buildings have now disappeared. Even the town clock was threatened, but the worthy citizens of Sheerness protested and it was allowed to remain. The ancient borough of Queenborough has been swallowed up and is now part of the Swale District Council.

Holiday-makers still come to Sheerness, attracted by the fine views across the Thames Estuary and the fact that it provides an

excellent base for exploring the rest of the island. Apart from the docks, which now handle a multitude of products, there is a vehicle and passenger ferry terminal providing a route to and from the Continent, via the Dutch port of Flushing. The town comprises three main areas: Mile Town, the commercial and shopping centre around the High Street; Marine Town, a largely residential area which is east of the High Street and extends to the sea front; and Bluetown, the area around the docks, so called because the residents used to use the paint from the naval dockyards to paint their houses. The esplanade provides a mile and a half of breezy promenade overlooking a sand and shingle beach, and Sheerness contains all the various shops and services of a busy modern town, plus an excellent open-air market (Tuesdays). There are a few hotels and plenty of guest houses.

About three miles south of Sheerness is Queenborough. It was originally known as Bynne, but the town was renamed by Edward III in honour of his wife, Queen Philippa, when he converted the town into a free borough. The post of Constable of Queenborough Castle (no longer standing) was held by many famous men, including John of Gaunt, father of Henry IV. A magnificent display of maces and regalia can be seen in the borough's ancient Guildhall which was erected in 1793 on the site of the old courthouse over which the Dutch flag flew in 1667. The English fleet, under Lord Howard, moored in Queenborough Harbour just before the attack of the Spanish Armada; a treasure chest, also in the Guildhall, was captured from a Spanish ship. The harbour has always been regarded as a safe haven for ships, and today it is extensively used by yachts and other small craft.

Across the harbour lies **Deadmans Island**, so called because it was used as a burial ground for the dead from ships in quarantine. Although surrounded by industry, the docks and steel mills of Sheerness in the north and the extensive area to the south used for storing imported cars and for light industry, Queenborough is perhaps the quietest and architecturally the most beautiful place on the island.

The road from Queenborough runs up the hill to the old village of Minster. The main feature of the village is Minster Abbey Church. In fact, it is really two churches – St Mary's and St Sexburga's. The northern half of the building is the nun's church and the southern half, the parish church. The gatehouse to the west is the only monastic building left of the once-great Minster Abbey.

Eastchurch lies a few miles east of Minster, hence the name - East of Minster Church. The early links with aeronautics are reflected in a stained-glass window in the parish church, commemorating C. S. Rolls and Cecil Grace, both of whom died in tragic flying accidents in 1910. Another link with flying is a splendid stone memorial to the early aviators which stands opposite the church. Just outside the village are the ruins of the 16th-C Shurland Hall, where the ill-fated Anne Boleyn and Henry VIII spent their honeymoon. Shurland Hall stands on private land and the public are not permitted to visit.

Eastchurch Memorial, Sheppey.

About two miles from Eastchurch, up on the north-eastern coast, is the holiday village of Warden, with hotels, guest houses, caravan sites, holiday camps, sandy beaches and low cliffs - an ideal place for families. The area has strong associations with smugglers and rumour has it that the local manor is linked to Shurland Hall by an as yet undiscovered tunnel. Many years ago the village of Warden was much larger and included a church, but this and many of the houses have vanished, victims of erosion by the sea. In fact, most of Sheppey's north coast is in great danger from the sea and massive defences are being prepared to prevent more land from slipping into it.

Further east on the coast is Leysdown-on-Sea, a sort of miniature Southend or Blackpool, with acres upon acres of caravans, chalets and holiday camps, fun fairs and amusement arcades. Its major attraction is a long expanse of sandy beach which gets very crowded during the summer months.

Halfway between Leysdown-on-Sea and Eastchurch, at Rides, is a sign pointing south to Harty Ferry. A narrow metalled road runs through the marshlands for four miles to the **Isle of Harty**. The Isle of Sheppey is practically three islands in one. Harty is almost completely separated from Sheppey by Capel Fleet, a freshwater creek controlled by sluice gates at Muswell Creek in the east and Bells Creek in

the west. Capel Fleet is now only a few yards wide but, at one time, before the road bridge was built, there used to be a ferry to the Isle of Harty from Oare, near Faversham, and a second ferry over Capel Fleet to the Isle of Sheppey. Apart from the farms, the church of St Thomas and the Ferry Inn are the only buildings on the little isle. The church was built in 1216 and there has been an inn on the present site since Elizabethan times. The ferry boat to the Kent mainland was in use until 1979. **Elmley Island** is the third 'island' on Sheppey, The Dray and Windmill Creek providing the island's boundaries; the village of Elmley is now almost deserted.

To see Sheppey one should either walk or hire a bicycle; there are many small tracks off the main road and plenty of footpaths along the coast and through the marshlands where a car cannot go. For the naturalist, the marshes will provide a variety of wild flowers, insects and birds not found in many other places in Britain. The importance of these marshes as an area of high conservation value is recognised by the Nature Conservancy Council, who manage a nature reserve at Shellness, on the extreme south-east tip of Sheppey, and the RSPB who also have a reserve at Elmley.

The waterways around Sheppey contain many small tidal islands and marshes: **Fowley Island** and **The Lilies** in the Swale; **Burntwick Island, Greenborough Marshes, Nor Marsh** and **Hoo Salt Marsh** in the River Medway. Most of these marshes are accessible at low water and provide the naturalist with the opportunity of observing the many different shore birds using them. The visitor to the Isle of Sheppey will find many other interesting things to do and places to see. It would be difficult not to find a sport that is not provided for on the island; golf, bowls, swimming, tennis, sailing and fishing are just a few of those offered. There are also cinemas and theatres, jazz and folk clubs, carnivals and village fêtes.

The South Coast

Thorney Island
West Sussex. Situated in Chichester Harbour just off the mainland near Emsworth, Thorney Island is about two miles long and one mile wide. Connected to the mainland by a bridge over a small creek called the Great Deep, it is flat and looks as though much of it has been reclaimed from the sea but, in fact, the opposite is true, as Thorney has lost much of its land to the sea in recent history.

The island seems to have been bypassed by most historical events. It is now owned by the Ministry of Defence and all information about its inhabitants and industry is classified. Apart from the three services, all of which use the island for one reason or another, some civilians do live there and it has recently become 'home' to quite a few Vietnamese 'boat people'. Being MOD property, there is no public access.

Hayling Island
Hampshire. Hayling Island lies two miles south of Havant between Chichester Harbour and Langstone Harbour. Shaped like an inverted T, it measures three-and-a-half miles north to south and four-and-a-half miles east to west across the southern coastline; the centre section of the island is only about half a mile wide. It is connected to the mainland by the Langstone Bridge, a long road bridge over the main channel linking the two harbours, and running alongside it are the remains of the old railway bridge, long since fallen into decay. The island consists of soft Reading clay and London clay in the north and Bracklesham beds in the south plus some chalk.

An axe-head dating from 2500 BC, now in the British Museum, was found on the island, indicating that early man at least hunted in the

The harbour, Queenborough, Isle of Sheppey.

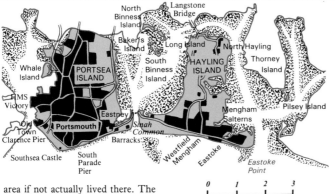

area if not actually lived there. The Celts, Saxons and, later, the Danes all left their mark on Hayling Island. The origin of the name is debatable: some sources say it derives from the Saxon *hal-ing*, meaning salt meadow; *The Oxford Dictionary of Place Names* lists it as 'the island of Haeglingas, after a Saxon tribe of that name'; and a third derivation, again from the Saxon, has it called *helige* or 'holy place'.

The Abbey of St Peter and St Mary was established on Hayling in AD 654, at one time housing over 900 monks and 1500 lay brothers. It stood, according to some sources, near the present church of St Peter's, but this is hotly disputed by many local historians who say that the site of the old abbey was on that part of the island off the south shore which was lost to the sea by flooding. Some charts show the name 'Church Rocks' in this area and there is a legend of bells having been heard ringing under the sea, so there may be some truth to the old abbey having been situated here. Perhaps one day some sub-aqua club will be sufficiently intrigued to find out the truth. The Danes destroyed everything on the island, including the abbey, during a raid in the 9th C.

After the Conquest the island was given to the Norman Abbey of Jumieges which held it until, in 1415, Henry V gave possession to Sheen Abbey. After the Dissolution it came into the hands of the Earl of Arundel, Henry Fitzalan. He died leaving two daughters, one of whom married Thomas Howard, Duke of Norfolk, and the Howard family remained the Lords of Hayling Island until 1825.

Many attempts have been made to commercialise and industrialise

North Hayling.

Hayling Island and all these endeavours have had to deal with the problem of access to and from the mainland. During the Victorian period, 'watering places' were springing up all along the south coast of England and on the Isle of Wight, and on Hayling Island the general idea was that, if the railway could be extended on to the island, then the wealthy tourists would follow. The Brighton line arrived at Havant in 1847 and a branch line to the island was planned. After several disasterous attempts (one line was washed away by the sea), the first train arrived on the island on 28 June 1867. The next step was to attract people to the island, and to this end the building of 16 imposing mansions, each with its own

grounds, was contemplated. This 'rich man's community' was to have been called Victoria Square and built on land that is now Hayling Park. A courageous idea but one that never became reality; lack of money and lack of interest by London's élite made sure that Hayling Island never became another Brighton.

The next idea was to make travelling between Portsea and Hayling a simple ferry-boat trip across Langstone Harbour. The SS *Hayling*, a 1000-passenger ship which could also carry tramcars, was to operate between the two islands, and Portsea's tramcars would simply run on to the ship and, once across the harbour, would continue through Hayling to the little town of Westfield. Unfortunately, the ship ran aground on a shingle bank and the whole idea was abandoned after it had taken 11 days to refloat her. Today, of course, a perfectly safe ferry shuttles back and forth between the two islands several times a day but it took several decades to make the plan operational after that first setback.

Hayling Island has four main areas: South Hayling, Sinah Beach, Eastoke and North Hayling. After crossing the bridge, the road leads south right down to the coast where it divides; to the right is Sinah Beach and to the left is Eastoke. Sinah Beach, containing the ferry terminal, a few houses and a golf course, is quiet, pretty and has no tourist facilities of any kind. There are several old houseboats on the north side of the road on the Sinah Lake inlet, most of which look as though the only thing holding them together is several coats of paint. Between the golf course and Black Point, sometimes referred to as Sandy Point, is a four-mile stretch of sand and shingle broken only by the lines of wooden breakwaters. The central

Langstone Bridge, Hayling Island.

area of the coast, at Westfield where the main roads join, contains a small fun fair and several hotels and guest houses. Further east between the Coast Guard look-out and Black Point, the whole coastline is dotted with holiday bungalows and amusement arcades.

The general development of the south of Hayling Island is a confused mess and could have been better controlled. Black, or Sandy, Point is not easy to get to, the way being blocked by many private roads and estates, but it, and the rest of the Chichester Harbour coastline, comprise mainly marshy creeks with yacht clubs and boatbuilders situated north of the hospital as far as Mengham Salterns. North Hayling is similar to East Mersea on Mersea Island – quiet and agricultural, with a small village and a church.

Hayling Island does not seem to have changed much over the years. Out of season it is very quiet, and even at the height of the holiday season it seems to be more of a weekend retreat than a fully fledged holiday resort. It has a large resident population of 15,295, but the great majority of people work either in Havant or Portsmouth and not on the island.

Langstone Harbour has several small islets, tiny sand and shingle ridges, situated close to Hayling Island: **Long Island, North Binness Island, Baker's Island** and **South Binness Island**. At low water it is difficult to see them since most of the harbour dries out twice a day, but at high water they stand a few feet above the sea.

Portsea Island

Hampshire. Looking like a mainland promontory, Portsea Island is situated between Hayling Island and Gosport, with Langstone Harbour on one side and Portsmouth Harbour on the other. Portsea is one of those islands from which, because they are so close and well connected to the mainland, it is impossible to get that 'island' feeling. Like Mersea, Sheppey and Canvey, it is a 'drive-on, drive-off', island and, as such, is rarely considered to be a 'true' island. Nevertheless, they are all islands and, in years gone by, communications were by boat only. Portsea, although assimilated into the mainland, is still a place of immense historic interest, having grown from a small 12th-C settlement to Britain's premier naval base.

The Portsea of today is totally dominated by the city of Portsmouth and the great majority of visitors know it only as the ferry departure point for the Isle of Wight. Portsmouth is an industrial, commercial and naval giant and by far the largest 'capital' of any of our offshore islands. A narrow channel called

The Round Tower, Old Town, Portsea.

Port Creek cuts off the island from the mainland, and over it three roads and one railway line now pass. In discussing the history of Portsea we are really talking about Portsmouth, since the city boundaries take in the whole island and part of the mainland as well.

The *Domesday Book* (c. 1086) makes no mention of the city and names only three manors – Buckland, Copnor and Fratton – on island, but during the 12th C the advantages of the Camber, a sheltered inlet just inside the harbour entrance, were recognised and a small town grew up around its shoreline, receiving its first charter from Richard I in 1194. No real attempt was made to fortify Portsmouth until 1481, when the Round Tower was constructed. Later Henry VII had a dry dock built nearby, the first in Europe, declaring it a Royal dockyard, and the growth of the naval dockyards led to a tremendous increase in population of the small town, and to more fortifications – Southsea Castle was built in 1544 and Fort Cumberland in 1747. The development of Southsea as a fashionable resort began in 1812 with the construction of elegant terraces and the promenade. Residential development on the island increased by leaps and bounds, and the population rose from 40,558 in 1811 to 159,251 in 1891; today it totals 198,000. Communications improved in 1847 with the opening of the Brighton-Portsmouth railway line; the Isle of Wight steam packet and the floating bridge betwen Portsmouth and Gosport had already been in operation for a few years.

Visitors will cross to the island by one of the three roads already mentioned, travelling through the new city centre (much of Portsmouth having been destroyed during the last war) down to the Old Town and dockyards. The Old Town is situated around the Point (the Portsmouth-Fishbourne car ferry

terminal is close by), once an area teeming with ale houses, brothels, sailors and press gangs. It still retains much of the old atmosphere with its narrow lanes, pretty houses and, of course, the Round Tower. This fort was one of a pair, the other being situated on the Gosport side of the harbour entrance, and a great chain, each link four feet long, connected the two forts and could be drawn taut by capstans to prevent enemy ships from entering the harbour. Leland commented on the 'mightie chayne of yron' in his itinerary of 1540, and it was in position until 1912. A few links are now in Southsea Castle and one is displayed in the City Museum.

Visitors are allowed into the Royal Dockyards but only to see HMS *Victory*, Nelson's flagship at Trafalgar, and the museum. There is a deep sense of history as soon as you pass through the main gates, not only because of the *Victory* but also because the yards are teeming with naval craft of all types, from submarines to destroyers. The *Victory* is a beautiful ship; about 226-ft long and 52-ft wide, she has a displacement of 3500 tons, and had a complement of 850 officers and men. She carried 104 guns on three decks and is the longest-serving ship in the world – built in 1765, she is still in commission as the flagship of the Commander-in-Chief, Portsmouth.

A little further north of the dockyards is a small islet named **Whale Island**, only a few acres in extent, now part of the naval base and, as such, out of bounds to the public. Other points of interest on this side of the island include: Quebec House, situated on the Point and once an early sea-bathing establishment; Broad Street, the many lanes leading off it and Grand Parade; and the Garrison Church, which used to be the military centre of Portsmouth. Since Portsmouth was also a garrison town there are several barracks, the two most impressive being Cambridge Barracks (now a grammar school) and

Clarence Barracks which is now the City Museum and Art Gallery.

Southsea's beginnings were due to military and naval overspill and it used to be referred to as 'the Village'. It has two piers and one of the longest seaside promenades in Britain as well as a rather unimpressive castle situated on the shore amid beautiful sunken gardens. The sea between Southsea and the Isle of Wight is known as Spithead and is the area of the Solent where the great naval reviews are held. Eastney, the area around Fort Cumberland, has, apart from the fort, two major tourist attractions -the Royal Marines' Museum and a Victorian pumping station.

The other main points of interest on or near Portsea are Farlington Marshes, to the north-east of the island, a vast area of mud flats which has become an important feeding ground for brent geese and other wildfowl during the winter; and in Fratton Road stands the original parish church of the island, St Mary's, rebuilt in 1889 by the generosity of W. H. Smith, son of the founder of the famous chain of bookstores, and First Lord of the Admiralty at the time.

Portsea seems to have connections with more than its fair share of famous writers: Charles Dickens was born at 393 Old Commercial Road, Portsmouth; Kipling spent several years at Southsea as a boy; H. G. Wells was an apprentice to a draper in King Street, Southsea and obviously drew on this experience for his novel *Kipps*; finally, Sir Arthur Conan Doyle lived in Southsea for seven years and it was here that he wrote his first book featuring Sherlock Holmes, while earning his living as the local doctor.

The Isle of Wight

Once part of Hampshire but now a county in its own right, the Isle of Wight is England's largest island. Measuring 23 miles long and 13 miles wide, the island is diamond-shaped, covering an area of 147 square miles, and is separated from the mainland by the Solent, a stretch of water which varies in width from one to six miles. The resident population is about 110,000, but during the summer months thousands of holiday-makers flock there, swelling this figure to a weekly average of 183,000. According to recent transport figures, more than seven million people cross the Solent each year; many, of course, are residents who work on the mainland, but the vast majority are tourists.

The coastline is deeply indented by bays, creeks, chines (deep clefts cut in the `cliffs by fast-flowing streams), caves and small harbours. The island is divided naturally into

two halves by a chalk ridge forming a central backbone running east-to-west from Culver Down to The Needles. The area to the north is underlain by Tertiary rock that is mostly clay with some sand and limestone, and the whole of this region is one of undulating lowlands. Most of the southern part of the island is composed of lower greensand (a kind of sandstone) rising to the highest points of the island along much of the south coast. The Needles, where the chalk ridge ends, are three giant stacks rising out of the sea off the western promontory, possibly the most famous rocks in Britain. There used to be a fourth stack, 'Lot's Wife', which crashed into the sea during a storm in 1764; it is recorded that the noise of this rock falling was heard on the mainland.

The island has four primary rivers: the Medina, the western Yar, the eastern Yar and Wooton Creek. The Medina is the main one, rising a few miles from the south coast and running north to emerge at Cowes, almost cutting the island in two.

The first inhabitants of the Isle of Wight were the 'Beaker Folk' who arrived around 1900 BC; several pieces of their distinctive pottery have been found here. Two thousands years later the island was invaded by the Belgae from the Low Countries who named the island *Wiht*, 'raised' or 'that which rises over the sea'. This is thought to refer to a time when there was a great inundation, resulting in the sinking of the ancient River Solent which separated the island from the mainland during the Bronze Age. The Romans, when they in turn arrived, translated this name to *Vectis*. After the Romans left Britain, the Jutes were the next invaders to see possibilities in the island; however, their relatively peaceful rule was shattered first by the South Saxons in AD 661 who defeated them but left them to administer the island, and then by the arrival of the Danes in 897; for about the next 100 years life on the island was disrupted by Viking raids.

The Isle of Wight formed part of the vast estate of Godwin, Earl of Wessex, who was second only to the King in wealth and power until his death in 1053. After the Conquest it was governed by a succession of Norman lords and one of them, Henry Beauchamp, Duke of Warwick, was actually crowned 'King of Vectis' by Henry VI, but it is doubtful if he was ever able to exercise any royal authority since sovereignty could not be held by anyone but the rightful king of England. In 1647 Charles I came to the Isle of Wight, fleeing from the English army now under the control of Parliament. The Governor, or

Captain, of the island at that time was Colonel Robert Hammond, whose allegiance was split between Parliament and the Crown. Hammond at first allowed the king as much freedom as he wished but, later, on orders from Parliament, confined him to his quarters in

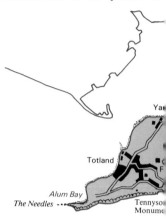

Carisbrooke Castle. After several abortive attempts to escape the king was finally taken back to London and was beheaded at Whitehall in 1649.

The gatehouse, Carisbrooke Castle, Isle of Wight.

After this the Isle of Wight does not feature largely in Britain's history until Queen Victoria purchased the Osborne estate and used it as a winter residence. The island, having gained royal favour, became the place to have a country home. Following closely in the steps of the wealthy came the tourists, first in a trickle and then in their thousands. The Isle of Wight is now one of Britain's foremost seaside resorts.

Cowes is probably the most widely known town on the island but it is, in fact, two very different towns - Cowes and East Cowes -divided by the River Medina. They derive their name from two sandbanks, called 'the cows', which were situated at either side of the mouth of the river. Cowes is the

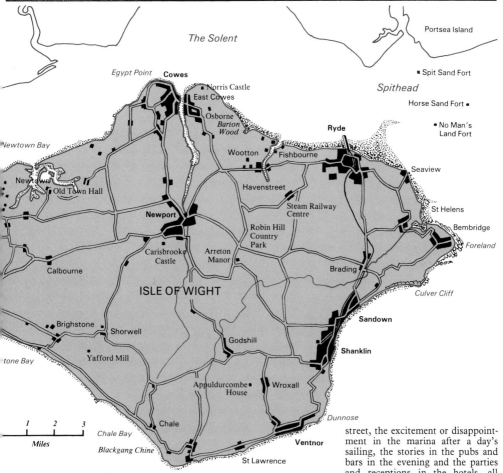

The Solent

Portsea Island

Egypt Point Cowes

Norris Castle
East Cowes

Osborne
Barton Wood

■ Spit Sand Fort

Spithead

Horse Sand Fort ■

■ No Man's Land Fort

Ryde

Newtown Bay

Wootton Fishbourne

Seaview

Newtown
Old Town Hall

Havenstreet

St Helens

Newport

Steam Railway Centre

Bembridge

Robin Hill Country Park

Foreland

Carisbrooke Castle

Arreton Manor

Calbourne

Brading

ISLE OF WIGHT

Culver Cliff

Brighstone

Shorwell

Sandown

Godshill

Shanklin

Yafford Mill

tone Bay

Appuldurcombe House

Wroxall

Miles 1 2 3

Chale

Dunnose

Chale Bay

Blackgang Chine

Ventnor

St Lawrence

St Catherine's Point

larger of the two towns and possesses a lot of Victorian charm, with narrow streets and picturesque architecture.

During the first week in August the town really comes alive when what seems to be the world and his boat arrive for 'Cowes Week' – the world's premier yachting event. This annual regatta is organised by the Royal Yacht Squadron, founded in 1812 by the Earl of Yarborough. The club has as its admiral the Duke of Edinburgh, and only the approximately 300 members, together with Her Majesty's ships of war in commission and Trinity House vessels when escorting royal yachts, are allowed to fly the white ensign and to take their vessels into all foreign ports without paying any harbour dues. None but members and officers of the Royal Navy may land their vessels at the stage in front of Cowes Castle, the club's headquarters.

During this hectic week, apart from the RYS regatta, eight other clubs also hold races, so at most times throughout the day the Solent

is so covered with sails that, at times, you can hardly see the water. Add to that the ferry boats, hydrofoils, hovercraft and all the other ships using the Solent each day and you can get some idea of the problems of being harbour master at Cowes.

Anyone with the slightest interest in sailing should visit Cowes during regatta week at least once in their lifetime. The hustle and bustle in the street, the excitement or disappointment in the marina after a day's sailing, the stories in the pubs and bars in the evening and the parties and receptions in the hotels, all make Cowes Week an unforgettable experience.

East Cowes is totally different from its sister across the river. Crossing the Medina is no problem at all, as there is a floating bridge and a regular ferry service. There are the boatbuilding yards and the large construction sheds of the helicopter and hovercraft industries on this side of the river. The town itself is drab and rather uninteresting, but on the

Osborne House, Isle of Wight.

outskirts to the east there are two fine houses, Norris Castle and Osborne House.

Norris Castle is privately owned but the grounds, including gardens, are open to the public. Half a mile down the road is Osborne House, built for Queen Victoria by Thomas Cubitt from designs by Prince Albert. The house is in the style of an Italian villa, with tall towers and a first-floor balcony, and the gardens are laid out in the Renaissance manner with terraces, fountains and statues. The pavilion wing (the Royal apartments) was completed in 1846, and the two eastern sections (Royal Household accommodation) in 1851. The Queen and Prince Albert spent a great deal of their private life at Osborne, preferring it to either Windsor or Balmoral.

After the Queen's death in 1901, the estate was presented to the nation by Edward VII and the apartments were opened to the public. They are exactly as the Queen left them and contain many of her personal items, paintings and souvenirs. Visitors can see the private rooms of the Royal Family, the State rooms and the beautiful gardens, particularly the terraces leading down to the sea.

One favourite tourist spot in the grounds is the Swiss Cottage. Erected in 1853, it belonged to the Royal children, who used it to learn all the aspects of running a house of their own - housekeeping, cooking, gardening and entertaining - often inviting their parents to tea, and cooking and serving everything themselves. The Swiss Cottage Museum contains all the things the children collected during their stays at Osborne - toys, curiosities, botanical specimens, etc. Behind the cottage is a miniature fortress built for Prince Arthur and used as a playground by all the children. Near the Swiss Cottage is Barton Manor, now part of the Osborne estate, 20 acres of beautiful gardens and vineyards. The wine from these, which can first be tasted, is on sale in the little shop on the estate.

Wooton Creek is tidal up as far as Wooton Bridge and is the most attractive river on the island, its banks covered with trees and wild flowers. Near its mouth, at Fishbourne, is the British Rail vehicle ferry terminal. Two places of interest in this area are Quarr Abbey and Havenstreet. The abbey was founded in 1132 by Bladwin de Redvers, Earl of Devon, whose family ruled the island for many generations. It was once an important Cistercian abbey but the scant remains show little evidence of this; the newer Benedictine abbey was begun in 1908. The name 'Quarr' is derived from the quarries at Binstead, and stone from these

The Town Hall and Wax Museum, Brading, Isle of Wight.

was used, not only to build the original abbey, but also to build Chichester Cathedral, Beaulieu Abbey and Porchester Castle. Havenstreet houses the Isle of Wight Steam Railway Centre with, in addition to the train rides, a fine display of railway relics.

To the north-east of here is Ryde, where people arrive on the passenger ferry and hovercraft from Portsmouth. The ferry is met by the train at the end of the 800-yd long pier, the railway line connecting with Brading, Sandown and Shanklin. The most striking buildings in Ryde are its churches, the most notable, and noticeable, being the parish church of All Saints, designed by Sir Gilbert Scott; the church and its 200-ft spire not only dominate the town, but the spire is also one of the first landmarks seen by travellers crossing the Solent. Ryde, like all the towns down this coast, was a Victorian seaside resort and it has not changed a great deal since then.

Take the coast road out of Ryde and through St Helens, Bembridge and Brading, instead of the main road directly to Sandown. Bembridge Harbour (sometimes referred to as Brading Haven) is a busy working harbour with many boat yards. This little bay used to extend as far inland as Brading, hence the alternative name, but the land was reclaimed from the Solent and Brading lost its waterfront but gained several hundred acres of land. The actual village of Bembridge seems to have been lost during the residential development that has taken place on the south side of the harbour in recent years. Of interest in this area are the Old Windmill, now owned by the National Trust, and the lifeboat station, situated in a little hut at the end of the pier.

Brading is one of the oldest towns on the island and contains the oldest house on the Isle of Wight, the Wax Museum. In the little town hall, sandwiched between the museum and the church, are three relics from a bygone age that once brought terror into the hearts of any

wrongdoers - the stocks, the whipping post and the town jail. The main pride of Brading and a tourist attraction is the Roman villa, discovered in 1880 at Morton Farm and said to be the finest collection of Roman remains in Britain. A large building has been constructed over the villa as protection, which also shields visitors from the weather.

Sandown, Shanklin, and Ventnor are the three main holiday centres made popular by the masses who flocked to the island after Queen Victoria came to live here. All are situated within a few miles of each other and all are similar in layout. Each has a pier and an esplanade backed by steep roads winding their way up the cliffs or downs, with houses and hotels perched on terraces overlooking the beaches with their shops, cafés, amusement arcades and deck chairs. They are not pretty towns, but neither have they succumbed to the crass commercialism of, say, Blackpool or Southend.

Ventnor has some charming houses, downs that rise 771 ft behind the town and, of course, the famous Undercliff, a landslip shelf running from St Catherine's Point to Dunnose sited between the towering cliffs and the sea. This area is famous for its associations with smuggling during the 18th and 19th centuries; at least two-thirds of the fishermen and quite a few farmers were engaged in this activity during that period. The Undercliff with its caves, chines and thick undergrowth was used as a landing point for illicit goods in order to outwit the excise men, who had a difficult time patrolling the area and an even harder time trying to find where the goods were hidden.

Of the three towns, Sandown, as the name suggests, has the best beaches and is backed by downs. Shanklin is really two communities, with the old village set back on top of the cliffs (where there is a chine), away from the holiday resort.

Opposite: *Winkle Street, Calbourne, Isle of Wight.*

Together with Ryde, these towns offer a traditional, unsophisticated British holiday with much to entertain the children during the day and a varied nightlife for adults in the pubs and bars in the evening.

A few miles north of Ventnor, near Wroxall, lies Appuldurcombe House, an imposing mansion that was once owned by Earl Godwin prior to the Norman Conquest. Between the 16th C and 19th C, the house was the seat of the Worsley family: Sir James Worsley was Keeper of the Wardrobe to Henry VIII, becoming the holder of all the important offices in the Isle of Wight, and the family made many alliances, by marriage, to some of the great families of England – the Nevilles, Herberts and Thynnes. Appuldurcombe has, unfortunately, been uninhabited since 1909 and the building has decayed to such an extent that only the shell now remains. Rose Macauley in her *Pleasure of Ruins* (1953) described the house as having 'disintegrated beautifully in all the morbid shades of a fading bruise'.

The coast runs along St Catherine's Down to Blackgang Chine, once an unspoiled wooded valley, but now the whole area has been turned into an amusement park, with bric-à-brac stalls, halls of mirrors, plastic gnomes and animals, a fun fair and a pirate ship. At night, with fairy lights everywhere, it looks like a giant Christmas tree.

Up the coast and inland from here is Yafford Mill, situated near the pretty village of Brighstone. This former flour mill itself is attractive and still has working machinery, but the whole atmosphere has been spoiled by commercialism, with playgrounds and picnic areas, gift shops and tea-rooms and (quoting from the brochure) 'Yafford seals living happily in their pool'.

In contrast, Calbourne Mill to the north, which is mentioned in the *Domesday Book*, is a fine museum of rural life. Everything has been kept as it was when the mill was a financially viable and important business, and the grounds around the mill contain a variety of wildfowl including several peacocks. Nearby, in the village of Calbourne, Winkle Street contains the most delightful row of houses on the island. Do not miss it, even if you have to push your way past crowds of artists and photographers all wanting to record this little gem.

The village of Freshwater is famous for being the home for many years of Alfred Lord Tennyson, the Victorian Poet Laureate; Farringford House, now a hotel, is where the poet lived. A granite memorial marks the area up on the downs, now called Tennyson Down, where he used to escape from unwelcome

Appuldurcombe House, near Wroxall, Isle of Wight.

tourists. If you continue west along the high ridge known as Main Bench, you will finally arrive at the western tip of the island, 440 ft above the sea overlooking Scratchell's Bay and **The Needles**. This is not the best position from which to view the latter as from here they tend to look smaller than they really are. Taking a boat trip around the rocks is a far better way to see them.

Alum Bay lies to the north-east of The Needles and much has been written about the unusual multi-coloured cliff face around it: 'Deep purplish-red, dusky blue, bright ochreous-yellow, grey approaching nearly white and absolute black, succeed each other as sharply as the stripes in silk' (Englefield). The cliff strata are vertically arranged and their tints are bright and varied. There is a multitude of tourist facilities on the cliff top, including a chairlift to take visitors down into the bay.

Standing on the eastern side of the western Yar, the little town of Yarmouth was once a port of some importance and, until 1832, returned two Members of Parliament. One of Henry VIII's castles, Yarmouth Castle, standing on the waterfront near to the ferry terminal for Lymington, is open to the public but is not as impressive as some others on the island. The George Hotel, near the castle, was once the home of one of Yarmouth's most distinguished residents – Sir Robert Holmes, Governor of the island (1667-1692), part-time buccaneer and one of the greatest seamen of his day. In the church there is a fine marble statue of him. It is said to have been originally intended to be a likeness of Louis XIV, and was on its way to Paris on board a French ship for the final sitting with the King –only the head remaining to be finished – when the ship was

captured by Sir Robert. He was so impressed by the statue that he had the sculptor fashion his head on to it instead of Louis'.

The Old Town Hall, Newtown.

A few miles east of Yarmouth is the tiny and, despite its name, ancient village of Newtown. Originally called Francheville, the village, or town as it was then, was razed to the ground by the French. In the 17th C it was important enough to have as its own Member of Parliament, John Churchill, later to become the first Duke of Marlborough, and 100 years ago Newtown was reputed to have one of the best harbours in the Isle of Wight, accommodating vessels of up to 500 tons. Today it comprises a scattering of cottages and a tiny town hall, and the once-fine harbour is now just a few creeks and marshland owned by the National Trust.

There is only one more place of importance – the 'capital' of the Isle of Wight, Newport, which received its first charter during the 12th C. Prior to this, Carisbrooke was almost certainly the principle town on the island, but after the Norman Conquest the more advantageous and accessible 'New Port' took precedence over the old Jute stronghold. The most remarkable old building in the town is the grammar school, dating from 1612, which was occupied for a time by Charles I

Arreton Manor, Isle of Wight.

during his negotiations with Parliament. The town itself looks like any other busy commercial centre, but there are one or two quiet little streets off the High Street with a lot to recommend them.

There is an interesting suggestion that Newport was the real town in Robert Browning's 'The Pied Piper of Hamelin'. It is said that Newport was once infested by rats which were duly exterminated by a man on the promise of a reward which was never paid; Browning supposedly transferred the story to Hamelin which had a similar tale. In certain reference books, the town in question is given as Newtown and, in this version, because the piper took all the children with him, that was why the French were able to attack so easily a generation later, as only the old men were left to defend the town. Whichever town it was, the story is unlikely to be true.

Carisbrooke Castle stands about one mile south of Newport, and first appears in recorded history as *Wihtgarasburgh*. A Roman settlement stood on the site of the present castle, and part of the foundations dates from this period. The 16th-C well-house contains a donkey-powered treadmill, and the old Governor's house is a fine museum.

Arreton Manor, about two miles east of Carisbrooke, was named in the 9th-C will of Alfred the Great, but the present house dates from 1595, and is possibly, with the exception of Osborne, the most impressive house on the island. There are several exhibitions and a museum inside the house plus a superb collection of dolls' houses and toys. Robin Hill Country Park, a mile north, has 80 acres of woodlands and meadows and over 100 species of animals. There are donkey rides, radio-controlled model boats, a commando-style assault course (for parents *and* children) plus a restaurant and bar. In good weather, it is the perfect place to take the family.

If you are interested in ornithology, Flamingo Park near Seaview east of Ryde, containing

hundreds of exotic birds and wildfowl, is worth a visit. If, on the other hand, you want to see or buy some local handicrafts, there is a pottery at Heasley Manor, near the village of Arreton, with an extensive range of gifts. For walkers and naturalists there is an excellent book published by the Isle of Wight Natural History Society which contains, apart from a complete list of all flora on the island, a botanical calender to guide you to the right places at the right time. There is no difficulty in gaining access to every part of the island, by car or public transport or on foot (public footpaths and long-distance trails are a main feature of the island).

The Isle of Wight offers all the normal sporting facilities found on the mainland – golf, tennis, bowling, squash, swimming and, of course, sailing – plus some first-rate fishing. Transportation to the island is either by car ferry, hydrofoil or hovercraft.

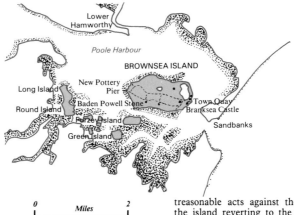

Brownsea Island

Dorset. Brownsea is the largest of the five main islands in Poole Harbour, one of the largest natural harbours in the world. Just inside its narrow entrance, a few hundred yards from Sandbanks, lies Brownsea, one-and-a-half miles long and one mile wide, extending over some 560 acres of woodland and

meadows with broad banks of rhododendrons.

The major part of Brownsea consists of Bagshot beds from the Eocene division, overlying London clay. It is these deposits of clay and gravel which have provided the island with various industries in the past. Copperas (green vitriol) was a substance used during the 16th C and 17th C for dyeing and tanning, and a small-scale industry extracting this substance existed on the island during this period. Alum was another product obtained from the same raw materials. Tobacco pipes were produced on Brownsea during the 18th C from various patches of pipe clay, and fire bricks were made in large quantities at about the same time. But the largest industry Brownsea has ever had was the production of salt-glazed drain-pipes in the 19th C; the large quantity of fragments littering the southern shore reveal the scale of this operation.

Although small, Brownsea has had a colourful history with records dating back to the reign of Edward the Confessor. Prior to the Norman Conquest, the island was part of the Manor of Studland and was known as *Brunei Insula* after Bruno, Lord of the Manor. The name has changed through the centuries from 'Brunei' to 'Brankse', 'Brunksay', 'Branksea' and finally to the present 'Brownsea'.

After the Conquest, William the Conqueror gave the Manor, including the island, to his half-brother, Robert, Earl of Mortain, who was later banished from Britain for treasonable acts against the King, the island reverting to the Crown. Thereafter, until the Dissolution, possession lay with the Abbey of Cerne. A small chapel dedicated to St Andrew was built on Brownsea during the 12th C but, by the mid-16th C, no trace of it remained. Henry VIII, in his attempt to fortify the whole of the south coast, had a gun fort built on Brownsea which now forms the base of the present castle tower.

In 1722, William Benson became the first of a long line of private owners when he paid £300 for the island. The local people called him 'Mad' Benson and he was in fact certified insane in 1741, but recovered his sanity one year later. It was widely believed that Benson practised black magic and, when a servant girl vanished, it was rumoured that he had sacrificed her to Satan. Fishermen said that they often heard blood-curdling screams ringing forth from the island and ghostly lights shimmering in the woods. Despite 'Mad' Benson's odd behaviour, it was he who cultivated Brownsea for the first time, planting more than 10,000 saplings and introducing rare plants and trees, and Brownsea owes much to him.

In 1852 Colonel William Petrie Waugh and his wife visited Brownsea and, while walking around the southern coast, Mary Waugh, who was an amateur geologist, mentioned to her husband that the clay sticking to their feet was, in her opinion, 'a valuable bed of china clay'. The colonel paid £13,000 for Brownsea and set about converting it into a comfortable home and profitable business; on the strength of Brownsea's 'valuable bed', a London bank put up £237,000 for the venture. The former gun fort was extended and renovated to make a castle, a church was built, a 14-acre site was cleared for a three-storeyed pottery, and a small village, called Maryland, was constructed for the pottery workers.

Unfortunately, it was discovered that the clay was of a low grade and only suitable for producing, for example, sanitation items such as drain-pipes, and not fine porcelain. Since drain-pipes would never produce the financial return needed on the capital invested, Colonel Waugh's little empire collapsed. Legal proceedings were instituted but the colonel and his wife had already disappeared (some reports say they fled to Spain), leaving the bank to collapse under the strain of such a loss.

Brownsea's next owner, the Rt. Hon. G. A. Cavendish-Bentinck MP, tried to salvage something out of the pottery industry by producing the only items possible from the clay - chimney pots, drain-pipes and ornamental figures - but in 1887, with the population of the island standing at 300, the venture once again proved unviable and the pottery was closed for the last time. Kenneth Balfour, also a Member of Parliament, became the next owner, and it was during his ownership that a disasterous fire broke out in the castle. Priceless paintings were destroyed in the blaze which left the building a smouldering wreck.

In 1901, a member of the wealthy

The Church, Brownsea Island.

tobacco family, Charles Van Raalte, purchased Brownsea, and a slow but steady transformation of the island began to take place, with the castle restored to even greater standard of luxury than before. Here over 30 servants were employed, and gardeners, boatmen, carriage drivers and even a resident 20-piece orchestra were hired to look after and entertain the many guests of the Van Raaltes, among whom were the Queen of Rumania, many of Queen Victoria's grandchildren and Prince Henry Maurice of Battenberg. A regular visitor to the island was Guglielmo Marconi, the inventor of the wireless radio, who met his future wife at one of Mrs Van Raalte's parties. In 1907, Lord Robert Baden-Powell held his first camp for Boy Scouts on Brownsea Island, an annual event that is still held today.

After the death of Charles Van Raalte the island passed to his son-in-law, Lord Howard de Walden, who sold it to Mrs Mary Florence Bonham-Cox-Christie in 1925 for £125,000. The new owner soon gave notice to all the islanders to pack and leave as soon as possible, and from that day no one was allowed to land on Brownsea. Mrs Bonham-Cox-Christie sealed off the island from the outside world and it quickly

reverted to its original wild state. Nothing was cultivated, animals wandered freely and anyone attempting to land was forcibly thrown back into the sea by one of the owner's few retainers. Even Peter Scott, the well-known naturalist, was refused permission to make a film of the rare plants and birds on Brownsea.

For the next 36 years the island remained a jungle and the castle was neglected and fell into decay, but at the same time Brownsea had become a wildlife sanctuary and, being undisturbed by man, birds and animals prospered and multiplied on the island. Mrs Bonham-Cox-Christie died in 1961 and her grandson gave the island to the Treasury in lieu of death duties, which in turn gave it to the National Trust. The cost of endowing the island (£100,000) was achieved by public appeal and the castle was purchased by the John Lewis Partnership as a holiday home for their staff. The money from that sale made it possible for the National Trust to turn back the overgrown tangle that had taken over and restore the island to its previous splendour. It now has a population of 21.

Visitors today land at the Town Quay on the east coast, where there is a little row of cottages on the

The Castle, Brownsea Island.

waterfront with a shop and a restaurant just behind. The castle is, unfortunately, not open to the public so they have to be content to gaze over the walls at this splendid residence. From the quayside the path leads past the castle towards the church, and a short way along this is The Look-out, a small wooden hut where visitors can gaze out over the lagoon and see the many species of waders and wildfowl that seek refuge here. The whole of the north coast of Brownsea is a nature reserve run by the Dorset Naturalists' Trust, who offer guided tours of the area every afternoon throughout the summer months.

The church, built by Colonel Waugh in 1853, stands about 200 yd from the castle, and in the graveyard there is a rather unusual Italianate well-head mounted over the grave of Mrs Cavendish-Bentinck. Leaving the church and heading up the hill on the south-shore path, the visitor will not only be surprised at the number of peacocks – there are over 150 – but also by their lack of fear when approached. The noise from these beautiful birds is devastating and the whole island rings with their screams, especially during the mating season towards the end of May.

At the top of the hill is Daffodil Field, a blaze of colour in April and a relic of Mrs Van Raalte's bulb-growing venture. From here the path goes west through the woods towards The Viewpoint. There are several trails leading down to the shore along this route but the best access to the beach is through the 'Scout Camp'. From this point there is a fine view of Furzey Island; Baden-Powell's memorial stone stands nearby.

The heathland and the woods on the south-west corner of the island are, surprisingly, favourite nesting areas for herring gulls. Walking through this area in late May will cause great commotion among the gulls and you will be lucky if you get through the area without being dived at by a few of the more aggressive males. The path is now almost at the western tip and passes several old clay workings and New Pottery Pier, the best place to tie up your dinghy if you arrive in your own boat, away from the dangerous currents of Brownsea Road to the east of the island. Between the clay workings and the old village of Maryland, the path is covered with fragments of terra-cotta pottery and is not all that easy to walk on. All that is left of the village are just a few broken-down walls and part of the factory that has been left standing in the undergrowth.

From here on, along the north side of Brownsea, the landscape changes dramatically with dark

forests of pine covering the whole area. The path now goes past the West and East Lakes, through the great marshy area on the north side of the path, which then winds its way through tunnels of rhododendrons until, finally, it emerges back at the church.

If you like to stroll along gently, taking a few photographs, watching the birds and sitting down occasionally to enjoy the view, then Brownsea needs at least four hours of your time, and that does not include the hour or so spent in the nature reserve. There are some excellent booklets in the island shop listing all the resident species of birds and mammals. There are at least eight of the latter breeding on the island, including more than 50 red squirrels, seven kinds of bat, pygmy shrew and sika deer. The bird population is numerous and includes cormorant, heron, Canada goose and oystercatcher.

Brownsea Island is open to the public every day between April and September, and boats run frequently throughout the day from Poole Quay and Sandbanks. The trip from Sandbanks takes only six minutes whereas it takes 30 minutes from Poole Quay.

The four other main islands in Poole Harbour are Furzey, Green, Round and Long Islands, all privately owned. **Furzey Island** lies a couple of hundred yards south-west of Brownsea and covers an area of 31 acres of which much is covered by dark woodlands; the highest point is only 30 ft above sea level. There are three houses; the main one was built in Purbeck stone by Lord and Lady Iliffe who owned the island during the 1930s. The island has had many owners during the last 100 years; it was bought in 1969 by the Midlands industrialist, Newton Mason, for £30,000, and, at the time of writing, was bought by Algernon Cluff for a reported price of £500,000 – but then that does include a colony of red squirrels and two wallabies! Landing on Furzey is not permitted without the owner's permission.

Green Island, covering only 20 acres, is situated a little further south-west and rises to a height of 50 ft. Like Furzey and Brownsea, it is covered in trees and rhododendrons. Once connected to the mainland by a causeway and formerly called St Helen's Island, it has no ancient recorded history but it is thought that, about 2000 years ago, Kimmeridge shale was worked there and domestic utensils, tombstones and ornaments produced.

Long Island and **Round Island**, to the west of Brownsea, are usually shown on most maps as one land mass; in fact, a strip of marshland separates them and this is only

covered at the high water of spring tides. Neither island is larger than 15 acres and contains no valuable agriculture or woodland, yet in the 1960s Mr Stanley Fowler from Birmingham paid £100,000 for them, a high price to pay for seclusion.

Thatcher Rock

Devon. Thatcher Rock, rising to 132 ft with an area of two acres, stands about a quarter of a mile from the Devon coast at the northern end of Torbay. It was purchased in 1967 by the Torquay Corporation from a Mr Whidborne, together with two other small rocks, the **Ore Stone** and the **Lead Stone** (also called Flat Rock). Thatcher Rock (the name probably comes from the fact that its outline looks like a straw-thatched roof) is a well-known local beauty spot, best seen from Marine Drive in Torquay, and is now a bird sanctuary. Although it is possible to land there, it is not always so easy to get off, as two youths found when they were marooned on the rock for several days in the 1930s. There are no buildings or ruins and no mention in historical records, except that the three were alluded to by Leland in 1550 as 'rocks in the sea'.

Burgh Island

Devon. Situated about 400 yd south of Bigbury-on-Sea, at the mouth of the River Avon, lies Burgh Island, 21 acres in extent rising to 160 ft above sea level. It is connected to the mainland at low water, and visitors may walk over the sands or, during the summer months, take the 'sea tractor' when the tide is in. In 1870, the island was well known as a picnic spot but, by 1890, the tea house and the inn were deserted. The advent of the motor car changed all this and soon crowds of tourists came each year to Bigbury-on-Sea and to Burgh Island.

Between 1910 and 1946 the island changed hands four times, first for £500, then £1000 and then for £5000, the purchaser on this occasion being a Midlands steel millionaire, Archibald Nettlefold. Nettlefold spent over £60,000 building a luxury 40-room hotel with its own swimming pool, and started to develop the island as a holiday resort. However, in 1946 he sold the island and the property for £36,500, and the property has since changed hands several times. The hotel still dominates Burgh Island; near it stands the Pilchard Inn, said to date back to 1395 and reputed to have been the haunt of smugglers in the 18th and 19th centuries. One of its most interesting features is the stone fireplace with carvings on either side depicting Tom Crocker, smuggler *and* excise officer.

The remains of an ancient chapel

Burgh Island.

Great Mew Stone

Devon. Great Mew Stone rises nearly 200 ft out of the water at the entrance to Wembury Bay, five miles south-east of Plymouth. Barely three acres in extent, it is hard to believe that this steep-sided crag would support anything other than goats or gulls. But Great Mew Stone has been included in this book because of one man – Sam Wakeham. Sam was, in fact, just one of several residents of Great Mew Stone in recorded history, but it is his life-style, recorded and documented, that makes this rock worthy of mention.

The rock became part of the Langdon Estate on the mainland, owned from 1555 to 1850 by the Calmady family. All Great Mew Stone residents were tenants of the family, and they were allowed to live rent-free for one purpose – to keep their master's table well stocked with fish and rabbits, and to protect the rabbits out of season so that the lord of the manor might enjoy an occasional day's hunting.

were discovered on the top of the island in 1959. First recorded in 1411, this was dedicated to St Michael and was known as 'St Michael-de-la-Burgh'. The island itself has been known by many names in the past – 'Borough', 'Burr' and 'Bur', all corruptions of the 15th-C 'la Burgh' – but it was more familiar to fishermen as St Michael's Rock. Camden wrote (1586), 'Where Avon's waters with the sea are mixed, St Michael firmly on a rock is fixt', and, in Thomas Westcote's *View of Devonshire* (1630), the author refers to 'St Michael's Island and Hope Bay, famous for fishing for Pilchards'. The name of the inn also indicates that the island was once a medieval net-fishing (seine) station. The site of the chapel was converted into a shelter for the 'huer', a man who signalled the approach of the pilchard shoals, about 170 years ago.

At one time there must have been a settled population on the north-east side of the island, as evidenced by the remains of several cottages. It was also frequented by wreckers as well as smugglers. In 1772, so the

tale goes, the *Chanteluope*, homeward bound from the West Indies, was wrecked on the island; all passengers and crew were lost, except for one unfortunate woman who had put on all her jewels before swimming to safety. When she reached the shore she was attacked and robbed and buried in the sand. Her attackers, in their haste, even cut off her fingers and ears to get her jewels.

Out of season the island is drab and inhospitable, but in the summer months it comes to life. The hotel is now converted into self-catering holiday flatlets, the inn opens for business and the sea tractor trundles over the sands at high tide carrying holiday-makers. At low water the neck of sand between the island and the mainland dries out and becomes so crowded that you would be hard pressed to find enough room to pitch a deck chair on the sands, never mind walking over to the island. The best time to visit is 'slightly out of season', when there is room to walk round the island and have a quiet drink in the inn.

Sam Wakeham had been living on the rock for many years when, in 1833, he married and took his wife to live there as well, enlarging his little cottage, said to contain stones from an ancient chapel which once stood on the rock. This chapel, dedicated to St Michael, would also have served as a lighthouse, such as those that existed on Drake's Island and numerous others around the coast. Sam's daily activities included fishing, collecting seagulls' eggs, catching crabs and rabbits. He was also aware of the profit to be made from tourists and, for their benefit, he cut two 'thrones' out of solid rock, so that visitors could sit and appreciate the splendid views extending from Bolt Head in the east to The Lizard in the west.

In 1834, when the *South Devon Monthly* published an article about the rock, Sam Wakeham wasted no time in penning a letter to the journal to make it known that 'if any genteelman what likes a wark, he can wark to the shoar at Wembury, and if they holds up there a white pocket hanchecuffs for a signal, ile cum off in me bote and fetch them to the island for two pens a pease.' He went on to say that these visitors could 'shut rabets at nine pens a pease' and that 'my missus hasent got no habjecksuns to boyll the kittle and hand the taypot out of the winder and put a tabell outside and everything humbell and cumfortabell.' And the tourists came from all over the country. Sam and his wife sold them bottles of porter and cups of tea, eggs and ham, casks of biscuits, cabbages and rabbits.

For many years Sam and his family (he had two children) lived

Burgh Island.

Great Mew Stone.

very well. It has been documented that he also did a bit of smuggling to supplement his income and that he had several caves and other hiding places for the illicit goods. However, in 1837, a visit from an exciseman pretending to be a tourist put paid to Sam's life on Great Mew Stone. A story appeared in the *Plymouth, Devonport and Stonehouse News* on 25 February of that year: 'Sam Wakeham has abdicated his throne on the Mew Stone and is about to retire into private life by plying as a boatman at the Barbican Steps. Sam has lived on the island for many years and there he waxed fat, espoused a wife and procreated two flourishing young ones. He lived as became him, like a prince, most folks supposing that he did so at the expense of his fat pigs and lean rabbits.'

Sam Wakeham had no successor as 'Lord of the Isle'. Offered with vacant possession, the Great Mew Stone was sold at auction for £500 and today is just another rock off our coast, something to gaze at while picnicking on the beach. Access is by boat only, so you either need your own boat or must persuade one of the boatmen at Newton Ferrers or the Barbican Steps, Plymouth to take you out to the island.

DRAKE'S ISLAND

Casemates

0   Miles   ¼

Drake's Island

Devon. Drake's Island is situated in the middle of Plymouth Sound, formed of hard volcanic rock, covering six acres and rising to a height of 96 ft. It was originally part of a rocky outcrop that ran into the Sound from

Mount Edgcumbe on the western side of the bay; most of this has been worn away by the sea but a little of it remains and can be seen at low water.

Known as the 'Bridge', this rocky ledge has been used to great advantage by the military in their efforts to defend Plymouth, since passage through the Sound on the western side of Drake's Island is impossible except for the smallest ships. Therefore, all defences could be concentrated on the eastern side of the Sound where there is a deep-water channel, and any attack on the town or the dockyards would have to be preceded by an attack on Drake's Island to silence the guns that cover this approach. Drake's Island has thus played a major role in the defence of Plymouth, the naval dockyards and, ultimately, England.

The island first appears in the records in 1135, when St Michael's Island, its original name, was transferred to the ownership of the priors of Plympton by the previous owners, the Norman family of Valletort. Although no remains are to be found today, a chapel dedicated to St Michael stood on the very top of the island. The name of the island was later changed to St Nicholas, patron saint of sailors.

During the 14th C, the island was used as a store for goods in transit and a bonded warehouse was built; provided that the goods were not offered for sale, no duty was charged. In 1550, the old chapel was demolished and, as a result of the wars with the French, fortifications were begun. About 1590, the name was changed once again, this time in honour of Plymouth's most famous son, Sir Francis Drake. Drake had come to know the island when he was a boy; in 1548, he, his father and other Protestants had taken refuge there when Plymouth was overrun by Catholic rebels. Many years later, in 1580, on his return from his historic voyage around the world, he anchored the *Golden Hind* near the island until he learned whether Queen Elizabeth was still alive and if she approved of his voyage. Had she not been alive *and* approving, Drake almost certainly would have sailed away because of his many enemies. The Queen, however, welcomed Drake and his 'stolen treasure'. Just how much treasure he brought back is not known but estimates of its worth vary between £1-2½ million in today's terms. One year later Sir Francis Drake became Mayor of Plymouth as well as advisor on maritime matters to the Queen. The people of Plymouth bestowed on him the office of 'Captain of the Island', but it is unlikely that he ever had time to take up this position.

In 1599, the island contained a garrison of 300 men, since the threat

of a retaliatory attack by the Spanish hung heavily over England at this time: the Armada had been defeated only 11 years previously and the two countries were still at war. The Civil War broke out in 1642 and Plymouth decided to back Cromwell, the town and the island successfully withstanding a siege by the Royalist troops, but after the Restoration many of the town's citizens were confined, with other political prisoners, on Drake's Island, which was used as a prison between 1660 and 1684. Its most notable detainee was Major-General John Lambert, who would have succeeded Cromwell as Lord Protector.

In 1701, more fortifications were erected, some remains of which can still be seen today – the entrance gate and small courtyard, the musket ledge and the musket wall – and the island's firepower at this time amounted to 23 32-pounders, six 18-pounders and two 13-inch mortars. For the next 260 years Drake's Island was truly a military fortress. The casemates, still there today, were built in 1860 and contained 29 guns, including six 80-pounders. The island was ready to repel any attack but, fortunately, no attack ever came and these massive guns were never fired except in practice. Concrete gun-emplacements on the top of the island date from World War I. The Ministry of Defence finally released the island in 1963 and gave it to the National Trust, who leased it to Plymouth as a youth training base.

For the sub-aqua enthusiast, Drake's Island has a tremendous appeal because of its history of shipwrecks, standing as it does near the main tidal flow of the River Tamar. These include the 70-gun HMS *Conqueror*, wrecked in 1760, and the *Paulsgrove*, an East Indiaman wrecked in 1637. One loss of an entirely different nature occurred in 1798, when a certain Mr Day from Suffolk claimed that he had invented a diving machine in which a man could live underwater for up to 12 hours. The experiment took place near the island in 28 fathoms (168 ft) on 20 June. Mr Day equipped his vessel with a hammock, watch, bottle of water and some biscuits and was full of confidence that the experiment would succeed and he would emerge from the sea 12 hours later. The crowds watched excitedly as the vessel sank below the waves. After 12 hours, attempts were made to locate Mr Day and his vessel but without success. No trace of either has ever been found.

Today, experiments of a more successful nature are taking place on the island, now known as 'Drake's Island Adventure Centre'. Groups of boys and girls come to the island for a wide range of adventure-based courses, covering sailing, rock climbing, marine biology and expeditions. The groups are made up of young people over 12 years old who come from a wide variety of backgrounds and environments: school and industry groups, Scouts, and Guides, foreign students and also individuals, sponsored by organisations and companies. There is dormitory accommodation for 96 students as well as recreational areas and lecture rooms, and the catering facilities are first class.

Visitors' trips to the island can be arranged between the end of May and the end of September when regular transport is available. They are shown a complete audio-visual presentation of the island and its various activities, and are given a conducted tour of the fortifications and the museum. A café and a shop are provided for refreshments.

The landing pier, the obvious place to begin a tour of the island, was built in 1939 in preparation for World War II; it used to have a narrow-gauge railway track to transport ammunition and supplies into the magazines. Access from the pier is literally through a door, built in Tudor times to make an invasion of the island almost impossible, since the door could be covered from the musket ledge up above. Through the courtyard, the first building to be seen is that of the commanding officer's house, now used by the island's staff as an administration centre. The barrack block beyond was constructed in 1830 and is still used for the same purpose, except that now students sleep there. Behind the commanding officer's house is the entrance tunnel to the casemates. There are various tunnels connecting the ammunition magazines with the gun emplacements, and this unique complex of stonework and tunnels shows the extent to which Britain went to defend herself in times of war. The highest ground on the island is occupied by the upper battery of World War I vintage. In 1978, four 11-inch guns were found buried on the upper battery, each one weighing 25 tons; when originally made in 1869 these were capable of penetrating 13-inch armour at 1000 yd.

At the front of the casemates on the north cliffs stands the oldest building on the island, an oubliette dungeon. Prisoners were dropped through an opening in the roof and simply left there to die, or so it seems since there was no other entrance or exit to the building other than the roof. On the other side of the island, behind the barrack block, is the western musket wall, constructed during the Civil War; it was, at that time, the only defence on that side of the island. Below the wall is the islet

Looe Island.

known as **Little Drake's Island**, connected to the main island by a sand ridge at low water and a popular spot with visitors because of its little beach; the only other beach on the island is near the landing pier. Also from this spot, a good view can be seen of the 'Bridge' and, particularly at low tide, the remains of a wartime barge.

Transport to the island is by boat from the Mayflower Steps, Plymouth, and information on adventure courses and holidays is available from The Mayflower Centre, Plymouth, Devon.

Looe Island

Cornwall. Looe Island lies about one mile south of West Looe, and is half a mile in circumference and 22½ acres in extent. The island has been known by many names in the past; Camden referred to it as St Michael's, Leland called it St Nicholas's and Carew knew it as St George's.

In the 1377 census of Cornwall the island was uninhabited and, when Leland visited the county in 1530, he mentioned St Nicholas's Isle, '6 or 7 acres in cumpace and feedeth conies [rabbits]'; Carew, in 1602, said the island contained 'a great abundance of sundry seafoule'. Looe Island was included in a charter incorporating West Looe, or Porbuan as it was known then, and was confirmed by Edward II during the 14th C.

At one time, the island abounded with rabbits and rats, the rats coming from the various ships wrecked on the rocks called **The Ranneys** at the eastern end of the island. Their numbers were very much depleted during the 19th C when the local inhabitants caught both rats and rabbits for food. Thomas Bond's *Sketches of East and*

West Looe (1823) states that 'a rat smothered with onions must no doubt be a delicate dish'. In 1823, the Finn family lived on the island, owned at that time by Sir Harry Trelawny; the Finns had previously been the tenants of Great Mew Stone, prior to Sam Wakeham.

Although only 22½ acres the island looks much bigger, with a hill rising to 150 ft and a rugged coastline indented with steep cliffs. The south-east coast slopes down to a promontory which is joined by a bridge to a small islet. Looe Island is now owned by two sisters, Evelyn and Babs Atkins, who originally came to Looe in 1964 to open a pottery but purchased the island instead. The story of how and why they bought it is told in a delightful book, *We Bought an Island* by Evelyn Atkins. Being privately owned, Looe Island can only be visited with permission from the owners.

Asparagus Islands

Cornwall. Situated in Kynance Cove, a few miles north-west of The Lizard, lie a group of rocks known locally as the Asparagus Islands, individually called **The Bellows**, **Asparagus Island** and **Gull Rock**. The National Trust now owns the islands along with much of the surrounding area and they have changed the name to Kynance Island. The Bellows and Asparagus Island are joined together and both are accessible from the mainland at low water, although climbing their steep sides is not easy. The group covers an area of about 14 acres, uninhabited except for birds, with a little soil and grass, which is slowly being eroded by the great number of tourists visiting the area.

Kynance Cove itself is a very pretty, steep-sided cleft cut into the cliffs which, on the western side of the cove, reach a height of about 200 ft. The whole area is extremely popular with geologists and rock climbers. There is a car park and a shop at the top of the cliffs and a pathway with steps leading down to the cove. Although steep, the cliffs are not at all difficult to climb, but care must be taken when approaching the cliff top since the area is not too stable and there are signs of landslip.

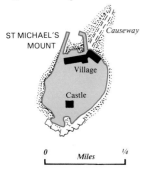

ST MICHAEL'S MOUNT

Causeway

Village

Castle

0 — Miles — ¼

St Michael's Mount

Cornwall. Situated in Mount's Bay about three miles east of Penzance and half-a-mile south of Marazion, St Michael's Mount rises out of the sea like a tiny jewelled stone. It is circular in shape and reaches a height of 300 ft, crowned by an ancient castle. According to an old Cornish legend, the archangel St Michael appeared before some fishermen on the western side of the island in about AD 500. In ancient times the island was widely known as a trading port; Pytheas, the navigator of Marseilles, recorded that, in about 320 BC, Cornish tin was exported to the Mediterranean from the island of 'Ictis', and Diodorus, the Sicilian historian, writing in about 31 BC, gave a more detailed account of Ictis and how tin was worked on the Cornish mainland and carried over, at low water, to it. From here it was purchased by merchants, probably the Veneti, a powerful sea-faring people from Brittany, and transported to Gaul.

The legends of the Mount Giants possibly came about as a result of pirates and robbers using the island as a base. One such story concerns Jack the Giant Killer and a giant called Cormoran, who would often wade ashore and steal cows and sheep from the mainland farms and carry them back to the island. Jack, a local boy, decided to trap the giant and one night he rowed out to the island while Cormoran slept. He dug a large pit and, when daybreak came, blew his horn and woke up the giant. Standing with his back to the sun, Jack proceeded to taunt Cormoran who came running out of his castle to get this foolish boy. In his rush

down the hill and blinded by the sun, he fell into the pit and died. The pit, or well, is still shown to visitors.

Tradition has it that both St Cadoc and St Keyne visited the Mount in the 6th C. Very little is known about the island during that era but, in 1086, records show that Brismar, a priest, owned it and that the chapel there was dedicated to St Michael. After the Norman Conquest, the abbot of Mount St Michel in Normandy built a priory here and in 1144 it was consecrated by the Bishop of Exeter. In 1275 an earth-quake destroyed the church and it was not rebuilt until sometime in the middle of the 14th C.

The stone causeway was constructed in 1427 by William Morton who then demanded the payment of a toll by all the ships who used the harbour. During the Middle Ages, St Michael's Mount became a place of pilgrimage and, for many who came, a difficult and dangerous climb to St Michael's Chair was necessary as a form of self-imposed penance. The original 'chair' was said to be first located on the spot where St Michael appeared to the fishermen, but it was later moved to the top of the church tower. Pilgrims waiting for the tide to turn would worship in a little chapel called The Virgin on the Rock, which was situated on the mainland side of the causeway. Today, about one-third of the way across lies a large stone, on which a wooden cross once stood to mark the site of the little chapel. It seems that either the stone has been moved or the level of the sea was lower in those days than it is today. The latter seems to be a more acceptable choice since William Borlase stated (1756) that Mount's Bay was once a great forest and that he himself had seen the stumps of trees at low water. The island, in fact, was once known as 'The Heugh [Hill] in the Wood'.

During the Wars of the Roses, both sides used the island. The Earl of Oxford, commander of the defeated Lancastrian army, escaped to France but soon returned with a fleet of ships and, in 1473, captured the Mount. For 26 weeks, the Earl withstood a siege by Edward IV but was forced to surrender by his own men who had been promised a pardon by the King. In 1497, the Mount became a base for Perkin Warbeck and his wife, Lady Catherine Gordon. Warbeck claimed to be one of the two princes supposedly murdered in the tower, thus the rightful heir to the throne, and, supported by the King of Scotland, he attempted to depose Henry VII. Leaving his wife on the island, he and his followers laid siege to Exeter but were defeated by the Earl of Devon. Although Warbeck

The Castle, St Michael's Mount.

was able to escape, he was later captured and imprisoned in the Tower where he confessed that he was not Richard, Duke of York, but the son of a boatman from Tournai. He was tried and executed in 1499. Lady Catherine was taken back to London where she became a favourite of the King.

After the dissolution of the monasteries, the Mount reverted to the Crown and was leased to various captains or governors. In 1588, the approach of the Spanish Armada was first signalled from the beacon on top of the church, and later, after the defeat of the Armada, Queen Elizabeth, in need of money to pay for her sailors and soldiers, sold the island to Robert Cecil, Earl of Salisbury and Secretary of State; it is not known whether he actually lived in the castle or even visited the island. In 1640, the Mount was again sold, this time to Sir Francis Bassett. Two years later the Civil War broke out with most of Cornwall declaring for the King, and Bassett became High Sheriff of Cornwall, taking a leading part in the battles against the Roundheads. When defeat seemed imminent, the son of the King, later Charles II, was moved for safety, first to St Michael's Mount and then to the Isles of Scilly, prior to being taken to Jersey. A room in the Mount's castle is still known as 'King Charles' Room'. The island was finally surrendered to the Roundheads in 1646, and a year later Parliament appointed Colonel John St Aubyn as military governor who later purchased the island from the Bassett family.

The St Aubyn family retained ownership of the island for 307 years until, in 1954, the Mount was given to the National Trust together with a large endowment to preserve the island for the future. The gift was subject to certain conditions - that part of the castle and gardens were leased back to the family - and the

Interior, The Castle, St Michael's Mount.

The Isles of Scilly

Situated 28 miles south-west of Land's End are a group of more than 140 small islands and rocks - the Isles of Scilly. The largest, St Mary's, is only three miles at its widest point and ten miles in diameter. Only six islands are inhabited - St Mary's, St Martin's, St Agnes, Gugh, Tresco and Bryher -with a total population of 2040. The total area for these six islands is 3568 acres and the other 130-odd islands in the group occupy an area of only 396 acres.

The Isles of Scilly consist mainly of granite, differing from the granite of Cornwall by being whiter and softer and containing minerals such as quartz, biotite, orthoclase and muscovite. Being soft, the granite has weathered into weird shapes, best seen on the southern coast of St Mary's. Where the granite has not been exposed, there is a thin covering of soil and a great deal of blown sand; this, combined with an excellent sunshine record, an adequate rainfall and the almost complete absence of air frost, enables the cultivation of a great variety of trees and plants normally seen only in sub-tropical areas or botanical gardens.

Root crops do extremely well in Scilly, and palm trees grow on most of the inhabited islands as do

Monterey pines from northern California. However, these islands should not be thought of as a 'sub-tropical paradise', the term used by most travel agents to describe Scilly. The weather in Scilly, like that of any other island, is extremely changeable. Although a mild climate prevails most of the time, the islands are prone to strong winds and violent gales, especially in the spring and autumn, and winter in Scilly can be a daunting experience.

It is not known just how long the islands have been separated from the British mainland, but most experts agree that it happened before the appearance of man, despite the legend of 'The Lost Land of Lyonesse' - the sequel to the story of King Arthur. After Mordred killed Arthur his followers were chased across Cornwall, finally reaching the western hills. Following their arrival, the land between these hills and Land's End - the Land of Lyonesse - was submerged, drowning the army of Mordred. The 'western hills' were the present Isles of Scilly.

Legends apart, Scilly has been subjected to many inundations in recorded history. Strabo, writing in about AD 18, stated that there were ten islands lying west of Britain, which he called the *Cassiterides*. In AD 240 Solinus, the Roman geographer, recorded one principle island, *Insula Sylina*, and, from then on, the islands were known only in the singular: 'Sylinancim', 'Sully', 'Sullya' and the modern 'Scilly'. William Borlase, visiting in 1752,

present Lord St Leven, John St Aubyn, still lives there with his family. The island, now with a resident population of 25, is open to the public on certain days each week throughout the year, but some rooms in the castle are only open during the summer months. During the holiday season, motor launches ply between Penzance and Marazion when the tide is high and the causeway covered, but, if you do visit the island by boat, you may decide not to buy a return ticket since the tide will probably have receded by the time you wish to return and you can then walk back to the mainland.

Once on the island the first thing that strikes you is the sheer height of the castle. From the mainland it towers up into the sky, but when you stand below in the little village square it seems ten times higher - a marvellous architectural and constructional achievement. Do not miss the opportunity to visit this beautiful building and the chapel, if only for the view from the battlements. Apart from the castle and a few attractive houses in the village, there is not much else of interest, but St Michael's Mount is one of the few islands in Britain which has a true 'fairy-tale' look. This is true not only on a warm summer's day when the flowers below the castle are blooming, but also on a damp January evening when the sea mist swirls around the bay and only the top of the castle is visible through the gloom.

Apart from the boat service from Penzance and Marazion, there is also a regular bus service to and from Marazion. Accommodation is no problem since Mount's Bay is a major holiday resort.

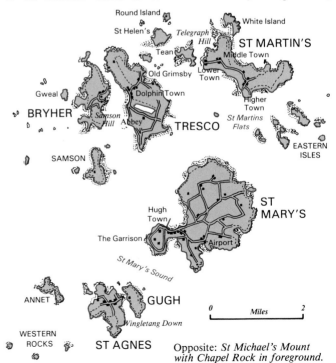

Round Island

St Helen's

White Island

Telegraph Hill

ST MARTIN'S

Tean

Middle Town

Old Grimsby

Lower Town

Gweal

Dolphin Town

Higher Town

BRYHER

Samson Hill

Abbey

St Martins Flats

TRESCO

SAMSON

EASTERN ISLES

Hugh Town

ST MARY'S

The Garrison

Airport

St Mary's Sound

ANNET

GUGH

Wingletang Down

0   Miles   2

WESTERN ROCKS

ST AGNES

Opposite: St Michael's Mount with Chapel Rock in foreground.

Hugh Town, St Mary's, in 1756.

stated that it was possible to walk on the sand flats from Bryher to St Mary's via Tresco and St Martin's, and that the ruins of houses and stone hedges could be seen in the sands at low water. In fact, dwellings from the Bronze Age and the Roman period have been found below the low-water mark, but this area is now covered by the sea, although when there are exceptionally low tides it is possible to wade where once men walked.

The first settlers probably arrived around 2000 BC, their origins being, like most of Britain's early visitors, around the Mediterranean. There are over 150 Bronze Age burial mounds in Scilly, three times as many found in the whole of Cornwall, and Iron Age culture is represented by a series of cliff fortifications, the most famous being Giant's Castle on the south-eastern side of St Mary's, best seen from the air when approaching the airport. Excavations suggest a date around 300 BC. Although people were clearly living here, no settlement sites have been found, only the cliff forts, giving greater credence to the theory of a great catastrophic inundation; they would have only used the high points of land for their burials and hill forts as was their custom on other islands and, like the Stone Age people before them, would have lived in the fertile valleys now beneath the sea.

The Roman invasion of Britain had little effect on Scilly. Some Roman coins have been found, and the only recorded event concerning the islands during this period was the banishment of two bishops, Instantius and Tiberianus, to Insula Sylina in AD 387. A settlement on Nornour indicates that there was a certain amount of Roman influence on the islands, since Roman brooches, rings and beads were found there in substantial quantities. After the Roman withdrawal from Britain a dark veil is drawn over the islands and, apart from a Celtic hermitage and some graves dating from around 700, nothing more is heard of Scilly until the late 10th C.

The Orkneyinga Saga records the journey of Olaf Tryggvesson, King of Norway, Denmark and Sweden, on his voyage of plunder to Northumberland, Scotland, Ireland, Wales and France. According to the saga, before Olaf's return to Norway he came to rest in Scilly and, hearing of an old fortune teller, reputed to be St Elid who could foresee the future, he became curious. He sent for one of his followers, dressed him in his clothes and bade the man to go to the fortune teller to declare that he was the King. When this man presented himself, the old man said, 'Thou art not the King but I advise thee to be faithful to thy King.' When he heard of this, Olaf became even more curious. He visited the old man himself and was told that he would become a renowned king and do celebrated deeds, and that he would bring many men to the faith and baptism. So that he would have no doubts as to the truth of this, he was told that, when he returned to his ships, many would conspire against him and a battle would follow in which many of his men would fall. He himself would be wounded almost to death, and carried upon a shield to his ship; yet, after seven days, he would be well of his wounds, and would immediately let himself be baptised. All the events foretold came true and Olaf went back to the saint and the saint baptised him and, on Olaf's orders, all his followers. On returning to Norway, he forced Christianity on all his subjects, usually at the point of a sword.

During the 15th C, Richard III ordered a survey of the islands to be carried out and it appears that, in time of peace, they were worth £2.00 but were worth nothing in time of war, since the cost of defending them far exceeded their value. One hundred years later this opinion changed and the islands were fortified as a precaution against the raids by Spain and marauding pirates, and in the latter part of the 16th C, Star Castle was built on St Mary's and the islands were leased to Francis Godolphin who was required to maintain a garrison there. During the Civil War, St Mary's was the last Royalist strong-hold; the King's son, later to be Charles II, took refuge in Star Castle prior to sailing to Jersey and safety. The island finally fell to Cromwell in 1651 when Admiral Blake took Tresco and controlled the approach to St Mary's.

After the Restoration Scilly reverted back to the Godolphin family and remained in their posession until 1834, when a new lease was granted to Augustus Smith, a Hertfordshire squire. He was an energetic landlord who re-organised the economy and industry of the islands. Shipbuilding became one of the more important financial bases as did the collection of kelp, and then, in 1865, Smith laid the foundations of the flower industry by sending narcissi packed in a hat box to London's Covent Garden where they fetched 7/6. The experiment came just at the right time since shipbuilding and kelping had come to an end as viable economic industries. By 1885, 65 tons of flowers were being shipped each year to Covent Garden, and in 1931 this figure had grown to over 1000 tons. Today, tourism has overtaken the flower trade in the economy of Scilly. Very little commerical fishing is done in the islands except for a few boats catching crab, lobster and crawfish –the boatmen can make more money by running trips to the islands than they can from fishing.

St Mary's

Visitors to the Isles of Scilly, arriving either by boat or helicopter, come first to St Mary's which, at 1554 acres, is the largest island in the group. The first impression from the air is similar to that of Orkney: low-lying and agricultural with neat, well-laid-out fields. Hugh Town, the 'capital', lies on a narrow isthmus which joins the main part of the island to the garrison. Both sides of this isthmus have sandy bays, Porth Cressa beach on the south and Town Beach on the north, the latter running past pretty granite-built houses. There are about 25 shops, a post office and Tourist Information office, and several hotels and guest houses, all of which blend into the general 'old world' appearance of the town. One of the more unusual buildings is Star Castle Hotel, converted from the original 16th-C fort. The conversion is very well done and from the outside no one would ever know that it was a hotel.

The resident population of St Mary's now numbers 1650, but in the summer months this is more than doubled by the influx of seasonal workers who come to look after the tourists. Tourists coming to Scilly fall roughly into two categories: the people who come for relaxation and are happy with sun, sand and sea; and the naturalists, hikers and birdwatchers. There is no lack of facilities for either category; there are plenty of restaurants, cafés, bars and sandy beaches as well as

A field of daffodils on St Mary's.

marvellous walks, superb views and an abundance of wildlife.

The garrison is best seen in the evening with the sun setting low over the Western Rocks. One walk is to start at Star Castle and follow the garrison walls round to Woolpack Point and then on to Morning Point; the whole panorama of the Isles of Scilly can be seen – a very pleasant way to spend an hour or two. It would be possible to complete a coastal walk round the main part of the island in one day, but it is better to split this up into two excursions. (Most hotels provide packed lunches since, once outside Hugh Town, there is not much in the way of refreshment facilities.) Start at the lifeboat station and take the coastal path past Harry's Walls and **Newford Island** and then walk up to Bar Point past **Taylor's Island** and Bant's Carn to the northern point of St Mary's. Continuing along the eastern side via Watermill Cove and **Toll's Island** takes you to Porth Hellick Point and Giant's Castle. The homeward stretch passes Tolman Point and then Old Town. This walk provides not only fabulous views but also goes past standing stones (at Porth Mellon and Macfarland's Down), burial chambers (at Bant's Carn, Innisidgen and Porth

Hellick Down) and two ancient fortifications, Harry's Walls and Giant's Castle.

But by far the most spectacular scenery on St Mary's is Peninnis Head, a high headland on the southern coast. The rocks on this rugged promontory have been weathered into magnificent shapes and giant blocks of granite are precariously balanced on top of each other – Tooth Rock, Monk's Cowl and the Kettle and Pans, all named as they are shaped. Pulpit Rock, which looks as though it could topple into the sea at any minute, is a truly splendid example of nature's design. The Atlantic crashes over the rocks, throwing sea spray over the whole headland and, although it can be very pleasant to picnic on the rocks on a warm sunny day, the time to really see nature at her best is on a day when a southerly gale is blowing.

On Friday evenings during the summer crews from the inhabited islands compete in a gig race. The tradition of gig racing dates back to the time when men from the islands competed for the right to pilot a vessel into the harbour; the man in the first gig to reach the ship got the job. Some of the boats are very old; the *Czar* (1879) from St Agnes, the

Golden Eagle (1870) and the *Bonnet* (1830) from St Mary's, can be seen on Town Beach when not in use. The local museum, in Church Street, contains a display of exhibits illustrating the history of the islands, and you should take time to visit this before touring.

One thing that Scilly is not short of is organised tours; there are coach tours, boat tours and walking tours. One of the most interesting is organised by a local naturalist, who apart from nature walks around St Mary's also leads sea trips to look at the flora and fauna on the other islands. If you are based on St Mary's, which is the most logical place to stay as there are not too many facilities on the other islands, there are twice daily trips from here to all the other inhabited islands in the group, and occasionally to some of the larger uninhabited ones.

Tooth Rock, St Mary's.

Tresco

At 735 acres, Tresco is the second largest island in Scilly and has a population of 155. Lying two miles north of Hugh Town, it is usually referred to as 'sub-tropical' but, although plants and trees from Australia, California, Chile, China and the Indian sub-continent do grow in the open, in no way could you describe the whole island as sub-tropical. Tresco does, in fact, have something of a 'split personality'; part of it is covered with exotic plants, a 'Kew Gardens without the glass', while the north is a rocky, barren moorland, broken only by Cromwell's Castle, built in 1651, on the north-western coast just below the older King Charles's Castle from which most of its stone-work came.

On the north coast is a remarkable geological phenomenon called Piper's Hole, a legendary haunt of smugglers. It is a large cave extending some 80 yd into the cliff near the water-line, containing a freshwater pool. Torches are essential to explore beyond the pool.

Town Beach, Hugh Town, St Mary's.

Cromwell's Castle, Tresco.

On the eastern side of the island are some attractive sandy bays leading down to Old Grimsby harbour. From this little village the road runs down to the modern Tresco Abbey built in 1835, near the ruins of the 12th-C priory. Continuing south past the gardens and the pools, a path leads to Oliver's Battery overlooking Crow Point; the battery was built by Admiral Blake to command the approach to St Mary's Pool during the Civil War.

St Martin's

One mile east of Tresco lies St Martin's and its dependent isle, **White** (pronounce 'wit') **Island.** These islands, covering 586 acres with a population of 80, are noted for their long sandy beaches. Those around St Martin's Bay on the northern side are possibly the finest in Scilly. The boat usually lands visitors at New Quay, below Higher Town, but also occasionally, depending on the tides, at Lower Town on the west coast. The great majority of monuments on the island are really not worth climbing the various hills to see.

The south-western side of St Martin's is very sandy while the eastern coast is rough and rocky, the interior being covered with heather, bracken and brambles. Rocks off White Island are frequented by seals. The geology also changes at this point and a seam of slate, not found anywhere else in Scilly, runs through the northern tip of the island. St Martin's, like most of the Isles of Scilly, is a place for the naturalist; the whole of the northern area, including White Island, is scheduled as a Site of Special Scientific Interest. Apart from tourism the main industry, as it is on most inhabited islands in the group, is flower-growing.

Bryher

Off the western side of Tresco, separated by a quarter of a mile of shallow water, lies Bryher, 327 acres in extent with a population of 55. The island is really a series of low granite hills, sloping gently to the sea on the eastern side, but more steeply and rugged on the Atlantic side. There are three landing places at two sites: The Quay and Landing Beach at Bryher Town, and Rushy Bay at the southern tip, all used at different tide levels. On the beach between The Quay and Samson Hill, stone hedges and the remnants of huts can be seen at exceptionally low spring tides, all that remains of a Bronze Age farming community that once occupied the flat agricultural land between Bryher and Tresco.

Bryher is very attractive with a variety of different landscapes and, once again, is of interest to the naturalist. Archaeologically speaking, the island seems to be sadly lacking in remains. **Shipman Head,** an islet separated from Bryher by a narrow channel, is the site of a cliff castle, but this rock is very difficult and dangerous to get to and visitors should not attempt to cross the channel, whatever the weather. Another small island near Bryher is **Gweal,** covering about 15 acres. The best way to see Bryher is to join one of the 'nature excursions' from St Mary's and be guided round this island by a local naturalist. These trips are excellent value since an unaccompanied visitor could spend a week here and still not find everything to be seen on these half-day tours.

St Agnes and Gugh

One-and-a-half miles south-west of St Mary's, across St Mary's Sound, are St Agnes and Gugh, two small islands (total 366 acres) with a combined population of 60.

Gugh, (pronounced 'hugh') the smaller of the two, is joined to St Agnes by a sand bar and is about 1200 yd long by 500 yd wide. The island is, however, very famous for its Bronze Age remains. The Old Man of Gugh, a nine-foot standing stone on Kittern Hill, and Obadiah's Barrow, a fine 'dolmen' (entrance grave) which originally had six capstones, are just two of the monuments worth seeing here. It is interesting, although probably coincidental, that the Old Man of Gugh stands on one of the most southerly pieces of land in Britain and that a similar stone stands on the island of Unst in Shetland, the most northerly point.

St Agnes's name is believed to come from the old Norse, *Hagni's nes* or 'Hagni's headland'. (Where the 'saint' in front of the name came from is anybody's guess; the islanders don't use the prefix when speaking of the island.) John Leland, librarian to Henry VIII, visited these isles in 1548 and recorded one story concerning St Agnes: during the 16th C, the whole population went to St Mary's, probably for a wedding although the reason is not known; on the way back, the weather changed and the boats sank, drowning most of the islanders.

The island is very pretty with coves and beaches and a delightful place called Beady Pool, so called because a ship carrying a cargo of 16th-C glass beads went down at this point and the tide has been washing them ashore ever since. However, they are not so easy to find now and the closest you are likely to come to seeing one is in the museum on St Mary's. Near the west coast is a well, reputed to be on the spot where St Warna landed in a coracle from Ireland during the 9th C. The lighthouse, erected in 1680, is one of the oldest in Britain. St Agnes is extremely popular with visiting birdwatchers; in fact, the Isles of Scilly are said to be as popular with ornithologists as Fair Isle.

The St Agnes lighthouse.

The little church at Lower Town was the second to be built on this site, the first one dating from 1685. Names on gravestones show that the

Men-a-vaur and Round Island viewed from Tresco.

majority of people on St Agnes were called Hicks, just as Jenkins was the most common name on Bryher, and as Bond was on St Martin's. The people of each island not only had nicknames but, at one time, it was also possible to discern one islander from another: St Agnes people were called 'Turks' and were generally short, dark and thickset; St Martin's men were 'Ginnicks' and most of them had ginger hair and were very tall; Bryher men were 'Thorns', or lop-sided people. R. L. Bowley, in his *The Fortunate Isles* (1945), stated that it was frequently claimed that 'whatever is done by the men of Bryher, it is aslant; that they walk askew, carry their heads slightly bent sideways, hold a cup or glass at an angle.' However, in recent times there have been many inter-island marriages and this has tended to dilute the special characteristics of individual islanders.

Of the uninhabited islands, only a few are worthy of a mention. They are usually classified into three sections, the Eastern Isles and the Western and the Northern Rocks. In addition, five individual islands stand out apart from these groups.

Annet, situated between St Agnes and the Western Rocks, is the principle nesting place in England of the Manx shearwater and storm petrel; puffins can still be seen and a colony of kittiwakes nests at the northern end. The island, covering only 53 acres, is closed during the nesting season (15 April–20 August). There are boat trips to Annet, and the best way to see it is to take an evening cruise around the island during the nesting season. There is no need to land, as the boat goes fairly close and you can see the birds without disturbing them.

Samson, the largest of the five at 95 acres, consists of two granite hills joined by a low sandy strip. The island is a few hundred yards south of Bryher and was inhabited up until

1855; the old cottages are still there, decayed and ruined, and one of them, on the west of South Hill, is traditionally reputed to be the home of 'Armorel', the heroine of Sir Walter Besant's novel, *Armorel of Lyonesse*. There are at least ten burial mounds on North Hill, mainly piles of stones of no real interest to the casual visitor, but one of them, on the east side of the hill, is worth a visit. This is a mound, 26 ft in diameter and 4 ft high, with a burial chamber 15 ft long by 6 ft wide and 3½ ft high. Only two capstones remain; the rest, like so many others, were used in the building of houses and hedges during the Middle Ages.

During the Napoleonic wars, 19 Samson men took over a French ship and attempted to sail her to Devonport and claim a reward. The ship went down near Land's End, drowning all aboard, and the island never really recovered from this severe blow; in the 1850s, the remaining inhabitants were evacuated to St Mary's. The best time to see Samson is in the early spring before the bracken takes over.

The three other islands lie between Tresco and St Martin's. **St Helen's** covers 49 acres and is roughly circular in shape. Although Leland called it 'St Lide's Isle', Borlase thought the true name was 'St Elid' or *Insula Sancti Elidii*. The island rises to a height of 144 ft, and there are the remains of an early Celtic hermitage on the south slope of the hill, believed by some to be that of St Elid, the fortune teller of the Orkneyinga Saga. During the 18th C, St Helen's housed sailors who were in quarantine from the plague, but the last inhabitants left in 1756. In summer, the island is covered in bracken, ling and English stonecrop. From the north-west point, birdwatchers have a good view of the island of **Men-a-vaur,** one of the finest sea-bird colonies in Scilly.

South-east of St Helen's lies **Tean,** 40 acres in extent with a jagged coastline, which has been utilised from ancient times, as evidenced by the several chamber tombs and burial mounds. It is not until 1684 that the island appears in any records; in that year, a Cornishman by the name of Nance leased the island and introduced kelping to the Isles of Scilly. Almost all the Atlantic islands and coastal regions of Britain were involved in kelping up to the late 19th C. Kelp is the ash that results from the burning of oarweed or seaweed and was used mainly in the manufacture of soap, alum and glass. It took 24 tons of seaweed to produce one ton of kelp, and at the time of Borlase's visit the price was £2.15 per ton, but three years prior to that the figure had been as low as £1.13 per ton. He stated that 'an industrious man may earn £5 or £6 during a kelping season' (May–August).

Kelping involved cutting the seaweed at low water, often many miles out to the sea on the rocky ledges that abound in this area, and bringing the cargo back to the beach so that it could be laid out to dry. After this, the men, having dug pits in the sand and lined them with stones, lit a fire of bracken and, when the flame was just right, put the seaweed into the fire. This seems to have been a skilled job since the seaweed had to be fed slowly on to the fire by a 'master burner'. When the embers died down, the fire was mixed and stirred and the melted kelp was left to settle in the bottom of the pit. Later, when cool, the lump of kelp would be taken out and stored ready for shipping.

Rising to a height of 136 ft, **Round Island** is a circular mound of granite about 300 yd north-east of St Helen's, and is known mainly for its lighthouse built in 1887. The area around its shores is extremely rock-strewn and the red light of the lighthouse has kept many ships out of trouble.

The Eastern Isles lie south of St Martin's and north-east of St Mary's. About 80 acres in total, the largest is **Great Ganilly** (33 acres). The other large islets or rocks are **Great Arthur, Little Arthur, Little Ganilly, Nornour, Great Ganinick, Little Ganinick, Menawethan, Great Innisvouls** and **Little Innisvouls.** These isles are very attractive in the spring and summer months, covered with wild flowers and grass, perfect for that 'get-away-from-it-all' picnic. At low tide some of them are joined together and the whole area becomes one large submerged sandbank. If you get the chance to visit this group, a landing on Great Ganilly would be your best choice, since at low water you can cross to Nornour from here

The Bishop Rock lighthouse.

and see its ancient settlement site, which dates from about 1200 BC through to AD 383.

The Western Rocks are, as the name suggests, the most westerly parts of Scilly. The largest are **Melledgan, Rosevean, Rosevear** and **Gorregan**, and other grim and forbidding rocks in the group include **Jacky's Rock, Dogs of Scilly, Retarrier Ledges** and Gilstone. A little further west is the famous **Bishop Rock** lighthouse, the tallest lighthouse in the British Isles.

The Northern Rocks, also known as the Norrad Rocks, are situated west of Bryher and include **Mincarlo, Illiswilgig, Scilly Rock** and **Maiden Bower.** Mincarlo (5 acres) is situated just over a mile south-west of Bryher and is scheduled as part of a Site of Special Scientific Interest. Permits are required to land there but, since the coast is dangerous and the tides run very strongly around the island, there are very few chances for visitors to land, even if they have a permit. Other islands in this group are **Great Minalto, Little Minalto, Castle Bryher** and **Seal Rock.**

Getting to any of the Isles of Scilly is not too difficult. The Isles of Scilly Steamship Company regularly operate launches to the inhabited islands and the St Mary's Boatmen's Association run twice-daily trips to not only the main islands but also occasionally to some of the uninhabited ones. Notices are displayed daily in Hugh Town and down on The Quay, indicating which islands can be visited on a particular day. Apart from St Mary's, there is some accommodation on the other islands if you want to get away from the crowds. Camping is allowed on a few specific sites but caravans and dormobiles are not permitted on the islands.

Since there are only 11 miles of roads on St Mary's, cars should not be brought to Scilly. Taxis are available and there is a carrier who delivers luggage to the hotels. The Isles of Scilly can be reached either by sea or by air. There is a ferry, the *Scillonian III*, which in the summer sails daily (except Sundays) from Penzance to St Mary's, taking about two-and-a-half hours. But for those who like to reach their holiday destinations quickly, British Airways Helicopters operate a regular service with a 32-seater Sikorsky helicopter from Penzance, which takes about 20 minutes.

The West Coast

Although only one or two can really be considered islands, there are many rocks between Land's End and the Bristol Channel. **The Brisons,** situated half a mile from Cape Cornwall and four miles north of Land's End, are two uninhabited rocks, the larger one rising to a height of 90 ft, with a total combined area of about eight acres. Access is by boat from Sennen Cove. **The Carracks** are two small rocks off the coast near Carn Naun Point about three miles west of St Ives.

Godrevy Island is situated three miles from St Ives across St Ives Bay and 300 yd from Godrevy Point. The island is 12 acres in extent and the only inhabitants are gulls, oyster-catchers and pipits. There are some grassy areas which, in springtime, are covered with primroses and sea thrift. A dangerous reef, extending out to the north-west for one mile, is called **The Stones,** and on this many ships have come to grief. On the 30 November 1854, the steamer *Nile* was totally wrecked with the loss of all lives and, under pressure from public and maritime groups, Trinity House finally erected a lighthouse in 1859. Initially operated by two keepers it is a white octagonal tower some 85-ft tall, but it became automatic and the keepers were withdrawn in 1939. Permission to land on the island is required from Trinity House, permits only being issued for those with valid reasons for going there; however, it is really not worth the effort and a fine view can be had from Godrevy Point on the mainland.

Four miles north-east of Godrevy Point, near Portreath, is a series of large rocks and small islets within a three-mile area of coastline; these are the **Crane Islands, Samphire Island, Gull Rock** and **Sheep Rock.** All are uninhabited with no recorded history, and the total land mass amounts to not more than a few acres. Between St Agnes Head and Newquay there are several more islands and rocks – **Carter's or Gull Rocks** off Penhale Point and **Trevelgue Head** in Newquay Bay. The latter is inhabited and there are the remains of a cliff castle and burial site. As its name suggests, it is really part of the headland and only an inundation has caused it to be separated from the mainland. A small bridge does, in fact, join it to the cliff top.

Further north between Park Head and Trevose Head is a series of tidal rocks and islets, most of them accessible at low tide, including the **Trescore Islands, Minnows Islands** and **Trethias Island.** Padstow Bay contains two fairly large rocks, **Gulland Rock** and **Newland** which is about four acres in extent and rises to about 120 ft. Access to both is by boat from Padstow Harbour. Getting on to any of these rocks is difficult in the best of weather and care must be taken, particularly when assessing the tide situation, so as not to be marooned. It is advisable to check with the local tourist office or boatmen before attempting a visit. Currents and tides are particularly strong around any rock or small islet.

Lundy
Devon. Lundy (Old Norse for 'puffin island') stands at the entrance to the Bristol Channel, 19 miles west of Morte Point. It is three miles long by about a half a mile wide and stands over 400-ft high. From the top of its tall cliffs there is an incredible view of England, Wales and the Atlantic. The western cliffs slope gradually down to the east coast which is more sheltered and contains trees and vegetation. Like most offshore islands the wind is the dominant factor on Lundy: an easterly can make it impossible for any boat to land.

Prehistoric remains have been

Godrevy Island.

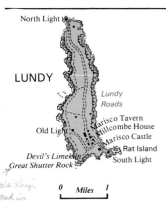

LUNDY

North Light

Lundy
Roads

Old Light

Marisco Tavern
Millcombe House
Marisco Castle
Rat Island
South Light

Devil's Limekiln
Great Shutter Rock

0   Miles   1

found on the island and during the early Middle Ages a Christian community existed there. The Vikings were extremely active in the Bristol Channel, and Lundy became a perfect base for their exploits. After the Norman Conquest the island was owned by Normans, the Marisco family, but during the 13th C, Henry III ousted them and the then head of the family, William de Marisco, was hanged, drawn and quartered for pirate activities.

Over the next few hundred years Lundy changed hands many times, from the Crown to private individuals, from private individuals to pirates. Occasionally it was difficult to tell who was a pirate and who was 'respectable': Sir Richard Grenville was warned by Queen Elizabeth I that she would confiscate the island unless he prevented pirates from using it as a base. Thomas Benson, Member of Parliament for Barnstaple, owned the island in the 18th C and in 1750 secured a contract from the Government to transport convicts to America. However, he dumped them on Lundy instead and put them to work building roads and walls. Much later, in 1925, Lundy was purchased by Martin Coles Harman, who introduced the deer, some Soay sheep and the precursors of the Lundy ponies, now registered as a

separate breed by the National Pony Society. In 1929, the Post Office closed down its services on the island and Harman began producing his own stamps to cover the cost of transporting the mail across to the mainland. These are still used today and many issues have become collectors' items over the years. When he tried to introduce his own coins - 'puffins' and 'half-puffins' -he fell foul of the Coinage Act and was brought to trial.

In 1968, the island once again came up for sale. The National Trust decided that it did not have the funds for the purchase but, in 1969, Jack Hayward, a Bahamas-based British property developer, donated the necessary £150,000 'in gratitude for all Britain had done for him'. The Landmark Trust was given the responsibility of administering the island which now has a population of 25.

Visitors will disembark at the landing beach on the south-eastern point near **Rat Island**. The road from the beach climbs up the cliffs to the Millcombe House Hotel and then doubles back towards the Battlements where, to the south, lies the Marisco castle. The road continues west towards St Helena's church and then turns north into what could be described as 'The Village', where you will find the Marisco Tavern and the island's shop. The road now runs west across to the old lighthouse.

By heading south-west you will reach the Devil's Limekiln and the **Great Shutter Rock**. The former is a natural hole on the cliff top, over 300 ft deep, and the latter is supposed to be the rock the Devil used to cover it. Be careful when approaching the Limekiln; 300 ft is a long way to fall.

Lying as it does on a busy seaway, Lundy has always been a danger to shipping, but it was not until 1819 that Trinity House erected the first lighthouse and keeper's quarters. The light, at 567 ft, was one of the highest in Britain and it proved too

high, often being hidden by low clouds when the weather was clear at sea level. Two other lighthouses were built in 1896, one at each end of the island. The foundations of a 4th-C chapel, dedicated to St Elen, a Welsh saint, can be seen in the cemetery next to the old lighthouse. The disused Battery, situated on the west side of the island, was built by Trinity House as a fog signal station in 1863. Below the cottages built for the gun crews is the firing platform with two George III cannons and the shell of the gunhouse.

Although over 420 different birds have been recorded on 'puffin island', there are only a few breeding puffins remaining. The grey seal breeds only in one place, in a sea cave on the south coast. The areas covered in rhododendrons and bracken are favoured by the sika deer which the sharp-eyed visitor will see occasionally. The Soay sheep usually keep to the north; but the ponies, a cross between New Forest and Welsh mountain breeds, can be seen everywhere.

Accommodation on Lundy is restricted to one small hotel, seven self-catering cottages plus accommodation for parties of up to 13 people in the old lighthouse and the keepers' quarters. There are also sites for about 20 campers.

Millcombe House, Lundy.

Transportation to the island is either by the island's own boat, the *Polar Bear*, which sails from Ilfracombe, or, during the summer months, the White Funnel Line's *Balmoral*, sailing out of several ports in the Bristol Channel. This ship carries 730 passengers and runs two or three times a week to the island via Ilfracombe.

A word of warning: with the hazards of wind and sea, landing on Lundy can be impossible on occasion, particularly if an east wind is blowing. However, visitors are often only told that a landing is not possible just as the ship approaches the island, and day trippers may find that, instead of spending several hours on this delightful island, the boat will circle Lundy and return to Ilfracombe. The owners will then refund only a small fraction of the fare paid which, if you have a large family, can be a sizeable sum.

The landing beach, Lundy.

Steep Holm from the eastern approach.

Steep Holm

Avon. Steep Holm, 1000 yd long by 450 yd wide, is situated in the Bristol Channel between the English and Welsh coasts and about five miles from Weston-super-Mare. High cliffs, rising to 256 ft, enclose all but the south-eastern side where they slope gradually down to a shingle beach. The island is an outcrop of carboniferous limestone, the cliffs containing the same strata as those exposed in the Avon Gorge at Bristol.

One legend about the origin of Steep Holm concerns a monster called the Giant of Gorm who fought with the Lord of Avon but was defeated. In his haste to run away, the giant fell into the Bristol Channel and drowned, his remains forming the islands of Steep Holm and Flat Holm.

The historian Gildas, author of *Liber Querulus De Excidio Britanniae (On the Destruction of Britain)*, is reputed to have stayed on the island around AD 540, and it is said that his ghost still walks in the ruins of the priory on certain moonlit nights. The earliest recorded occupation of the island was in 914, when the Danes landed on the Welsh coast and planned to attack King Edward the Elder's army which was successfully repelling even more Danes invading the east coast. Edward then met the second invaders at Hereford and once again the Danes were defeated, having to retreat to the Bristol Channel. The remnants of the Danish army took refuge on

Steep Holm where they remained until they ran out of food, and many died of starvation before the rest could finally leave.

The earliest remains on Steep Holm that can be readily dated are those of the priory. Built around the time of the Conquest and dedicated to St Michael, it appears to have been abandoned about 1270. The attraction of islands for the early Christian clergy has been noted throughout the research for this book and one wonders if the attraction had more to do with practical living than with religion. The solitude would certainly have been of importance, but these islands also had large colonies of sea birds and an abundance of fish right on the doorstep. For a small number of people, there would have been an unlimited supply of food, all year round. (For many centuries, communities in the Western Isles, Iceland, Orkney and Shetland have lived on sea birds and their eggs when fishing and crofting was impossible because of the weather.) With such sustenance so close at hand, the monks would certainly have had more time for their religious duties. Those on Steep Holm also had time to grow herbs; they introduced a tall biennial called alexanders *(Smyrnium olusatrum)*, which now covers part of the island.

Not much is known of the island during medieval times. In 1786 Steep Holm was owned by John Freke Willes of Northamptonshire, and in 1831 it became the property of Charles Kemeys Kemey-Tynte,

Baron Wharton of Halswell. The family leased the island to a succession of tenants until, in 1976, the Hon. Mrs Ziki Robertson, daughter of Lady Wharton, sold the island to the Kenneth Allsop Memorial Trust, set up in memory of the author and naturalist who died in 1973. The Trust is involved with extensive conservation work to preserve the island's ecology from development and abuse, and groups of young people from the International Voluntary Service and other organisations have been working on its restoration.

Apart from the priory the visitor will find plenty to see. There are five Victorian batteries complete with guns, as well as eight or nine sea caves of varying sizes, and a blowhole. Of particular interest are Steep Holm's slow worms which not only grow to amazing lengths (one was reported in 1978 to be 39 inches long although the average size is about 16-20 inches) but, unlike other slow worms, the ones here are blue. Over 462 different birds were recorded on the island in 1977, and for the botanist there is the wild peony (naturalised nowhere else in the British Isles), the caper spurge and the rare wild leek. Steep Holm has been scheduled a Site of Special Scientific Interest by the Nature Conservancy Council, and it is also a registered ringing centre for the British Trust for Ornithology.

Visitors are welcome, and during the summer months a regular twice-weekly (Saturday and Sunday) ferry service operates from Weston-super-Mare. There are self-catering holidays available, either for the weekend or for the week.

The Hilbre Islands

Merseyside. The Hilbre group consists of three small islands situated in the Dee Estuary about one mile from the shoreline between West Kirby and Hoylake. **Hilbre Island**, the largest and most northerly in the group, is approximately 11 acres in extent; **Little Hilbre Island**, or Middle Island, covers about fives acres; and **Little Eye** is no more than half an acre. The tide surrounds and separates them for about six hours out of every twelve. When the tide recedes, it is possible to walk from the mainland to all three islands.

The Hilbre group is part of the Bunter sandstone ridge which continues south-east, occasionally outcropping in rocky banks such as the **Tanskey Rocks, Seldom Seen Rocks** and **Caldy Blacks**, all visible only at low water. The islands contain many examples of 'pebblebeds' and fossils from the Ordovician, Silurian and Carboniferous ages. Cliffs on the two larger islands rise to a height of 56 ft on the

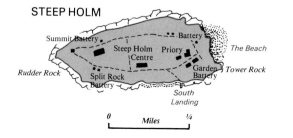

STEEP HOLM

Summit Battery
Battery
Steep Holm Centre
Priory
The Beach
Rudder Rock
Garden Battery
Tower Rock
Split Rock Battery
South Landing

0   Miles   ¼

North Scale, Isle of Walney.

south-west sides, running down to rocky shores on the north and east sides.

From historical documents it is known that the islands were once much larger than they are now. Maps of the 16th and 17th C show one island named Hilbre about one square mile in extent, and in the 16th C 4000 foot soldiers and 200 horse troops encamped there before voyaging to Ireland, hardly possible if the island had been the same size as it is today. It is also thought that a small religious community was established on Hilbre prior to the arrival of the Norsemen in AD 905; after the Norman Conquest the island was given to the Abbey of St Evroul in Normandy, who maintained a small cell and a shrine dedicated to St Hildeburgh.

There are several buildings on Hilbre Island including some stone and wooden cottages, a bird observatory, canoe club, the remains of a lifeboat station complete with slipway, and other buildings originally erected to house the keeper and staff of the telegraph station. The islands, along with the whole of the Dee Estuary, have been designated a Grade I Site of Special Scientific Interest, and many ornithologists believe the islands to be one of the finest sites in England for observing and photographing the many different species of wading birds that winter in this area. Over 1000 birds are ringed annually and 221 different species have been recorded. There is also a large colony of grey seals that haul out on a sandbank close to the islands, their numbers varying between 100 and 200 throughout the year.

A permit is required to visit the Hilbres and notices have been erected at Dee Lane, West Kirby and Stanley Road, Hoylake, giving information on the tides and how to obtain a permit. Being neither fenced in or walled off and with easy access as low water, thousands of visitors had been crossing to the islands each weekend throughout the summer months. Their numbers reached such proportions that it is hoped to restrict them by requiring permits, to prevent the destruction of the entire ecosystem of the area. It is possible that, if people ignore the permit regulations, as regrettably many do, the Hilbres could become a statutory wildlife reserve and all visits to the islands prohibited by law.

Isle of Walney

Cumbria. Situated on the western side of Morecambe Bay and separated from Barrow-in-Furness by a narrow channel, the Isle of Walney is ten miles long and under one mile wide, with a population of 11,000. Connected to the mainland by a bridge, it was only inhabited by a few fishermen and farmers until, in the early 19th C, the growth of industry in Barrow-in-Furness led to its development as a residential area. Vickerstown, built by the shipbuilding company of that name for

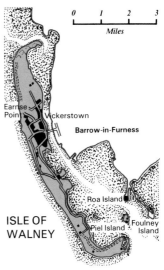

their employees, is situated in the middle of the island near the bridge. Apart from the development of the original town, both the northern and southern sections of Walney have been preserved and the establishment of a nature reserve at the southern end has gone a long way to stopping the growth of urban development on this little oasis. Although extremely close to a major industrial area, the island is considered to be a fine example of a diverse complex of habitats of outstanding scientific and educational value.

Walney consists of ancient rocks of sedimentary and volcanic origin, mainly sandstone, limestone and mudstone, overlaid with shingle and sand. Being under the influence of westerly Atlantic air streams, the average annual rainfall is 41 inches with an average maximum temperature of 75° F. The Walney Nature Reserve in the south contains the largest colony of herring gulls and lesser black-backed gulls in the British Isles, about 10,000 pairs of each. But the north and south of the island are not only of interest to ornithologists; there is also a varied plant and animal life. In the north, rabbits are numerous, as are foxes, shrews, weasels and stoats, and the most important species, in terms of rarity, is the natterjack toad (*Bufo calamita*), distinguishable from the common toad by the yellow stripe down the middle of its back.

The west or Atlantic coast is almost one continuous stretch of sandy beach, very popular with holiday-makers, while the area between the island and the mainland contains salt marshes, sand flats and dunes. There are also a few dependent isles here: **Piel Island** (containing the remains of an ancient castle), **Sheep Island, Foulney Island** and **Roa Island**. The last two are, in fact, now part of the mainland.

Isle of Man

An ancient kingdom with its own parliament, the Isle of Man has, as Lord of Man, the reigning United Kingdom monarch. A popular resort island with good ferry links to mainland Britain.

The Isle of Man lies in the Irish Sea, 32 miles long by 13½ miles wide lying on a north-east/south-west axis, and has an area of 145,325 acres, extending as far north as the Lake District and as far west as Bodmin. The nearest point on the mainland to the island is Burrow Head, 18 miles north.

The name is of uncertain origin: the Romans referred to it as *Mona*, the Irish and Welsh as *Mannan*, but it may be derived from *Manannan Beg Mac Lir*, a Celtic sea god.

The first inhabitants were mesolithic, probably from northern France. Agriculture began to develop with the neolithic culture when stone burial cairns, such as the Meayll Hill Circle and Cashtal yn Ard, were built. The Bronze Age peoples built smaller individual cairns, among them The Giants Grave at St John's and Cronk ny Arrey Lhaa. About 200 BC Celtic Iron Age folk came to the Isle of Man and built large hill forts, for

St Patrick's Isle, Peel.

example those at Cronk Sumark and Chapel Hill, Balladoole, suggesting a period of instability.

Following the Roman invasion of Britain, life became more settled since, although there is no evidence of a Roman presence on the island, their galleys in the Irish Sea would have discouraged raiders. A Manx-Celtic, circular, unfortified dwelling at Ballakaighen, Arbory, occupied during this period, was excavated by Bersu, an eminent German archaeologist interned on the island during World War II. In the past, the site would have consisted of two round houses (the largest being some 90 ft in diameter) with turf roofs supported on timber frameworks around central hearths. A model of the larger dwelling can be seen in the Manx Museum, Douglas.

During the 5th C the Christian missionaries came. St Ninian was probably the first, although it may have been St Patrick who is said to have landed on St Patrick's Isle, Peel, and founded a church there in AD 444. His nephew Germanus, first Bishop of Man, established the Cathedral Church of St German on the same site. Later missionaries were St Brigid - the village of Bride is dedicated to her - and MacCuill, to whom Maughold Church is dedicated, as well as Ronan and Brendan, followers of St Columba. By the 6th C the Christian Church was well established, and small simple chapels called 'keeills' were built all over the island, examples of which can be seen at Lag ny Keeilley (with a ruined hermit's cell nearby) on the west slope of Cronk ny Arrey Lhaa, in addition to three restored keeills in Maughold churchyard, once the site of a Celtic monastery.

Land was held under the *udal* system, with each chieftain owning a small area which was passed on to his descendants; the prefix *Balla*, common on Man, means 'homestead'. Four homesteads were amalgamated into one *treen* (200 - 400 acres), each probably responsible for one keeill. After the arable land had been accounted for, the rest of the land, called *intack*, was used as rough grazing.

Inscriptions in ogham scripts have been found cut in pillar stones and probably date from the 5th or 6th centuries. Most of the stones are in the typical Old Celtic language,

although one, from Knock-y-Dooney, is notable for being bilingual, repeating the inscriptions in late Roman capitals. Similar ogham stones have been found in Wales - on Caldey Island, for example. Many of these stones are now in the Manx Museum, as is the 'Calf of Man Crucifixion', a unique and very fine example of 8th-C Christian art, in a style derived from that of the eastern Mediterranean.

The tranquil Celtic Christian period came to an end, around the year AD 800, with the arrival of the Norsemen, who came initially to raid, and later to settle. They were pagan, practising ceremonies such as boat burials, when the chief was interred in his boat with all his belongings needed for the journey to Valhalla. There are such burial sites at Balladoole and Knock-y-Dooney, although there is now little to see.

The Isle of Man's fertile northern plain is an area where many Norse names survive, the settlers having intermarried with the Celts and adopted Christianity. It was not until 1079, the beginning of the reign of Godred Crovan (son of Harold the Black of Iceland, the legendary 'King Orry') that Man again enjoyed stability under Norwegian suzerainty. He established the Kingdom of Man and the Isles, administering the Hebrides from the House of Keys on the Isle of Man, and his descendants ruled this kingdom until 1265. There was, however, a great deal of family rivalry, which resulted in Godred II and Somerled, his brother-in-law, fighting a great sea battle near Colonsay in 1158. Godred was defeated and was forced to surrender sovereignty over the Sudreys ('southern isles'), which left him with the Nordreys ('northern isles') and Man, a rather fragmented empire. Further power struggles ensued, with successive kings pledging their allegiance to the English sovereign. The last King of Man and the Isles was Magnus who, after Haakon's defeat by Alexander of Scotland at the Battle of Largs in 1263, declared his allegiance to Alexander. Following Magnus's death in 1265 a treaty was signed, and Norway finally relinquished Man and the Isles to Scotland.

There are many beautiful cross slabs dating from the period of

Norse rule, a number of which are kept in the parish churches of Andreas, Braddan, Jurby, Onchan, Maughold and Michael. Remains of Norse houses, which had low stone walls, steep turf or thatch roofs and central hearths, can be seen at Braaid and at Cronk ny Merriu, Port Grenaugh.

The short period of Scottish rule - initially under Alexander III, and later under Margaret 'Maid of Norway' - was an unsettled time. The last descendant of Godred Crovan, King Magnus's son Godred, was killed leading an unsuccessful rebellion. In 1291 Man came under English suzerainty, later to be seized by Robert the Bruce and held by him from 1313 to 1329. In 1333 it was taken by Edward III and, since then, all Lords of Man have been English.

At first the island was run as a feudal society, with the Manx as

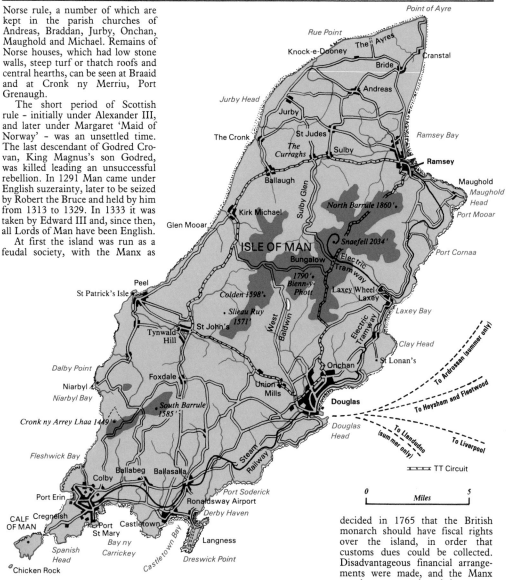

tenants, paying rent to their lord. The year 1405 marked the start of the period of the Stanleys as Lords of Man which lasted until 1736. John Stanley II (ruled 1414-37) instituted significant reforms at a Tynwald Court held at Castle Rushen in 1423 and, for the first time, laws were written and disputes settled by jury.

James Stanley I, seventh Earl of Derby (ruled 1627-51), who became known as *Y Stanlagh Moar*, the 'Great Stanley', appointed a Manx man, Edward Christian, as Governor. Illiam Dhone, a distant cousin of Christian, led a revolt during the Lord's absence, eventually having to surrender control to Parliament. Charles Stanley, eighth Earl of Derby, belatedly seeking revenge,

had Illiam Dhone, who was in prison for debt, executed at Hango Hill, Castletown. An appeal cleared his name posthumously, and he became a popular Manx hero, a focus for the discontent felt at the time.

The last of the Stanleys was James Stanley II, tenth Earl of Derby. With Bishop Wilson, who came to the island in 1698 and did much to improve welfare, agriculture, industry and education, he passed an act that became known as the 'Manx Magna Carta', which gave tenants security of tenure for perpetuity on payment of the 'Lord's Rent', a fixed yearly sum, effectively bringing the feudal system to an end.

In order to control the vast smuggling 'industry' on Man, it was

decided in 1765 that the British monarch should have fiscal rights over the island, in order that customs dues could be collected. Disadvantageous financial arrangements were made, and the Manx people were not pleased; it was not until 1866, during Lord Loch's governorship, that a more satisfactory position was secured with the British Exchequer.

The Isle of Man is well known for its TT Races, tail-less cats, punishment by the birch and low income tax, but its status in relationship to the United Kingdom and Europe is often not clearly understood. The Isle of Man is an ancient kingdom. It is not, and never has been, part of the United Kingdom, nor is it a colony. It is a Crown Possession; the British monarch is also the Lord of Man, represented on the island by the Lieutenant-Governor.

In 1979 celebrations marked the millennium of the Tynwald parliament, the oldest continuous assembly in the world, dating from the

Tynwald ceremony.

rule of Godred Crovan in the 11th C. The name 'Tynwald' is derived from the Old Norse *Thing-vollr* meaning 'assembly field'. On the Isle of Man it makes its own laws, collects its own taxes (including VAT) and controls its own expenditure. Bills passed at Tynwald require only the Royal Assent, and a special committee set up by the British Home Secretary deals with this. The United Kingdom Parliament, which legislates for the monarch (as Lord of Man), may pass laws which affect the island, but these are usually restricted to such matters as defence, shipping and so on, and Tynwald is *always* consulted.

In 1894 the 'Common Purse' arrangement was designed to over-come difficulties in the levying and collecting of customs and excise duties. Under this agreement Tynwald maintains its customs duties more or less in line with those of the United Kingdom who, in turn, agree to collect them and charge the island a fee based on a percentage of the total amount. The Isle of Man is not a full member of the EEC, only having a special relationship with the Community to the limited extent necessary to ensure free movement of goods and the observance of normal conditions of competition in trade.

Tynwald is the symbol of Manx independence. It has come to mean two things: the Assembly, consisting of the 24 Keys (elected repre-sentatives); and the Legislative Council, similar in function to the House of Lords and consisting of the Lieutenant-Governor, the Lord Bishop, HM Attorney General and eight members elected by the Keys. The origin of 'Keys' is not clear – it may be a reference to men who 'unlock' the law; the Statute Book of 1417 mentions *Claves Manniae et Claves Legis*, the 'Keys of Man and the Law'. Their number bears no relationship to the 17 parishes in six sheadings (divisions). The Govern-ment building is in Douglas.

Another meaning of Tynwald is 'the hill', a tiered mound on the site of a Bronze Age tumulus at St John's; it is said that the hill contains a handful of soil from each parish. Until World War I no new law took force until it had been read out at Tynwald Hill on 5 July, Old Mid-summer's Day. The tradition still continues although each bill now passes into law when given the Royal Assent. A Processional Way, 360-ft long, connects the hill with the Royal Chapel of St John's. In accordance with ancient practice the pathway is spread with rushes and, after a service, the members of Tynwald take their places on the hill, arranged in order of rank, and a resumé of the new laws are read in Manx and English by the Deemsters (judges). This type of open-air assembly dates from the Norse occupation of Iceland in the 10th C, although that particular 'tynwald' was abandoned 150 years ago.

The national symbol, the 'Three Legs of Man', has its earliest known representation on the 14th-C Pillar Cross in Maughold churchyard. It is possibly derived from the Greek cross – such a device was used on coinage in Sicily in the 4th C – but any link between this and Man seems tenuous. It is thought more likely to be of Norse origin.

Other obvious differences be-tween the island and mainland Bri-tain are the Manx bank notes and coinage (although British currency is readily accepted), postage stamps and lower postal charges, and its atmosphere of spirited free enter-prise, in part resulting from the 'across the board' rate of income tax of 20.5 per cent. Small cornershops, old-fashioned road signs, old buses, trams and steam trains create an impression reminiscent of Britain in the 1950s. For beer drinkers, the licensing hours (12.00–22.00 or later) and the quality of beer brewed on the island – virtually all 'real ale' and controlled by the Manx Beer Act which allows only malt, hops and sugar to be used – make the island seem close to paradise.

Not so attractive is the sprawling development of the towns, especially in the south, and the quite extra-ordinary ostentation of some of the new houses which demonstrate a

The harbour and brewery, Castletown.

total lack of sensitivity to the natural, if modest, beauties of the landscape.

For those who might consider this a fine place to live there are no restrictions on entry, but employment is strictly controlled by a system of work permits giving preference to residents who now number 65,000. Health, social security and unemployment benefits are arranged on a reciprocal basis with the United Kingdom. There is full employment, but property is expensive.

The largest single generator of income, and a rapid growth area, is in the financial sector, accounting for almost 30 per cent of the Gross National Income; manufacturing provides a further 12 per cent and tourism 11 per cent. Professional and scientific services and construction are also important, but agriculture and fishing produce less than three per cent. This last, although a tiny part of the economy, is a traditional Manx industry, currently employing about 450 people. Herring is the main catch, being processed over oak chips into delicious Manx kippers, and scallops, white fish and prawns are also taken.

Geologically the island is primarily a slate massif with granitic intrusions. The fertile northern plain is an area of glacial drift with a hilly terminal moraine running from Jurby to Bride, and the extreme northern tip is a raised beach. There is carboniferous limestone around Castletown, and Triassic sandstone around Peel. Except for the higher ground, most of the land is covered with varying depths of boulder clay and sand. Climate is typically maritime, with mild winters and cool summers, the sunniest period being May to August the wettest October to January. Snow seldom settles for long.

Over 100 species of birds breed on the island and 250 different species have been observed, with the coastal areas, such as The Ayres and Langness, providing the most interesting habitat. Half a mile off the south-west tip is the **Calf of Man**, a rocky island of 616 acres, administered by the Manx Museum and the Manx National Trust as a bird sanctuary and nature reserve. Many of the birds found on the Isle of Man nest on the Calf where the steep slate cliffs are particularly attractive to sea birds. It is an ideal place for the study of migration, being on one of western Britain's migration routes, and has long been recognised as an important area for noting such movements through the Irish Sea area. Manx shearwater, once extinct on the Isle of Man, have now re-established themselves here. Since 1959 organised ornithological

Snaefell mountain railway.

work has been carried out on the Calf, generally from spring to autumn each year, and in 1962 it became an officially recognised observatory. The Calf, apart from the lighthouse complex, is in the charge of a warden. Visits are by arrangement only, and access is by small boats from Port Erin and Port St Mary.

The range of flora present on the Isle of Man suggests that the land-bridge with Great Britain persisted after the Ice Age, and only a limited number of species crossed before the island was formed. Of most interest are the plants of the Curraghs wetlands. The mountain flora is comparable with that of North Wales, and, in the south, fuchsia grows in many hedges. Ragwort is the national flower, and grows everywhere.

The unique tail-less Manx cat is a mutation preserved in the limited genetic environment of the island. The true Manx is called a 'rumpie'; those with short tails are 'stumpies'. Also peculiar to Man are Loghtan sheep, possibly related to the Soay sheep of St Kilda; most of the rams produce four horns.

The Isle of Man steam railway, running from Douglas to Port Erin via Castletown, was opened in 1874, and one of the locomotives dating from that year, the 'Loch', is still operational. The electric tramway runs from Douglas to Ramsey via Laxey, sections of it dating from 1893, and the electric mountain railway from Laxey to Snaefell summit (2032 ft) was built in 1895. Since 1876, horse-drawn trams have run along Douglas promenade. All these services operate from May to September and, together with an excellent bus service, allow the visitor to travel the island without a car.

Many street name signs are bilingual; although Manx Gaelic is not in common use, an enthusiastic minority is working to ensure its preservation. There has also been a resurgence of interest in traditional

song and dance. Manx folk dancing, although having some of the characteristics of other Celtic dances, has a style of its own and, in contrast to some of the Manx songs which are often rather sad, the dances are lively, gay and often vigorous. There are dances for various occasions, such as the Manx courting dance ('Return the Blow'), the Manx wedding dance ('Peter O'Tavy'), and dances for the different seasons of the year: 'Hunt the Wren' is a traditional dance commemorating the custom of hunting the wren of St Stephen's on Boxing Day; 'Hop Tu Naa' is a processional dance performed during the Celtic New Year, Hollantide, on 12 November; and one of the oldest dances, the 'Dirk Dance', was traditionally performed on state occasions before the Kings of Man. The usual accompaniment is the fiddle or violin, though mouth music is sometimes used.

The Tourist Trophy ('TT') Races.

The Tourist Trophy motorcycle races, the 'TT' Races, date from 1907, are held in early June, and attract enormous numbers of enthusiastic supporters. The present 37¾-mile road circuit, starting and finishing at Douglas, has remained virtually unchanged since 1911, although surfaces have been smoothed, crash barriers installed and all sorts of safety considerations taken into account. Not with-

Douglas: the Tower of Refuge is on the extreme right.

standing this, it is a tough course. The first race was won at an average speed of 35 mph, and the present lap record stands at 115 mph. Most of motorcycling's 'greats' have ridden here; Geoff Duke, John Surtees, Phil Read and Giacomo Agostini are a few in recent memory. There are also motor car and bicycle races among a myriad of other sporting events on the island.

The Isle of Man, long geared to tourism, has countless holiday attractions. The tourist office in Douglas offers a large range of literature, much of it free. What follows is a general introduction, with only the major or unusual items receiving a word of description.

The capital is Douglas, built around a bay on the east coast. It is the main administrative, business and holiday centre, a solid Victorian town with a promenade of hotels painted in every pastel shade, as well as fairy lights, amusements, a sandy

The Inner Harbour, Douglas.

beach and pleasant pedestrian shopping streets. The harbour and ferry terminal are at the southern end, with the attractive red-brick steam railway station behind. The excellent Manx Museum and Library should both be visited. There is also the Gaiety Theatre, cinemas, a casino and aquadrome and much more. It is all brash, breezy and friendly.

The Tower of Refuge on **Conister or St Mary's Rock** in Douglas Bay was built in 1832 by Sir William Hillary, founder of the Royal National Lifeboat Institution. Douglas had one of the first lifeboats in the British Isles, a station being established in 1802, with the present one dating from 1874.

The town merges into Onchan in the north. In Onchan church there is an almost perfect round-headed slab cross with interfacing work, and on 4 February 1781 Captain Bligh of the *Bounty* was married here. To the north-west is the beautiful and tiny church of St Lonan's, founded in the 5th C, with a wheel cross dating from this time in the churchyard. Laxey, to the north, is a pretty touring centre, with a small harbour and a shingle beach nestling in the cliffs. The glen was once mined for lead and zinc blende, and the 72-ft diameter Laxey Wheel ('The Lady Isabella', named after the Governor's wife) was used to pump water up 1500 ft out of workings 1350 ft below sea level. It was commissioned in 1854, and was designed by Robert Casement. The water was siphoned to the top of the wheel up a 24-inch cast-iron tube from the intake, and a series of rods transferred the power (a maximum of 185 hp) to pumps situated up the

The Laxey Wheel.

glen. Mining operations ceased in 1919, but the wheel was 'rescued' in the late 1930s, and is now restored, turning but no longer pumping.

Port Cornaa and Port Mooar are small sheltered bays, beyond which is the lighthouse at Maughold Head, 212 ft above high water to the light. The church here has a fine collection of cross slabs. To the north-west, Ramsey, built around a small harbour and with long sandy beaches, is a useful touring centre.

The northern end of the island is a fertile plain with some low hills around Bride. There are fine collections of cross slabs in the churches at Andreas and Jurby, and the old Church of St Mary de Ballaugh at The Cronk, dating from the 17th C, built on the site of earlier buildings, has an unusual porch, an ancient font, and an 11th-C runic cross. To the east are the Curraghs wetlands. At Kirk Michael the

Gothic-style church dating from 1834 also has a notable collection of cross slabs, and to the south of here is the attractive Glen Mooar Bay.

One of the most pleasing small towns on the island is Peel on the west coast. Dominated by the ruined castle and cathedral on **St Patrick's Isle**, sheltering Peel Bay from the west, the town is built to the east of the harbour, full of fishing boats and with kipper factories at the rear. Each July the first Viking landings (in AD 798) are commemorated here with a rowdy but good-natured celebration.

To the south is the lovely Niarbyl Bay with some tiny thatched fishermen's cottages, but for the most part the coast consists of steep cliffs. In the south-west Port Erin spills into Port St Mary in an unattractive sprawl of random development. The two towns are popular holiday and boating centres, and at Port Erin there is a marine biological station, the island being noted for the clear clean waters that surround it, making it ideal for skin diving. Cregneish to the south is an open-air museum – a collection of crofters' cottages beautifully preserved – and to the south-west are The Chasms, vertical rifts along the top of the cliffs. The road continues down to Calf Sound where, beyond the rocky Calf of Man which rises to 421 ft, is the lighthouse on **Chicken Rock**, so named because of the storm petrels which nest there – 'Mother Carey's chickens'.

Castle Rushen, Castletown.

Castletown is attractively sited on the west side of a wide bay, a compact town clustered around Castle Rushen, the harbour and brewery. The present limestone castle is 600 years old, erected on the site of an earlier fortress built, in the 11th C perhaps by Godred Crovan, and was the island's centre of government until the 19th C. Down by the harbour is the Nautical Museum with a schooner-rigged yacht, the *Peggy*, in its boathouse. Higher up the Silver Burn, at Ballasalla, are the remains of Rushen Abbey, dating from 1134.

Peel Viking ceremony.

East of the town is King William's College, the island's public school. At the northern end of Langness is the circular Derby Fort, built by the third Earl of Derby and strengthened by the seventh Earl in 1647. Behind Derbyhaven is Ronaldsway, the Isle of Man airport. The coast to the north is rocky and steep, with just a couple of small sandy bays. The mountainous centre of the island is excellent for walking with some pleasant glens and many prehistoric sites and ancient chapels to see. St John's, scene of the annual Tynwald ceremony, is the most important inland town.

The summit of Snaefell affords excellent views – on a fine day Ireland, Scotland, England and Wales can be seen – but the summit itself has been spoiled by radio transmitters and antennae.

Since its inauguration in 1829, the Isle of Man Steam Packet Company has served the island well, in all conditions and with an enviable safety record – only once has a ship foundered with loss of life. The company operates regular sailings from Liverpool (3¾ hours), and in summer there are services from Ardrossan, Fleetwood and Llandudno (passengers only). Another company, Manx Line, operates a roll-on/roll-off stabilised and air-conditioned ferry from Heysham in Lancashire. The crossing time is also about 3¾ hours and continues winter and summer. No touring caravans are allowed on the island. Flights to Ronaldsway operate from all major British airports.

The Isle of Man is ideal for a family holiday, with lots to do and see. The scenery is pleasant without ever being breathtaking, there is much of historical interest, and the trams and trains are irresistible. Its most enviable asset, however, is its independence.

Cregneish open-air museum.

The Channel Islands

Lying closer to France than England, with their own parliaments, the Channel Islands are a Crown possession, visited by thousands of British tourists each year — an integral part of 'offshore Britain'.

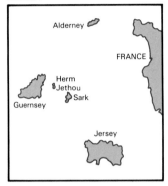

The main islands in the group are Jersey, Guernsey, Alderney, Sark, Herm and Jethou, with a total area of 76 square miles, and a total population of 128,000. They are situated about 110 miles south of Southampton and between eight and 30 miles west of the Cherbourg peninsula in France. The islands are mainly composed of granite; on Jersey the pink Mont Mado granite prevails, but in Guernsey one only finds blue and grey granite. Other rocks throughout the group include shale, diorites and volcanic conglomerates.

More than 250,000 years ago, before the Great Ice Age, primitive man lived in the area we now know as the Channel Islands. At that time they were not islands at all but joined to both England and France (the English Channel was just a river known at the Hurd Deep), and these early Stone Age (Acheulian) men had been forced to move southwards to this region to escape the advancing ice. Before the last ice age, Neanderthal man inhabited the same area. Flint tools, a fireplace and the bones of animals dating from about 100,000 BC were found in a cave in St Bredlade's Bay, Jersey, in 1912. After the last ice age the sea began to rise and, around 5500 BC, England was separated from the Continent.

The Channel Islands continued to be part of France for another 1000 years, until they were also cut off by the rising sea to form the present islands, and by 3500 BC neolithic man had colonised them, their dolmans (burial chambers) dating from this period. The Unelli, a tribe from Eastern Gaul, were the next

settlers, arriving about 300 BC. The Romans called the islands *Riduna, Sarnia* and *Caecarea* (respectively, Alderney, Guernsey and Jersey), and Christianity came to the region during the 6th C when Celtic priests from Cornwall settled in Jersey.

From AD 800, the islands were subjected to frequent attacks by the Norsemen, culminating in 911 with Hrolf (Rollo), son of Earl Rognvald, taking control of the present-day Normandy, and it was formally granted to Rollo by the King of the Franks, Charles the Simple, on condition that he restricted his ambitions to here. At that time Normandy did not include the Channel Islands, but these were added in 937 by Rollo's son, William Longsword.

Before long the Norse language was assimilated into the language of the French Normans, and the old Norse feudal system endured in these islands. There exists, even today, a curious form of appeal, *Clameur de Haro.* When a Channel Islander feels he has been wronged or trespassed by a neighbour, he may cry out, in the presence of two witnesses, *Haro! Haro! Haro! À l'aide mon Prince, on me fait tort.'* The alleged offence must stop immediately and the matter be decided by the court. The word 'Haro' probably derives from Rollo's Norse name, 'Hrolf'. This form of appeal has been used many times, most recently in 1976.

William the Conqueror.

The allegiance of the Channel Islands fluctuated between Normandy and England until, in 1106, Henry I of England took possession of the whole of Normandy after defeating his brother Robert. Normandy remained united with England until, in 1259, Henry III renounced all his French possessions except for Gascony and the Channel Islands. In 1360 the French agreed

to the claim of the English Crown to the Channel Islands and, from that day, the islanders have given their allegiance only to the Sovereign of England, their 'Duke'. Even today, many islanders give the loyal toast as 'The Queen, our Duke.' They will also say that they are not part of England but that England is part of the Channel Islands since it was their Duke, William the Conqueror, who took over England.

The German occupation of the Channel Islands has been well documented. On 30 June 1940 they landed on Guernsey, and one day later the German commandant arrived in Jersey. Occupation orders were printed in the local newspapers, all transport was commandeered and British servicemen still on the islands were interned. The Germans anticipated that, within a few weeks, they would be in England; in fact, some of the soldiers, who had been told they were invading British soil, actually thought they were in England and were extremely impatient to get to London and spend their money. The occupational forces began to fortify all the islands, especially Alderney and Guernsey. Gun emplacements and observation towers were built everywhere, most of which are still there today.

By 1944 the German forces in the Channel Islands had been cut off from their supply lines in France by the Allied landings in Normandy. Obtaining food and fuel then became a real problem for both the invaders and the islanders. In the end, the troops were searching the islands for anything to eat; cats, dogs, dead fish and other scarcely edible items were pounced upon. The islanders had visits from the Red Cross ships bringing food parcels from Australia and New Zealand but, even so, life was not easy for anyone in the Channel Islands during the last months of the war. Many islanders had been sent to camps in France and Germany, many were shot for resistance activities and some openly collaborated with the Germans. On 8 May 1945, the German occupational forces surrendered and the islanders started to rebuild their homes and their lives.

Although English is the official language, a Norman-French patois used to be spoken in all the islands but has completely disappeared from Alderney and to a great extent from Guernsey and Jersey. It is, however, still spoken by some on Sark. The islands are independent of the United Kingdom in all aspects except defence and matters of foreign diplomacy, and are only associate members of the EEC. They have their own parliaments, currencies and postage stamps, the last two issued by the two Bailiwicks of

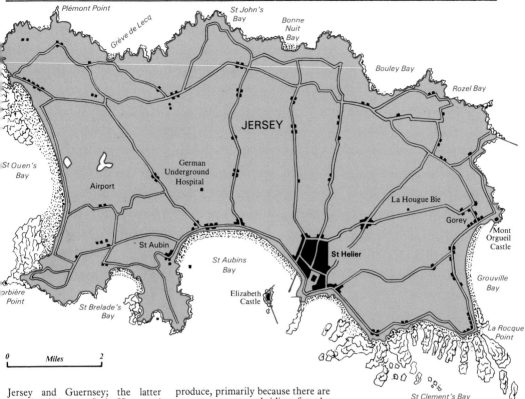

St Clement's Bay

Jersey and Guernsey; the latter includes Alderney, Sark, Herm and Jethou. All but Herm and Jethou (which are leased to tenants by the Bailiwick of Guernsey) have their own independent local governments called 'States'.

Anyone wishing to take advantage of the Channel Islands' low taxation, and high sunshine record, by becoming resident must first become a landowner. Unfortunately property is enormously expensive and, in the case of Jersey, you would also have to have a millionaire-class income as immigrants there must satisfy financial prerequisites before being allowed to settle. Guernsey operates a two-level housing system, on a local and an open-market basis. Would-be residents to Guernsey have only to find enough money to be able to afford a house on the open market which, according to a local estate agent, will cost between £100,000 and £500,000. There are, however, restrictions to the open market, in that whatever has been designated 'local' cannot be sold to a non-resident and the open market cannot be added to. Land is therefore at a premium on these islands and very few more houses may be built.

The general cost of living is higher than in the United Kingdom due to the great cost of importing most necessities. Even home-grown produce such as butter, fruit and vegetables cost more than imported

produce, primarily because there are no government subsidies for the Channel Islands and nothing from the EEC. But then, if you can afford to live here, you can afford to pay a little extra for the privilege.

Jersey

Jersey is the largest island in the group, measuring about ten miles long by six miles wide with a resident population of 74,000. It reaches a height of 450 ft on the north coast and gently slopes down through wooded valleys to the long sweeping beaches in the south. Visually, it looks like rural southern

England, but with smaller fields. Tourism is the island's largest industry, followed by banking and finance. There seems to be more limited companies registered in Jersey than there are inhabitants, all taking advantage of the tax laws. Dairy farming, potato, cauliflower and tomato crops, plus some flower growing, are the mainstays of agriculture.

The climate of Jersey differs slightly to that of the other islands, being closer to the French coast and

The north coast of Jersey.

having high cliffs on the north and west coasts protecting it from the Atlantic storms. The yearly sunshine average is 1941 hours with an average maximum temperature of 47°F in winter and 69°F in summer. Rainfall averages 34.31 inches annually.

The main population centre is St Helier at the eastern end of St Aubins Bay on the south coast, guarded by Elizabeth Castle in the bay and by the ramparts of Fort Regent on land. Over half the total island population lives in the town, which is basically a holiday resort, with hotels, guest houses, bars, restaurants, gift shops and a sandy beach. It is not a pretty place, being more of an 'urban Blackpool'. Royal Square, or Peirson's Place as it is called locally, is now a pedestrian precinct, one of the few picturesque areas in the town. It was here that the 'Battle of Jersey' took place in 1781, when the French, under the command of Rullecourt, landed at night and advanced on St Helier, taking control of the Royal Court (the Government) and demanding the surrender of Jersey. However, a certain Major Peirson, acting commander of Elizabeth Castle, decided otherwise and attacked the French. The battle was a bloody one but eventually Peirson's men won the day and the French were defeated. Both commanding officers were killed in the battle and were buried at St Helier's Church, Major Peirson inside, Rullecourt outside. The old, attractive houses still remain, and the States Chamber, public library, church and Royal Court also attract interest. Apart from this one small area, St Helier proper has little to offer architecturally, and outside the town the spread of urban bungalows detracts from what, at one time, must have been a very pretty area.

The islet on which **Elizabeth Castle** stands used to be called 'L'ilet de St Helier', so called after a hermit of that name who came to Jersey in the 6th C and lived on this tiny isle. He was killed by pirates in AD 555 but miracles that had been allegedly performed by him after his death resulted in his canonisation. The castle was built in 1551 and the islet renamed Elizabeth Castle. Today it is connected to Jersey by a stone causeway 1100 yd long, which is dry for about five hours at low water but is covered to a depth of 12-15 ft at high tide. However, by using several wartime amphibious vehicles tourists can get on and off Elizabeth Castle when the causeway is under water. Visitors should remember that the tides in the Channel Islands have some of the largest rises and falls in the world, almost 40 ft between high and low water.

Mount Orgueil, Jersey.

Several notable persons have stayed at the castle, among them Sir Walter Raleigh, who lived there between 1600 and 1603 while he was Governor of Jersey. The future Charles II stayed in the castle for two months in 1646 after fleeing from England via the Isles of Scilly during the Civil War. Three years later, he returned to Jersey, having been proclaimed king by Jersey and the Scots. The castle today contains displays depicting the various personalities who took part in the history of Jersey, as well as tableaux of historic events.

Fort Regent, a once majestic Napoleonic fortress covering 22 acres on the hill to the east of the town, has now been converted into a gigantic sports and entertainment complex, containing swimming pools, bars, museum, restaurant, concert hall and conference centre. Just below the fort, in Pier Street, is the Jersey Museum, open all year round with exhibits of Victoriana, natural and maritime history, the island's stamps and coins, maps and old photographs. Perhaps the most visited room in the museum is the Lillie Langtry Room. The famous society beauty and actress was born Emilie Charlotte Le Bretan, the daughter of the Dean of Jersey, in 1853. After marrying Edward Langtry, she moved to London and became notorious for her relationships with the Prince of Wales, later to become Edward VII, and the playwright, Oscar Wilde. She died in 1929 and is buried in St Saviour's churchyard.

Jersey's internal bus service is, as on most islands, sufficient for the inhabitants but not for the roving tourist. Special coach tours do operate to specific areas of interest and are excellent value if you only want to spend a couple of days. outside St Helier. But if you really wish to see everything Jersey has to offer, then you must hire a car. There are 36 car-hire companies in St Helier and over 500 miles of narrow twisting roads on the island. There is one problem in driving in Jersey: there are no name signs for any village, no street names outside St Helier and few directional signs, so make sure you have a good map before you start out.

Leaving St Helier, take the tunnel road under Fort Regent out on to the coast road heading east to St Clement's Bay. At high tide many rocks protrude from the bay; at low water the view is totally different with hundreds of rocks and islets filling it between Le Nez and La Rocque Points. These rocks extend out into the sea towards the Cherbourg peninsula and are probably what is left of the landbridge that once joined Jersey to France.

Jersey has a whole series of dependent isles lying between its shores and the French coast. **Les Minquiers** is a large group of islets, rocks and reefs situated 16 miles south of Jersey and 21 miles from the French coast. **Maitresse Ile,** the largest of the group, although not inhabited has some cottages and a customs house; Jersey fishermen use the island occasionally and islanders with boats often go there for a picnic. The other main group of islands is **Ecréhos**, 70 acres in area and lying midway between Jersey's north-east coast and the Cherbourg peninsula; **Marmoutier, Maitre Ile** and **Blanque Ile** are the largest. Marmoutier has several summer houses, but no one lives permanently on any of these islands. There is an abundance of marine life in the rocks and lagoons of both groups.

The next stretch of coastline between La Rocque Point and Gorey measures only two miles, yet between these two points there are no fewer than six Martello towers, two forts and a magnificent castle, clearly indicating that it was considered important during the French wars. The little village of Gorey and its delightful harbour make a nice change from the commercialism of St Helier and is probably the best place to use as a touring base. The castle – Mont Orgueil ('Mount Pride') – dominates the whole area, dwarfing the harbour and the village, and undoubtedly the best time to see Gorey is at night when the castle floodlights are on, giving a fairy-tale look to the area. Mont Orgueil is first mentioned in historical records in 1292 and over the years has been a fortress, Governor's residence and state prison. In 1907, the castle was handed over to the States of Jersey who repaired it and opened it to the public.

Instead of continuing on the main road, which turns inland at this point, take the little coast road to St Catherines Bay where, just round the headland, is a large granite rock called Geoffrey's Leap. According to legend, condemned prisoners were thrown off this rock to the reefs below, but one prisoner named Geoffrey survived the fall and was by law a free man. Filled with bravado, Geoffrey attempted to repeat the jump; needless to say, he did not survive.

Between Geoffrey's Leap and Rozel Bay are a series of pretty and reasonably secluded bays, although during the summer months they do tend to get a bit crowded and Rozel Bay itself, being one of the most picturesque in Jersey, is very crowded all summer. The whole of the north coast between Rozel and Plémont Point is, rough and rocky and over 400 ft high in places. Because of the lack of a coast road at this point and a certain amount of quarrying, it is not easy to get to some of the best places by car, and so hiking is recommended here. Care must be taken when near the cliffs since they are high, steep and prone to landslides.

Turning south, past the race course, the road runs down to St Ouen's (pronounced 'one') Bay, a long crescent of sand spanning the entire west coast. Facing out into the Atlantic, it is ideal for surfers, but only the strongest of swimmers should attempt these rollers since the currents are extremely dangerous. Seaweed is collected along this coast; the local word for this activity is *vraicing, vraic* being the Norman-French name for this particular seaweed. The bay terminates at Corbière Point, a series of jagged rocks and a lighthouse. This is without doubt the most attractive part of the island - wind-swept and rocky with superb sunsets. Between Corbière and St Helier the coast comprises sandy beaches, sand dunes and hotels, attracting the most tourists as it has everything for those who enjoy sun, sand and sea, as well as entertainment in the evening.

The interior of Jersey is mainly agricultural land but there are a few places which should be visited. North-east of St Helier is a remarkable museum, La Hougue Bie, the

La Hougue Bie, Jersey.

site of magnificent neolithic tomb built about 3000 BC. The tomb is covered by an enormous mound of earth and rubble, 40 ft high and 180 ft in diameter. Inside the mound, there is a passageway 33 ft long, leading to the central burial chamber, similar to that at Maeshowe in Orkney and just as well preserved. On top of the mound there are two medieval chapels which look like a single chapel from outside. The Chapel of Notre Dame de la Clarté was built during the 12th C and the Jerusalem Chapel was incorporated into it during the 16th C.

Another place of interest is located at Meadow Bank, east of St Peters Valley - the German underground hospital. Tunnelled out of solid rock during the World War II occupation, the hospital is certainly one of the finest engineering achievements left by the Germans in the whole of the Channel Islands, and is, not surprisingly, Jersey's most visited tourist attraction. Although designed to be twice its present size, thousands of Russian slaves took two-and-a-half years to

construct the part that remains, many of them dying because of their labours. Everything has been left as it was at the end of the war - the equipment in the operating theatres, the beds in the wards, the administrator's office - and, through the clever use of light and sound, it feels as though you are there with the Germans in 1944. In the incomplete tunnels, the sounds of slaves chipping away at the granite and the constant dripping of water from the roof seem all too real.

Guernsey

The difference between Jersey and Guernsey is immediately apparent from the air: Guernsey appears to be virtually covered in glass - mile upon square mile of greenhouses reflect the sun's rays like a giant mirror - and Guernsey is not as wooded as Jersey although pockets of elm do exist in many places. With a resident population of 54,650, it is situated 20 miles north-west of Jersey and covers an area of 25 square miles. Shaped like a triangle with the northern point cut off, it is seven miles north-to-south, seven

Corbière Point, Jersey.

miles across the southern coast, and the blunt end in the north is about two miles wide.

St Peter Port on the east coast is the capital and is situated in a steep sloping valley cut through the high cliffs. Its architecture is a mixture of many periods, all blending well with each other. St Peter Port is comfortable, modernised yet retaining much of the past.

The Town Church, down on the esplanade, is certainly the finest in the Channel Islands, with a 12th-C chancel and a 15th-C south chapel. Behind the church is one of the largest covered markets on any island. Here you can walk through great halls lined with shops and stalls selling flowers, fruit, vegetables, meat and fish. It is here that the great Channel Island delicacy –the ormer or 'sea-ear' - is sold, a local shellfish found only in these waters and protected by law.

St Peter Port, Guernsey.

Guarding the town and harbour is a magnificent 13th-C castle, Castle Cornet, which contains three museums and an armoury, all open daily with conducted tours every morning. It originally stood on a tidal island but this was later connected to the mainland by a breakwater. Opposite the castle, on the south side of the town near the top of Hauteville Road, stands Hauteville House, home of Victor Hugo, the 19th-C French writer, who lived in Guernsey from 1855 to 1870; the house has been preserved by the City of Paris as a memorial and museum. At the top of Smith Street is the Royal Court, where the island's parliament meets. Here visitors are able to see the workings of the States and also the island's most important documents - the original charters which spell out the

special privileges that enable the islanders to determine their own laws and taxation, and those which allow the relief of import duty.

Guernsey's main source of revenue is tourism, having surpassed the previously important tomato and flower-growing industries. Dairy

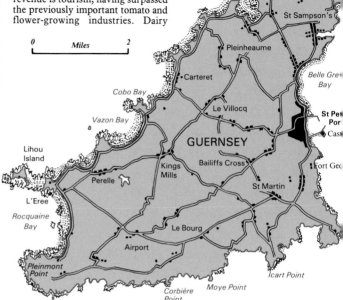

farming is still a major activity, producing milk and butter from the world-famous Guernsey cows. As on Jersey, Guernsey will not allow the importation of any cattle; even if a Guernsey cow has to be sent to another island it will never be allowed back again, thus keeping the breed pure and free from disease. International banking has also become of primary importance on Guernsey, tax exiles from the United Kingdom being encouraged to settle on the island. In 1969 a new, and highly profitable, industry was formed when Guernsey became responsible for its own postal system and a special philatelic bureau was set up to cope with the millions of orders from stamp collectors and dealers all over the world.

Outside St Peter Port, the architecture changes; there are still fine old houses and cottages but the general look is one of suburbia. Most of the farmhouses are very large and all have granite facings which were added in the 1820s. The German fortifications on Guernsey seem, surprisingly, to have been designed with some care, often incorporating a Napoleonic tower or earlier fort or building in a way that looks natural - no doubt to fool Allied bombers rather than for any aesthetic reasons.

To see Guernsey, the visitor will not need to hire a car; the bus service is good and the island is small enough to walk from one coast to the other in a few hours. To give some idea of the variety of interesting historic remains and the magnificent

Aerial view of Guernsey.

landscapes to be seen on this small island, two suggested walks and a series of specific sites have been included.

Starting in St Peter Port at the La Vallette Esplanade, there is a coastal path that runs down to Jerbourg Point and then west along the south coast all the way to Torteval, a walking distance of a convoluted 19 miles. Depending on how energetic you feel, all or part of this walk is possible in one day and you can catch the bus back to town should you get tired. The first part takes you up over Fort George, now a housing estate, and down to Fermain Bay, its beach having two caves and a natural arch, all accessible at low water. From Fermain Bay to Jerbourg Point the distance is about two miles with steep cliffs all the way, broken only by a few small coves. From this point you turn west round Moulin Huet Bay which contains the **Pea Stacks** (Le Tas de Pois d'Amont) - four isolated rocks -as well as the **Cradle Rocks** and the **Dog and Lion Rocks.** Saints Bay is next with its tiny harbour and beach. Up now to Icart Point, past the Martello tower, where the cliffs reach 250 ft, and from here the straight path runs all the way to Torteval and Pleinmont Point. Petit Bot Bay, about one mile west of Icart Point, is a good place to relax.

During the rest of the walk the scenery is the most untouched and beautiful on the whole island. The path runs through Corbière past the Prévôté and Mont Hérault Watch Houses to Le Souffleur - the finest blowhole in the Channel Islands, best seen and heard about two hours after low water. Half a mile north of Pleinmont Point, opposite La Grosse Rock, is a circular indentation in the ground about 30 ft across known as La Table des Pions. This is where the pions (footmen) sat and feasted during a ceremony called La Chevauchée de St Michel, which was carried out every three years until 1837. It involved walking along the roads on the island, assuring that rights of way were maintained and also acted as an inspection of the roads' condition. From here it is only a pleasant and relaxing bus ride back to town, taking a route through the southern interior of the island.

To begin the second walk, a round trip of 15 miles, take Grange Road out of St Peter Port and walk right across the centre of the island to L'Erée and **Lihou Island,** a distance of almost seven miles. The island, 18 acres in extent and privately owned, is connected to Guernsey by a causeway that is above water for a few hours at each low tide. During the 19th C it was used for the collection and burning of *vraic* (seaweed). Lihou's first recorded inhabitants were monks from

St Peter Port, Guernsey, viewed from Castle Cornet.

the Abbey of Mont St Michel, who founded a small priory called Notre Dame de la Roche in the 12th C. For those who have also visited Orkney, there is a surprise; sheep found on North Ronaldsay,

Victoria Tower, Guernsey.

living on seaweed, can also be seen on Lihou, wandering about on the rocky foreshore. During the 1930s, Lihou was advertised for sale in *The Times:* the price — just £5.00. To return to St Peter Port, take the coast road north to Cobo Bay, and then walk inland back to town.

There are other places of interest to visit on Guernsey, including the Candie Museum (which has exhibits of local history) and the Victoria Tower overlooking St Peter Port. The two guns in front of the tower are from World War I. When the German invasion of 1940 became inevitable, the government of Guernsey decided to bury these two museum pieces just in case the Germans might think they were going to be used against them; nearly 40 years later, someone remembered them and they were dug up and put on display. Kings Mills, a very pretty village near Vazon Bay, is where the islanders once brought their corn for grinding. La Gran' Mère du Chimquière, situated outside St Martin's churchyard, is a 6th-C megalithic menhir (monumental stone). Le Creux des fées is a megalithic tomb in the middle of the L'Erée promontory.

For the tourist, Guernsey has more to offer than all the other Channel Islands put together: beautiful landscapes, excellent museums and monuments, easy transportation, good beaches and superb sports facilities, especially for those who like messing about in boats. There are also some excellent restaurants and most pubs do very good and inexpensive meals.

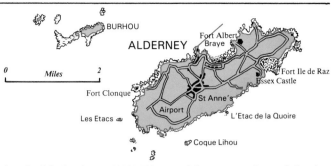

Alderney

Alderney, three-and-a-half miles long and one mile wide, is the most northerly island in the group and the closest to France. Situated 21 miles north-east of Guernsey and just eight miles from Cap de la Hague in France, Alderney has a climate that is more bracing than the other Channel Islands. The waters surrounding it contain some of the most dangerous currents in the group; tides run as fast as eight miles per hour, particularly in the stretch of water known as the 'Race' which separates the island from the French coast. Alderney rises to a height of 294 ft and has a population of 1690.

There are three dependent isles – **Ortac, Burhou** and **Renonpuet** –as well as a group of rocks called **Les Casquets**, all situated to the north and west of Alderney. Ortac, four miles west, is six acres in extent and rises to a height of 60 ft. It is of special interest to ornithologists as it is the home of several hundred gannets. Les Casquets (30 acres) are the traditional site of the sinking of *The White Ship* in which Prince William, son and heir of Henry I, lost his life in 1120. For 18 years during the 19th C, a family of eight lived here and looked after the light-houses.

The earliest structures found on Alderney date from about 2000 BC but most were destroyed during the 19th C, the stones being used for the building of the forts and the break-water. Visitors will be amazed at the

length of the breakwater (2850 ft) in relation to this small island, being nearly as long as the island is wide. It was built in 1864 to protect a large fleet of British warships; however, the advent of steam-powered ships made it redundant as soon as it was completed.

The island has only one town, the very French St Anne's, with narrow, granite-paved streets and some pretty houses, which is without doubt the most attractive in the Channel Islands. Royal Connaught Square is a delight to walk through, even at the height of the tourist season. Tourism on Alderney is more controlled than on the other islands, primarily because there is accommodation for only 2000 holiday-makers; the States are very careful not to expand this quantity, and there are restrictions on building hotels and few plans are approved. Consequently, Alderney is an extremely quiet island with never more than 4000 people on it at any one time. There is space to walk, time to sit and enjoy the scenery, and time to drink since, unlike the other islands in the group, the bars on Alderney stay open from 9.00 a.m. right through to 1.00 the next morning.

The only safe anchorage is Braye Harbour and a certain number of moorings are available for visitors' boats. The local fishermen operate from here and, although it is not a busy harbour, there is usually some

activity at most times of the day. Being the nearest of the Channel Islands to both France and England it is also the most heavily fortified; there are 11 forts around the coast, most of them built during the 1860s except Essex Castle, to the south of Longy Bay, which was completed during the 13th C and rebuilt in the 16th C. Today, two of the forts have been converted into flats, another (Fort Corblets) has been incorporated into a beautiful private residence, and a fourth is used by the local Scout troop; the rest lie empty, some in ruins.

Because of its position, the Germans built more fortifications here than on the other islands although, when their invasion was imminent, the islanders voted to abandon their island home rather than live under German rule. There are dozens of bunkers, gun emplacements and control towers remaining and, although they are not attractive or useful, they are part of the island's history. The islanders sometimes put the bunkers to good use in the summer by holding 'bunker parties' on the flat concrete tops; if it should rain, everyone goes underground and the music and dancing continues.

St Anne's offers little in the way of tourist facilities – just reasonably priced accommodation, good food and lots of duty-free drinks. Naturalists will find Alderney particularly attractive – birds and wild flowers will be your only companions once you head out of town – and artists and photographers will also enjoy the beautiful landscapes and deserted beaches. You should take care on the cliffs as many of the German fortifications have become overgrown with bracken and gorse and are difficult to see until it is too late. There are a few sports facilities on the island (golf, tennis and squash) plus a cinema show once a week and the usual summer carnivals.

R. M. Lockley, a writer with a great affinity to all islands (*see* Skokholm), once defined his perfect island as, 'large enough to walk around, small enough to love.' Alderney is exactly that.

St Anne's, Alderney.

Fort Clonque, Alderney.

SARK
Eperquerie
Port du Moulin
BRECQHOU
Havre
Gosselin
La Coupée
LITTLE SARK
Venus Bath
L'Etac de Sark
0   Miles   2

Sark

Eight miles east of Guernsey is an island of less than 1400 acres and a population of about 500 – Sark. It is a high plateau reaching over 360 ft, and is in fact almost two islands, joined by a narrow isthmus called La Coupée which separates Sark from Little Sark. The island is, in effect, a 'private kingdom', owned and ruled by a feudal lord, the Seigneur. The fief of Sark was first granted to Helier de Carteret of Jersey by Queen Elizabeth I in 1565, the only condition being that the island should be settled by 40 men loyal to the English Crown. Tenancies were allocated to them and the present-day owners of these 40 farms constitute the parliament of Sark, presided over by the Seigneur who has the right of veto.

All the feudal rights of the Seigneur would be far too numerous to list but some of the privileges enjoyed by the Lord of Sark, to the exclusion of the other islanders, are that no one may own a car on Sark, except the Seigneur; no one may own a bitch on Sark, except the Seigneur; no one may own doves on Sark, except the Seigneur.

Visitors who take the day-trip tour from Guernsey will find it difficult, tiring and virtually impossible to see all that Sark has to offer in just a few hours, even if you hire one of the expensive horse-drawn carriages. There are magnificent views of superb bays, wild and rugged cliffs, caves and rock pools which the carriage drivers do not attempt to show to visitors.

It is therefore certainly worth spending a few days on this attractive island in order to appreciate its beauty. Venus' Bath, on the southern tip of Little Sark, is not easy to find, and at high tide the sea covers it, but the effort is worth it when you finally arrive there with enough time for a swim. Port Gorey harbour on Little Sark should be visited, as should Happy Valley and Havre Gosselin on the west coast of Sark opposite the island of **Brecqhou.** The caves in this area are magnificent but the climb down is steep and a little dangerous. Port du Moulin has natural arches, a rocky cove and the **Les Autelets** rocks, and Eperquerie Common on the northern tip is ideal for a family picnic, sunbathing, swimming, walks or even fishing. The eastern coast is not as dramatic as the Atlantic side but includes some quiet coves and beaches. Accommodation is available on Sark at several hotels and guest houses as well as at three pubs.

Creux Harbour, Sark.

Herm and Jethou

Between Sark and St Peter Port in Guernsey lie two small islands, Herm and Jethou, both situated about five miles east of Guernsey and half a mile from each other.

One-and-a-half miles in circumference, Jethou covers 44 acres and is conical, rising to 268 ft. It has been inhabited throughout history; it is said that convicted smugglers and pirates were hanged from gibbets and witches burned there. Its most famous resident was Sir Compton Mackenzie who leased the island until 1934 after his residence on Herm. Today, a house and a few other buildings remain, and at the highest point are the vestiges of ancient cultivated fields and hedges. The island today is privately owned and landing is not permitted.

Herm is one-and-a-half miles long and half a mile wide, covering an

The Seigneurie, Sark.

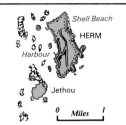

area of 500 acres. This is another island that fits Lockley's definition of the perfect island. Its name derives from the Latin *erimus* meaning 'open and fruitless', but today nothing could be further from the truth.

Neolithic man left behind several dolmans, and Roman pottery and tiles have also been unearthed. In AD 565, St Magloire built a small chapel on the reef between Herm and the **Crevichon Rock**, which lies near Jethou. During the 11th C, Robert I, Duke of Normandy, gave the island to the Abbey of Mont St Michel, and the still-standing St Tugdual's Chapel dates from about 1480.

Stone quarrying was carried out on a large scale in the past, and Herm granite was exported to mainland Britain in great quantities between 1815 and 1850, after which the industry declined; visitors today would be hard pressed to find any evidence of it. In 1889, the lease of Herm was sold to Prince Blücher von Wahlstatt who immediately set about changing the island; roads were laid, the old manor house was converted into a castellated mansion, the gardens were redesigned and planted with tropical plants and eucalyptus trees and, of all things, wallabies were introduced. During World War I, the Prince was interned by the British as an enemy alien. After the war Compton Mackenzie obtained the lease and, for three years, lived in the manor house he called 'the ugliest building in Europe'. Mackenzie also hated the constant stream of tourists whom he called 'those 20th-C cannibals'.

The island today is almost totally self-sufficient, with a large dairy farm and a hotel, as well as a restaurant, café and bars for the 100,000 day visitors that come to the island each year. All of this has been made possible by the efforts of one man, Major Peter Wood. A person of great character and determination, Major Wood - or 'King Peter' as he is affectionately known - leased the island in 1949 when Herm was, in his words, 'a derelict, run-down and overgrown island'. With his wife and family, he set about making it not only hospitable but also economically viable. Great care has been taken in converting and redesigning the hotel and cottages, and

one is reminded of Portmeirion in Wales. The archways, walled courtyards and crenellations on Herm all have an Italian flavour.

About 60 people live on the island as permanent residents but this figure swells in the summer months to cope with the thousands of tourists, and everyone works for the Major, either in the hotel, on the farm or in the various tourist facilities. Although Herm is part of the Bailiwick of Guernsey and therefore entitled to the services of the police and firemen, the island has its own fire-fighting service and its own regulations since it would take too long for those services to reach them from Guernsey.

The visitor lands at Herm Harbour at high water, or at the Rosière Steps at low water. The hotel is the first building to be seen. In the garden in front of it is a small circular building, now used as a potting shed, but it was originally a prison during the quarrying days where inebriated workers could be locked up for the night. Past the hotel as you head north, is the little shopping piazza containing the island's post office, gift shop and pub. Until recently, all mail posted on Herm carried a special Herm stamp to cover the cost of the boat journey between the island and Guernsey but, when the Bailiwick of Guernsey took over the postal service, the Herm stamps were discontinued and Major Wood had to open a Guernsey post office. This represented quite a considerable loss of revenue since the Herm stamps had been in demand by collectors and dealers all over the world. It is now illegal to put a Herm stamp on a letter or postcard even if you also

put on the correct Guernsey stamp.

The island contains a great variety of landscapes - golden beaches, fine cliffs, moorland, meadows, woodland, sand dunes, and rocky outcrops - and a leisurely walk round Herm will not take long. You do not have to worry about being late for the boat, since all the signposts on the island give the time (in minutes) it will take to walk from that point back to the harbour. Shell Beach, as its name implies, is composed of tiny shells, many of which are said to have been carried across the Atlantic from the Caribbean. At the northern end of the island, the dunes, or Herm Common as it is known, contain many megalithic remains including a cromlech (burial chamber). To complete the circuit, you should walk to the top of the island, past the Manor House and the chapel, through the farm and down to the south coast. Alternatively, there is a small path running round the island within a few yards of the sea. Boats from Guernsey run every hour to Herm during the day, but you should not try to see this in just two or three hours. Ideally Herm is a place for staying a few days, to relax, to do some fishing, to see the island in your own time and, best of all, to enjoy the warm, quiet evenings when all the other tourists have gone back to Guernsey.

Each of the Channel Islands has something different to offer and, if you are lucky and have your own boat, the whole of the Channel Islands can be your playground. Transportation to the Channel Islands is available from a variety of sea and air services.

The Village, Herm.

Wales

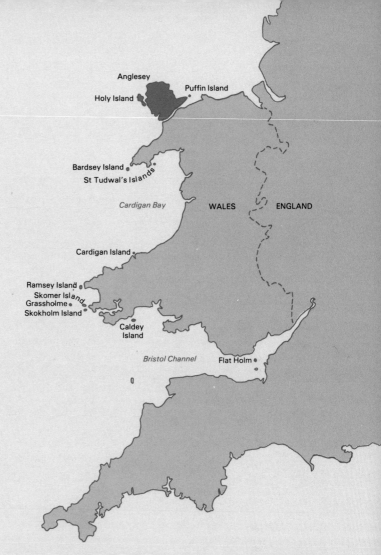

From Anglesey in the north to Flat
Holm in the south these few Welsh
islands are remarkable in their
diversity and interest.

Anglesey
Holy Island
Puffin Island

Bardsey Island
St Tudwal's Islands

Cardigan Bay

WALES   ENGLAND

Cardigan Island

Ramsey Island
Skomer Island
Grassholme
Skokholm Island

Caldey
Island

Bristol Channel   Flat Holm

Anglesey

Gwynedd. The derivation of the
name 'Anglesey' is probably from
Old Norse, but whether it is *Anglesey*, 'isle of the Angles', or *Ongulls-ey*,
a 'fjord' or 'strait', is not clear. Its
Welsh name is *Ynys Môn*, from the
ancient Briton word *Bon*, meaning
'end'.

With an area of 176,692 acres, the
land is low-lying, mainly composed
of the most extensive tract of pre-
Cambrian rocks in the British Isles,
known as the Mona Complex. The
highly altered series of rocks
comprises three main groups: the
gneisses; the bedded series; and the
more recent plutonic intrusions.
Vast earth movements caused folds
and overfolds which often collapsed
along their axes, frequently leaving
the oldest rock at the surface and
burying the newer types; such folds
can be seen in the cliff face at South
Stack. This was all subject to
extensive erosion which scraped
these old ribs away, leaving the flat

landscape that can be seen today.

Around Benllech and along part
of the Menai Strait there are deposits
of carboniferous limestone which is
thought to have, at one time, covered
the whole area. During the glacial
period, ice was pushed across
Anglesey from the north-east,
scouring the land and depositing
erratics from the Lake District and
possibly from as far away as Ailsa
Craig.

Anglesey was once the granary of
Wales – its fertile soil was said to be
able to produce grain enough for the
whole country, and it became known
as *Môn, Mam Cymru*, 'Anglesey,
Mother of Wales'. The growing
season is long, thanks to its maritime
position and low elevation. Severe
air frosts are virtually unknown,
rainfall is moderate but the wind,
unbroken by hills, is persistent.
Between the 15th and 18th centuries
as many as 3000 head of black cattle
were exported from Anglesey each
year, being swum across the Menai
Strait by cattle drovers. Today the

emphasis in farming is on beef cattle
as well as dairy cattle, and on the
production of early fat lambs. Much
of the land is pasture, green and
lush, and there is little rough
grazing, about 12 per cent of the
total farmland.

The island is rich in prehistoric
remains, with many neolithic burial
chambers and cairns still to be seen.
Bronze Age finds include tools
found in a cinerary urn at Lland-
dyfnan which suggest a link with the
builders of Stonehenge. The great
hoard of Llyn Cerrig Bach, dating
from the 2nd C BC to the 1st C AD,
consisted of chariot fittings, swords,
arrowheads, tools, shackles and an
engraved shield-boss, and may be a
relic of the last stand of the Celtic
people against the Roman invaders
who came in the 1st C AD during
the reign of Nero. The Roman
historian Tacitus described the Celts
as 'fearful' and as practising 'horrid
rites'.

When the Romans withdrew in
about AD 410, the Celtic culture,

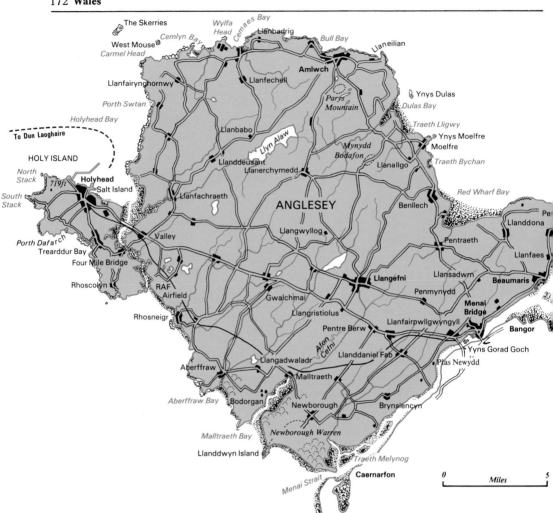

suppressed during occupation, re-emerged. For 750 years the Princes of Gwynedd, including Llewellyn the Great, had their stronghold at Aberffraw in the south-west of Anglesey, creating an independent kingdom that finally succumbed to the English king, Edward I, in 1283.

Anglesey's proximity to Ireland, and its vital position on the trade routes, made it an important religious and cultural centre. In the 6th C Maelgwyn Gwynedd allowed St Cybi to found a monastery in the Roman fort at Holyhead, and St Seriol also founded one at Penmon in the south-east of the island. These two monks, described in Matthew Arnold's poem 'East and West', often met to discuss religious affairs, arranging a venue in the centre of Anglesey. St Cybi became known as *Cybi Felyn* ('the dark') because he walked eastwards in the morning and westwards home, always facing the sun, and became suntanned. St Seriol was *Seriol Wyn* ('the fair') because his journey kept his back to

the sun. The Holy Well of St Seriol and the remains of his cell still survive at Penmon. During the 9th C the Viking raids began, continuing until they settled and were converted to Christianity in the 11th C.

Anglesey was created a shire, along with Caernarfon, Merioneth and Flint, in 1284, its hundreds (ancient measures of land) being framed on the ancient Welsh 'cantrefi', and was part of the private estate of the Crown until it joined the English realm in 1536. English became the language of administration, reducing the status of Welsh.

The outbreak of civil war in 1642 saw Anglesey firmly on the side of the King, his supporters holding out at Beaumaris until June 1646 although Charles I had been held by the Scots since early May. The history of Anglesey has since been that of the rest of Wales.

The Welsh were initially 'Celtic' Christians, becoming 'Latin' Christians during the Middle Ages,

and part of the reformed Anglican Church after the Reformation. In the mid-17th C Anglesey had no Nonconformist minister, and the majority of Welsh people were indifferent to what was seen as an essentially English phenomenon, but by the 18th C John Wesley's Methodism was adopted with great vigour and tailored to their own needs. In 1811 the Welsh Methodists officially left the Anglican Church to become Nonconformists in the 'Great Schism', and evangelists such as John Elias were hailed as Welsh heroes. It was once said of Anglesey that, if it were roofed over, it would be 'one giant Methodist Chapel'. Present Welsh education, radicalism and liberalism in politics and much Welsh music and culture all have their roots in the Nonconformist movement.

Anglesey, now with a population of 60,000, is a stronghold of the Welsh language (Holy Island and the coastal areas less so), although all the people are bilingual. Welsh is now

Britannia Bridge, rebuilt after the fire of 1970.

taught in the schools – in contrast to the 19th C when it was actively suppressed. In common with the rest of rural Wales, and the Scottish islands, the lack of job opportunities causes emigration among young people while ·incomers tend to be older and non-Welsh speaking, and it is because of this gradual erosion of Welsh culture that there is the occasional burst of violent nationalism – such as the burning of holiday homes. Like the Gaelic-speaking area in Scotland, the Welsh-speaking area, *Bro Gymraeg*, has been pushed to the 'western fringe'.

For the visitor unfamiliar with Wales, the 'Welshness' of Anglesey soon becomes apparent. The love of song and poetry is a common link through all levels of society – support for *Eisteddfodau* (local and national gatherings for music and poetry competitions) is strong, and even the Saturday-night 'sing-song' in the pub will demonstrate quite an extensive musical knowledge. Out of this wealth of natural talent came, in the 18th C, Goronwy Owen, one of Anglesey's most famous sons, since acknowledged as one of the greatest bards of his time although his verse came from a longing for home while in Williamsburg, Virginia, where he died in obscurity in about 1770, his genius unrecognised. The Morris brothers of Anglesey, great patrons of the arts who grew up at Dulas Bay, did much to try and promote Goronwy Owen, complaining, when

his works did not appear, that they lived in 'an age more fertile in ignorance than the past'. Their many hundreds of letters, collected and published, give a great insight into the social life and attitudes of the time.

Anglesey is joined to the mainland by two well-known and much photographed bridges. The first to be opened was Thomas Telford's elegant Menai Suspension Bridge in 1826, the central span of which is 579 ft long and 100 ft above high water, so designed to allow sailing ships to pass unhindered through the Strait. Its total length is 1265 ft, and it cost £120,000 to build. It originally had four iron chains anchored in tunnels in rock instead of the present two steel ones; the bridge, except for the stonework, was reconstructed in 1938-40. Until it was built the island was served by ferries.

Twenty-four years later Sir William Fairburn and Robert Stephenson built the Britannia Railway Bridge, to the west of Telford's structure. The original design consisted of two rectangular tubes 1500 ft long through which the trains travelled, constructed from wrought-iron plates weighing over 10,000 tons, and supported by five towers. Floating them into position on pontoons, they were then raised by a hydraulic press in the 230-ft Britannia Tower to a clearance of 100 ft above high water. The cost was £600,000. The bridge

was closed for two years after suffering serious fire damage in 1970; the famous tubes were subsequently replaced with open track, and a roadway was later incorporated to cope with increasing traffic.

Anglesey has 124 miles of coastline – the main attraction for the thousands of holiday-makers who visit each summer. The town of Menai Bridge (Porthaethwy) is a major touring centre, with accommodation, tourist office, good sea fishing, annual regatta (August) and fair (October) among the many attractions. A summer ferry runs to Bangor and Beaumaris. A path leads to **Church Island**, where there is a 14th-C church on the site of the original building founded in the 7th C by St Tysilio. Lying to the east of the Britannia Bridge, in the Strait among a group of rocks and skerries known as the **Swellies**, is **Ynys Gorad Goch**, the 'island of the red weir'. It is, in fact, two small islands linked by a causeway: on the western outcrop is a house; on the eastern Tern Island is a smoke tower (for herring), workshop and a store house with a cosy two-seat 'privy'. From the 13th C until 1915 a commercial fishery was operated on Ynys Gorad Goch, originally supplying fish for the monasteries of Anglesey, the island being owned by the Bishop of Bangor until 1888, and the two fish-traps (weirs) can still be seen. Between 1800 and 1920 it was occupied by the Madoc Jones family

Ynys Gorad Goch in the Menai Strait.

who raised seven children there, and latterly supplemented their income by providing 'whitebait teas' for visitors at the price of one shilling. During the big spring and autumn tides of the equinoxes the island is awash and the buildings have often been flooded. Ynys Gorad Goch is privately owned, but can be viewed from Anglesey or the Menai Bridge, or from the trip boats from Beaumaris that ply the Strait.

To the west of Menai Bridge is Llanfairpwllgyngyll(gogerychwyrn-drobwllllantysiliogogogoch). The second part of the name was probably added in the 19th C to attract tourists, and all together it means: 'St Mary's Church in the hollow of the white hazel near a rapid whirlpool and the church of St Tysilio near the red cave.' Platform tickets with the full name can be bought at what was once the station. There are fine views from the nearby Marquess of Anglesey's Column, built in 1816, and Telford's two-storey octagonal tollhouse can be seen by the A5 which was the last public turnpike road in Britain.

The area around Llanddaniel Fab was once a centre of worship for the Druids, and a mile to the east is the Bryncelli Ddu burial chamber (the 'mound in the dark grove'), the present grassy mound replacing the

original which was cleared during excavation, when human remains and tools were uncovered. The Bronze Age chamber, with a tall pillar and a stone (a replica) carved with zig-zags and a maze-like pattern, is probably the most impressive passage grave in Wales. Nearby Plas Newydd, by the shore of the Menai Strait, is a fine 18th-C mansion built of Moelfre marble, the family home of the Marquess of Anglesey now owned by the National Trust and open to the public; among its attractions are a Rex Whistler mural and a military museum. The old church of Llanidan, St Nidans, also overlooking the Strait, is of considerable interest; the stoup (holy-water basin) in the back porch is said to have healing powers. To the west are earthworks, a burial chamber and a stone circle, and to the south, at Foel, a ferry operated from 1425 to 1849. At the extreme southern tip of Anglesey is Abermenai Point; until the 13th C there was a causeway to the mainland here, which was later replaced by a ferry.

Newborough Warren is a National Nature Reserve, a vast area of dunes covered with marram – from the 16th C until the outbreak of World War II a major industry thrived here making mats and

baskets from the grass. In the forest to the west are the remains of medieval houses; the village of Rhosyr has lain buried beneath sand since a great storm in 1331. To the west of the beach is Llanddwyn Island, a peninsula with a lighthouse built in 1873 at the tip; it too is a National Nature Reserve. The cottages around the harbour are used by the Nature Conservancy Council and house an exhibition. The ruined priory was founded by St Dwynwen, the patron saint of Welsh lovers.

The Afon Cefni spills into a fine sandy bay beyond the village of Malltraeth, home of the bird artist, Charles Tunnicliffe RA, from 1947 until his death in 1979. Called the 'finest English practitioner since Thomas Bewick', he wrote about his life here in his book, *Shorelands Summer Diary*. At Pen-y-parc to the west of the estuary, there is a well-preserved promontory fort. Llangad-waladr church has a fine stained-glass window and a memorial to Cadfan, a 7th-C Welsh leader. Aberffraw to the west was the capital of the Princes of Gwynedd from the 7th C to the 13th C, although no trace of their palace remains. Traeth Mawr, a fine sandy beach, is nearby. On a tiny tidal island in Porth Cwyfan, one mile south-west, stands a church, built on 7th-C foundations and restored in 1893, where services were arranged to suit the tides.

Above Porth Trecastell, a beautiful sandy cove, is Barclodiad y Gawres, the 'Giantess's Apronful', five ancient carved stones that were uncovered in the original chambered cairn, now protected by a modern concrete dome. Two miles north-east is the impressive Ty Newydd Cromlech, a neolithic burial chamber with a massive capstone supported by three uprights, the earth covering having long since disappeared.

Rhosneigr is an area of beautiful beaches, rocks and dunes, with a golf course by Afon Crigyll, the haunt of 18th-C wreckers. Aeroplane-spotters are attracted to this area by Valley RAF Station, the Advanced Jet Flying School, Strike Command Missile Practice Camp and the Air-Sea Rescue base. Built as a fighter base in 1941, RAF Valley was enlarged to receive US servicemen in 1943. The village of Valley is to the north where the main A5 crosses to Holy Island on Telford's 1300-yd Stanley Embankment, opened in 1823. To the south-west is Four Mile Bridge, where crossings were made at low tide before the bridges were built. Cytiau'r Gwyddelod nearby is the site of ancient hut circles.

In 1775, Rev. Nicholas Owen, in his *History of Anglesey*, wrote: 'Holyhead, in Welsh "Caergybi", is a small sea-port town, situated near

Plas Newydd, Anglesey.

St Cwyfan, near Aberffraw, Anglesey.

the extremity of an island in the Irish sea, joined to the north west part of the Isle of Anglesey, by a stone bridge of one arch, called Rhyd-pont Bridge.' His description rather understated the long-standing importance of the harbour of **Holy Island** on the route between Wales (and England) and Ireland. The Romans recognised its strategic position when they built a fort here in the 3rd C AD, and, in the 6th C, St Cybi built a church inside the fortress walls which still stand today. The present church is mainly 15th – 17th C and contains windows by Burne-Jones and William Morris. That most 'English' of institutions, the Women's Institute, had its beginnings at a meeting held in 1911 at the Station Hotel, organised by Mrs Alfred Watt from Canada, and the very first organised Women's Institute in the country was formed at Llanfairpwllgwyngyll in June 1915.

The earliest recorded packet boat to Ireland sailed from Holyhead in 1573. The long breakwater, which makes a fine walk, was completed in 1873, and the harbour was rebuilt in 1880. It is now a modern container port and the terminal for the Dun Laoghaire (Irish Republic) car ferry. The town is a busy cosmopolitan place, the most populous area of

Anglesey and, if not always in itself attractive, it is a spirited base from which to tour. There is sailing, angling, a sports centre, Tourist Information office and all the services of a major town. **Salt Island**, formerly Ynys Gybi, once had a salt-house where the mineral was extracted from sea water. In the early 18th C, Queen Anne gave permission for rock salt to be added but, by 1775, 'for want of proper management the work had fallen into decay'. To the south-east of the town there is much heavy industry, and beyond is Penrhos, a nature reserve. Near here, at low tide, turf from the remains of one of the many drowned forests of West Wales was once dug for fuel. Inland, over-looking the aluminium works, is Trefignath burial chamber, where urns containing human bones were found.

The highest point on Anglesey is Holyhead Mountain, 719 ft high, commanding views of Ireland, the Isle of Man, Snowdonia and Cumbria, the summit of which was once an ancient fortress. On the south-west slope, above South Stack, is Cytiau'r Gwyddelod, the 'Irish-men's huts', remains of about 20 hut circles occupied during the late Iron Age and early Roman periods – there is, however, no particular evidence

to suggest they were occupied by the Irish. South Stack cliffs, by the lighthouse built in 1808, are an RSPB reserve. Nine species of sea bird nest here, including puffins and the rare chough. Ellen's Tower, a small 19th-C castellated structure, is now an information centre. The cliffs, sheer to 400 ft in places, show clearly the folds of the Mona Complex, and are of great geological importance. An array of coastal flora grows on them, particularly colourful in spring and early summer.

South Stack lighthouse.

The west coast of Holy Island is rocky, with many attractive bays, much frequented by skin divers. At the southern end of the island is Rhoscolyn, which once had marble-quarrying and oyster-catching industries. The water from St Gwenfaen's Well, on Rhoscolyn Head, is traditionally supposed to cure mental disorders.

There are fine sandy bays along the north-west coast of Anglesey, although swimmers should be wary of strong currents near Traeth y Gribin. Carmel Head, wild and rocky, overlooks **The Skerries** (*Ynysoedd y Moelrhoniaid*, 'isle of porpoises'), where William Trench, a merchant of Dublin, erected a lighted beacon in 1716 which consumed 100 tons of coal each year, and was the last privately owned lighthouse in the country. Until the 19th C, passing ships had to pay a toll. The new light is visible for 29 miles, and warns mariners of submerged reefs and The Skerries themselves; three miles west is a major tanker route.

Cemlyn Bay, a sheltered shingle spit, is now a bird sanctuary owned by the National Trust, but between 1828 and 1919 it was a lifeboat station. Near Hen Borth, to the west, is Llanrhwydrys Church, founded on this site in AD 570. To the east the surroundings are dominated by the massive blocks of Wylfa Nuclear Power Station, the largest of the Magnox type, although its output has been down-rated from a planned 1180 megawatts to 840 megawatts. In 1979, in the world league of 158 nuclear stations, it was 134th for efficiency.

Cemaes sits snugly behind a fine

Holyhead, Anglesey.

sandy and sheltered bay, once a shipbuilding and smuggling centre; the small harbour was built in the late 19th C. The church at Llanbadrig was built on the site of an earlier chapel dedicated to St Patrick who, according to legend, was shipwrecked on **Middle Mouse** rocks (Ynys Badrig). Beacons on the coast to the west of Porth Wen, and to the west of Bull Bay, measure nautical miles (6078 ft).

Amlwch is a resort, market town and sea-angling centre, and in the early 19th C was the most populous area of Anglesey, its inhabitants working in the copper mines of Parys Mountain and in the tobacco industry. The harbour, established in 1793, was used for exporting the copper, and ships were also once built here. The harbour has now been revived with the building of the marine terminal (which received an RIBA award), and the single-buoy mooring two miles off shore, accommodating tankers of over 500,000 tons. A three-foot diameter pipeline carries oil the 78 miles to Cheshire; it has all been buried and there is no detrimental effect on the environment.

Point Lynas lighthouse, established in 1835 and situated on the small peninsula sheltering Porth Eilean, marks the north-east tip of Anglesey. To the south Mynydd Eilian rises to 580 ft, giving superb views along the coast, and the 15th-C St Eilian's Church contains some interesting relics, including a studded chest and tongs for separating fighting dogs.

The eastern coast of Anglesey is characterised by wide expanses of sand between the rocky headlands from whence, in the 18th C, great quantities of herring were caught. **Ynys Dulas**, a mile outside Dulas Bay, has a 19th-C beacon tower, a place of refuge for mariners. Dulas's new church, replacing the ruined St Gwenllwyfo Church, contains the font, oak screen and brass from the older building, and also has some fine 15th and 16th-C Flemish glass. The aforementioned Morris brothers grew up on a farm over-

looking the bay. Traeth Lligwy, to the south, is an excellent beach, and further south are the remains of Din Lligwy, the 4th-C residence of a chieftain, consisting of two circular and seven rectangular huts with a burial chamber nearby; it was excavated in 1908, when the remains of 30 people were found.

Moelfre is famous for its lifeboat station, established in 1830, which has been involved in many memorable rescues on a coast notorious for shipwrecks. One such tragic incident concerned the iron sailing ship *Royal Charter* which, when returning to Liverpool from Australia, was driven on to the rocks in October 1859 with the loss of 452 lives. Many of those drowned were gold prospectors, whose washed-up bodies were said to have been looted, contributing to the prosperity of Moelfre and its hinterland. The *Royal Charter* memorial is at Llanallgo. About three miles inland is Mynydd Bodafon, rising steeply to 504 ft, and giving excellent views over the coast; on its slopes are ancient cairns and the remains of a medieval homestead.

Benllech, the birthplace of Goronwy Owen, the celebrated bard, is a popular resort with a sandy beach and ample facilities. South-east is the vast expanse of sand of Red Wharf Bay (Traeth Coch), overlooked by Castell-mawr, an early British fortress. To the east of the bay is Llanddona, where parts of the original 7th-C church of St Dona are incorporated into the present building. Nearby is the pretty church of Llaniestyn, and north-east, below the fort of Bwrdd Arthur, is the tiny church of St Michael, overlooking the sea. At the eastern tip of Anglesey, called Trwyn Du ('black nose'), is a lighthouse built in 1837, which now operates automatically; there was a lifeboat station here between 1832 and 1915.

Puffin Island, also known as Ynys Seiriol and Priestholm, about one-half mile off the point, has the remains of a monastery founded in the 6th C by St Seriol. Puffins still nest on the island, but numbers have

declined. At the north-east end is an old telegraph station, once a link in the Holyhead – Liverpool chain. The island can be seen from the trip boats that operate from Beaumaris.

A monastery was founded at Penmon in the 6th C, the priory buildings and Norman church (rebuilt in the 12th C) making an attractive group. There are also two fine Celtic crosses, St Seriol's Well nearby, a 17th-C dovecote, and the foundations of St Seriol's cell. Beaumaris Castle and the two Menai bridges were all built from limestone quarried in this area. The whole Penmon area is particularly attractive, and the views of the mountains on the mainland are superb. During the 18th C poor people dredged 'remarkably large' oysters off the coast here, and seaweed was collected and burned, to become kelp for making soap and glass (*see* The Isles of Scilly). Today, fishing boats dredge for mussels. To the south-west is Llanfaes, once a busy port where Llewelyn founded a monastery in 1237, and site of a battle in AD 811 when Egbert, King of Wessex, defeated the Welsh.

Castle Street, Beaumaris.

Strategically placed towards the eastern end of the Menai Strait is Beaumaris, a salty and sedate town with a sturdy moated castle, built in 1298 by Edward I of England in response to the attack on Caernarfon during Prince Madog's rebellion four years earlier. Together with Caernarfon, it effectively closed the Strait, separating the Welsh from their vital Anglesey grain supplies. Beaumaris withstood seige during Owain Glyndwr's rebellion in the early 15th C (after which the town was walled) and, later, supporters of Charles I held out in the castle until finally yielding to Major-General Hytton in June 1646, after the fall of Caernarfon and Conway towards the close of the Civil War. The town,

Puffin Island.

Beaumaris Castle, Anglesey.

once a thriving port and ship-building centre, is now a deservedly popular resort, with some very fine period buildings, beautifully preserved: the Courthouse, built in 1614, the Gaol (1829), the 14th-C Church of SS Mary and Nicholas, Ye Olde Bull's Head (1472), the Tudor Rose dating from 1400, the 17th-C cottages in Wexham Street, and Victoria Terrace - all are outstanding. The town was granted its charter in 1294 by Edward I, and the name *beaumarais* describes the 'beautiful marsh' that is now The Green. The waterfront, where trade

flourished in Tudor times, is now packed with anchored yachts.

Away from the coast, Anglesey undulates gently. Most of the land is lush and green, and narrow lanes wind among fields of grazing cattle and sheep. The atmosphere is definitely Welsh, but it is a unique area, a gentler landscape than mainland Wales. In the north-west, Llanfechell is a village conservation area, with a fine square and an unusual Norman church. In the north-east is Parys Mountain, during the 18th C the world's most famous copper mine, employing

1500 people. The ore was taken by pack horse to Amlwch for shipping to Swansea and when it ran out the mountain was abandoned; it is still covered with shafts, tunnels, a ruined windmill and, lower down, a Cornish-type engine house. It is probably the most spectacular copper mine in Britain, a lunar landscape of browns, greens, yellows, oranges and pinks, quite a sight when the sun shines, but depressing on a dull day when the despoliation is more apparent.

To the north-west of the Llyn Alaw reservoir is the tiny church of Llanbabo, which contains a 14th-C carving of St Pabo. At Llanddeusant, to the west, there are two windmills, built in the 18th C along with many others on the island, taking advantage of the persistent unchecked winds off the sea. The village of Gwalchmai further south was the first on Anglesey to have electricity, generated by watermill, and is the site of the Annual Agricultural Show held in August.

Until 1760 Llangefni was the furthest navigable point of the Afon Cefni. It is a market town surrounded by beautiful woods and is Anglesey's administrative centre, with a theatre company and a sports and recreation complex. St Cyngar's Church has an engraved 5th-C gravestone, and Llangristiolus Church to the south-west has a 13th-C chancel arch and a 12th-C font. Pentre Berw was the centre of Anglesey's brief coal-mining industry, supplying fuel for the mines at Parys Mountain.

Penmynydd, north-west of Menai Bridge, has fine 17th-C almshouses, now renovated as dwellings, and the Church of St Gredifael, dating from the 6th C but rebuilt in the 12th and 14th centuries. The Tudor monarchs were descended from Owain Tudor, born in Penmynydd in 1400.

Wales' largest island is seen by many travelling to Holyhead, who think it both dull and flat. Those who take the trouble to leave the main roads and explore further will be amply rewarded and pleasantly surprised.

Bardsey Island

Gwynedd. Named after the Norse warrior, Bardr, Bardsey Island is accurately described in Welsh as *Ynys Enlli*, 'the island in the tide-race'. It lies two miles south-west of the tip of the Lleyn Peninsula, separated from the mainland by the fierce tides of Bardsey Sound, which in times of storm can isolate the island for weeks.

Bardsey is 1¾ miles long by three-quarters of a mile at the widest point, and covers 444 acres. Geologically, it is basically a large fault-breccia in part of the Lleyn complex which consists of gneiss, meta-

The Beaumaris waterfront, Anglesey.

Bardsey Island, from the south.

morphosed grits and shales, and pillow lavas and tuffs, all crushed and distorted into a *mélange* of crush-conglomerates and lenticular strips. There are also gabbro and granite intrusions.

The eastern side of the main body of the island rises to a ridge 550 ft high, green and grey and blustery, with fine views of Snowdon, Anglesey and the Wicklow Mountains of Ireland. The western side is low-lying meadow and rough pasture, still retaining the old field system. A few trees grow around the withy beds, where willow shoots were once cut to make lobster pots. On its southern peninsula stands the square red-and-white striped lighthouse built in 1821, with a cluster of buildings at its foot. An unsurfaced road runs from the lighthouse, past the landing place, to the remains of the Augustinian Abbey of St Mary, with farm buildings, church and manse nearby. Along the road are six farmhouses, surprisingly large and solid, having been rebuilt by the third Baron Newborough during the 1870s, and several smaller buildings including the old school.

According to Arthurian legend Bardsey was the home of Merlin the Wizard. On a stormy night, when the sea lashes the rocks with spray and the dark Atlantic storm clouds race overhead, the legend is easy to believe. During the 6th C the island, along with others on the west coast, became a sanctuary from which missionaries of the Celtic church journeyed into Britain and Europe to convert the heathen. The original abbey here was founded by St Cadfan in AD 516, and St Dubricius died here in 612. Following the Battle of Chester in 615, the ousted monks of Bangor-Is-Coed re-established their college on Bardsey,

and it may be these brothers and their successors who are the 20,000 saints said to be buried on the island. They left no memorials, but from time to time bones are uncovered. During the Middle Ages Bardsey became a place of pilgrimage, three visits to the island being considered the equivalent of one to Rome.

The present visible remains of the abbey probably date from the 13th C. Following the dissolution of the monasteries, the island lost its former importance, and was inhabited by farmers, fishermen and, at one time, pirates. In the 19th C, when the population numbered over 100, a 'King of Bardsey' was appointed by the Barons Newborough

(owners since the 16th C) to settle local disputes. The last 'King' was Love Pritchard, introduced at the 1924 Pwllheli National Eisteddfod as a Welshman 'from overseas'.

The island has again been farmed since 1972, the present residents numbering three. One farmhouse is 'Ty Pellaf', where the 'King' used to live, and sheep and Connemara ponies are grazed. Other inhabitants are the lighthouse keepers and the wardens for the bird observatory, which uses as its base 'Cristin', the 19th-C farmhouse which is sometimes available as holiday accommodation. The observatory was established in 1953; since that time there have been over 3000 visitors.

'Cristin' and the schoolhouse, Bardsey.

The Abbey of St Mary, Bardsey.

Over 40 species of birds breed here (including the rare chough) and many migrants use the island as as a staging post. In all, over 250 species have been recorded. The oceanic Manx shearwater has one of its major breeding sites here, some 3000 pairs staying from March to September. They nest in burrows, which, on dark nights, echo with their eerie cooing noises as birds return from fishing expeditions.

Of great concern to the wardens of the observatory has been the effect of the powerful beams of light emitted by the lighthouse, often attracting great clouds of migrating birds, many of which kill themselves by flying at the lantern. It is not uncommon for 100 or more corpses to be found scattered around the lighthouse buildings after such an occurrence. Experiments with a 'decoy light' on a mast 150 yd east of the lighthouse are being conducted with the co-operation of Trinity House, and this may lessen the fatalities. The rich bird life of the island gives credence to another suggested origin of the name Bardsey – a derivation of 'Birdsey'.

For such a small island, the flora is rich and varied, with such rarities as Wilson's filmy-fern, sea pea and small-flowered buttercup. There are also hops and herbs, perhaps brought to the island by the monks. In the spring, the cliffs and mountain slopes are bright with gorse and thrift, and a recent survey recorded 280 varieties of lichen. The rocky shoreline provides shelter for the grey seals which breed in the sea caves.

In 1975 the island was offered for sale for £103,050. The Observatory Council had an overdraft and it seemed possible that Bardsey could fall into unsympathetic hands. It was to secure its future that the Bardsey Island Trust was incorporated in 1977 and, with financial help from the World Wildlife Fund, the Countryside Commission, the Nature Conservancy Council and

thousands of individuals, the Trust purchased the island in March 1979. Bardsey will now be 'preserved, protected and improved for the benefit of the general public. Visitors are welcome, provided their numbers do not exceed that compatible with its function as a nature reserve and farm.'

The nearest harbour is Aberdaron; enquire here and at Pwllheli about trips to Bardsey in the summer, weather permitting. The tiny islands to the east of Aberdaron Bay are **Ynys Gwylan-fawr** and **Ynys Gwylan-bâch**. They have a combined area of about 20 acres and, for obvious reasons, are sometimes called the 'Gull Islands'.

St Tudwal's Islands

Gwynedd. Two miles south-east of Abersoch are two islands, the name of which is taken from that of Tugdual, Bishop of Treguier, who fled there from Brittany in the 6th C, following the collapse of the Roman Empire. The islands are composed of Ordovician sedimentary rock, with grassy tops, low craggy cliffs and deep sea caves inhabited by grey seals. Puffins nest here, and these, with rabbits, were once harvested. A disused lighthouse stands on the western isle.

On **St Tudwal's Island East**, the larger of the two, covering 26 acres, evidence of habitation over a period of 1800 years has been discovered, from Roman times until 1887. This was the year in which Father Henry Balie Hughes failed to found a monastery, and the only evidence remaining of his work is the chapel, a converted barn originally built when the island was farmed in the 18th C. Recent excavations have also uncovered the extensive remains of a 13th-C chapel on the site of the sanctuary built by Tugdual. It is possible that Edward I may have visited the island in 1284

when it was probably inhabited by secular canons associated with Bardsey. In 1410 a priory of Augustinian canons was known to be present, but during the 16th C it was the haunt of pirates, one with the fine name of 'Morgan Irish'. During World War II, the islands were used as an unofficial bombing target. They are now privately owned.

Cardigan Island

Dyfed. This is a cliff-girt island of some 40 acres, composed of Ordovician sedimentary rock, rising to a height of 170 ft in the west and situated a little over 100 yd from the mainland to the north of where the River Teifi enters the sea. Although the western point has been heavily eroded, the majority of the surface is grassy, and thick with bluebells in the spring. A small flock of Soay sheep, introduced by the West Wales Naturalists' Trust, are grazed. Traces of field divisions can be found, and there is a small pond.

Cardigan Island has been kept as a nature reserve since 1944, and was purchased by the WWNT in 1963. There are about 900 nesting pairs of herring gull, and numerous other sea birds. Until treatment with the exterminator Warfarin killed them off in 1968, there was a brown rat colony of over 1000, thought to have originated from the SS *Hereford*, wrecked off the island in 1934. Access is by permit only but, for trips around the island, enquire at St Dogmaels.

Ramsey Island

Dyfed. In Welsh this island is called *Ynys-Dewi*, 'St David's island'; in old Norse it was either *Hrafn-ey*, 'Hrafn's island', or *Hranfsaa*, 'raven's isle'. With an area of 650 acres, it lies half a mile off the Pembrokeshire coast near St David's, across the swift-flowing and treacherous waters of Ramsey Sound. Off the southern tip of the

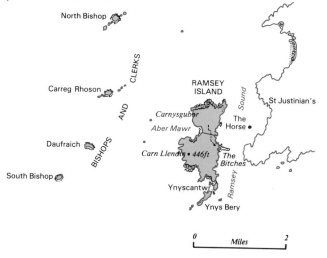

island are **Ynyscantwr** (the 'chanter's isle'), **Ynys Bery** ('falcon's isle', once known as 'Margery Island') and numerous rocks and skerries. On the east coast, jutting into Ramsey Sound are **The Bitches**, dangerous rocks where the St David's lifeboat was lost in 1910 when it went to the aid of the ketch *Democrat* of Barnstaple. Twelve people were miraculously saved, but three lifeboatmen drowned. In the middle of the Sound is another hazard, a rock called **The Horse.**

About two miles to the west of Ramsey are the **Bishops and Clerks**, a series of islets and rocks long feared by mariners – men have often been marooned on them for days after their ships struck them. A lighthouse has stood as a warning on the **South Bishop** (Em-sger) since 1839. They are a natural sanctuary for sea birds; puffins were once harvested, and sheep were ferried over for summer grazing.

The soil on Ramsey is shallow, being on a base of Cambrian slate, and the highest point is 446 ft at the summit of Carn Llendin. There were two chapels on the island, dedicated to St Devanus (who came to Britain in AD 186) and St Justinian. It is said that a well with healing water sprang from the spot where the followers of the latter cut off his head, and he was buried at St Justinian's after walking over the Sound carrying his head.

Ramsey was owned by the Bishop of St David's from very early times, and has been let to farmers since the 12th C. Rabbits were introduced in the 13th C, the flesh being considered a delicacy at that time, but their presence soon ruined the pastures. At the end of the 18th C the farmhouse was built, in the 1890s a cornmill with a 14-ft waterwheel was operating and, in 1908, at the north end on the site of earlier houses, the bungalow was erected.

The Ecclesiastical Commissioners sold Ramsey to Winford Philips, later Lord St David, in 1904, who leased it to various farming families, none of whom met with much success. In 1935 it was purchased by L. D. Whitehead, industrialist and humanitarian, who built the sheltered landing place. Unfortunately he died three years later, but his bailiff, Bert Griffiths, continued to farm and make improvements, such as introducing the first tractor; he grew seed corn during the war, and finally left in 1947. The next tenants continued with the improvements until the last people to farm Ramsey, Phil Davies and his family, took over in 1953 and stayed 10 years, installing a generator and providing holiday accommodation for visitors. In 1961 the island received its first visit by a reigning monarch, when Queen Elizabeth II came ashore from the royal yacht for

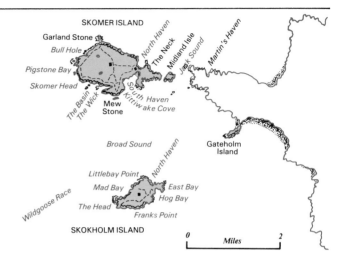

a picnic. The island was, for a time, leased by the RSPB as a reserve. At the time of writing Ramsey is inhabited, in the summer only, by a warden, and deer and goats are kept there. Once again, it is up for sale, and the future is uncertain.

There are daily landing trips during the summer from St Justinian's.

Skomer Island

Dyfed. Named *Skalmey* by the Norsemen in reference to its cloven shape, by the 18th C it was called Skomer Island. Measuring two miles by 1¼ miles, it has an area of 722 acres. **Midland Isle**, just off its eastern tip across the narrow Little Sound, adds another 21 acres, and the two lie about one-third of a mile off the mainland near Martin's Haven, across Jack Sound. Skomer is a cliff-bound tableland (with several rock ridges outcropping west to east) about 200 ft high, rising to a

maximum of 260 ft near the centre, joined by a narrow and precipitous isthmus to The Neck.

The island is composed mainly of volcanic rock and ash beds of the lower Silurian age, a succession of flows with bands of clays, marls and quartzite interbedded. The platform top of the island was eroded preglacially by the sea, although the 'Irish Sea Glacier' caused little erosion but deposited boulder clay and erratics. The rise in sea level following the melting of the ice separated Skomer from the mainland, and the full force of the Atlantic, sweeping in unchecked, began to cut along lines of weakness, creating narrow inlets, Midland Isle and The Neck. The soil is ideal for burrowing; rabbits, puffins and especially Manx shearwaters take advantage of this to such an extent that, in places, the ground is riddled with holes.

95,000 pairs of the oceanic Manx

Manx shearwater, numerous on Skomer.

North Haven, Skomer.

shearwaters nest on Skomer; on dark nights their characteristic eerie cooing echoes around the island as they return from their nocturnal fishing trips. They breed here from March to September, spending the winter in South America. In addition there are over 6000 pairs of puffins nesting here (although at one time there were as many as 50,000 pairs), as well as a major predator of the Manx shearwater, puffin and other sea birds, the great black-backed gull, of which there are now about 80 pairs. In all, about 120 species of birds are recorded on the island each year, and in excess of 200 flowering plants and ferns are present.

There are only five species of land mammal present – rabbit, long-tailed field-mouse, common and pygmy shrews and, of particular interest, the unique Skomer vole *(Clethrionomys glareolus skomerensis)*, a type of bank vole that is longer than usual with a lighter colour and different skull shape; it was 'discovered' in 1897 by Robert Drane, the Cardiff naturalist. It is quite tame and, if found, will allow itself to be handled. Rabbits were introduced to the island around 1300, the carcasses and skins having been 'exported' until the mid-1950s, and grey seals breed here, often being seen near the **Garland Stone** to the north. Four square miles of sea around the island (and part of the Pembrokeshire coast) are now kept as a marine nature reserve.

Skomer was farmed during the Iron Age, and evidence of the ancient field systems and huts is still visible in the south by The Wick, as well as a promontory fort on The Neck which also dates from this period. There is little recorded history until the 13th C, when the island was uninhabited and used for grazing, rearing rabbits and harvesting sea birds.

During the late 16th C it formed part of the estates of Sir John Perrot, Lord Deputy of Ireland. The ruined farm buildings and enclosures, probably dating from the late 18th C, were rebuilt and enlarged in 1843 by Charles Philipps of St Brides, who made extensive use of ships' timbers cast up on the shore, and also improved the landing place in North Haven. The island was then farmed intensively, with threshing and chaffing machines being driven by horses (the 'horse course' can still be seen by the south-west corner of the old barn). Near North Haven, below the monolith known as the Harold Stone, are the remains of a lime kiln where limestone, delivered by sea, was fired for use as fertiliser. Visitors began to stay on the island around 1900 when the extent of the sea-bird colonies became widely known, but by 1909 they were causing so much disturbance that they were banned by the Neales, who had leased Skomer from the then owner, Lord Kensington.

Walter Sturt of Exeter purchased the island in 1922, his daughter marrying Reuben Codd who was to be the last man to farm Skomer. Despite gallant efforts, farming activity ceased about 1950, and a severe storm in 1954 damaged the farmhouse which soon fell into ruin. The island was then owned by an industrialist, and visiting naturalists were ferried to the island by Reuben Codd.

In 1959 the Nature Conservancy Council purchased the island and built the warden's house and laboratory at North Haven, leasing the whole as a nature reserve to the West Wales Naturalists' Trust (who, as the West Wales Field Society, have

had an interest in Skomer since 1946). A warden is resident from March to October, and the old cowshed at the farm is used as simple accommodation for members of the WWNT.

Skomer is open to visitors each day from April to September (although not on Mondays before August) but numbers are limited, a landing fee is charged and no dogs are allowed. A small boat leaves from Martin's Haven, weather permitting, and landing may be difficult. There is a nature trail and an excellent guide book.

Grassholme Island

Dyfed. The name derives from the Old Norse for 'grass island'. This is Wales' most distant island, lying seven miles due west of Skomer, part of the system of lava flows which stretch 26 miles from St Ishmael's through Skomer to The Smalls, eight miles further west.

Grassholme is also a famous gannetry owned and managed by the RSPB, having expanded from 60 breeding pairs in 1820 to over 15,000 pairs (1974), making it the largest concentration in England and Wales. At a distance the colony appears like a patch of snow on the northern side – at close range, the smell of guano can be overpowering. Puffins, of which there were 125,000 pairs in 1890, are now found in much smaller numbers, their over-intensive burrowing having caused erosion of the top soil, exposing bedrock. The first prosecution under the Wild Birds Protection Act of 1880 was made when a party of seamen from the Royal Navy boat *Sir Richard Fletcher* landed on the island and senselessly destroyed thousands of birds and eggs. They were fined a total of £22-17-0d.

Although its exposed position makes landing difficult, sheep were once grazed on Grassholme's green surface. Lack of fresh water, however, has made human habitation impossible, and many shipwrecked seamen have spent a wretched time marooned here with no shelter, waiting for the sea to calm before they could be rescued. In 1893 the *Ellen* of Caernarfon, a schooner bound from Norway to Cardigan, sank off the island but the crew of five, the injured captain and the pilot all managed to get ashore. Except for the unfortunate captain, they were rescued by line from a boat launched by the steam trawler *Birda* – when the sea calmed a few days later and a landing could be made, the captain was found dead.

During World War II, Grassholme was used as a practice-bombing target until protests brought it to a halt. Stringent new safety regulations have restricted the activities of some of the boatmen who used to take visitors; for

Grassholme Island, showing the gannetry.

transport to the island, enquire at Dale.

The Smalls, a rocky outcrop to the west, have been marked by a light since 1776 when John Phillips of Cardiganshire and his engineer, Henry Whiteside, built a timber octagonal tower on legs. The present lighthouse dates from 1857.

Skokholm Island

Dyfed. The name is Old Norse, meaning the 'island in the sound'. It is composed of sandstone with an area of 240 acres, four miles east of Dale, and west of the Wildgoose tide-race. From the 12th C the island was managed as a rabbit warren but, popularised by the writings of R. M. Lockley in the 1930s, in 1939 it became the first bird observatory in Britain. It has been owned by the Dale Castle Estate since 1745 and is now leased to the West Wales Naturalists' Trust (of which Lockley was co-founder). The small and rough farmhouse dates from 1760; it was built on the site of an earlier building and reflects Skokholm's poor farming potential. A lime kiln was also built at this time, and deer were kept (unsuccessfully).

In 1905 the island was let to John 'Bulldog' Edwards, a fiery but compassionate man who farmed vigorously until 1912. He then left the island due to a traumatic experience at the time of the birth of his first child in 1910: his wife's labour began during a storm, and Edwards barely made the crossing to Gateholm Island to fetch the midwife, returning just in time for the delivery.

R. M. Lockley leased Skokholm in 1927, keeping some sheep, studying sea birds and writing of his

island life. In 1928 he salvaged coal, fittings and the figurehead from the *Alice Williams*, wrecked off the island, and fixed this handsome piece to the rockface overlooking South Haven, where it still remains. The lighthouse at The Head was built in 1916, and the keepers are now the island's only permanent inhabitants.

The island is a sanctuary for birds, including colonies of Manx shearwater (35,000 pairs), puffin (5000 pairs), storm petrel (5000 pairs), razorbill, guillemot and gull. Usually seen around the island are gannet, cormorant, shag and kittiwake, and about 150 different species of bird have been recorded.

A warden is present from April to October, accommodation is available and courses on birdwatching and the history and natural history of the island are run. There is also census and migration-watch work carried out. Trips to land on Skokholm can only be made by arrangement with the National Park Office, Haverfordwest and the courses are arranged by the WWNT. For trips around the island, enquire at Dale and Solva Quay.

Gateholm Island

Dyfed. This is the small uninhabited tidal island of 20 acres to the west of Marloes, where John 'Bulldog' Edwards made his storm-tossed landing from Skokholm in 1910. The island provides valuable shelter during easterlies, the boats being pulled up on a flat rock. At the seaward end there was once a settlement, possibly of monastic origin, where over 100 hut circles have been found. In the early 18th C the island was owned by Charles

Philipps, and stayed in his family until sold to Lord Kensington in the 1890s. Sheep are grazed on its grassy summit.

Caldey Island

Dyfed. From the Old Norse *keld* (a 'spring') and *ey* ('island'), in Welsh the name is *Ynys Pŷr*, the 'island of St Pŷr'. One-and-a-half miles by three-quarters of a mile, it has an area of 500 acres, with limestone in the north and sandstone in the south, rising to a height of 180 ft in both the south-east and south-west. It lies just over half a mile south of Giltar Point on the mainland, and two miles south of the popular resort of Tenby.

The island now belongs to monks of the strict Cistercian order known as Trappists who, as far as is possible, are self-sufficient within the confines of the monastery. They run a productive mixed farm of 350 acres, and, since 1953, have produced perfume from the gorse and lavender that grows in profusion here.

Evidence of former occupation dates back to 10,000 BC: Mid-Stone Age tools were found in Nanna's Cave, and Bronze Age implements and Roman pottery have also been unearthed. The Celtic missionary Pyro came to the island in the 6th C, occupying a cell close to the freshwater spring where a small community was soon established. Pyro was later succeeded by Samson, who came to the island from Llantwit and later became the first Bishop of Dol, in Brittany. It seems probable these Celtic monks were killed sometime during the 10th C by the Danish invaders who gave the island its present name. The old priory and St Illtud's church were

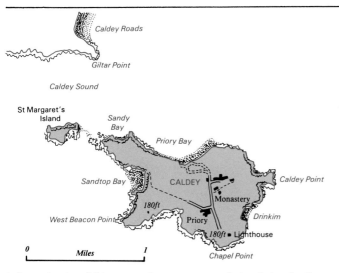

serves the score or so other islanders. It is Celtic in plan (the foundations may date from the 6th C) and is a substantial primitive building, restored in 1838 and again in 1906. The Ogham Stone, a 6th-C relic, is kept in the nave of St Illtud's Church. Unearthed near the well in the 18th C, its inscriptions, which have their roots in Latin but use a series of dots to represent vowels, originated sometime between the 6th and 9th centuries. Various translations have been suggested; one possibility indicates a reference to St Dubricius, reputed to be the founder of Llandaff Cathedral, who died on Bardsey Island in AD 612.

The lighthouse, built in 1828 and now automatic, stands above Chapel Point in the south-east from where there are fine views over the island and, on a clear day, it is possible to see Lundy 30 miles to the south, the Gower to the east and the mainland to the north and west. The prevailing winds, and gales, sweep in unchecked from the south-west where the next landfall is Florida, over 3000 miles away. Sandtop Bay and the more sheltered Priory Bay are good sandy beaches, the latter being safe for bathing.

Off the western tip of Caldey, once connected by a causeway, is **St Margaret's Island** (14 acres). During the 19th C, limestone was quarried there and several houses were occupied, but it is now administered by the West Wales Naturalists' Trust as a nature

built on the site of this community in 1113, probably by Benedictine monks from St Dogmaels, near Cardigan, who occupied the island from 1131 until the dissolution of the monasteries in 1534.

After several changes of ownership it was purchased in 1897 by Rev. W. Done Bushell who restored the priory and the churches, St Illtud's and St David's. In 1906 it was bought for Dom Aelred Carlyle, leader of a small community of Anglican Benedictines, and it was they who, in 1912, built the present Romanesque, red-tiled and turreted

monastery designed by J. Coats Carter. The extravagance of the exterior belies an elegantly simple interior which is more in harmony with the life of the monks, and the whole stands in a cluster with earlier buildings, surrounded by trees for shelter. In 1928 the Benedictines moved to Prinknash, near Gloucester, and in the following year monks of the Trappist order, from Chimay in Belgium, took residence. In keeping with their beliefs, they still do not allow women to enter the monastery.

The parish church of St David

Caldey Abbey.

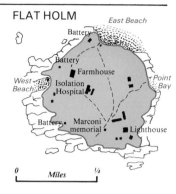

FLAT HOLM

The sea cliffs of Caldey.

reserve. Landing is difficult – there is a tide-race between St Margaret's and Giltar Point and it is unsafe to try to cross from Caldey at low tide, therefore permission is required. There is a large colony of cormorants (the largest in Wales), now numbering over 300 pairs.

Between the Spring Bank Holiday and September, boats run regularly every weekday (and on some Saturday afternoons in summer) from Tenby to Caldey. There are also boat trips around Caldey and St Margaret's from Tenby and Saundersfoot.

On the top of **St Catherine's Island,** which can be reached across Tenby beach at low tide, is a fort built between 1868 and 1875, part of a defensive scheme for Milford Haven devised when it was thought the French might invade. The fort was designed to house 11 guns and a garrison of 60 men; it is now a zoo. Other fortifications were built around the harbour including those on **Thorn Island** (1852-59; now a hotel), and **Stack Rock** (1859-67), the latter fairly difficult of access and so in a well-preserved state. The standard of building and the materials used have made the fortresses virtually indestructible; collectively they are sometimes referred to as 'Palmerston's Follies'. Information about them all can be obtained from the Pembrokeshire Coast National Park Office.

Sully Island

South Glamorgan. This is a low green tidal hump, situated near Barry, which can be reached on foot at low tide; do *not* attempt to cross when the rocks are awash. It lies in an area of great interest to geologists; the nearby cliffs at Lavernock show layered deposits of green, grey and blackish marls of the Triassic system known as the Sully Beds, laid down when the area was covered by the sea.

A prehistoric fort, later used by the Romans, was sited at the higher eastern end of the island. Roman gold and silver coins were found here in 1899.

Flat Holm

South Glamorgan. Two-and-three-quarter miles south-east of Lavernock Point, Flat Holm is roughly circular, with a diameter of about 550 yd. It has an area of 57 acres, with a flat top tilting from a little above sea level in the west to 76 ft in the east, thus exposing the whole surface to the prevailing salt-laden winds. The coast is cliff- and rock-bound with a few patches of shingle and, due to its exposed position and the extreme tidal range in the area, landing is difficult. Geologically it is the northern extremity of the carboniferous limestone of the Mendips (Somerset), overlaid in places with red clay.

To the south is the main deep-

water part of the Bristol Channel, and it seems probable that a light was maintained on the island by the Romans. In 1738 William Crispe built a 70-ft tower with a lighted beacon. The tower height was raised to 90 ft, and an oil lantern installed in 1819, and in 1823 it was purchased by Trinity House. The light was subsequently improved, and in 1908 a foghorn station was built, the whole installation now manned by three men.

It is not clear who were the earliest inhabitants of Flat Holm, although it has been suggested that part of a human skeleton found in gravel to the north of the farmhouse is neolithic. St Cadoc is reputed to have visited the island in the 6th C, and two inscribed stones discovered here, thought to date from the 6th to 9th centuries, tend to confirm the possibility of a monastic settlement. Two early graves have also been uncovered, said to have contained the corpses of the murderers of Thomas à Becket.

The Danes took refuge here in 917 after being defeated at Watchet in Somerset; many died of hunger before the island was evacuated (*see also* Steep Holm). Pottery relics, dating from the 12th, 14th and 16th centuries, that have been unearthed around the farmhouse confirm occupation and farming activities for at least 700 years. During the 18th C the island was a regular haunt of smugglers. The farmhouse, which once served as an inn, was built in the mid-18th C and was occupied until the 1960s; to the south-east of it are the ruins of a cholera isolation hospital dating from 1896, which replaced a temporary building erected ten years earlier.

Increasing worries about possible French aggression in the 1860s resulted in the fortification of this strategically placed island, and four gun batteries were built, along with underground bunkers and tunnels. While these are still in a reasonable state of repair, the barracks, built at the same time, are now in an advanced state of decay. During World War II, 350 soldiers were stationed on the island to man dual-

Flat Holm.

purpose anti-aircraft/anti-ship guns, searchlights and radar, and at this time Flat Holm had a NAAFI, post office, library and concert hall. This occupation left many scars in the form of dug-outs, concrete structures and emplacements, and sandbags brought to the island introduced many alien plant species. In 1976 Trinity House leased it to South Glamorgan County Council, who have declared it as a Local Nature Reserve.

On 11 May 1897 an historic event in the field of telecommunications took place on Flat Holm, when Marconi and his assistant Kemp transmitted the first wireless message across water to Lavernock Point. A memorial, erected on the island in 1976, marks the spot from where the message is thought to have originated. There is also a commemorative plaque at Lavernock Church.

Over 180 species of flowering plants and ferns have been recorded on the island, and large colonies of herring gulls and lesser black-backed gulls have established themselves since they first came from Steep Holm, four miles to the south, in 1954. Lack of adequate ground cover and the dominance of the gulls limits the numbers of land birds present.

Flat Holm was declared a nature reserve in October 1977. The lease on the island has been purchased by the South Glamorgan County Council, who are at present investigating various management schemes, although it is certain that access will be restricted. Landings must not be made without the lease-holder's permission.

Useful addresses

All of these organisations have provided help in the preparation of this book. The publishers wish to thank them for their assistance.

Auriegny Air Services Ltd
Alderney, Channel Islands

British Airways
Victoria Terminal, Buckingham Palace Road, London SW1

British Tourist Authority
239 Old Marylebone Road, London NW1

Caledonian MacBrayne Ltd
The Pier, Gourock, Strathclyde

English Tourist Board
4 Grosvenor Gardens, London SW1

Essex Naturalists' Trust
Fingringhoe Wick Nature Reserve, Fingringhoe, Colchester, Essex

Highland and Islands Development Board
27 Bank Street, Inverness IV1 1QR

Isle of Man Steam Packet
PO Box 5, Douglas, Isle of Man

Isle of Man Tourist Office
Victoria Street, Douglas, Isle of Man

Isle of Wight Natural History and Archaeological Society
66 Carisbrooke Road, Newport, Isle of Wight

Loganair Ltd
St Andrew's Drive, Glasgow Airport, Glasgow

Manx Line Ltd
Sea Terminal, Douglas, Isle of Man

Manx Museum and National Trust
Douglas, Isle of Man

Nature Conservancy Council
19-20 Belgrave Square, London SW1

National Trust
42 Queen Anne's Gate, London SW1

National Trust for Scotland
5 Charlotte Square, Edinburgh EH2 4DU

Northern Lighthouse Board
George Street, Edinburgh

P & O Ferries Ltd
PO Box 5, Aberdeen

Royal National Lifeboat Institute
21 Ebury Street, London SW1

Royal Society for the Protection of Birds
The Lodge, Sandy, Bedfordshire

Scottish Tourist Board
23 Ravelston Terrace, Edinburgh

Trinity House
Tower Hill, London EC3

Wales Tourist Board
2 Fitzalan Road, Cardiff

Western Ferries Ltd
Kennacraig, Strathclyde

West Wales Naturalists' Trust
7 Market Street, Haverfordwest, Dyfed

Index

LUNDY: (Ancient Monuments, from D.O.E. 'List of National Importance'), 1971
from (England)

Burial Mound: (Megalithic?), mound south of Widow's Tenement: SS 135 465

Camps and Settlements:
  Prehistoric settlement at North End: SS 133 477
  Bull's Paradise Settlement Site: SS 136 441
  Prehistoric settlement site south of St Helen's Chapel: SS 132 442.

Ecclesiastical Building:
  Lundy, St Helen's Chapel and cemetery, remains of: SS 132 442.

Castles and Fortifications:
  Lundy, Brazen Ward, remains of battery: SS 139 468
  Lundy, Marisco Castle: SS 141 437
  Lundy, battery at North East Point: SS 135 480

Deserted Villages, Settlements and Moated Sites:
  Lundy, Settlement sites near Halfway Wall SS 136 458
  Lundy, Settlement sites West of Tibbett's Hill: SS 135 462
  Lundy, Widow's Tenement, medieval settlement site: SS 135 468

Other Secular Sites and Buildings:
  Lundy, revetment walls and platform above
      Jenny's Cove: SS 133 458
  Lundy, The Old Lighthouse: SS 132 442.

LUNDY: some sights of Lundy (from Arthur Mee's 'DEVON' (The King's England).
The Shutter Rock, on which a battleship was wrecked in 1906.

The Templar Rock, like a man's face.
The Constable Rock, rising 800 feet on the extreme north.
The Hen and Chickens group of rocks.
The Devil's Limekiln, a 250-foot-wide cavity
The 19th Century granite church of St Helen, with a statue of the patron saint
    over the entrance (built for the Heaven family who owned the island in Victorian times.

Sir Lewis STUCLEY died on Lundy in 1620 (mad and melancholy) after his betrayal of
    Sir Walter Raleigh circa 1618. He had gone to the island to seek sanctuary
    from public hatred (that could not so easily be shown to James I).